FICTION

The Elements of the Short Story

Jane Bachman Gordon   **Karen Kuehner**

New York, New York   Columbus, Ohio   Chicago, Illinois   Peoria, Illinois   Woodland Hills, California

Cover illustration: Emilio Pettoruti/SuperStock

Acknowledgments begin on page 453, which is to be considered an extension
of this copyright page.

Send all Inquiries to:
Glencoe/McGraw-Hill
8787 Orion Place
Columbus, OH 43240

ISBN :   0-8442-5915-2 (student edition):   0-8442-5991-8 (softbound)
ISBN :   0-8442-5934-9 (teacher's edition): 0-8442-5990-X (softbound)

Printed in the United States of America

2 3 4 5 6 7 8 9 10   100 / 055   08 07 06 05 04 03

CONTENTS

PREFACE

For more than thirty thousand years, through drawing, sculpture, pantomime, dance, and language, human beings have told stories. It is probable that the first stories were communicated through cave paintings, followed shortly by the pantomime and dance reenactments of tribal triumphs such as a successful hunt. An Egyptian papyrus dating from around 2600 B.C. notes that the sons of the great pharaoh Cheops amused their father by telling him stories. In nearly all cultures a body of myths deals with such topics as the creation of the world, its peoples, and its phenomena. The oldest literary works of the western world, Homer's *Iliad* and *Odyssey*, are long poems comprised of episodes similar in length to short stories and containing the legendary exploits of heroic Greek and Trojan super-heroes. The parables of the Bible are essentially short or short-short stories. So, too, are fairy tales, fables, and folk tales.

A story can be as simple as a joke or an anecdote, or as complex as a short novel. If you think about it for a moment, your daily conversations are filled with stories, long and short, true or fictional. The stories you *tell* allow you to share your experiences with others, perhaps to instruct or entertain or frighten or inspire them. The stories you *hear* enable you to learn about people and places different from your own and to compare your lives with that of others.

What are short stories? And why do we human beings respond so eagerly to them? The answer to the second question is simple. Young or old, we want to know the answer to this question: "What happened next?" The answer to the first can also be simple: a short story is a short narrative. If it contains some five hundred words, it is usually categorized as a short-short story. If its length reaches fifteen thousand words, it may be considered a novella, a short novel.

The real answer to that first question, however, is not so simple as total word length. Edgar Allan Poe, often credited with creating the modern short story, described it as "a short prose narrative, requiring from a half-hour to one or two hours in its perusal." As a definition, that might be a good beginning, but it is incomplete. It doesn't begin

v

to encompass the sophistication of most short stories. The majority of—and some say the best—short stories

- *are "consciously made."* Many story ideas come from events in the author's life or from the pages of the daily newspaper. Instead of simply retelling what occurred, skillful writers often rearrange the chronology, change or combine characters, move or invent setting—all to achieve some desired end.

- *have a formal structure.* The story has a form—a beginning, middle, and end.

- *exhibit causality.* The establishment of causes and effects reveals why characters act as they do and what the results of their actions are.

- *develop and end inevitably.* All actions, the happenings or the series of events in a story, should seem inevitable. This is particularly true of the ending.

- *establish an atmosphere.* The mood of a short story should complement the characters and their actions.

Poe recognized his description was incomplete. Writing in 1847, he asserted that the "skillful artist" does not fashion "his thoughts to accommodate his incidents, but having deliberately conceived a certain *single effect* to be wrought, he then invents such incidents, he then combines such events, and discusses them in such a tone as may best serve him in establishing this preconceived effect."

Stories can simultaneously convey experiences both individual *and* universal. Universal experiences are those that would be familiar to people from any period of time and in any country. They include being part of a family, growing up, finding one's place in the world, falling in love, overcoming obstacles, and/or accepting success or failure. What storytellers do is to particularize experiences, creating characters who are specific, unique individuals. Storytellers dramatize a concrete struggle that their fictional characters encounter, then choose the resolution that would logically occur to their particular character. The result is a narrative whose individual characters engage your interest and whose experiences often parallel your own. A skillful storyteller enables you to identify with one or more characters, become concerned about their situation, intrigued by their actions, and perhaps instructed by the resolution of their conflicts.

OBJECTIVES OF THE ANTHOLOGY

In putting together this anthology, we had five primary goals:

- to enable students to learn about the basic elements of fiction and how these elements contribute to the creation of an artistic whole

- to acquaint students with the wide variety of authors who write in English

- to promote students' awareness of the cultures represented by these writers

- to provide students with an opportunity to apply their knowledge to the oral and written analysis of short fiction

- to encourage students to respond to literature on both an emotional and an intellectual level

STORY SELECTIONS

In selecting the stories for this anthology, we limited our choices to stories originally written in English. Certainly we do not suggest that those are the most worthy; the achievements of Chekhov, Tolstoy, de Maupassant, Borges, and others are rightly celebrated. But we wanted readers to read words actually chosen by the author, not those of a translator—no matter how talented.

The stories emphasize writers of the twentieth century. In addition to such recognized writers as Cather, O'Connor, Welty, and Hurston, the table of contents also acknowledges the contributions of modern women to the short story; the twentieth century has seen a flowering of female short story writers. We have also included African-American, Asian, Native American, and Hispanic American writers. Geographically, the table of contents ranges from the United States to Canada, Ireland, England, and India.

FEATURES OF THE BOOK

Organization. The book is divided into seven major sections. Each of the first six chapters focuses on one of the elements of fiction: plot, setting, character, point of view, theme, and style and symbol. The seventh chapter presents eight stories, two in each of the following types of popular fiction: Westerns, Detective and Mystery stories, Fantasy and Science Fiction, and Ghost and Horror stories. A Glossary of literary terms follows the last chapter.

Discussion of Literary Elements. Each of the first six chapters begins with a general discussion of the featured element. Pertinent literary terms appear in **boldface** followed by definitions.

Biographical Sketch. Preceding each of the stories is a short sketch of the author that includes relevant personal data as well as the titles and publication dates of important works. The sketch concludes with questions or suggestions a reader should consider while reading the story.

Footnotes. Some readers see the footnoting of a work as an annoying disruption of the reading process. We disagree. Our experience suggests that many readers find it even more annoying to wonder about a word, a reference, or a foreign phrase. We have included a footnote for anything that might impede a reader's ability to understand the meaning of or a nuance in a story.

Questions for Discussion. The discussion questions following each story emphasize the element focused on in the chapter but are not limited to it. They also highlight important issues in the stories. Questions about the various elements are cumulative; that is, questions in the chapter on setting will also include questions about plot; questions in the character chapter will also focus on plot and setting.

Topics for Writing. Some suggested writing topics follow the discussion questions. Some tap into the reader's personal response to the story or to the reader's personal experiences. Others focus on the short story element discussed. A few ask the reader to go beyond the immediate story and consider universal implications.

Synthesis. At the end of each chapter are questions that ask for consideration of more than one story at a time. Readers may consider these questions in a class discussion or write about them. Although the synthesis questions are specifically directed to the stories in a particular chapter, we encourage readers to continue to think about them as they move from one chapter to another. Their purpose is to encourage the making of connections between or among stories, to see similarities and differences, and to make judgments.

Popular Fiction stories. This section is divided into four categories, each an important type of popular fiction.

Glossary. The glossary contains all the terms defined earlier in the text.

Chapter One

PLOT

The term *short story* is a relatively recent one. For example, Nathaniel Hawthorne's 1837 collection of stories was titled *Twice-Told Tales*. Today, the term *tale* suggests a simple narrative, told in chronological order. In the past, a short work was sometimes called a *sketch*. Today, *sketch* implies the narration of only a single brief scene. When you tell a friend how you got an A on an English paper, you are telling an *anecdote*—a simple narrative told in an interesting way. What differentiates the short story from the tale, the sketch, or the anecdote is plot.

Plot has been defined as "an author's careful arrangement of incidents in a narrative to achieve a desired effect." In telling your best friend *what happened* when you tried to buy tickets for a concert, your narration might include losing your way, running out of gas, giving a friend a ride to work, paying $10 to park the car, standing in line for hours, and discovering at the box office that you didn't have enough money to buy the tickets. Although it would be a long, sad, or humorous story—perhaps entitled "My Rotten Day"—the narrative would not illustrate the concept of plot. One ingredient is missing.

CAUSALITY

A plot is a series of actions, often presented in chronological order, but the ingredient a plot has that a story lacks is *causality*. In a narrative with a plot, there is little that happens without a cause. For example, consider the following two events: The baby cried and the dog growled. There is no causal relationship suggested between these two events. The substitution of one word, however, not only creates a complex sentence but establishes a relationship: Because the baby cried, the dog growled. To transform the concert ticket anecdote into a short story, a writer would need to state or imply causes for *why* he

1

or she got lost, ran out of gas, and failed to have enough money to pay for both the parking and the tickets. Suppose that the writer's point in writing "My Rotten Day" was to portray the careless incompetence of the main character. If so, the writer would almost certainly omit mentioning the lift that the main character gave to a friend. Why? Because that action does not fit the incompetent character's image and would undercut the writer's portrait of an undependable and impulsive person.

CONFLICT

Even with the addition of causality, however, the concert ticket anecdote lacks another important ingredient. Traditionally, plots grow out of a **conflict**—an internal or an external struggle between the main character and an opposing force.

When a story includes **internal conflict,** the main character is in conflict with himself or herself. For example, the writer of the concert ticket anecdote might establish that the main character was not careless or impetuous, but subconsciously did not want to attend that concert. What appeared to be careless actions actually were due to a war with self. In Chapter 1, "The Intruder" illustrates the internal struggle of a main character.

In contrast, an **external conflict** can occur between the central character and either another character, society, or natural forces, including fate. The most common **external force** is another character. In Frank O'Connor's "First Confession," for example, the young main character is in conflict both with other characters and with society.

In Chapter 2, an example of external conflict with nature occurs in "The Wedding Gift." In a variation of this conflict, a main character's destiny—as in "Sweat"—is controlled by a force mightier than his or her free will.

PLOT STRUCTURE

One graphic way to describe the **structure,** or architecture, of a fictional plot is to envision it as a pyramid. Although the nineteenth-century German critic Gustav Freytag developed the diagram on page 3 to illustrate the structure of ancient Greek and Shakespearean plays, it can be applied to nearly all narratives, including the novel and the short story.

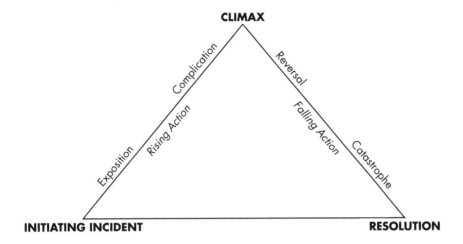

Note the label *exposition* as used in the diagram. This term is important both to writing and to literature. Synonymous with *explanation,* exposition is one of the four basic modes of expression; description, narration, and persuasion are the other three. Much of the world's everyday writing—reports, doctor's notes, memos, magazine articles—is exposition. In literature, however, **exposition** refers to the explanatory information a reader needs to comprehend the situation in the story. Exposition establishes the setting, the major characters and perhaps some minor ones, the situation, and any necessary background information about what happened before the story began.

The **initiating incident** is the event that changes the situation established in the exposition and sets the conflict in motion. In Frank O'Connor's story, Jackie's blissful young life changes when he is sent to Mrs. Ryan to be prepared for his first communion.

In the **rising action,** various episodes occur that develop, complicate, or intensify the conflict. In movies, the word *action* usually suggests high-speed chases, adventurous deeds, or violence. In a story, an action can be any of those acts, but also it can be as subtle as a raised eyebrow, a hidden smile, or even an impulsive purchase.

Climax has been defined in a number of ways: the point of greatest conflict, the emotional high point, the turning point in the plot, or the point at which one of the opposing forces gains the advantage. A story's climax often requires the main character to choose some form of action that will either worsen or improve his or her situation.

The Irish writer James Joyce labeled the revelation resulting from the climax an **epiphany.** For Joyce, the term designated "an event in which the essential nature of something—a person, a situation, an object—was suddenly perceived."

The events that follow the climax are known as the **falling action.** In novels, this section of the written work may be fairly long; in short stories it tends to be fairly brief. Approximately 10 percent of the total length of "The Intruder" comprises the falling action.

The falling action leads into the **resolution** or **denouement** of the story. The term *resolution* sometimes refers to all the events that follow the climax, including the denouement. *Dénouement* is a French word that means the "unknotting" or the untying of a knot. Some critics use it to denote the actual ending of the story—the final one or two paragraphs. Other critics think that the ending of a story should "tie up" all the loose ends in the story. (Although this may seem tidy and practical, it does not always represent what writers do.)

The American critic Laurence Perrine has suggested that there are three kinds of endings: happy, unhappy, and indeterminate. In a happy ending, the main character is the winner: the ugly duckling turns into a swan; the sleeping princess awakens at the kiss of the handsome prince; young Jackie in "First Confession" has a triumphant first encounter with an understanding priest. In an unhappy ending, the main character does not gain so spectacularly. The indeterminate endings of many modern short stories are those that are neither happy nor unhappy. Given the horrors that have occurred during the last century, many twentieth-century writers are pessimistic or cynical about the human condition. Seeing life as, at best, ambiguous, they reject altogether the possibility of happy endings. The characters in many modern stories struggle to come to terms with life. And though they rarely triumph, they may be allowed to reach an uneasy understanding concerning the forces that oppose them.

Most readers prefer happy endings. We like to be reassured that our struggles will not be in vain, that good can triumph over evil. Yet there is a danger in such thinking—particularly if holding such an attitude blinds us to the facts of the story. Imagine a story, for example, about a Jewish man who lives in Germany during the 1930s, who has been involved in underground activities, whose activities are known to the Nazi authorities, whose colleagues have been arrested and imprisoned, and who is trying to escape to a neutral country. Is this story likely to have a happy ending? As the reader, you may want to see that character happy and free and living a contented life, but given the totality of his circumstances, a happy ending seems more than improbable. Indeed, logic suggests that a more realistic result of his choices and actions will be capture, imprisonment, and even death.

Have you ever finished the ending of a story and said to yourself, "I sure didn't see *that* ending coming!"? The American short story writer O. Henry was noted for the unexpected twists of his endings, but he was not always praised for them. Surprise endings are legitimate if the author has prepared you for them. An author may use the device of foreshadowing or the superior power of the opposing force or the nature of the main character to do so. However, when the solution to a conflict is completely unexpected, readers are likely to feel cheated. Such conclusions are sometimes referred to as **deus ex machina** endings—a term deriving from Greek drama in which the conflict could be resolved only through divine intervention. In such drama the actor portraying the god (*deus*) or goddess (*dea*) was actually lowered onto the platform stage by means of a mechanical device (*machina*) similar to a crane. Then, in front of the audience, the god or goddess briskly sorted out the problem and provided a solution. Today, unrealistic *deus ex machina* endings are considered forced or contrived, weakening a story's impact.

In summary, a plot has six structural components: exposition, initiating incident, rising action, climax, falling action, and the resolution or denouement. These components may be of varying length, although the exposition and rising action usually are the longest sections, while the falling action and resolution usually are the shortest.

TECHNIQUES IN STORYTELLING

Authors employ a number of techniques in telling their stories. They include flashback, foreshadowing, suspense, and coincidence. Their effective use in storytelling draws the reader in and compels him or her to follow the action closely.

The **flashback**—the presentation of material that occurred before the events of the story—interrupts the chronology and often provides important exposition. If a story begins in the middle of the action or at a moment of great dramatic intensity, the author needs to return to an earlier point in the events to update the reader. In movies, a flashback often is signaled by a slow fade or dissolve; in literature, an extra space in the text may signal a change from the present to the past. Flashbacks can occur in the narration or the dialogue, with one or more characters revealing information.

Another technique used by writers, **foreshadowing,** gives hints or clues that suggest or prepare the reader for events that occur later in a work. Foreshadowing can be done through setting, as in "Sweat," with the increasing heat foreshadowing the increasingly hot anger of both main characters; through action, as in "The Intruder," with Kenneth's careful cleaning of his gun; or through a character's thoughts or speech.

Using the technique of foreshadowing, a writer can create **suspense**—the feeling of anxious anticipation, expectation, or uncertainty that creates tension and maintains the reader's interest. In "First Confession," for example, the events that temporarily prevent the young narrator from making his confession build suspense.

Finally, writers can use **coincidence**—the chance occurrence of two things at the same time or place—to denote the workings of Fate in a person's life. But this technique must be employed carefully. Coincidence can weaken a story if it seems too improbable; however, in a humorous story, far-fetched coincidences often accentuate or promote the comedy.

SUMMARY

This chapter introduction provides you with both concepts and terms to discuss the craft of a short story writer. The discussions of causality and conflict establish the essential principles on which narrative is based; the description of plot structure demonstrates *how* authors develop their stories; the discussion of techniques reveals how authors vary the chronology, provide hints of future action, sustain interest, and introduce the idea of chance or fate in the character's lives. With the exception of conflict, which illuminates the major issue of the story, your discussion of the concepts presented in this chapter will focus more on *how* the author crafted his or her story, not its meaning. Then, as you continue your study of the short story, you will realize that meaning emerges from the interaction between action and character.

THE INTRUDER

ANDRE DUBUS (born 1936)

Andre Dubus was born in Lake Charles, Louisiana. After graduating from McNeese State College in 1958, Dubus was commissioned a lieutenant in the Marine Corps, where he began to write seriously. In 1964 he left the service and enrolled in the famed Writer's Workshop at the University of Iowa. From 1966 through 1984, Dubus taught modern fiction and creative writing at Bradford College in Massachusetts. He has been a visiting professor at a number of colleges and universities, among them Boston University and the University of Alabama.

While at the University of Iowa, Dubus finished his novel *The Lieutenant* (1967). Although the actor Burt Lancaster bought the movie rights to the novel and hired Dubus to write the screenplay, the movie was never produced. The experience persuaded Dubus that screenwriting did not give him the challenge he wanted. With the exception of *Voices from the Moon* (1984), a novella, Dubus's subsequent publications have been essays or collections of short stories, a form he prefers. In addition to contributing stories to such periodicals as *Sewanee Review, Midwestern University Quarterly, Sage, New Yorker, Viva,* and *Ploughshares,* Dubus is represented in four editions of *Best American Short Stories* and in *O. Henry Prize Stories.* His short story collections include *Separate Flights* (1975), *Adultery and Other Choices* (1977), *Finding a Girl in America* (1980), *The Times Are Never So Bad* (1983), *We Don't Live Here Anymore* (1984), and *The Last Worthless Evening* (1986).

In July 1986, Dubus stopped to help the occupants of a disabled car on the side of the road. As he stood talking with the driver and a passenger, Dubus was hit by another car. His right leg was shattered and his left leg had to be amputated above the knee. Dubus spent the next several years in physical therapy, finally accepting that he would spend the rest of his life in a wheelchair. In 1996 he told a reporter that friends, family members, and prayer sustain him: "If I can get to mass in the morning, I usually got the gloominess knocked." The accident turned him away from fiction until 1996, however, when he published *Dancing After Hours,* his most acclaimed collection, from which "The Intruder" is taken. In this story, the protagonist Kenneth is a shy 13-year-old who reacts to what he perceives as an extreme situation. Has Kenneth read the situation correctly? Are his actions justifiable?

■

Because Kenneth Girard loved his parents and his sister and because he could not tell them why he went to the woods, his first moments there were always uncomfortable ones, as if he had left the house to commit a sin. But he was thirteen and he could not say that he was going to sit on a hill and wait for the silence and trees and sky to close in on him, wait until they all became a part of him and thought and memory ceased and the voices began. He could only say that he was going for a walk and, since there was so much more to say, he felt cowardly and deceitful and more lonely than before.

He could not say that on the hill he became great, that he had saved a beautiful girl from a river (the voice then had been gentle and serious and she had loved him), or that he had ridden into town, his clothes dusty, his black hat pulled low over his sunburned face, and an hour later had ridden away with four fresh notches on the butt of his six-gun, or that with the count three-and-two and the bases loaded, he had driven the ball so far and high that the outfielders did not even move, or that he had waded through surf and sprinted over sand, firing his Tommy gun and shouting to his soldiers behind him.

Now he was capturing a farmhouse. In the late movie the night before, the farmhouse had been very important, though no one ever said why, and sitting there in the summer dusk, he watched the backs of his soldiers as they advanced through the woods below him and crossed the clear, shallow creek and climbed the hill that he faced. Occasionally, he lifted his twenty-two-caliber rifle and fired at a rusty tin can across the creek, the can becoming a Nazi face in a window as he squeezed the trigger and the voices filled him: *You got him, Captain. You got him.* For half an hour he sat and fired at the can, and anyone who might have seen him could never know that he was doing anything else, that he had been wounded in the shoulder and lost half his men but had captured the farmhouse.

Kenneth looked up through the trees, which were darker green now. While he had been watching his battle, the earth, too, had become darker, shadowed, with patches of late sun on the grass and brown fallen pine needles. He stood up, then looked down at the creek, and across it, at the hill on the other side. His soldiers were gone. He was hungry, and he turned and walked back through the woods.

Then he remembered that his mother and father were going to a party in town that night and he would be alone with Connie. He liked being alone, but, even more, he liked being alone with his sister. She was nearly seventeen; her skin was fair, her cheeks colored, and she had long black hair that came down to her shoulders; on the right side of her face, a wave of it reached the corner of her eye. She was the most beautiful girl he knew. She was also the only person with whom, for his entire life, he had been nearly perfectly at ease. He could be silent with her or he could say whatever occurred to him and he never had to think about it first to assure himself that it was not foolish or, worse, uninteresting.

Leaving the woods, he climbed the last gentle slope and entered the house. He leaned his rifle in a corner of his room, which faced the quiet blacktop road, and went to the bathroom and washed his hands. Standing at the lavatory, he looked into the mirror. He suddenly felt as if he had told a lie. He was looking at his face and, as he did several times each day, telling himself, without words, that it was a handsome face. His skin was fair, as Connie's was, and he had color in his cheeks; but his hair, carefully parted and combed, was more brown than black. He believed that Connie thought he was exactly like her, that he was talkative and well liked. But she never saw him with his classmates. He felt that he was deceiving her.

He left the house and went into the outdoor kitchen and sat on a bench at the long, uncovered table and folded his arms on it.

"Did you kill anything?" Connie asked.

"Tin cans."

His father turned from the stove with a skillet of white perch in his hand.

"They're good ones," he said.

"Mine are the best," Kenneth said.

"You didn't catch but two."

"They're the best."

His mother put a plate in front of him, then opened a can of beer and sat beside him. He sat quietly, watching his father at the stove. Then he looked at his mother's hand holding the beer can. There were veins and several freckles on the back of it. Farther up her forearm was a small yellow bruise; the flesh at her elbow was wrinkled. He looked at her face. People said that he and Connie looked like her, so he supposed it was true, but he could not see the resemblance.

"Daddy and I are going to the Gossetts' tonight," she said.

"I know."

"I wrote the phone number down," his father said. "It's under the phone."

"Okay."

His father was not tall either, but his shoulders were broad. Kenneth wondered if his would be like that when he grew older. His father was the only one in the family who tanned in the sun.

"And *please*, Connie," his mother said, "will you go to sleep at a reasonable hour? It's hard enough to get you up for Mass when you've had a good night's sleep."

"Why don't we go into town for the evening Mass?"

"No. I don't like it hanging over my head all day."

"All right. When will y'all be home?"

"About two. And that doesn't mean read in bed till then. You need your sleep."

"We'll go to bed early," Connie said.

His father served fried perch and hush puppies onto their plates and they had French bread and catsup and Tabasco sauce and iced tea. After dinner, his father read the newspaper and his mother read a *Reader's Digest* condensation, then they showered and dressed, and at seven-thirty, they left. He and Connie followed them to the door. Connie kissed them; then he did. His mother and father looked happy, and he felt good about that.

"We'll be back about two," his mother said. "Keep the doors locked."

"Definitely," Connie said. "And we'll bar the windows."

"Well, you never know. Y'all be good. G'night."

"Hold down the fort, son," his father said.

"I will."

Then they were gone, the screen door slamming behind them, and Connie left the sunporch, but he stood at the door, listening to the car starting and watching its headlights as it backed down the trail through the yard, then turned into the road and drove away. Still he did not move. He loved the nights at the camp when they were left alone. At home, there was a disturbing climate about their evenings alone, for distant voices of boys in the neighborhood reminded him that he was not alone entirely by choice. Here, there were no sounds.

He latched the screen and went into the living room. Connie was sitting in the rocking chair near the fireplace, smoking a cigarette. She looked at him, then flicked ashes into an ashtray on her lap.

"Now don't you tell on me."

"I didn't know you did that."

"Please don't tell. Daddy would skin me alive."

"I won't."

He could not watch her. He looked around the room for a book.

"Douglas is coming tonight," she said.

"Oh." He picked up the *Reader's Digest* book and pretended to look at it. "Y'all going to watch TV?" he said.

"Not if you want to."

"It doesn't matter."

"You watch it. You like Saturday nights."

She looked as if she had been smoking for a long time, all during the summer and possibly the school year, too, for months or even a year without his knowing it. He was hurt. He laid down the book.

"Think I'll go outside for a while," he said.

He went onto the sunporch and out the door and walked down the sloping car trail that led to the road. He stopped at the gate, which was open, and leaned on it. Forgetting Connie, he looked over his shoulder at the camp, thinking that he would never tire of it. They had been there for six weeks, since early June, his father coming on Friday evenings and leaving early Monday mornings, driving sixty miles to their home in southern Louisiana. Kenneth fished during the day, swam with Connie in the creeks, read novels about baseball, and watched the major league games on television. He thought winter at the camp was better, though. They came on weekends and hunted squirrels, and there was a fireplace.

He looked down the road. The closest camp was half a mile away, on the opposite side of the road, and he could see its yellow-lighted windows through the trees. *That's the house. Quiet now. We'll sneak through the woods and get the guard, then charge the house. Come on.* Leaning against the gate, he stared into the trees across the road and saw himself leading his soldiers through the woods. They reached the guard. His back was turned and Kenneth crawled close to him, then stood up and slapped a hand over the guard's mouth and stabbed him in the back. They rushed the house and Kenneth reached the door first and kicked it open. The general looked up from his desk, then tried to get his pistol from his holster. Kenneth shot him with his Tommy gun. *Grab those papers, men. Let's get out of here.* They got the papers and ran outside and Kenneth stopped to throw a hand grenade through the door. He reached the woods before it exploded.

He turned from the gate and walked toward the house, looking around him at the dark pines. He entered the sunporch and latched the screen; then he smelled chocolate, and he went to the kitchen. Connie was stirring a pot of fudge on the stove. She had changed to a fresh pale blue shirt, the tails of it hanging almost to the bottom of her white shorts.

"It'll be a while," she said.

He nodded, watching her hand and the spoon. He thought of Douglas coming and began to feel nervous.

"What time's Douglas coming?"

"Any minute now. Let me know if you hear his car."

"All right."

He went to his room and picked up his rifle; then he saw the magazine on the chest of drawers and he leaned the rifle in the corner again. Suddenly his mouth was dry. He got the magazine and quickly turned the pages until he found her: she was stepping out of the surf on the French Riviera, laughing, as if the man with her had just said something funny. She was blond and very tan and she wore a bikini. The photograph was in color. For several moments he looked at it; then he got the rifle and cleaning kit and sat in the rocking chair in the living room, with the rifle across his lap. He put a patch on the cleaning rod and dipped it in bore cleaner and pushed it down the barrel, the handle of the rod clanging against the muzzle. He worked slowly, pausing often to listen for Douglas's car, because he wanted to be cleaning the rifle when Douglas came. Because Douglas was a tackle on the high school football team in the town, and Kenneth had never been on a football team, and never would be.

The football players made him more uncomfortable than the others. They walked into the living room and firmly shook his father's hand, then his hand, beginning to talk as soon as they entered, and they sat and waited for Connie, their talking never ceasing, their big chests and shoulders leaned forward, their faces slowly turning as they looked at each picture on the wall, at the designs on the rug, at the furniture, passing over Kenneth as if he were another chair, filling the room with a feeling of strength and self-confidence that defeated him, paralyzing his tongue and even his mind, so that he merely sat in thoughtless anxiety, hoping they would not speak to him, hoping especially that they would not ask: *You play football?* Two of them had, and he never forgot it. He had answered with a mute, affirming nod.

He had always been shy and, because of it, he had stayed on the periphery of sports for as long as he could remember. When his teachers forced him to play, he spent an anxious hour trying not to become involved, praying in right field that no balls would come his way, lingering on the outside of the huddle so that no one would look up and see his face and decide to throw him a pass on the next play.

But he found that there was one thing he could do and he did it alone, or with his father: he could shoot and he could hunt. He felt that shooting was the only thing that had ever been easy for him. Schoolwork was, too, but he considered that a curse.

He was not disturbed by the boys who were not athletes, unless, for some reason, they were confident anyway. While they sat and waited for Connie, he was cheerful and teasing, and they seemed to like him. The girls were best. He walked into the living room and they stopped their talking and laughing and all of them greeted him and sometimes they said: "Connie, he's so cute," or "I wish you were three years older," and he said: "Me, too," and tried to be witty and usually was.

He heard a car outside.

"Douglas is here," he called.

Connie came through the living room, one hand arranging the wave of hair near her right eye, and went into the sunporch. Slowly, Kenneth wiped the rifle with an oily rag. He heard Douglas's loud voice and laughter and heavy footsteps on the sunporch; then they came into the living room. Kenneth raised his face.

"Hi," he said.

"How's it going?"

"All right."

Douglas Bakewell was not tall. He had blond hair, cut so short on top that you could see his scalp, and a reddish face, and sunburned arms, covered with bleached hair. A polo shirt fit tightly over his chest and shoulders and biceps.

"Whatcha got there?" Douglas said.

"Twenty-two."

"Let's see."

"Better dry it."

He briskly wiped it with a dry cloth and handed it to Douglas. Quickly, Douglas worked the bolt, aimed at the ceiling, and pulled the trigger.

"Nice trigger," he said.

He held it in front of his waist and looked at it, then gave it to Kenneth.

"Well, girl," he said, turning to Connie, "where's the beer?"

"Sit down and I'll get you one."

She went to the kitchen. Douglas sat on the couch and Kenneth picked up his cleaning kit and, not looking at Douglas, walked into his bedroom. He stayed there until Connie returned from the kitchen; then he went into the living room. They were sitting on the couch. Connie was smoking again. Kenneth kept walking toward the sunporch.

"I'll let you know when the fudge is ready," Connie said.

"All right."

On the sunporch, he turned on the television and sat in front of it. He watched ten minutes of a Western before he was relaxed again, before he settled in his chair, oblivious to the quiet talking in the living room, his mind beginning to wander happily as a gunfighter in dark clothes moved across the screen.

By the time the fudge was ready, he was watching a detective story, and when Connie called him, he said: "Okay, in a minute," but did not move, and finally she came to the sunporch with a saucer of fudge and set it on a small table beside his chair.

"When that's over, you better go to bed," she said.

"I'm not sleepy."

"You know what Mother said."

"*You're* staying up."

"Course I am. I'm also a little older than you."

"I want to see the late show."

"No!"

"Yes, I am."

"I'll tell Daddy."

"He doesn't care."

"I'll tell him you wouldn't listen to me."

"I'll tell him you smoke."

"Oh, I could *wring* your neck!"

She went to the living room. He tried to concentrate on the Western, but it was ruined. The late show came on and he had seen it several months before and did not want to see it again, but he would not go to bed. He watched absently. Then he had to urinate. He got up and went into the living room, walking quickly, only glancing at them once, but when he did, Connie smiled and, with her voice friendly again, said: "What is it?"

He stopped and looked at her.

"*Red River.*"

He smiled.

"I already saw it," he said.

"You watching it again?"

"Maybe so."

"Okay."

He went to the bathroom and when he came back, they were gone. He went to the sunporch. Connie and Douglas were standing near the back door. The television was turned off. Kenneth wondered if Connie had seen *Red River.* If she had not, he could tell her what had happened during the part she missed. Douglas was whispering to Connie, his face close to hers. Then he looked at Kenneth.

"'Night," he said.

"G'night," Kenneth said.

He was gone. Kenneth picked up the saucer his fudge had been on and took it to the kitchen and put it in the sink. He heard Douglas's car backing down the trail, and he went to the sunporch, but Connie was not there, so he went to the bathroom door and said: "You seen *Red River*?"

"Yes."

"You taking a bath?"

"Just washing my face. I'm going to bed."

He stood quietly for a moment. Then he went into the living room and got a magazine and sat in the rocking chair, looking at the people in the advertisements. Connie came in, wearing a robe. She leaned over his chair and he looked up and she kissed him.

"Good night," she said.

"G'night."

"You going to bed soon?"

"In a minute."

She got her cigarettes and an ashtray from the coffee table and went to her room and closed the door. After a while, he heard her getting into bed.

He looked at half the magazine, then laid it on the floor. Being awake in a house where everyone else was sleeping made him lonely. He went to the sunporch and latched the screen, then closed the door and locked it. He left the light on but turned out the one in the living room. Then he went to his room and took off everything but his shorts. He was about to turn out the light when he looked at the chest of drawers and saw the magazine. He hesitated. Then he picked it up and found the girl and looked at the exposed tops of her breasts and at her navel and below it. Suddenly he closed the magazine and raised his eyes to the ceiling, then closed them and said three Hail Mary's. Without looking at it, he picked up the magazine and took it to the living room, and went back to his bedroom and lay on his belly on the floor and started doing push-ups. He had no trouble with the first eight; then they became harder, and by the fifteenth he was breathing fast and his whole body was trembling as he pushed himself up from the floor. He did one more, then stood up and turned out the light and got into bed.

His room extended forward of the rest of the house, so that, from his bed, he could look through the window to his left and see the living room and Connie's bedroom. He rolled on his back and pulled the sheet up to his chest. He could hear crickets outside his window.

He flexed his right arm and felt the bicep. It seemed firmer than it had in June, when he started doing push-ups every night. He closed his eyes and began the Lord's Prayer and got as far as *Thy kingdom come* before he heard it.

Now it was not the crickets that he heard. He heard his own breathing and the bedsprings as his body tensed; then he heard it again, somewhere in front of the house: a cracking twig, a rustle of dried leaves, a foot on hard earth. Slowly, he rolled on his left side and looked out the windows. He waited to be sure, but he did not have to; then he waited to decide what he would do, and he did not have to wait for that either, because he already knew, and he looked at the far corner of the room where his rifle was, though he could not see it, and he looked out the window again, staring at the windows of the living room and Connie's room, forcing himself to keep his eyes there, as if it would be all right if the prowler did not come into his vision, did not come close to the house; but listening to the slow foot-steps, Kenneth knew that he would.

Get up. Get up and get the rifle. If you don't do it now, he might come to this window and look in and then it'll be too late.

For a moment, he did not breathe. Then, slowly, stopping at each sound of the bedsprings, he rolled out of bed and crouched on the floor beneath the window. He did not move. He listened to his breathing, for there was no other sound, not even crickets, and he began to tremble, thinking the prowler might be standing above him, looking through his window at the empty bed. He held his breath. Then he heard the footsteps again, in front of the house, closer now, and he thought: *He's by the pines in front of Connie's room.* He crawled away from the window, thinking of a large, bearded man standing in the pine trees thirty yards from Connie's room, studying the house and deciding which window to use; then he stood up and walked on tiptoes to the chest of drawers and moved his hand over the top of it until he touched the handful of bullets, his fingers quickly closing on them, and he picked up the rifle and took out the magazine and loaded it, then inserted it again and laid the extra bullets on the chest of drawers. Now he had to work the bolt. He pulled it up and back and eased it forward again.

Staying close to the wall, he tiptoed back to the window, stopping at the edge of it, afraid to look out and see a face looking in. He heard nothing. He looked through the windows in the opposite wall, thinking that if the prowler had heard him getting the rifle, he could have run back to the road, back to wherever he had come from, or he could still be hiding in the pines, or he could have circled to the rear of the house to hide again and listen, but there was no way of knowing, and he would have to stand in the room, listening, until his father came home. He thought of going to wake Connie, but he was afraid to move. Then he heard him again, near the pines, coming toward the house. He kneeled and pressed his shoulder against the wall, moving his face slightly, just enough to look out the screen and see the prowler walking toward Connie's window, stopping there and looking over his shoulder at the front yard and the road, then reaching out and touching the screen.

Kenneth rose and moved away from the wall, standing close to his bed now; he aimed through the screen, found the side of the man's head, then fired. A scream filled the house, the yard, his mind, and he thought at first it was the prowler, who was lying on the ground now, but it was a high, shrieking scream; it was Connie, and he ran into the living room, but she was already on the sunporch, unlocking the back door, not screaming now, but crying, pulling open the wooden door and hitting the screen with both hands, then stopping to unlatch it, and he yelled: "Connie!"

She turned, her hair swinging around her cheek.

"Get away from me!"

Then she ran outside, the screen door slamming, the shriek starting again, a long, high wail, ending in front of the house with "*Douglas, Douglas, Douglas!*" Then he knew.

Afterward, it seemed that the events of a year had occurred in an hour, and, to Kenneth, even that hour seemed to have a quality of neither speed nor slowness, but a kind of suspension, as if time were not passing at all. He remembered somehow calling his father and crying into the phone: "I shot Douglas Bakewell," and because of the crying, his father kept saying: "What's that, son? What did you say?" and then he lay facedown on his bed and cried, thinking of Connie outside with Douglas, hearing her sometimes when his own sounds lulled, and sometimes thinking of Connie inside with Douglas, if he had not shot him. He remembered the siren when it was far away and their voices as they brought Connie into the house. The doctor had come first, then his mother and father, then the sheriff; but, remembering, it was as if they had all come at once, for there was always a soothing or questioning face over his bed. He remembered the footsteps and hushed voices as they carried the body past his window, while his mother sat on the bed and stroked his forehead and cheek. He would never forget that.

Now the doctor and sheriff were gone and it seemed terribly late, almost sunrise. His father came into the room, carrying a glass of water, and sat on the bed.

"Take this," he said. "It'll make you sleep."

Kenneth sat up and took the pill from his father's palm and placed it on his tongue, then drank the water. He lay on his back and looked at his father's face. Then he began to cry.

"I thought it was a prowler," he said.

"It was, son. A prowler. We've told you that."

"But Connie went out there and she stayed all that time and she kept saying '*Douglas*' over and over; I heard her—"

"She wasn't out there with *him*. She was just out in the yard. She was in shock. She meant she wanted Douglas to be there with her. To help."

"No, *no*. It was *him*."

"It was a prowler. You did right. There's no telling what he might have done."

Kenneth looked away.

"He was going in her room," he said. "That's why she went to bed early. So I'd go to bed."

"It was a prowler," his father said.

Now Kenneth was sleepy. He closed his eyes and the night ran together in his mind and he remembered the rifle in the corner and thought: *I'll throw it in the creek tomorrow. I never want to see it again.* He would be asleep soon. He saw himself standing on the hill and throwing his rifle into the creek; then the creek became an ocean, and he stood on a high cliff and for a moment he was a mighty angel, throwing all guns and cruelty and sex and tears into the sea.

QUESTIONS FOR DISCUSSION

1. How would you describe the relationships between the various members of this family? Cite reasons or quotations.

2. Why does Kenneth like being at the family's cottage, or camp?

3. What might be some reasons for Kenneth's imaginary exploits?

4. What is the initiating incident in the story?

5. What conflicts can you discern in this story?

6. What is the climax of the story?

7. What details foreshadow the climax of the plot?

8. What prompts Kenneth to fire at the intruder?

9. His father assures Kenneth that the prowler was not Douglas. Do you agree? Why or why not?

10. Who is the greater victim—Douglas or the intruder?

11. Working in small groups, discuss how you think the killing will change Kenneth's life. Be prepared to explain your answer.

12. In what sense might the story contain more than one intruder?

13. How does the final sentence of the resolution tie together many of the important ideas and details of the story?

TOPICS FOR WRITING

1. Describe a time when you were faced with a dangerous situation. What was your reaction at the time?

2. Could the shooting have been prevented? If so, how? If not, why not? Discuss this question in an essay of opinion.

3. Working in a small group, identify the paragraphs containing the exposition. Remember: exposition is not limited to the opening paragraphs.

4. In an essay, analyze how Dubus creates suspense in the paragraphs immediately before the shooting.

FIRST CONFESSION

FRANK O'CONNOR (1903–1966)

Born Michael Francis O'Donovan in Cork, Ireland, Frank O'Connor was the only child of an Irish family too poor to provide him with much formal education. By age twelve, O'Connor had written a collection of poems, biographies, and essays about history. O'Connor observed later, "I was intended by God to be a painter, but I was very poor and pencil and paper were the cheapest."

At sixteen, O'Connor joined the Irish Republican Army and fought in the civil war from 1919 to 1921. Although a 1921 treaty ended English occupation, O'Connor was imprisoned for continuing the fight. In prison, O'Connor continued his self-education. When he was released in 1923, O'Connor became a librarian; he also began submitting short stories to *Irish Statesman*, the most important literary magazine in Ireland. When his first collection of short stories, *Guests of the Nation* (1931), was published, O'Connor—concerned that his political past would be held against him—adopted his beloved mother's maiden name as his pen name.

From 1935 to 1939, O'Connor was codirector of Dublin's famed Abbey Theatre; he wrote several one-act plays celebrating Irish history and nationalism. He also began to write poetry and to translate old Irish literature and poetry into English from the Gaelic. O'Connor resigned his position at the Abbey over the issue of censorship.

During World War II, though Ireland was officially neutral, O'Connor worked as a writer/broadcaster for the Ministry of Information. In the 1950s, O'Connor came to the United States as a visiting professor at Harvard University, Northwestern University, and Stanford University, but missing his native land, he returned to Ireland.

Best known today for his short stories that capture both the voice and soul of Ireland, O'Connor also wrote poetry, biography, literary criticism, two autobiographies, travel books, various translations of Irish poetry and tales, and several books of history. For his varied and extensive output, O'Connor is often considered one of Ireland's premier writers. In "First Confession," a story first published in *Traveller's Samples* (1951), O'Connor captures the voice and the experience of a young sinner. Why does Jackie fear his first confession? Do you find the ending satisfying?

■

All the trouble began when my grandfather died and my grandmother—my father's mother—came to live with us. Relations in the one house are a strain at the best of times, but, to make matters worse, my grandmother was a real old countrywoman and quite unsuited to the life in town. She had a fat, wrinkled old face, and, to Mother's great indignation, went round the house in bare feet—the boots had her crippled, she said. For dinner she had a jug of porter[1] and a pot of potatoes with—sometimes—a bit of salt fish, and she poured out the potatoes on the table and ate them slowly, with great relish, using her fingers by way of a fork.

Now, girls are supposed to be fastidious, but I was the one who suffered most from this. Nora, my sister, just sucked up to the old woman for the penny she got every Friday out of the old-age pension, a thing I could not do. I was too honest, that was my trouble; and when I was playing with Bill Connell, the sergeant-major's son, and saw my grandmother steering up the path with the jug of porter sticking out from beneath her shawl I was mortified. I made excuses not to let him come into the house, because I could never be sure what she would be up to when we went in.

When Mother was at work and my grandmother made the dinner I wouldn't touch it. Nora once tried to make me, but I hid under the table from her and took the bread-knife with me for protection. Nora let on to be very indignant (she wasn't, of course, but she knew Mother saw through her, so she sided with Gran) and came after me. I lashed out at her with the bread-knife, and after that she left me alone. I stayed there till Mother came in from work and made my dinner, but when Father came in later Nora said in a shocked voice: "Oh, Dadda, do you know what Jackie did at dinnertime?" Then, of course, it all came out; Father gave me a flaking;[2] Mother interfered, and for days after that he didn't speak to me and Mother barely spoke to Nora. And all because of that old woman! God knows, I was heart-scalded.[3]

Then, to crown my misfortunes, I had to make my first confession and communion. It was an old woman called Ryan who prepared us for these. She was about the one age with Gran; she was well-to-do, lived in a big house on Montenotte, wore a black cloak and bonnet, and came every day to school at three o'clock when we should have

---

1 **porter:** short for *porter's ale*; a strong, dark-brown beer.

2 **flaking:** beating.

3 **heart-scalded:** disgusted.

been going home, and talked to us of hell. She may have mentioned the other place as well, but that could only have been an accident, for hell had the first place in her heart.

She lit a candle, took out a new half-crown,[4] and offered it to the first boy who would hold one finger—only one finger!—in the flame for five minutes by the school clock. Being always very ambitious I was tempted to volunteer, but I thought it might look greedy. Then she asked were we afraid of holding one finger—only one finger!—in a little candle flame for five minutes and not afraid of burning all over in roasting hot furnaces for all eternity. "All eternity! Just think of that! A whole lifetime goes by and it's nothing, not even a drop in the ocean of your sufferings." The woman was really interesting about hell, but my attention was all fixed on the half-crown. At the end of the lesson she put it back in her purse. It was a great disappointment; a religious woman like that, you wouldn't think she'd bother about a thing like a half-crown.

Another day she said she knew a priest who woke one night to find a fellow he didn't recognize leaning over the end of his bed. The priest was a bit frightened—naturally enough—but he asked the fellow what he wanted, and the fellow said in a deep, husky voice that he wanted to go to confession. The priest said it was an awkward time and wouldn't it do in the morning, but the fellow said that last time he went to confession, there was one sin he kept back, being ashamed to mention it, and now it was always on his mind. Then the priest knew it was a bad case, because the fellow was after making a bad confession and committing a mortal sin. He got up to dress, and just then the cock crew in the yard outside, and—lo and behold!—when the priest looked round there was no sign of the fellow, only a smell of burning timber, and when the priest looked at his bed didn't he see the print of two hands burned in it? That was because the fellow had made a bad confession. This story made a shocking impression on me.

But the worst of all was when she showed us how to examine our conscience. Did we take the name of the Lord, our God, in vain? Did we honor our father and our mother? (I asked her did this include grandmothers and she said it did.) Did we love our neighbors as ourselves? Did we covet our neighbor's goods? (I thought of the way I felt about the penny that Nora got every Friday.) I decided that, between one thing and another, I must have broken the whole ten commandments, all on account of that old woman, and so far as I

---

4 **half-crown:** a coin worth two shillings and sixpence; no longer used.

could see, so long as she remained in the house I had no hope of ever doing anything else.

I was scared to death of confession. The day the whole class went I let on to have a toothache, hoping my absence wouldn't be noticed; but at three o'clock, just as I was feeling safe, along comes a chap with a message from Mrs. Ryan that I was to go to confession myself on Saturday and be at the chapel for communion with the rest. To make it worse, Mother couldn't come with me and sent Nora instead.

Now, that girl had ways of tormenting me that Mother never knew of. She held my hand as we went down the hill, smiling sadly and saying how sorry she was for me, as if she were bringing me to the hospital for an operation.

"Oh, God help us!" she moaned. "Isn't it a terrible pity you weren't a good boy? Oh, Jackie, my heart bleeds for you! How will you ever think of all your sins? Don't forget you have to tell him about the time you kicked Gran on the shin."

"Lemme go!" I said, trying to drag myself free of her. "I don't want to go to confession at all."

"But sure, you'll have to go to confession, Jackie," she replied in the same regretful tone. "Sure, if you didn't, the parish priest would be up to the house, looking for you. 'Tisn't, God knows, that I'm not sorry for you. Do you remember the time you tried to kill me with the bread-knife under the table? And the language you used to me? I don't know what he'll do with you at all, Jackie. He might have to send you up to the bishop."

I remember thinking bitterly that she didn't know the half of what I had to tell—if I told it. I knew I couldn't tell it, and understood perfectly why the fellow in Mrs. Ryan's story made a bad confession; it seemed to me a great shame that people wouldn't stop criticizing him. I remember that steep hill down to the church, and the sunlit hillsides beyond the valley of the river, which I saw in the gaps between the houses like Adam's last glimpse of Paradise.

Then, when she had maneuvered me down the long flight of steps to the chapel yard, Nora suddenly changed her tone. She became the raging malicious devil she really was.

"There you are!" she said with a yelp of triumph, hurling me through the church door. "And I hope he'll give you the penitential psalms, you dirty little caffler."[5]

---

5 **caffler:** mocker, one who jeers. A variant of the verb *to cavil.*

I knew then I was lost, given up to eternal justice. The door with the colored-glass panels swung shut behind me, the sunlight went out and gave place to deep shadow, and the wind whistled outside so that the silence within seemed to crackle like ice under my feet. Nora sat in front of me by the confession box. There were a couple of old women ahead of her, and then a miserable-looking poor devil came and wedged me in at the other side, so that I couldn't escape even if I had the courage. He joined his hands and rolled his eyes in the direction of the roof, muttering aspirations in an anguished tone, and I wondered had he a grandmother too. Only a grandmother could account for a fellow behaving in that heartbroken way, but he was better off than I, for he at least could go and confess his sins; while I would make a bad confession and then die in the night and be continually coming back and burning people's furniture.

Nora's turn came, and I heard the sound of something slamming, and then her voice as if butter wouldn't melt in her mouth, and then another slam, and out she came. God, the hypocrisy of women! Her eyes were lowered, her head was bowed, and her hands were joined very low down on her stomach, and she walked up the aisle to the side altar looking like a saint. You never saw such an exhibition of devotion; and I remembered the devilish malice with which she had tormented me all the way from our door, and wondered were all religious people like that, really. It was my turn now. With the fear of damnation in my soul I went in, and the confessional door closed of itself behind me.

It was pitch-dark and I couldn't see priest or anything else. Then I really began to be frightened. In the darkness it was a matter between God and me, and He had all the odds. He knew what my intentions were before I even started; I had no chance. All I had ever been told about confession got mixed up in my mind, and I knelt to one wall and said: "Bless me, father, for I have sinned; this is my first confession." I waited for a few minutes, but nothing happened, so I tried it on the other wall. Nothing happened there either. He had me spotted all right.

It must have been then that I noticed the shelf at about one height with my head. It was really a place for grown-up people to rest their elbows, but in my distracted state I thought it was probably the place you were supposed to kneel. Of course, it was on the high side and not very deep, but I was always good at climbing and managed to get up all right. Staying up was the trouble. There was room only for my knees, and nothing you could get a grip on but a sort of wooden moulding a bit above it. I held on to the moulding and repeated the words a little louder, and this time something happened all right. A slide was slammed back; a little light entered the box, and a man's voice said: "Who's there?"

"'Tis me, father," I said for fear he mightn't see me and go away again. I couldn't see him at all. The place the voice came from was under the moulding, about level with my knees, so I took a good grip of the moulding and swung myself down till I saw the astonished face of a young priest looking up at me. He had to put his head on one side to see me, and I had to put mine on one side to see him, so we were more or less talking to one another upside-down. It struck me as a queer way of hearing confessions, but I didn't feel it my place to criticize.

"Bless me, father, for I have sinned; this is my first confession," I rattled off all in one breath, and swung myself down the least shade more to make it easier for him.

"What are you doing up there?" he shouted in an angry voice, and the strain the politeness was putting on my hold of the moulding, and the shock of being addressed in such an uncivil tone, were too much for me. I lost my grip, tumbled, and hit the door an unmerciful wallop before I found myself flat on my back in the middle of the aisle. The people who had been waiting stood up with their mouths open. The priest opened the door of the middle box and came out, pushing his biretta[6] back from his forehead; he looked something terrible. Then Nora came scampering down the aisle.

"Oh, you dirty little caffler!" she said. "I might have known you'd do it. I might have known you'd disgrace me. I can't leave you out of my sight for one minute."

Before I could even get to my feet to defend myself she bent down and gave me a clip across the ear. This reminded me that I was so stunned I had even forgotten to cry, so that people might think I wasn't hurt at all, when in fact I was probably maimed for life. I gave a roar out of me.

"What's all this about?" the priest hissed, getting angrier than ever and pushing Nora off me. "How dare you hit the child like that, you little vixen?"

"But I can't do my penance with him, father," Nora cried, cocking an outraged eye up at him.

---

6 **biretta:** a stiff, square cap with three or four upright projecting ridges.

"Well, go and do it, or I'll give you some more to do," he said, giving me a hand up. "Was it coming to confession you were, my poor man?" he asked me.

"'Twas, father," said I with a sob.

"Oh," he said respectfully, "a big hefty fellow like you must have terrible sins. Is this your first?"

"'Tis, father," said I.

"Worse and worse," he said gloomily. "The crimes of a lifetime. I don't know will I get rid of you at all today. You'd better wait now till I'm finished with these old ones. You can see by the looks of them they haven't much to tell."

"I will, father," I said with something approaching joy.

The relief of it was really enormous. Nora stuck out her tongue at me from behind his back, but I couldn't even be bothered retorting. I knew from the very moment that man opened his mouth that he was intelligent above the ordinary. When I had time to think, I saw how right I was. It only stood to reason that a fellow confessing after seven years would have more to tell than people that went every week. The crimes of a lifetime, exactly as he said. It was only what he expected, and the rest was the cackle of old women and girls with their talk of hell, the bishop, and the penitential psalms. That was all they knew. I started to make my examination of conscience, and barring the one bad business of my grandmother it didn't seem so bad.

The next time, the priest steered me into the confession box himself and left the shutter back the way I could see him get in and sit down at the further side of the grille from me.

"Well, now," he said, "what do they call you?"

"Jackie, father," said I.

"And what's a-trouble to you, Jackie?"

"Father," I said, feeling I might as well get it over while I had him in good humor, "I had it all arranged to kill my grandmother."

He seemed a bit shaken by that, all right, because he said nothing for quite a while.

"My goodness," he said at last, "that'd be a shocking thing to do. What put that into your head?"

"Father," I said, feeling very sorry for myself, "she's an awful woman."

"Is she?" he asked. "What way is she awful?"

"She takes porter, father," I said, knowing well from the way Mother talked of it that this was a mortal sin, and hoping it would make the priest take a more favorable view of my case.

"Oh, my!" he said, and I could see he was impressed.

"And snuff, father," said I.

"That's a bad case, sure enough, Jackie," he said.

"And she goes round in her bare feet, father," I went on in a rush of self-pity, "and she knows I don't like her, and she gives pennies to Nora and none to me, and my da sides with her and flakes me, and one night I was so heart-scalded I made up my mind I'd have to kill her."

"And what would you do with the body?" he asked with great interest.

"I was thinking I could chop that up and carry it away in a barrow I have," I said.

"Begor,[7] Jackie," he said, "do you know you're a terrible child?"

"I know, father," I said, for I was just thinking the same thing myself. "I tried to kill Nora too with a bread-knife under the table, only I missed her."

"Is that the little girl that was beating you just now?" he asked.

"'Tis, father."

"Someone will go for her with a bread-knife one day, and he won't miss her," he said rather cryptically. "You must have great courage. Between ourselves, there's a lot of people I'd like to do the same to but I'd never have the nerve. Hanging is an awful death."

"Is it, father?" I asked with the deepest interest—I was always very keen on hanging. "Did you ever see a fellow hanged?"

"Dozens of them," he said solemnly. "And they all died roaring."

"Jay!" I said.

"Oh, a horrible death!" he said with great satisfaction. "Lots of the fellows I saw killed their grandmothers too, but they all said 'twas never worth it."

He had me there for a full ten minutes talking, and then walked out the chapel yard with me. I was genuinely sorry to part with him, because he was the most entertaining character I'd ever met in the religious line. Outside, after the shadow of the church, the sunlight was like the roaring waves on a beach; it dazzled me; and when the frozen silence melted and I heard the screech of trams on the road my heart soared. I knew now I wouldn't die in the night and come back, leaving marks on my mother's furniture. It would be a great worry to her, and the poor soul had enough.

---

7 **begor:** Irish form of the English exclamation *begad,* or "By God." Also, *begorra* or *begorrah.*

Nora was sitting on the railing, waiting for me, and she put on a very sour puss when she saw the priest with me. She was mad jealous because a priest had never come out of the church with her.

"Well," she asked coldly, after he left me, "what did he give you?"

"Three Hail Marys," I said.

"Three Hail Marys," she repeated incredulously. "You mustn't have told him anything."

"I told him everything," I said confidently.

"About Gran and all?"

"About Gran and all."

(All she wanted was to be able to go home and say I'd make a bad confession.)

"Did you tell him you went for me with the bread-knife?" she asked with a frown.

"I did to be sure."

"And he only gave you three Hail Marys?"

"That's all."

She slowly got down from the railing with a baffled air. Clearly, this was beyond her. As we mounted the steps back to the main road she looked at me suspiciously.

"What are you sucking?" she asked.

"Bullseyes."[8]

"Was it the priest gave them to you?"

"'Twas."

"Lord God," she wailed bitterly, "some people have all the luck! 'Tis no advantage to anybody trying to be good. I might just as well be a sinner like you."

---

8 **Bullseyes:** round, hard candies.

QUESTIONS FOR DISCUSSION

1. What details suggest that the story takes place in Ireland?

2. Describe Jackie, the narrator of this story. Support your description with evidence from the story.

3. What kind of relationship does Jackie have with each of his parents?

4. What information does O'Connor include in the exposition, the first six paragraphs?

5. Working with a partner, identify the events that constitute the rising action.

6. How does O'Connor create suspense in this story?

7. As Nora and Jackie walk to the chapel, Jackie compares the "sunlit hillsides beyond the valley of the river" to "Adam's last glimpse of Paradise." Why is this comparison particularly appropriate?

8. O'Connor is particularly celebrated for the humor underlying many of his stories. In a small group, identify what in this story you find humorous.

9. What seems to be the major conflict in the story?

TOPICS FOR WRITING

1. Using the existing dialogue, retell the priest's encounter with Jackie from the point of view of the priest.

2. Write about a personal experience that you feared would turn out badly.

3. In a group, identify any events in the first six paragraphs that foreshadow the conclusion and explain how they do so.

4. In an essay, discuss what seems to be the most likely moment of climax in the story and why.

SWEAT

ZORA NEALE HURSTON (1891–1960)

Zora Neale Hurston was born in Eatonville, Florida, the first all-black township incorporated in the United States. After her widowed father remarried, Hurston left home and lived with a variety of relatives before taking a job as the personal maid of an actress in a traveling drama troupe. By 1918, she had left the troupe and completed her high school education in Baltimore. Between 1918 and 1924, she occasionally took courses at Howard University. At the suggestion of a professor, Hurston successfully submitted one of her short stories to a New York publication. Hurston moved to New York and, in 1928, graduated from Barnard College. She soon became one of the brighter literary stars of the artistic movement known as the Harlem Renaissance.

One of her Barnard professors, impressed with a paper she wrote, sent it to the renowned anthropologist Franz Boas. Boas arranged for Hurston to begin graduate work in anthropology at Columbia University. She returned to the South for her field work and eventually published two books containing folklore, short stories, and anthropological material: *Mules and Men* (1935) and *Tell My Horse* (1938), whose contents focused on the culture of the Caribbean. While living in the Caribbean, Hurston completed her second and greatest novel: *Their Eyes Were Watching God* (1937). Hurston's writing of dialect reflects her extensive research and accurately represents the speech patterns and pronunciation her characters would use.

During the 1930s Hurston worked on musical productions based on the folklore she collected; she also collaborated with Langston Hughes on a play, *Mule Bone*, but quarreled with him before it could be produced. After publishing her autobiography, *Dust Tracks on a Road* (1942), Hurston was soon writing articles for mainstream magazines. In 1948, however, she was accused of a crime she had not—indeed, could not have—committed. Deeply humiliated by the publicity, she chose to disappear from public view. In the remaining years of her life, she was briefly employed as a cleaning woman, a librarian, a journalist, and a substitute teacher. Hurston died in 1960.

In "Sweat" (1926), Hurston explores the plight of Delia, married to a brutish and unfaithful husband. Why has her marriage failed? Is the resolution to Delia's unhappiness the result of her actions or the working of fate?

■

It was eleven o'clock of a Spring night in Florida. It was Sunday. Any other night, Delia Jones would have been in bed for two hours by this time. But she was a washwoman, and Monday morning meant a great deal to her. So she collected the soiled clothes on Saturday when she returned the clean things. Sunday night after church, she sorted them and put the white things to soak. It saved her almost a half day's start. A great hamper in the bedroom held the clothes that she brought home. It was so much neater than a number of bundles lying around.

She squatted on the kitchen floor beside the great pile of clothes, sorting them into small heaps according to color, and humming a song in a mournful key, but wondering through it all where Sykes, her husband, had gone with her horse and buckboard.

Just then something long, round, limp and black fell upon her shoulders and slithered to the floor beside her. A great terror took hold of her. It softened her knees and dried her mouth so that it was a full minute before she could cry out or move. Then she saw that it was the big bull whip her husband liked to carry when he drove.

She lifted her eyes to the door and saw him standing there bent over with laughter at her fright. She screamed at him.

"Sykes, what you throw dat whip on me like dat? You know it would skeer me—looks like a snake, an' you knows how skeered Ah is of snakes."

"Course Ah knowed it! That's how come Ah done it." He slapped his leg with his hand and almost rolled on the ground in his mirth. "If you such a big fool dat you got to have a fit over a earth worm or a string, Ah don't keer how bad Ah skeer you."

"You aint got no business doing it. Gawd knows it's a sin. Some day Ah'm gointuh drop dead from some of yo' foolishness. 'Nother thing, where you been wid mah rig? Ah feeds dat pony. He aint fuh you to be drivin' wid no bull whip."

"You sho is one aggravatin' nigger woman!" he declared and stepped into the room. She resumed her work and did not answer him at once. "Ah done tole you time and again to keep them white folks' clothes outa dis house."

He picked up the whip and glared down at her. Delia went on with her work. She went out into the yard and returned with a galvanized tub and set it on the washbench. She saw that Sykes had kicked all of the clothes together again, and now stood in her way truculently, his whole manner hoping, *praying,* for an argument. But she walked calmly around him and commenced to re-sort the things.

"Next time, Ah'm gointer kick 'em outdoors," he threatened as he struck a match along the leg of his corduroy breeches.

Delia never looked up from her work, and her thin, stooped shoulders sagged further.

"Ah aint for no fuss t'night, Sykes. Ah just come from taking sacrament at the church house."

He snorted scornfully. "Yeah, you just come from de church house on a Sunday night, but heah you is gone to work on them clothes. You aint nothing but a hypocrite. One of them amen-corner Christians—sing, whoop, and shout, then come home and wash white folks' clothes on the Sabbath."

He stepped roughly upon the whitest pile of things, kicking them helter-skelter as he crossed the room. His wife gave a little scream of dismay, and quickly gathered them together again.

"Sykes, you quit grindin' dirt into these clothes! How can Ah git through by Sat'day if Ah don't start on Sunday?"

"Ah don't keer if you never git through. Anyhow, Ah done promised Gawd and a couple of other men, Ah aint gointer have it in mah house. Don't gimme no lip neither, else Ah'll throw 'em out and put mah fist up side yo' head to boot."

Delia's habitual meekness seemed to slip from her shoulders like a blown scarf. She was on her feet; her poor little body, her bare knuckly hands bravely defying the strapping hulk before her.

"Looka heah, Sykes, you done gone too fur. Ah been married to you fur fifteen years, and Ah been takin' in washin' fur fifteen years, Sweat, sweat, sweat! Work and sweat, cry and sweat, pray and sweat!"

"What's that got to do with me?" he asked brutally.

"What's it got to do with you, Sykes? Mah tub of suds is filled yo' belly with vittles more times than yo' hands is filled it. Mah sweat is done paid for this house and Ah reckon Ah kin keep on sweatin' in it."

She seized the iron skillet from the stove and struck a defensive pose, which act surprised him greatly, coming from her. It cowed him and he did not strike her as he usually did.

"Naw you won't," she panted, "that ole snaggle-toothed black woman you runnin' with aint comin' heah to pile up on *mah* sweat and blood. You aint paid for nothin' on this place, and Ah'm gointer stay right heah till Ah'm toted out foot foremost."

"Well, you better quit gittin' me riled up, else they'll be totin' you out sooner than you expect. Ah'm so tired of you Ah don't know whut to do. Gawd! how Ah hates skinny wimmen!"

A little awed by his new Delia, he sidled out of the door and slammed the back gate after him. He did not say where he had gone, but she knew too well. She knew very well that he would not return until nearly daybreak also. Her work over, she went on to bed but not to sleep at once. Things had come to a pretty pass!

She lay awake, gazing upon the debris that cluttered their matrimonial trail. Not an image left standing along the way. Anything like flowers had long ago been drowned in the salty stream that had been pressed from her heart. Her tears, her sweat, her blood. She had brought love to the union and he had brought a longing after the flesh. Two months after the wedding, he had given her the first brutal beating. She had the memory of his numerous trips to Orlando with all of his wages when he had returned to her penniless, even before the first year had passed. She was young and soft then, but now she thought of her knotty, muscled limbs, her harsh knuckly hands, and drew herself up into an unhappy little ball in the middle of the big feather bed. Too late now to hope for love, even if it were not Bertha it would be someone else. This case differed from the others only in that she was bolder than the others. Too late for everything except her little home. She had built it for her old days, and planted one by one the trees and flowers there. It was lovely to her, lovely.

Somehow, before sleep came, she found herself saying aloud: "Oh well, whatever goes over the Devil's back, is got to come under his belly. Sometime or ruther, Sykes, like everybody else, is gointer reap his sowing." After that she was able to build a spiritual earthworks against her husband. His shells could no longer reach her. *Amen*. She went to sleep and slept until he announced his presence by kicking her feet and rudely snatching the covers away.

"Gimme some kivah heah, an' git yo' damn foots over on yo' own side! Ah oughter mash you in yo' mouf fuh drawing dat skillet on me."

Delia went clear to the rail without answering him. A triumphant indifference to all that he was or did.

The week was full of work for Delia as all other weeks, and Saturday found her behind her little pony, collecting and delivering clothes.

It was a hot, hot day near the end of July. The village men on Joe Clarke's porch even chewed cane listlessly. They did not hurl the caneknots[1] as usual. They let them dribble over the edge of the porch. Even conversation had collapsed under the heat.

---

1 **caneknots:** the inedible part of the sugar cane stalk.

"Heah come Delia Jones," Jim Merchant said, as the shaggy pony came 'round the bend of the road toward them. The rusty buckboard was heaped with baskets of crisp, clean laundry.

"Yep, " Joe Lindsay agreed. "Hot or col', rain or shine, jes ez reg'lar ez de weeks roll roun' Delia carries 'em an' fetches 'em on Sat'day."

"She better if she wanter eat," said Moss. "Syke Jones aint wuth de shot an' powder hit would tek tuh kill 'em. Not to *huh* he aint."

"He sho' aint," Walter Thomas chimed in. "It's too bad, too, cause she wuz a right pritty lil trick when he got huh. Ah'd uh mah'ied huh mahseff if he hadnter beat me to it."

Delia nodded briefly at the men as she drove past.

"Too much knockin' will ruin *any* 'oman. He done beat huh 'nough tuh kill three women, let 'lone change they looks," said Elijah Moseley. "How Syke kin stommuck dat big black greasy Mogul[2] he's layin' roun' wid, gits me. Ah swear dat eight-rock[3] couldn't kiss a sardine can Ah done thowed out de back do' 'way las' yeah. "

"Aw, she's fat, thass how come. He's allus been crazy 'bout fat women," put in Merchant. "He'd a' been tied up wid one long time ago if he could a' found one tuh have him. Did Ah tell yuh 'bout him come sidlin' in' roun' *mah* wife—bringin' her a basket uh peecans outa his yard fuh a present? Yessir, mah wife! She tol' him tuh take em right straight back home, cause Delia works so hard ovah dat wash tub she reckon everything on de place taste lak sweat an' soapsuds. Ah jus' wisht Ah'd a caught 'im 'roun' dere! Ah'd a' made his hips ketch on fiah down dat shell road."

"Ah know he done it, too. Ah sees 'im grinnin' at every 'oman dat passes," Walter Thomas said. "But even so, he useter eat some mighty big hunks uh humble pie tuh git dat lil' 'oman he got. She wuz ez pritty ez a speckled pup! Dat wuz fifteen yeahs ago. He useter be so skeered uh losin' huh, she could make him do some parts of a husband's duty. Dey never wuz de same in de mind."

"There oughter be a law about him," said Lindsay. "He aint fit tuh carry guts tuh a bear."

Clarke spoke for the first time. "Taint no law on earth dat kin make a man be decent if it aint in 'im. There's plenty men dat takes a wife lak dey do a joint uh sugar-cane. It's round, juicy an' sweet when

---

2 **Mogul:** an important person, probably meant ironically.

3 **eight-rock:** the eight ball in pool. Here, a metaphor for a black person.

dey gits it. But dey squeeze an' grind, squeeze an' grind an' wring tell dey wring every drop uh pleasure dat's in 'em out. When dey's satis-fied dat dey is wrung dry, dey treats 'em jes lak dey do a cane-chew. Dey throws 'em away. Dey knows whut dey is doin' while dey is at it, an' hates theirselves fuh it but they keeps on hangin' after huh tell she's empty. Den dey hates huh fuh bein' a cane-chew an' in de way."

"We oughter take Syke an' dat stray 'oman uh his'n down in Lake Howell swamp an' lay on de rawhide till they cain't say Lawd a' mussy.' He allus wuz uh ovahbearin' niggah, but since dat white 'oman from up north done teached 'im how to run a automobile, he done got too biggety to live—an' we oughter kill 'im," Old man Anderson advised.

A grunt of approval went around the porch. But the heat was melting their civic virtue and Elijah Moseley began to bait Joe Clarke.

"Come on, Joe, git a melon outa dere an' slice it up for yo' cus-tomers. We'se all sufferin' wid de heat. De bear's done got *me!*"

"Thass right, Joe, a watermelon is jes' whut Ah needs tuh cure de eppizudicks,"[4] Walter Thomas joined forces with Moseley. "Come on dere, Joe. We all is steady customers an' you aint set us up in a long time. Ah chooses dat long, bowlegged Floridy favorite."

"A god, an' be dough. You all gimme twenty cents and slice way," Clarke retorted. "Ah needs a col' slice m'self. Heah, everybody chip in. Ah'll lend y'll mah meat knife."

The money was quickly subscribed and the huge melon brought forth. At that moment, Sykes and Bertha arrived. A determined silence fell on the porch and the melon was put away again.

Merchant snapped down the blade of his jackknife and moved toward the store door.

"Come on in, Joe, an' gimme a slab uh sow belly an' uh pound uh coffee—almost fuhgot 'twas Sat'day. Got to git on home." Most of the men left also.

Just then Delia drove past on her way home, as Sykes was order-ing magnificently for Bertha. It pleased him for Delia to see.

"Git whutsoever yo' heart desires, Honey. Wait a minute, Joe. Give huh two bottles uh strawberry soda-water, uh quart uh parched ground-peas, an' a block uh chewin' gum."

With all this they left the store, with Sykes reminding Bertha that this was his town and she could have it if she wanted it.

---

4 **eppizudicks:** from *epizootic,* relating to an outbreak of disease among animals.

The men returned soon after they left, and held their watermelon feast.

"Where did Syke Jones git da 'oman from nohow?" Lindsay asked.

"Ovah Apopka. Guess dey musta been cleanin' out de town when she lef'. She don't look lak a thing but a hunk uh liver wid hair on it."

"Well, she sho' kin squall," Dave Carter contributed. "When she gits ready tuh laff, she jes' opens huh mouf an' latches it back tuh de las' notch. No ole grandpa alligator down in Lake Bell aint got nothin' on huh."

Bertha had been in town three months now. Sykes was still paying her room rent at Della Lewis'—the only house in town that would have taken her in. Sykes took her frequently to Winter Park to "stomps."[5] He still assured her that he was the swellest man in the state.

"Sho' you kin have dat lil' ole house soon's Ah kin git dat 'oman outa dere. Everything b'longs tuh me an' you sho' kin have it. Ah sho' 'bominates uh skinny 'oman. Lawdy, you sho' is got one portly shape on you! You kin git *anything* you wants. Dis is *mah* town an' you sho' kin have it."

Delia's work-worn knees crawled over the earth in Gethsemane and up the rocks of Calvary[6] many, many times during these months. She avoided the villagers and meeting places in her efforts to be blind and deaf. But Bertha nullified this to a degree, by coming to Delia's house to call Sykes out to her at the gate.

Delia and Sykes fought all the time now with no peaceful interludes. They slept and ate in silence. Two or three times Delia had attempted a timid friendliness, but she was repulsed each time. It was plain that the breaches must remain agape.

The sun had burned July to August. The heat streamed down like a million hot arrows, smiting all things living upon the earth. Grass withered, leaves browned, snakes went blind in shedding and men and dogs went mad. Dog days!

Delia came home one day and found Sykes there before her. She wondered, but started to go on into the house without speaking, even

---

5 **stomps:** dances, especially loud and lively ones.

6 **Gethsemane . . . Calvary:** In the New Testament, the Garden of Gethsemane was the site of Jesus' agony, betrayal, and arrest; Calvary, or Golgotha, was the place near Jerusalem where Jesus was crucified.

though he was standing in the kitchen door and she must either stoop under his arm or ask him to move. He made no room for her. She noticed a soap box beside the steps, but paid no particular attention to it, knowing that he must have brought it there. As she was stooping to pass under his outstretched arm, he suddenly pushed her backward, laughingly.

"Look in de box dere Delia, Ah done brung yuh somethin'!"

She nearly fell upon the box in her stumbling, and when she saw what it held, she all but fainted outright.

"Syke! Syke, mah Gawd! You take dat rattlesnake 'way from heah! You *gottuh*. Oh, Jesus, have mussy!"

"Ah aint gut tuh do nuthin' uh de kin'—fact is Ah aint got tuh do nothin' but die. Taint no use uh you puttin' on airs makin' out lak you skeered uh dat snake—he's gointer stay right heah tell he die. He wouldn't bite me cause Ah knows how tuh handle 'im. Nohow he wouldn't risk breakin' out his fangs 'gin *yo'* skinny laigs."

"Naw, now Syke, don't keep dat thing 'roun' heah tuh skeer me tuh death. You knows Ah'm even feared uh earth worms. Thass de biggest snake Ah evah did see. Kill 'im Syke, please."

"Doan ast me tuh do nothin' fuh yuh. Goin' 'roun' tryin' tuh be so damn asterperious. Naw, Ah aint gonna kill it. Ah think uh damn sight mo' uh him dan you! Dat's a nice snake an' anybody doan lak 'im kin jes' hit de grit."

The village soon heard that Sykes had the snake, and came to see and ask questions.

"How de hen-fire did you ketch dat six-foot rattler, Syke?" Thomas asked.

"He's full uh frogs so he caint hardly move, thass how Ah eased up on 'm. But Ah'm a snake charmer an' knows how tuh handle 'em. Shux, dat aint nothin'. Ah could ketch one eve'y day if Ah so wanted tuh."

"Whut he needs is a heavy hick'ry club leaned real heavy on his head. Dat's de bes' way tuh charm a rattlesnake."

"Naw, Walt, y'll jes' don't understand dese diamon' backs lak Ah do," said Sykes in a superior tone of voice.

The village agreed with Walter, but the snake stayed on. His box remained by the kitchen door with its screen wire covering. Two or three days later it had digested its meal of frogs and literally came to life. It rattled at every movement in the kitchen or the yard. One day as Delia came down the kitchen steps she saw his chalky-white fangs curved like scimitars hung in the wire meshes. This time she did not run away with averted eyes as usual. She stood for a long time in the doorway in a red fury that grew bloodier for every second that she regarded the creature that was her torment.

That night she broached the subject as soon as Sykes sat down to the table.

"Syke, Ah wants you tuh take dat snake 'way fum heah. You done starved me an' Ah put up widcher, you done beat me an Ah took dat, but you done kilt all mah insides bringin' dat varmint heah."

Sykes poured out a saucer full of coffee and drank it deliberately before he answered her.

"A whole lot Ah keer 'bout how you feels inside uh out. Dat snake aint goin' no damn wheah till Ah gits ready fuh 'im tuh go. So fur as beatin' is concerned, yuh aint took near all dat you gointer take ef yuh stay 'roun' *me.*"

Delia pushed back her plate and got up from the table. "Ah hates you, Sykes," she said calmly. "Ah hates you tuh de same degree dat Ah useter love yuh. Ah done took an' took till mah belly is full up tuh mah neck. Dat's de reason Ah got mah letter fum de church an' moved mah membership tuh Woodbridge—so Ah don't haftuh take no sacrament wid yuh. Ah don't wantuh see yuh 'roun' me atall. Lay 'roun' wid dat 'oman all yuh wants tuh, but gwan 'way fum me an' mah house. Ah hates yuh lak uh suck-egg dog."[7]

Sykes almost let the huge wad of corn bread and collard greens he was chewing fall out of his mouth in amazement. He had a hard time whipping himself up to the proper fury to try to answer Delia.

"Well, Ah'm glad you does hate me. Ah'm sho' tiahed uh you hangin' ontuh me. Ah don't want yuh. Look at yuh stringey ole neck! Yo' rawbony laigs an' arms is enough tuh cut uh man tuh death. You looks jes' lak de devvul's doll-baby tuh *me.* You cain't hate me no worse dan Ah hates you. Ah been hatin' *you* fuh years."

"Yo' ole black hide don't look lak nothin' tuh me, but uh passle uh wrinkled up rubber, wid yo' big ole yeahs flappin' on each side lak uh paih uh buzzard wings. Don't think Ah'm gointuh be run 'way fum mah house neither. Ah'm goin' tuh de white folks bout *you,* mah young man, de very nex' time you lay yo' han's on me. Mah cup is done run ovah."

Delia said this with no signs of fear and Sykes departed from the house, threatening her, but made not the slightest move to carry out any of them.

---

7 **suck-egg dog:** a dog that steals and eats eggs.

That night he did not return at all, and the next day being Sunday, Delia was glad she did not have to quarrel before she hitched up her pony and drove the four miles to Woodbridge.

She stayed to the night service—"love feast"—which was very warm and full of spirit. In the emotional winds her domestic trials were borne far and wide so that she sang as she drove homeward,

> "Jurden water, black an' col'
>   Chills de body, not de soul
> An' Ah wantah cross Jurden in uh calm time."

She came from the barn to the kitchen door and stopped.

"Whut's de mattah, ol' satan, you aint kickin' up yo' racket?" She addressed the snake's box. Complete silence. She went on into the house with a new hope in its birth struggles. Perhaps her threat to go to the white folks had frightened Sykes! Perhaps he was sorry! Fifteen years of misery and suppression had brought Delia to the place where she would hope *anything* that looked towards a way over or through her wall of inhibitions.

She felt in the match safe behind the stove at once for a match. There was only one there.

"Dat niggah wouldn't fetch nothin' heah tuh save his rotten neck, but he kin run thew whut Ah brings quick enough. Now he done toted off nigh on tuh haff uh box uh matches. He done had dat 'oman heah in mah house too."

Nobody but a woman could tell how she knew this even before she struck the match. But she did and it put her into a new fury.

Presently she brought in the tubs to put the white things to soak. This time she decided she need not bring the hamper out of the bedroom: she would go in there and do the sorting. She picked up the pot-bellied lamp and went in. The room was small and the hamper stood hard by the foot of the white iron bed. She could sit and reach through the bedposts—resting as she worked.

"Ah wantah cross Jurden in uh calm time." She was singing again. The mood of the "love feast" had returned. She threw back the lid of the basket almost gaily. Then, moved by both horror and terror, she sprang back toward the door. *There lay the snake in the basket!* He moved sluggishly at first, but even as she turned round and round, jumped up and down in an insanity of fear, he began to stir vigorously. She saw him pouring his awful beauty from the basket upon the bed, then she seized the lamp and ran as fast as she could to the kitchen. The wind from the open door blew out the light and the darkness added to her terror. She sped to the darkness of the yard, slamming the door after her before she thought to set down the lamp. She did not feel safe even on the ground, so she climbed up in the hay barn.

There for an hour or more she lay sprawled upon the hay a gibbering wreck.

Finally she grew quiet, and after that, coherent thought. With this, stalked through her a cold, bloody rage. Hours of this. A period of introspection, a space of retrospection, then a mixture of both. Out of this an awful calm.

"Well, Ah done de bes' Ah could. If things aint right, Gawd knows taint mah fault."

She went to sleep—a twitch sleep—and woke up to a faint gray sky. There was a loud hollow sound below. She peered out. Sykes was at the wood-pile, demolishing a wire-covered box.

He hurried to the kitchen door, but hung outside there some minutes before he entered, and stood some minutes more inside before he closed it after him.

The gray in the sky was spreading. Delia descended without fear now, and crouched beneath the low bedroom window. The drawn shade shut out the dawn, shut in the night. But the thin walls held back no sound.

"Dat ol' scratch[8] is woke up now!" She mused at the tremendous whirr inside, which every woodsman knows, is one of the sound illusions. The rattler is a ventriloquist. His whirr sounds to the right, to the left, straight ahead, behind, close under foot—everywhere but where it is. Woe to him who guesses wrong unless he is prepared to hold up his end of the argument! Sometimes he strikes without rattling at all.

Inside, Sykes heard nothing until he knocked a pot lid off the stove while trying to reach the match safe in the dark. He had emptied his pockets at Bertha's.

The snake seemed to wake up under the stove and Sykes made a quick leap into the bedroom. In spite of the gin he had had, his head was clearing now.

"Mah Gawd!" he chattered, "ef Ah could on'y strack uh light!"

The rattling ceased for a moment as he stood paralyzed. He waited. It seemed that the snake waited also.

---

8 **ol' scratch:** one of the names for the devil; here, it refers to the snake.

"Oh, fuh de light! Ah thought he'd be too sick"—Sykes was muttering to himself when the whirr began again, closer, right underfoot this time. Long before this, Sykes' ability to think had been flattened down to primitive instinct and he leaped—onto the bed.

Outside Delia heard a cry that might have come from a maddened chimpanzee, a stricken gorilla. All the terror, all the horror, all the rage that man possibly could express, without a recognizable human sound.

A tremendous stir inside there, another series of animal screams, the intermittent whirr of the reptile. The shade torn violently down from the window, letting in the red dawn, a huge brown hand seizing the window stick, great dull blows upon the wooden floor punctuating the gibberish of sound long after the rattle of the snake had abruptly subsided. All this Delia could see and hear from her place beneath the window, and it made her ill. She crept over to the four-o'clocks[9] and stretched herself on the cool earth to recover.

She lay there. "Delia, Delia!" She could hear Sykes calling in a most despairing tone as one who expected no answer. The sun crept on up, and he called. Delia could not move—her legs were gone flabby. She never moved, he called, and the sun kept rising.

"Mah Gawd!" She heard him moan, "Mah Gawd fum Heben!" She heard him stumbling about and got up from her flower-bed. The sun was growing warm. As she approached the door she heard him call out hopefully, "Delia, is dat you Ah heah?"

She saw him on his hands and knees as soon as she reached the door. He crept an inch or two toward her—all that he was able, and she saw his horribly swollen neck and his one open eye shining with hope. A surge of pity too strong to support bore her away from that eye that must, could not, fail to see the tubs. He would see the lamp. Orlando with its doctors was too far. She could scarcely reach the Chinaberry tree, where she waited in the growing heat while inside she knew the cold river was creeping up and up to extinguish that eye which must know by now that she knew.

---

9 **four-o'clocks:** a small plant whose flowers open in late afternoon and close in early morning.

QUESTIONS FOR DISCUSSION

1. Does the setting of "Sweat" affect or reflect the events of the plot?

2. Describe Delia and Sykes's marriage.

3. Explain Sykes's attitude toward the "white folks' clothes."

4. Working in a small group, list the details established in the first section that foreshadow the end of the story.

5. What purpose does the second section of the story serve? Does it advance the plot? Reveal character? Suggest theme? Be prepared to defend your response.

6. Identify and discuss the appropriateness of the biblical references in section three, paragraph three: "Delia's work-worn knees crawled over the earth in Gethsemane and up the rocks of Calvary many, many times during these months."

7. Why does Sykes bring the rattlesnake home? Does the snake represent something more than just a snake?

8. In the final section, Delia finds only one match left in the match safe. What is the significance of this detail to the resolution of the plot?

9. To what does that "cold river" in the final sentence refer?

TOPICS FOR WRITING

1. Bertha persuades the local sheriff to arrest Delia for murder. List reasons Delia should not be indicted for Sykes's death.

2. Hurston has divided "Sweat" into several sections. Working with a partner, write a paper that discusses how each section contributes to the resolution of the story.

3. "Sweat" contains several references to creatures other than the rattlesnake. Working in a small group, list each creature, the person each is associated with, and what that association suggests.

4. This story was written more than 70 years ago. In an essay, discuss any aspects of the work that might now be considered politically incorrect.

5. In 1960, forgotten by all but a few, Hurston was buried in an unmarked grave in Fort Pierce, Florida. In an essay, explain why she is regarded today as one of the twentieth century's most important African-American voices.

SYNTHESIS QUESTIONS

1. Choose the story ending you liked best or least. Explain your choice.

2. Reread the stories by Dubus and O'Connor. For which main character do you have the most sympathy? Explain your answer.

3. The motif of parents and children is an important one in many of these stories. Analyze the success or failure of a parent in one of the stories in this chapter.

4. Choose one of the techniques of fiction—flashbacks, foreshadowing, suspense, or coincidence—and discuss which author used it most skillfully.

5. Read at least one more story by one of the authors in this chapter, and, in an essay, analyze the story's plot structures.

6. Suppose that you are going to make a film of one of the stories in this chapter. What would be your opening scene? Would you use flashbacks? Would you use a narrator along with dialogue, or dialogue only? What kind of background music, if any, would you choose? Block out the scene on paper.

7. Outline a plot for a short story based on something that you have recently observed in school, at home, on a bus, or in your neighborhood, or base the outline on a historical event.

8. Discuss an important epiphany experienced by one of the characters in these stories.

9. Choose three of the stories in this chapter and discuss which, if any, has a *deus ex machina* ending.

Chapter Two

SETTING

> In the days of King Alfred there lived a poor woman, whose cottage
> was in a remote country village, many miles from London.

Thus begins the old nursery tale "Jack and the Beanstalk." The sentence describes the **setting** of the tale—that is, the time (in the days of King Alfred) and the place (a cottage in a remote country village far from London). From the earliest times, storytellers have opened their narratives by telling of the setting, and generations of children have grown up intrigued by stories that begin "long ago in a faraway kingdom" or "one fine day in a hut by the sea."

Shakespeare, whose plays were performed on a bare stage with few props, conveyed setting through dialogue: "Ay, now am I in Arden," Rosalind says in *As You Like It*, "the more fool I: when I was at home, I was in a better place but travelers must be content." In *The Two Gentlemen of Verona*, Speed, a servant, says to one of the gentlemen, "welcome to Milan!" Near the beginning of *Hamlet*, an officer relieving a soldier on watch says, "'Tis now struck twelve; get thee to bed, Francisco." Such lines help to orient the viewer or reader and to anchor a story in time and space.

ASPECTS OF SETTING

Setting can be general (a city in the Midwest in the late nineteenth century), specific (a three-story mansion on Pine Street in Chicago in 1885), or very detailed (the darkened parlor of that mansion at four o'clock on the first Tuesday in December). Setting usually functions as more than a backdrop for a story, however.

Although writers do not always indicate setting in the first lines of their work, all of the authors in this chapter do so. In Thomas King's "Borders," the narrator announces that he and his mother are "going

45

to go to Salt Lake City to visit my sister who had left the reserve [reservation], moved across the line, and found a job." In his story "The Wedding Gift," Thomas Raddall is brief and straightforward: "Nova Scotia, in 1794. Winter," he writes. Not until paragraph ten does E. Annie Proulx reveal the initial setting of "Electric Arrows": "We are at the kitchen table . . . waiting for the pie to cool." The setting expands from there, however, both in time and space. Most authors continue to add details of setting throughout a story.

Setting creates certain expectations in readers. The description of the interior of a spaceship triggers an entirely different set of anticipations than does a description of an urban street corner, a whaling ship, a hospital room, an English country house, or a Viking settlement. Obviously, a writer cannot violate the limitations of a setting; throughout a work, Vikings must act and speak appropriately in their environment, for example, just as alien invaders from space must do in theirs. Characters in a historical setting cannot speak or act as if they know about twentieth-century people or events; readers would find it odd to read of a seventeenth-century doctor referring to germs, for example, or a description of a gas fire in a story set in the Middle Ages.

Regional Literature

When writers focus most or all of their writing on a specific locality or geographic region, their writing is sometimes known as **regional literature.** Zora Neale Hurston's and Eudora Welty's focus on the American South mark their stories in part as regional literature. Modern regionalists might include Tony Hillerman, whose detective stories are set in the American Southwest.

A closely related term is **local color,** which describes a late nineteenth-century American literary movement characterized by a focus on setting, as well as on customs, dialects, and attitudes of a specific region.

PURPOSES OF SETTING

Setting may serve a number of purposes, such as influencing action, defining character, and contributing to mood.

Influencing Action

In his powerful novel *Native Son,* Richard Wright describes the effect of an impoverished and racist setting on Bigger, the main character:

Sometimes, in his room or on the sidewalk, the world seemed to him a strange labyrinth even when the streets were straight and the walls were square; a chaos which made him feel that something in him should be able to understand it, divide it, focus it. But only under the stress of hate was the conflict resolved. He had been so conditioned in a cramped environment that hard words or kicks alone knocked him upright and made him capable of action—action that was futile because the world was too much for him. It was then that he closed his eyes and struck out blindly, hitting what or whom he could, not looking or caring what or who hit back.

In Raddall's "The Wedding Gift," the frigid setting helps to determine the decision the main character makes, one that affects the outcome of the story. In Proulx's "Electric Arrows," the Moon-Azures are so inept at becoming part of the rural setting into which they have just moved that the local inhabitants view them with amusement and some contempt.

Defining Character

Setting can help define the psychological, cultural, and economic states of the characters, as well as their social status. In Mark Twain's *The Adventures of Huckleberry Finn*, Huck encounters the Grangerford's parlor:

There was a big fireplace that was bricked on the bottom, and the bricks was kept clean and red by pouring water on them and scrubbing them with another brick; sometimes they wash them over with red water-paint that they call Spanish-brown. . . . There was a clock on the middle of the mantelpiece, with a picture of a town painted on the bottom half of the glass front, and a round place in the middle of it for the sun, and you could see the pendulum swinging behind it. It was beautiful to hear that clock tick. . . .

Well, there was a big outlandish parrot on each side of the clock, made out of something like chalk, and painted up gaudy. By one of the parrots was a cat made of crockery, and a crockery dog by the other; . . . There was a couple of big wild-turkey wing fans spread out behind those things. On the table in the middle of the room was a kind of a lovely crockery basket that had apples and oranges and peaches and grapes piled up in it, which was much redder and yellower and prettier than real ones is, but they warn't real because you could see where pieces had got chipped off and showed the white chalk, or whatever it was, underneath.

Contrast this setting with a setting from Tom Wolfe's *Bonfire of the Vanities:*

> The Bavardages' dining room walls had been painted with so many coats of burnt-apricot lacquer, fourteen in all, they had the glassy brilliance of a pond reflecting a campfire at night. The room was a triumph of nocturnal reflections, one of many such victories by Ronald Vine, whose forte was the creation of glitter without the use of mirrors. Mirror Indigestion was now regarded as one of the gross sins of the 1970s. So in the early 1980s, from Park Avenue to Fifth, from Sixty-second Street to Ninety-sixth, there had arisen the hideous cracking sound of acres of hellishly expensive plate-glass mirror being pried off the walls of the great apartments. No, in the Bavardages' dining room one's eyes fluttered in a cosmos of glints, twinkles, sparkles, highlight, sheens, shimmering pools, and fiery glows that had been achieved in subtler ways, by using lacquer, glazed tiles in a narrow band just under the ceiling cornices, gilded English Regency furniture, silver candelabra, crystal bowls, School of Tiffany vases, and sculpted silverware that was so heavy the knives weighed on your fingers like saber handles.

It is worth noting that Huck is impressed with the Grangerfords' parlor in the Midwest, which is filled with the sorts of objects thought to be fashionable in their social class in the nineteenth century, though to the reader it seems the epitome of bad taste. The Bavardages, while certainly at the opposite end of the economic scale from the Grangerfords, have decorated their dining room as their twentieth-century New York society dictates, and it serves as a symbol of the materialistic world in which Sherman McCoy, the main character of *The Bonfire of the Vanities,* moves.

In King's "Borders," geography and a national boundary help to strengthen the main character's resolve. In Proulx's "Electric Arrows," early photographs depicting a farm that has dwindled to its present few acres and the description of an old neighboring homestead rouse memories in the native inhabitants and shape the lives and attitudes of the natives and of the city dwellers newly arrived.

Contributing to Mood

Setting has a strong influence on the atmosphere of a story, as it does in Charlotte Brontë's *Jane Eyre,* for example, or in Stephen King's books. The famous description of Miss Havisham's room in Charles

Dickens's *Great Expectations* describes a ghastly atmosphere, which appalls the narrator:

> Certain wintry branches of candles on the high chimney-piece faintly lighted the chamber, or, it would be more expressive to say, faintly troubled its darkness. It was spacious, and I dare say had once been handsome, but every discernible thing in it was covered with dust and mould, and dropping to pieces. The most prominent object was a long table with a table-cloth spread on it, as if a feast had been in preparation when the house and the clocks all stopped together. An épergne or centre-piece of some kind was in the middle of this cloth; it was so heavily overhung with cobwebs that its form was quite undistinguishable; and, as I looked along the yellow expanse out of which I remember its seeming to grow, like a black fungus, I saw speckled-legged spiders with blotchy bodies running home to it, and running out from it, as if some circumstance of the greatest public importance had just transpired in the spider community.

In "Borders," the duty-free store, its parking lot, and the customs office contribute to the humor. In "The Wedding Gift," the setting creates a tension-filled atmosphere.

SUMMARY

Setting is so important that some readers base their literary likes and dislikes largely on the environment in a work—the future, early Rome, the English countryside, medieval France, Los Angeles in the thirties, Detroit today, Cairo yesterday. Whatever the scene, the details of setting can influence the action, the characterizations, and the mood of a work. Though his words have become a cliché, the author who first penned "It was a dark and stormy night" had the right idea. He was merely setting the scene for a work he hoped would be full of suspense.

THE WEDDING GIFT

THOMAS RADDALL (1903–1994)

Thomas Raddall was born in Kent, England, and moved with his parents to Canada in 1913. His father, a British Army captain, was killed in France in 1918 during World War i, prompting Raddall to leave his Halifax, Nova Scotia, school in the tenth grade and enlist as a wireless operator. He went to work as a bookkeeper in a wood-pulp mill in 1923, and his first short story appeared in *Maclean's* magazine in 1928. He became a full-time writer ten years later.

He completed eight novels, six collections of short stories, and several volumes of history. His interest in local and eighteenth-century history is evident in many of his works, which include *His Majesty's Yankees* (1929), *Roger Sudden* (1944), *The Wedding Gift and Other Stories* (1947), and *The Nymph and the Lamp* (1950. He won the Governor-General's Award for the best Canadian fiction book of the year in 1944 for *The Pied Piper of Dipper Creek and Other Tales,* and in 1949 and 1958 he won the same award for nonfiction. *In My Time* (1976) is the title of his autobiography.

Raddall's knowledge of Nova Scotia and its winters is apparent in this story. As you read, notice how he creates atmosphere through description.

■

Nova Scotia, in 1794. Winter. Snow on the ground. Two feet of it in the woods, less by the shore, except in drifts against Port Marriott's barns and fences; but enough to set sleigh bells ringing through the town, enough to require a multitude of paths and burrows from doors to streets, to carpet the wharves and the decks of the shipping, and to trim the ships' yards with tippets of ermine. Enough to require fires roaring in the town's chimneys, and blue wood smoke hanging low over the roof tops in the still December air. Enough to squeal under foot in the trodden places and to muffle the step everywhere else. Enough for the hunters, whose snowshoes now could overtake the floundering moose and caribou. Even enough for the always-complaining loggers, whose ox sleds now could haul their cut from every part of the woods. But not enough, not nearly enough snow for Miss Kezia Barnes, who was going to Bristol Creek to marry Mr. Hathaway.

Kezia did not want to marry Mr. Hathaway. Indeed she had told Mr. and Mrs. Barclay in a tearful voice that she didn't want to marry anybody. But Mr. Barclay had taken snuff and said "Ha! Humph!" in the severe tone he used when he was displeased; and Mrs. Barclay had sniffed and said it was a very good match for her, and revolved the cold blue eyes in her fat moon face, and said Kezia must not be a little fool.

There were two ways of going to Bristol Creek. One was by sea, in one of the fishing sloops. But the preacher objected to that. He was a pallid young man lately sent out from England by Lady Huntingdon's Connexion,[1] and seasick five weeks on the way. He held Mr. Barclay in some awe, for Mr. Barclay had the best pew in the meetinghouse and was the chief pillar of godliness in Port Marriott. But young Mr. Mears was firm on this point. He would go by road, he said, or not at all. Mr. Barclay had retorted "Ha! Humph!" The road was twenty miles of horse path through the woods, now deep in snow. Also the path began at Harper's Farm on the far side of the harbor, and Harper had but one horse.

"I shall walk," declared the preacher calmly, "and the young woman can ride."

Kezia had prayed for snow, storms of snow, to bury the trail and keep anyone from crossing the cape to Bristol Creek. But now they

---

1 **Connexion:** The British spelling for "connection." In the context of the story, it means "religious denomination." It was first used in this sense by John Wesley, founder of Methodism.

were setting out from Harper's Farm, with Harper's big brown horse, and all Kezia's prayers had gone for naught. Like any anxious lover, busy Mr. Hathaway had sent Black Sam overland on foot to find out what delayed his wedding, and now Sam's day-old tracks marked for Kezia the road to marriage.

She was a meek little thing, as became an orphan brought up as househelp in the Barclay home; but now she looked at the preacher and saw how young and helpless he looked so far from his native Yorkshire, and how ill-clad for this bitter trans-Atlantic weather, and she spoke up.

"You'd better take my shawl, sir. I don't need it. I've got Miss Julia's old riding cloak. And we'll go ride-and-tie."

"Ride and what?" murmured Mr. Mears.

"I'll ride a mile or so, then I'll get down and tie the horse to a tree and walk on. When you come up to the horse, you mount and ride a mile or so, passing me on the way, and you tie him and walk on. Like that. Ride-and-tie, ride-and-tie. The horse gets a rest between."

Young Mr. Mears nodded and took the proffered shawl absently. It was a black thing that matched his sober broadcloth coat and smallclothes,[2] his black woollen stockings and his round black hat. At Mr. Barclay's suggestion he had borrowed a pair of moose-hide moccasins for the journey. As he walked a prayer-book in his coat-skirts bumped the back of his legs.

At the top of the ridge above Harper's pasture, where the narrow path led off through gloomy hemlock woods, Kezia paused for a last look back across the harbor. In the morning sunlight the white roofs of the little lonely town resembled a tidal wave flung up by the sea and frozen as it broke against the dark pine forest to the west. Kezia sighed, and young Mr. Mears was surprised to see tears in her eyes.

She rode off ahead. The saddle was a man's, of course, awkward to ride modestly, woman-fashion. As soon as she was out of the preacher's sight she rucked her skirts and slid a leg over to the other stirrup. That was better. There was a pleasant sensation of freedom about it, too. For a moment she forgot that she was going to Bristol Creek, in finery second-hand from the Barclay girls, in a new linen shift and drawers that she had sewn herself in the light of the kitchen candles, in white cotton stockings and a bonnet and shoes from Mr. Barclay's store, to marry Mr. Hathaway.

---

2 **smallclothes:** men's close-fitting knee breeches worn in the eighteenth century.

The Barclays had done well for her from the time when, a skinny weeping creature of fourteen, she was taken into the Barclay household and, as Mrs. Barclay so often said, "treated more like one of my own than a bond-girl from the poorhouse." She had first choice of the clothing cast off by Miss Julia and Miss Clara. She was permitted to sit in the same room, and learn what she could, when the schoolmaster came to give private lessons to the Barclay girls. She waited on table, of course, and helped in the kitchen, and made beds, and dusted and scrubbed. But then she had been taught to spin and to sew and to knit. And she was permitted, indeed encouraged, to sit with the Barclays in the meetinghouse, at the convenient end of the pew, where she could worship the Barclays' God and assist with the Barclay wraps at the beginning and end of the service. And now, to complete her rewards, she had been granted the hand of a rejected Barclay suitor.

Mr. Hathaway was Barclay's agent at Bristol Creek, where he sold rum and gunpowder and corn meal and such things to the fishermen and hunters, and bought split cod—fresh, pickled, or dry—and ran a small sawmill, and cut and shipped firewood by schooner to Port Marriott, and managed a farm, all for a salary of fifty pounds, Halifax currency, per year. Hathaway was a most capable fellow, Mr. Barclay often acknowledged. But when after fifteen capable years he came seeking a wife, and cast a sheep's eye[3] first at Miss Julia, and then at Miss Clara, Mrs. Barclay observed with a sniff that Hathaway was looking a bit high.

So he was. The older daughter of Port Marriott's most prosperous merchant was even then receiving polite attentions from Mr. Gamage, the new collector of customs, and a connection of the Halifax Gamages, as Mrs. Barclay was fond of pointing out. And Miss Clara was going to Halifax in the spring to learn the gentle art of playing the pianoforte, and incidentally to display her charms to the naval and military young gentlemen who thronged the Halifax drawingrooms. The dear girls laughed behind their hands whenever long solemn Mr. Hathaway came to town aboard one of the Barclay vessels and called at the big house under the elms. Mrs. Barclay bridled at Hathaway's presumption, but shrewd Mr. Barclay narrowed his little black eyes and took snuff and said "Ha! Humph!"

---

3 **cast a sheep's eye:** looked longingly at.

It was plain to Mr. Barclay that an emergency had arisen. Hathaway was a good man—in his place; and Hathaway must be kept content there, to go on making profit for Mr. Barclay at a cost of only £50 a year. 'Twas a pity Hathaway couldn't satisfy himself with one of the fishermen's girls at the Creek, but there 'twas. If Hathaway had set his mind on a town miss, then a town miss he must have; but she must be the right kind, the sort who would content herself and Hathaway at Bristol Creek and not go nagging the man to remove and try his capabilities elsewhere. At once Mr. Barclay thought of Kezia—dear little Kezzie. A colorless little creature but quiet and well-mannered and pious, and only twenty-two.

Mr. Hathaway was nearly forty and far from handsome, and he had a rather cold, seeking way about him—useful in business of course—that rubbed women the wrong way. Privately Mr. Barclay thought Hathaway lucky to get Kezia. But it was a nice match for the girl, better than anything she could have expected. He impressed that upon her and introduced the suitor from Bristol Creek. Mr. Hathaway spent two or three evenings courting Kezia in the kitchen—Kezia in a quite good gown of Miss Clara's, gazing out at the November moon on the snow, murmuring now and again in the tones of someone in a rather dismal trance, while the kitchen help listened behind one door and the Barclay girls giggled behind another.

The decision, reached mainly by the Barclays, was that Mr. Hathaway should come to Port Marriott aboard the packet schooner on December twenty-third, to be married in the Barclay parlor and then take his bride home for Christmas. But an unforeseen circumstance had changed all this. The circumstance was a ship, "from Mogador in Barbary"[4] as Mr. Barclay wrote afterwards in the salvage claim, driven off her course by gales and wrecked at the very entrance to Bristol Creek. She was a valuable wreck, laden with such queer things as goatskins in pickle, almonds, wormseed,[5] pomegranate skins, and gum arabic, and capable Mr. Hathaway had lost no time in salvage for the benefit of his employer.

As a result he could not come to Port Marriott for a wedding or anything else. A storm might blow up at any time and demolish this fat prize. He dispatched a note by Black Sam, urging Mr. Barclay to

---

4 **"from Mogador in Barbary"**: Mogador is a seaport in Morocco, one of the former Barbary States, which were once a refuge for pirates.

5 **wormseed**: a tropical American plant yielding an oil.

send Kezia and the preacher by return. It was not the orthodox note of an impatient sweetheart, but it said that he had moved into his new house by the Creek and found it "extream empty lacking a woman," and it suggested delicately that while his days were full, the nights were dull.

Kezia was no judge of distance. She rode for what she considered a reasonable time and then slid off and tied the brown horse to a maple tree beside the path. She had brought a couple of lamp wicks to tie about her shoes, to keep them from coming off in the snow, and she set out afoot in the big splayed tracks of Black Sam. The soft snow came almost to her knees in places and she lifted her skirts high. The path was no wider than the span of a man's arms, cut out with axes years before. She stumbled over a concealed stump from time to time, and the huckleberry bushes dragged at her cloak, but the effort warmed her. It had been cold, sitting on the horse with the wind blowing up her legs.

After a time the preacher overtook her, riding awkwardly and holding the reins in a nervous grip. The stirrups were too short for his long black-stockinged legs. He called out cheerfully as he passed, "Are you all right, Miss?" She nodded, standing aside with her back to a tree. When he disappeared ahead, with a last flutter of black shawl tassels in the wind, she picked up her skirts and went on. The path climbed and dropped monotonously over a succession of wooded ridges. Here and there in a hollow she heard water running, and the creak of frosty poles underfoot, and knew she was crossing a small stream, and once the trail ran across a wide swamp on half-rotten corduroy,[6] wind-swept and bare of snow.

She found the horse tethered clumsily not far ahead, and the tracks of the preacher going on. She had to lead the horse to a stump so she could mount, and when she passed Mr. Mears again she called out, "Please, sir, next time leave the horse by a stump or a rock so I can get on." In his quaint old-country accent he murmured, "I'm very sorry," and gazed down at the snow. She forgot she was riding astride until she had passed him, and then she flushed, and gave the indignant horse a cut of the switch. Next time she remembered and swung her right leg back where it should be, and tucked the skirts modestly about her ankles; but young Mr. Mears looked down at the snow anyway, and after that she did not trouble to shift when she overtook him.

_____
6 **corduroy:** a road made of logs laid down crosswise.

The ridges became steeper, and the streams roared under the ice and snow in the swales. They emerged upon the high tableland between Port Marriott and Bristol Creek, a gusty wilderness of young hardwood scrub struggling up amongst the gray snags of an old forest fire, and now that they were out of the gloomy softwoods they could see a stretch of sky. It was blue-gray and forbidding, and the wind whistling up from the invisible sea felt raw on the cheek. At their next meeting Kezia said, "It's going to snow."

She had no knowledge of the trail but she guessed that they were not much more than half way across the cape. On this high barren the track was no longer straight and clear, it meandered amongst the meager hardwood clumps where the path-makers had not bothered to cut, and only Black Sam's footprints really marked it for her unaccustomed eyes. The preacher nodded vaguely at her remark. The woods, like everything else about his chosen mission field, were new and very interesting, and he could not understand the alarm in her voice. He looked confidently at Black Sam's tracks.

Kezia tied the horse farther on and began her spell of walking. Her shoes were solid things, the kind of shoes Mr. Barclay invoiced as "a Common Strong sort, for women, Five Shillings"; but the snow worked into them and melted and saturated the leather. Her feet were numb every time she slid down from the horse and it took several minutes of stumbling through the snow to bring back an aching warmth. Beneath her arm she clutched the small bundle which contained all she had in the world—two flannel nightgowns, a shift of linen, three pairs of stout wool stockings—and of course Mr. Barclay's wedding gift for Mr. Hathaway.

Now as she plunged along she felt the first sting of snow on her face and, looking up, saw the stuff borne on the wind in small hard pellets that fell amongst the bare hardwoods and set up a whisper everywhere. When Mr. Mears rode up to her the snow was thick in their faces, like flung salt.

"It's a nor-easter!" she cried up to him. She knew the meaning of snow from the sea. She had been born in a fishing village down the coast.

"Yes," mumbled the preacher, and drew a fold of the shawl about his face. He disappeared. She struggled on, gasping, and after what seemed a tremendous journey came upon him standing alone and bewildered, looking off somewhere to the right.

"The horse!" he shouted. "I got off him, and before I could fasten the reins some snow fell off a branch—startled him, you know—and he ran off, over that way." He gestured with a mittened hand. "I must fetch him back," he added confusedly.

"No!" Kezia cried. "Don't you try. You'd only get lost. So would I. Oh, dear! This is awful. We'll have to go on, the best we can."

He was doubtful. The horse tracks looked very plain. But Kezia was looking at Black Sam's tracks, and tugging his arm. He gave in, and they struggled along for half an hour or so. Then the last trace of the old footprints vanished.

"What shall we do now?" the preacher asked, astonished.

"I don't know," whispered Kezia, and leaned against a dead pine stub in an attitude of weariness and indifference that dismayed him.

"We must keep moving, my dear, mustn't we? I mean, we can't stay here."

"Can't stay here," she echoed.

"Down there—a hollow, I think. I see some hemlock trees, or are they pines?—I'm never quite sure. Shelter, anyway."

"Shelter," muttered Kezia.

He took her by the hand and like a pair of lost children they dragged their steps into the deep snow of the hollow. The trees were tall spruces, a thick bunch in a ravine, where they had escaped an old fire. A stream thundered amongst them somewhere. There was no wind in this place, only the fine snow whirling thickly down between the trees like a sediment from the storm overhead.

"Look!" cried Mr. Mears. A hut loomed out of the whiteness before them, a small structure of moss-chinked logs with a roof of poles and birch-bark. It had an abandoned look. Long streamers of moss hung out between the logs. On the roof shreds of birch-bark wavered gently in the drifting snow. The door stood half open and a thin drift of snow lay along the split-pole floor. Instinctively Kezia went to the stone hearth. There were old ashes sodden with rain down the chimney and now frozen to a cake.

"Have you got flint and steel?" she asked. She saw in his eyes something dazed and forlorn. He shook his head, and she was filled with a sudden anger, not so much at him as at Mr. Barclay and that—that Hathaway, and all the rest of menkind. They ruled the world and made such a sorry mess of it. In a small fury she began to rummage about the hut.

There was a crude bed of poles and brushwood by the fireplace—brush wood so old that only a few brown needles clung to the twigs. A rough bench whittled from a pine log, with round birch sticks for legs. A broken earthenware pot in a corner. In another some ash-wood frames such as trappers used for stretching skins. Nothing else. The single window was covered with a stretched moose-bladder, cracked and dry-rotten, but it still let in some daylight while keeping out the snow.

She scooped up the snow from the floor with her mittened hands, throwing it outside, and closed the door carefully, dropping the bar into place, as if she could shut out and bar the cold in such a fashion. The air inside was frigid. Their breath hung visible in the dim light from the window. Young Mr. Mears dropped on his wet knees and began to pray in a loud voice. His face was pinched with cold and his teeth rattled as he prayed. He was a pitiable object.

"Prayers won't keep you warm," said Kezia crossly.

He looked up, amazed at the change in her. She had seemed such a meek little thing. Kezia was surprised at herself, and surprisingly she went on, "You'd far better take off those wet moccasins and stockings and shake out the snow of your clothes." She set the example, vigorously shaking out her skirts and Miss Julia's cloak, and she turned her small back on him and took off her own shoes and stockings, and pulled on dry stockings from her bundle. She threw him a pair.

"Put those on."

He looked at them and at his large feet, hopelessly.

"I'm afraid they wouldn't go on."

She tossed him one of her flannel nightgowns. "Then take off your stockings and wrap your feet and legs in that."

He obeyed, in an embarrassed silence. She rolled her eyes upward, for his modesty's sake, and saw a bundle on one of the low rafters—the late owner's bedding, stowed away from mice. She stood on the bench and pulled down three bearskins, marred with bullet holes. A rank and musty smell arose in the cold. She considered the find gravely.

"You take them," Mr. Mears said gallantly. "I shall be quite all right."

"You'll be dead by morning, and so shall I," she answered vigorously, "if you don't do what I say. We've got to roll up in these."

"Together?" he cried in horror.

"Of course! To keep each other warm. It's the only way."

She spread the skins on the floor, hair uppermost, one overlapping another, and dragged the flustered young man down beside her, clutched him in her arms, and rolled with him, over, and over again, so that they became a single shapeless heap in the corner farthest from the draft between door and chimney.

"Put your arms around me," commanded the new Kezia, and he obeyed.

"Now," she said, "you can pray. God helps those that help themselves."

He prayed aloud for a long time, and privately called upon heaven to witness the purity of his thoughts in this strange and shocking situation. He said "Amen" at last; and "Amen," echoed Kezia, piously.

They lay silent a long time, breathing on each other's necks and hearing their own hearts—poor Mr. Mears' fluttering in an agitated way, Kezia's steady as a clock. A delicious warmth crept over them. They relaxed in each other's arms. Outside, the storm hissed in the spruce tops and set up an occasional cold moan in the cracked clay chimney. The down-swirling snow brushed softly against the bladder pane.

"I'm warm now," murmured Kezia. "Are you?"

"Yes. How long must we stay here like this?"

"Till the storm's over, of course. Tomorrow, probably. Nor'easters usually blow themselves out in a day and a night, 'specially when they come up sharp, like this one. Are you hungry?"

"No."

"Abigail—that's the black cook at Barclay's—gave me bread and cheese in a handkerchief. I've got it in my bundle. Mr. Barclay thought we ought to reach Bristol Creek by supper time, but Nabby said I must have a bite to eat on the road. She's a good kind thing, old Nabby. Sure you're not hungry?"

"Quite. I feel somewhat fatigued but not hungry."

"Then we'll eat the bread and cheese for breakfast. Have you got a watch?"

"No, I'm sorry. They cost such a lot of money. In Lady Huntingdon's Connexion we—"

"Oh well, it doesn't matter. It must be about four o'clock—the light's getting dim. Of course, the dark comes very quick in a snowstorm."

"Dark," echoed young Mr. Mears drowsily. Kezia's hair, washed last night for the wedding journey, smelled pleasant so close to his face. It reminded him of something. He went to sleep dreaming of his mother, with his face snug in the curve of Kezia's neck and shoulder, and smiling, and muttering words that Kezia could not catch. After a time she kissed his cheek. It seemed a very natural thing to do.

Soon she was dozing herself, and dreaming, too; but her dreams were full of forbidding faces—Mr. Barclay's, Mrs. Barclay's, Mr.

Hathaway's; especially Mr. Hathaway's. Out of a confused darkness Mr. Hathaway's hard acquisitive gaze searched her shrinking flesh like a cold wind. Then she was shuddering by the kitchen fire at Barclay's, accepting Mr. Hathaway's courtship and wishing she was dead. In the midst of that sickening wooing she wakened sharply.

It was quite dark in the hut. Mr. Mears was breathing quietly against her throat. But there was a sound of heavy steps outside, muffled in the snow and somehow felt rather than heard. She shook the young man and he wakened with a start, clutching her convulsively.

"Sh-h-h!" she warned. "Something's moving outside." She felt him stiffen.

"Bears?" he whispered.

Silly! thought Kezia. People from the old country could think of nothing but bears in the woods. Besides, bears holed up in winter. A caribou, perhaps. More likely a moose. Caribou moved inland before this, to the wide mossy bogs up the river, away from the coastal storms. Again the sound.

"There!" hissed the preacher. Their hearts beat rapidly together.

"The door—you fastened it, didn't you?"

"Yes," she said. Suddenly she knew.

"Unroll, quick!" she cried . . . "No, not this way—your way."

They unrolled, ludicrously, and the girl scrambled up and ran across the floor in her stockinged feet, and fumbled with the rotten door-bar. Mr. Mears attempted to follow but he tripped over the nightgown still wound about his feet, and fell with a crash. He was up again in a moment, catching up the clumsy wooden bench for a weapon, his bare feet slapping on the icy floor. He tried to shoulder her aside, crying "Stand back! Leave it to me!" and waving the bench uncertainly in the darkness.

She laughed excitedly. "Silly!" she said. "It's the horse." She flung the door open. In the queer ghostly murk of a night filled with snow they beheld a large dark shape. The shape whinnied softly and thrust a long face into the doorway. Mr. Mears dropped the bench, astonished.

"He got over his fright and followed us here somehow," Kezia said, and laughed again. She put her arms about the snowy head and laid her face against it.

"Good horse! Oh, good, good horse!"

"What are you going to do?" the preacher murmured over her shoulder. After the warmth of their nest in the furs they were shivering in this icy atmosphere.

"Bring him in, of course. We can't leave him out in the storm."
She caught the bridle and urged the horse inside with expert clucking
sounds. The animal hesitated, but fear of the storm and a desire for
shelter and company decided him. In he came, tramping ponderously
on the split-pole floor. The preacher closed and barred the door.

"And now?" he asked.

"Back to the furs. Quick! It's awful cold."

Rolled in the furs once more, their arms went about each other
instinctively, and the young man's face found the comfortable nook
against Kezia's soft throat. But sleep was difficult after that. The horse
whinnied gently from time to time, and stamped about the floor. The
decayed poles crackled dangerously under his hoofs whenever he
moved, and Kezia trembled, thinking he might break through and
frighten himself, and flounder about till he tumbled the crazy hut
about their heads. She called out to him "Steady, boy! Steady!"

It was a long night. The pole floor made its irregularities felt
through the thickness of fur; and because there seemed nowhere to
put their arms but about each other the flesh became cramped, and
spread its protest along the bones. They were stiff and sore when the
first light of morning stained the window. They unrolled and stood up
thankfully, and tramped up and down the floor, thrashing their arms
in an effort to fight off the gripping cold. Kezia undid her bundle in a
corner and brought forth Nabby's bread and cheese, and they ate it
sitting together on the edge of the brushwood bed with the skins
about their shoulders. Outside the snow had ceased.

"We must set off at once," the preacher said. "Mr. Hathaway will
be anxious."

Kezia was silent. She did not move, and he looked at her curiously.
She appeared very fresh, considering the hardships of the previous day
and the night. He passed a hand over his cheeks and thought how
unclean he must appear in her eyes, with this stubble on his pale face.

"Mr. Hathaway—" he began again.

"I'm not going to Mr. Hathaway," Kezia said quietly.

"But—the wedding!"

"There'll be no wedding. I don't want to marry Mr. Hathaway.
'Twas Mr. Hathaway's idea, and Mr. and Mrs. Barclay's. They wanted
me to marry him."

"What will the Barclays say, my dear?"

She shrugged. "I've been their bond-girl ever since I was fourteen, but I'm not a slave like poor black Nabby, to be handed over,
body and soul, whenever it suits."

"Your soul belongs to God," said Mr. Mears devoutly.

"And my body belongs to me."

He was a little shocked at this outspokenness but he said gently, "Of course. To give oneself in marriage without true affection would be an offense in the sight of heaven. But what will Mr. Hathaway say?"

"Well, to begin with, he'll ask where I spent the night, and I'll have to tell the truth. I'll have to say I bundled with you in a hut in the woods."

"Bundled?"

"A custom the people brought with them from Connecticut when they came to settle in Nova Scotia. Poor folk still do it. Sweethearts, I mean. It saves fire and candles when you're courting on a winter evening. It's harmless—they keep their clothes on, you see, like you and me—but Mr. Barclay and the other Methody people are terrible set against it. Mr. Barclay got old Mr. Mings—he's the Methody preacher that died last year—to make a sermon against it. Mr. Mings said bundling was an invention of the devil."

"Then if you go back to Mr. Barclay—"

"He'll ask me the same question and I'll have to give him the same answer. I couldn't tell a lie, could I?" She turned a pair of round blue eyes and met his embarrassed gaze.

"No! No, you mustn't lie. Whatever shall we do?' he murmured in a dazed voice. Again she was silent, looking modestly down her small nose.

"It's so very strange," he floundered. "This country—there are so many things I don't know, so many things to learn. You—I—we shall have to tell the truth, of course. Doubtless I can find a place in the Lord's service somewhere else, but what about you, poor girl?"

"I heard say the people at Scrod Harbor want a preacher."

"But—the tale would follow me, wouldn't it, my dear? This—er—bundling with a young woman?"

"'Twouldn't matter if the young woman was your wife."

"Eh?" His mouth fell open. He was like an astonished child, for all his preacher's clothes and the new beard on his jaws.

"I'm a good girl," Kezia said, inspecting her foot. "I can read and write, and know all the tunes in the psalter. And—and you need someone to look after you."

He considered the truth of that. Then he murmured uncertainly, "We'd be very poor, my dear. The Connexion gives some support, but of course—"

"I've always been poor," Kezia said. She sat very still but her cold fingers writhed in her lap.

He did something then that made her want to cry. He took hold of her hands and bowed his head and kissed them.

"It's strange—I don't even know your name, my dear."

"It's Kezia—Kezia Barnes."

He said quietly. "You're a brave girl, Kezia Barnes, and I shall try to be a good husband to you. Shall we go?"

"Hadn't you better kiss me, first?" Kezia said faintly.

He put his lips awkwardly to hers; and then, as if the taste of her clean mouth itself provided strength and purpose, he kissed her again, and firmly. She threw her arms about his neck.

"Oh, Mr. Mears!"

How little he knew about everything! He hadn't even known enough to wear two or three pairs of stockings inside those roomy moccasins, nor to carry a pair of dry ones. Yesterday's wet stockings were lying like sticks on the frosty floor. She showed him how to knead the hard-frozen moccasins into softness, and while he worked at the stiff leather she tore up one of her wedding bed-shirts and wound the flannel strips about his legs and feet. It looked very queer when she had finished, and they both laughed.

They were chilled to the bone when they set off, Kezia on the horse and the preacher walking ahead, holding the reins. When they regained the slope where they had lost the path, Kezia said, "The sun rises somewhere between east and southeast, at this time of year. Keep it on your left shoulder a while. That will take us back towards Port Marriott."

When they came to the green timber she told him to shift the sun to his left eye.

"Have you changed your mind?" he asked cheerfully. The exercise had warmed him.

"No, but the sun moves across the sky."

"Ah! What a wise little head it is!"

They came over a ridge of mixed hemlock and hardwood and looked upon a long swale full of bare hackmatacks.

"Look!" the girl cried. The white slot of the axe path showed clearly in the trees at the foot of the swale, and again where it entered the dark mass of the pines beyond.

"Praise the Lord!" said Mr. Mears.

When at last they stood in the trail, Kezia slid down from the horse.

"No!" Mr. Mears protested.

"Ride-and-tie," she said firmly. "That's the way we came, and that's the way we'll go. Besides, I want to get warm."

He climbed up clumsily and smiled down at her.

"What shall we do when we get to Port Marriott, my dear?"

"Get the New Light preacher to marry us, and catch the packet for Scrod Harbor."

He nodded and gave a pull at his broad hat brim. She thought of everything. A splendid helpmeet for the world's wilderness. He saw it all very humbly now as a dispensation of Providence.

Kezia watched him out of sight. Then, swiftly, she undid her bundle and took out the thing that had lain there (and on her conscience) through the night—the tinderbox[7]—Mr. Barclay's wedding gift to Mr. Hathaway. She flung it into the woods and walked on, skirts lifted, in the track of the horse, humming a psalm tune to the silent trees and the snow.

---

7 **tinderbox:** a metal box for holding tinder, some highly inflammable substance, such as decayed wood or burnt cloth, used to make a fire. A tinderbox usually also holds flint and steel with which to strike a spark to ignite the tinder.

QUESTIONS FOR DISCUSSION

1. What aspect of setting is most important to the story—the year, the season, or the country?

2. What has Kezia done to assure that she and Mr. Mears will have to wrap up together to stay warm?

3. Is the climax foreshadowed in any way, or is it a surprise?

4. Basically, what gives Kezia the advantage over Mears?

5. What did you learn about Nova Scotian society in 1794 from this story?

TOPICS FOR WRITING

1. What will the Barclays and Mr. Hathaway think and say when they discover that Kezia and Mr. Mears are married, and how will they discover the marriage? Write a scene in which the three of them learn what has happened.

2. In a short paper, analyze how the author achieves the mood or atmosphere of the story.

3. In a paragraph or two, describe how aspects of the story contribute to the 1700s setting.

BORDERS

THOMAS KING (born 1943)

Thomas King was born in Sacramento and raised in Roseville, California. Of Greek and Cherokee descent, King writes of contemporary Native American characters and concerns with understanding and humor.

He attended Sierra Junior college and Sacramento State University and received a B.A. degree in English in 1970 and an M.A. degree in 1972 from California State University at Chico. He has worked as an ambulance driver, a croupier in a casino, and a draftsman for Boeing Aircraft in Seattle, and he once worked his way to Australia and New Zealand on a tramp steamer.

In 1973, he became associate dean for student services at Humboldt State University and four years later became coordinator of the history of the Indians of the Americas program at the University of Utah. In 1980, he accepted a position at the University of Lethbridge in Alberta as assistant professor of Native studies. After receiving his Ph.D. degree from the University of Utah in 1986, he was an associate professor at the University of Minnesota and in 1993–1994 worked as story editor for the CBC in Toronto. He now teaches at the University of Guelph in Ontario, Canada.

His books include *Medicine River* (1990), set in a fictional Alberta town next to the Blackfoot reservation; *Green Grass, Running Water* (1993)—the title of which is a reference to the language of the many treaties that promised Native Americans that they would hold the land "as long as the grass is green and the water runs"; *One Good Story, That One* (1993), from which "Borders" is taken; and several anthologies. He has also written radio scripts titled *The One about Coyote Going West*, *Medicine River*, and *Borders*, several teleplays, and a screenplay.

The setting of the following story is the platform from which King launches his barbs toward bureaucracy.

■

When I was twelve, maybe thirteen, my mother announced that we were going to go to Salt Lake City to visit my sister who had left the reserve, moved across the line, and found a job. Laetitia had not left home with my mother's blessing, but over time my mother had come to be proud of the fact that Laetitia had done all of this on her own.

"She did real good," my mother would say.

Then there were the fine points to Laetitia's going. She had not, as my mother liked to tell Mrs. Manyfingers, gone floating after some man like a balloon on a string. She hadn't snuck out of the house, either, and gone to Vancouver or Edmonton or Toronto to chase rainbows down alleys. And she hadn't been pregnant.

"She did real good."

I was seven or eight when Laetitia left home. She was seventeen. Our father was from Rocky Boy[1] on the American side.

"Dad's American," Laetitia told my mother, "so I can go and come as I please."

"Send us a postcard."

Laetitia packed her things, and we headed for the border. Just outside of Milk River, Laetitia told us to watch for the water tower.

"Over the next rise. It's the first thing you see."

"We got a water tower on the reserve," my mother said. "There's a big one in Lethbridge, too."

"You'll be able to see the tops of the flagpoles, too. That's where the border is."

When we got to Coutts, my mother stopped at the convenience store and bought her and Laetitia a cup of coffee. I got an Orange Crush.

"This is real lousy coffee."

"You're just angry because I want to see the world."

"It's the water. From here on down, they got lousy water."

"I can catch the bus from Sweetgrass. You don't have to lift a finger."

"You're going to have to buy your water in bottles if you want good coffee."

There was an old wooden building about a block away, with a tall sign in the yard that said "Museum." Most of the roof had been blown away. Mom told me to go and see when the place was open. There were boards over the windows and doors. You could tell that the place was closed, and I told Mom so, but she said to go and check

---

1 **Rocky Boy**: an Indian reservation.

anyway. Mom and Laetitia stayed by the car. Neither one of them moved. I sat down on the steps of the museum and watched them, and I don't know that they ever said anything to each other. Finally, Laetitia got her bag out of the trunk and gave Mom a hug.

I wandered back to the car. The wind had come up, and it blew Laetitia's hair across her face. Mom reached out and pulled the strands out of Laetitia's eyes, and Laetitia let her.

"You can still see the mountain from here," my mother told Laetitia in Blackfoot.

"Lots of mountains in Salt Lake," Laetitia told her in English.

"The place is closed," I said. "Just like I told you."

Laetitia tucked her hair into her jacket and dragged her bag down the road to the brick building with the American flag flapping on a pole. When she got to where the guards were waiting, she turned, put the bag down, and waved to us. We waved back. Then my mother turned the car around, and we came home.

We got postcards from Laetitia regular, and, if she wasn't spreading jelly on the truth, she was happy. She found a good job and rented an apartment with a pool.

"And she can't even swim," my mother told Mrs. Manyfingers.

Most of the postcards said we should come down and see the city, but whenever I mentioned this, my mother would stiffen up.

So I was surprised when she bought two new tires for the car and put on her blue dress with the green and yellow flowers. I had to dress up, too, for my mother did not want us crossing the border looking like Americans. We made sandwiches and put them in a big box with pop and potato chips and some apples and bananas and a big jar of water.

"But we can stop at one of those restaurants, too, right?"

"We maybe should take some blankets in case you get sleepy."

"But we can stop at one of those restaurants, too, right?"

The border was actually two towns, though neither one was big enough to amount to anything. Coutts was on the Canadian side and consisted of the convenience store and gas station, the museum that was closed and boarded up, and a motel. Sweetgrass was on the American side, but all you could see was an overpass that arched across the highway and disappeared into the prairies. Just hearing the names of these towns, you would expect that Sweetgrass, which is a nice name and sounds like it is related to other places such as Medicine Hat and Moose Jaw and Kicking Horse Pass, would be on the Canadian side, and that Coutts, which sounds abrupt and rude, would be on the American side. But this was not the case.

Between the two borders was a duty-free shop where you could buy cigarettes and liquor and flags. Stuff like that.

We left the reserve in the morning and drove until we got to Coutts.

"Last time we stopped here," my mother said, "you had an Orange Crush. You remember that?"

"Sure," I said. "That was when Laetitia took off."

"You want another Orange Crush?"

"That means we're not going to stop at a restaurant, right?"

My mother got a coffee at the convenience store, and we stood around and watched the prairies move in the sunlight. Then we climbed back in the car. My mother straightened the dress across her thighs, leaned against the wheel, and drove all the way to the border in first gear, slowly, as if she were trying to see through a bad storm or riding high on black ice.

The border guard was an old guy. As he walked to the car, he swayed from side to side, his feet set wide apart, the holster on his hip pitching up and down. He leaned into the window, looked into the back seat, and looked at my mother and me.

"Morning, ma'am."

"Good morning."

"Where you heading?"

"Salt Lake City."

"Purpose of your visit?"

"Visit my daughter."

"Citizenship?"

"Blackfoot," my mother told him.

"Ma'am?"

"Blackfoot," my mother repeated.

"Canadian?"

"Blackfoot."

It would have been easier if my mother had just said "Canadian" and been done with it, but I could see she wasn't going to do that. The guard wasn't angry or anything. He smiled and looked towards the building. Then he turned back and nodded.

"Morning, ma'am."

"Good morning."

"Any firearms or tobacco?"

"No."

"Citizenship?"

"Blackfoot."

He told us to sit in the car and wait, and we did. In about five minutes, another guard came out with the first man. They were talking as they came, both men swaying back and forth like two cowboys headed for a bar or a gunfight.

"Morning, ma'am."

"Good morning."

"Cecil tells me you and the boy are Blackfoot."

"That's right."

"Now, I know that we got Blackfeet on the American side and the Canadians got Blackfeet on their side. Just so we can keep our records straight, what side do you come from?"

I knew exactly what my mother was going to say, and I could have told them if they had asked me.

"Canadian side or American side?" asked the guard.

"Blackfoot side," she said.

It didn't take them long to lose their sense of humor, I can tell you that. The one guard stopped smiling altogether and told us to park our car at the side of the building and come in.

We sat on a wood bench for about an hour before anyone came over to talk to us. This time it was a woman. She had a gun, too.

"Hi," she said. "I'm Inspector Pratt. I understand there is a little misunderstanding."

"I'm going to visit my daughter in Salt Lake City," my mother told her. "We don't have any guns or beer."

"It's a legal technicality, that's all."

"My daughter's a Blackfoot, too."

The woman opened a briefcase and took out a couple of forms and began to write on one of them. "Everyone who crosses our border has to declare their citizenship. Even Americans. It helps us keep track of the visitors we get from the various countries."

She went on like that for maybe fifteen minutes, and a lot of the stuff she told us was interesting.

"I can understand how you feel about having to tell us your citizenship, and here's what I'll do. You tell me, and I won't put it down on the form. No-one will know but you and me."

Her gun was silver. There were several chips in the wood handle and the name "Stella" was scratched into the metal butt.

We were in the border office for about four hours, and we talked to almost everyone there. One of the men bought me a Coke. My mother brought a couple of sandwiches in from the car. I offered part of mine to Stella, but she said she wasn't hungry.

I told Stella that we were Blackfoot and Canadian, but she said that that didn't count because I was a minor. In the end, she told us that if my mother didn't declare her citizenship, we would have to go back to where we came from. My mother stood up and thanked Stella for her time. Then we got back in the car and drove to the Canadian border, which was only about a hundred yards away.

I was disappointed. I hadn't seen Laetitia for a long time, and I had never been to Salt Lake City. When she was still at home, Laetitia would go on and on about Salt Lake City. She had never been there, but her boyfriend Lester Tallbull had spent a year in Salt Lake at a technical school.

"It's a great place," Lester would say. "Nothing but blondes in the whole state."

Whenever he said that, Laetitia would slug him on his shoulder hard enough to make him flinch. He had some brochures on Salt Lake and some maps, and every so often the two of them would spread them out on the table.

"That's the temple.² It's right downtown. You got to have a pass to get in."

"Charlotte says anyone can go in and look around."

"When was Charlotte in Salt Lake? Just when the hell was Charlotte in Salt Lake?"

"Last year."

"This is Liberty Park. It's got a zoo. There's good skiing in the mountains."

"Got all the skiing we can use," my mother would say. "People come from all over the world to ski at Banff. Cardston's got a temple, if you like those kinds of things."

"Oh, this one is real big," Lester would say. "They got armed guards and everything."

"Not what Charlotte says."

"What does she know?"

Lester and Laetitia broke up, but I guess the idea of Salt Lake stuck in her mind.

The Canadian border guard was a young woman, and she seemed happy to see us. "Hi," she said. "You folks sure have a great day for a trip. Where are you coming from?"

---

2 **the temple:** the Mormon temple at Temple Square, the headquarters of the Mormon Church.

"Standoff."

"Is that in Montana?"

"No."

"Where are you going?"

"Standoff."

The woman's name was Carol and I don't guess she was any older than Laetitia. "Wow, you both Canadians?"

"Blackfoot."

"Really? I have a friend I went to school with who is Blackfoot. Do you know Mike Harley?"

"No."

"He went to school in Lethbridge, but he's really from Browning."

It was a nice conversation and there were no cars behind us, so there was no rush.

"You're not bringing any liquor back, are you?"

"No."

"Any cigarettes or plants or stuff like that?"

"No."

"Citizenship?"

"Blackfoot."

"I know," said the woman, "and I'd be proud of being Blackfoot if I were Blackfoot. But you have to be American or Canadian."

When Laetitia and Lester broke up, Lester took his brochures and maps with him, so Laetitia wrote to someone in Salt Lake City, and, about a month later, she got a big envelope of stuff. We sat at the table and opened up all the brochures, and Laetitia read each one out loud.

"Salt Lake City is the gateway to some of the world's most magnificent skiing.

"Salt Lake City is the home of one of the newest professional basketball franchises, the Utah Jazz.

"The Great Salt Lake is one of the natural wonders of the world."

It was kind of exciting seeing all those color brochures on the table and listening to Laetitia read all about how Salt Lake City was one of the best places in the entire world.

"That Salt Lake City place sounds too good to be true," my mother told her.

"It has everything."

"We got everything right here."

"It's boring here."

"People in Salt Lake City are probably sending away for brochures of Calgary and Lethbridge and Pincher Creek right now."

In the end, my mother would say that maybe Laetitia should go to Salt Lake City, and Laetitia would say that maybe she would.

We parked the car to the side of the building and Carol led us into a small room on the second floor. I found a comfortable spot on the couch and flipped through some back issues of *Saturday Night* and *Alberta Report*.

When I woke up, my mother was just coming out of another office. She didn't say a word to me. I followed her down the stairs and out to the car. I thought we were going home, but she turned the car around and drove back towards the American border, which made me think we were going to visit Laetitia in Salt Lake City after all. Instead she pulled into the parking lot of the duty-free store and stopped.

"We going to see Laetitia?"

"No."

"We going home?"

Pride is a good thing to have, you know. Laetitia had a lot of pride, and so did my mother. I figured that someday, I'd have it, too.

"So where are we going?"

Most of that day, we wandered around the duty-free store, which wasn't very large. The manager had a name tag with a tiny American flag on one side and a tiny Canadian flag on the other. His name was Mel. Towards evening, he began suggesting that we should be on our way. I told him we had nowhere to go, that neither the Americans nor the Canadians would let us in. He laughed at that and told us that we should buy something or leave.

The car was not very comfortable, but we did have all that food and it was April, so even if it did snow as it sometimes does on the prairies, we wouldn't freeze. The next morning my mother drove to the American border.

It was a different guard this time, but the questions were the same. We didn't spend as much time in the office as we had the day before. By noon, we were back at the Canadian border. By two we were back in the duty-free shop parking lot.

The second night in the car was not as much fun as the first, but my mother seemed in good spirits, and, all in all, it was as much an adventure as an inconvenience. There wasn't much food left and that was a problem, but we had lots of water as there was a faucet at the side of the duty-free shop.

One Sunday, Laetitia and I were watching television, Mom was over at Mrs. Manyfingers's. Right in the middle of the program, Laetitia turned off the set and said she was going to Salt Lake City, that life around here was too boring. I had wanted to see the rest of the program and really didn't care if Laetitia went to Salt Lake City or not. When Mom got home, I told her what Laetitia had said.

What surprised me was how angry Laetitia got when she found out that I had told Mom.

"You got a big mouth."

"That's what you said."

"What I said is none of your business."

"I didn't say anything."

"Well, I'm going for sure, now."

That weekend, Laetitia packed her bags, and we drove her to the border.

Mel turned out to be friendly. When he closed up for the night and found us still parked in the lot, he came over and asked us if our car was broken down or something. My mother thanked him for his concern and told him that we were fine, that things would get straightened out in the morning.

"You're kidding," said Mel. "You'd think they could handle the simple things."

"We got some apples and a banana," I said, "but we're all out of ham sandwiches."

"You know, you read about these things, but you just don't believe it. You just don't believe it."

"Hamburgers would be even better because they got more stuff for energy."

My mother slept in the back seat. I slept in the front because I was smaller and could lie under the steering wheel. Late that night, I heard my mother open the car door. I found her sitting on her blanket leaning against the bumper of the car.

"You see all those stars," she said. "When I was a little girl, my grandmother used to take me and my sisters out on the prairies and tell us stories about all the stars."

"Do you think Mel is going to bring us any hamburgers?"

"Every one of those stars has a story. You see that bunch of stars over there that look like a fish?"

"He didn't say no."

"Coyote went fishing, one day. That's how it all started." We sat out under the stars that night, and my mother told me all sorts of stories. She was serious about it, too. She'd tell them slow, repeating parts as she went, as if she expected me to remember each one.

Early the next morning, the television vans began to arrive, and guys in suits and women in dresses came trotting over to us, dragging microphones and cameras and lights behind them. One of the vans had a table set up with orange juice and sandwiches and fruit. It was for the crew, but when I told them we hadn't eaten for a while, a really skinny blonde woman told us we could eat as much as we wanted.

They mostly talked to my mother. Every so often one of the reporters would come over and ask me questions about how it felt to be an Indian without a country. I told them we had a nice house on the reserve and that my cousins had a couple of horses we rode when we went fishing. Some of the television people went over to the American border, and then they went to the Canadian border.

Around noon, a good-looking guy in a dark blue suit and an orange tie with little ducks on it drove up in a fancy car. He talked to my mother for a while, and, after they were done talking, my mother called me over, and we got into our car. Just as my mother started the engine, Mel came over and gave us a bag of peanut brittle and told us that justice was a damn hard thing to get, but that we shouldn't give up.

I would have preferred lemon drops, but it was nice of Mel anyway.

"Where are we going now?"

"Going to visit Laetitia."

The guard who came out to our car was all smiles. The television lights were so bright they hurt my eyes, and, if you tried to look through the windshield in certain directions, you couldn't see a thing.

"Morning, ma'am."

"Good morning."

"Where are you heading?"

"Salt Lake City."

"Purpose of your visit?"

"Visit my daughter."

"Any tobacco, liquor, or firearms?"

"Don't smoke."

"Any plants or fruit?"

"Not any more."

"Citizenship?"

"Blackfoot."

The guard rocked back on his heels and jammed his thumbs into his gun belt. "Thank you," he said, his fingers patting the butt of the revolver. "Have a pleasant trip."

My mother rolled the car forward, and the television people had to scramble out of the way. They ran alongside the car as we pulled away from the border, and, when they couldn't run any farther, they stood in the middle of the highway and waved and waved and waved.

We got to Salt Lake City the next day. Laetitia. was happy to see us, and, that first night, she took us out to a restaurant that made really good soups. The list of pies took up a whole page. I had cherry. Mom had chocolate. Laetitia said that she saw us on television the night before and, during the meal, she had us tell her the story over and over again.

Laetitia took us everywhere. We went to a fancy ski resort. We went to the temple. We got to go shopping in a couple of large malls, but they weren't as large as the one in Edmonton, and Mom said so.

After a week or so, I got bored and wasn't at all sad when my mother said we should be heading back home. Laetitia wanted us to stay longer, but Mom said no, that she had things to do back home and that, next time, Laetitia should come up and visit. Laetitia said she was thinking about moving back, and Mom told her to do as she pleased, and Laetitia said that she would.

On the way home, we stopped at the duty-free shop, and my mother gave Mel a green hat that said "Salt Lake" across the front. Mel was a funny guy. He took the hat and blew his nose and told my mother that she was an inspiration to us all. He gave us some more peanut brittle and came out into the parking lot and waved at us all the way to the Canadian border.

It was almost evening when we left Coutts. I watched the border through the rear window until all you could see were the tops of the flagpoles and the blue water tower, and then they rolled over a hill and disappeared.

QUESTIONS FOR DISCUSSION

1. Why do you think the narrator's mother refused to declare herself Canadian?

2. The author inserts several flashbacks. What is their purpose and what is the effect on the main narrative?

3. Is the main character struggling against humans, nature, or society?

4. Who or what is satirized in the story?

5. How do you think the television reporters find out about the narrator and his mother?

6. Who wins the dispute and why?

7. Why does Mel think the narrator's mother is "an inspiration to us all"?

TOPICS FOR WRITING

1. Analyze the dialogue in this story. In a short paper, tell what it reveals about the characters and about their relationships. Include whether you find the dialogue believable.

2. Would this story have been more appropriate in a chapter on character or theme? In a short paper, give reasons for your opinion.

3. Write a news story describing the setting and the action as you found it when you arrived on the scene with the other reporters.

ELECTRIC ARROWS

E. ANNIE PROULX (born 1935)

E. Annie Proulx was born in Norwich, Connecticut, the oldest of five girls. She attended Colby College, received her B.A. from the University of Vermont and her M.A. from Sir George Williams (now Concordia) University in Montreal. She wrote nonfiction "how-to" books for many years while raising three sons. Her first volume of short stories, *Heart Songs and Other Stories,* from which the following story is taken, was published in 1988. The nine stories in that volume are set in northern New England.

Her first novel, *Postcards* (1992), is also set in New England, and her second novel, *The Shipping News* (1993), is set in Newfoundland, which she came to know on a visit there. Her novel *Accordion Crimes* appeared in 1997.

She has won many honors and awards, including a National Endowment for the Arts grant in 1991, a PEN/Faulkner Award for Fiction in 1993 for *Postcards,* the Chicago Tribune's Heartland Prize for Fiction in 1993, and the Pulitzer Prize for fiction and a National Book Award in 1994 for *The Shipping News.* A reviewer for the *Chicago Tribune* said of *The Shipping News:* "Her plot rushes out of a confluence between the force of the characters and their environment to buoy you on. The result is that rare creation, a lyric page turner."

Both setting and character are important in "Electric Arrows." The setting is a small New England community, long inhabited by the same families but now the focus of developers and city dwellers—particularly the Moon-Azures, husband and wife, who revel in the country life, the history of its inhabitants, and, at times, its artifacts.

■

1

"You tell me," says Reba, wrapped up in her blue sweater with the metal buttons. She's wearing the gray sweatpants again. Her head is tipped back steeply on the long neck column as she looks up at me, her narrow rouged mouth like a red wire. "Tell me why anybody in his right mind would sit in The Chicken swilling beer, watching fat men wrestle until midnight, why?"

I think, so they don't have to sit around in the kitchen and look at moldy pictures.

Aunt pulls one out as thick as a box lid. I see milkweed blowing, the house set square on a knob of lawn, each nailhead hard, the shadows of the clapboards like black rules.

There is a colorless, coiled hair on Reba's sweater sleeve.

"I couldn't believe it, open the door of that place and there you are," she says.

Aunt's finger traces along the side of the picture, over the steep maples, over a woman with two children standing in the white road. Aunt smells of lemon lotion and clothes worn two days to save on laundry detergent. The faces in the photograph are round plates above dark shoulders, smiles like fern fronds. The woman holds a blurred baby, she holds him forever. The other child is unsmiling, short and stocky, a slap of black hair across his forehead. He died of cholera a few weeks after they took the photograph.

Aunt points to the baby and says, "That's your father." He is unfocused, leached by the far sunlight. She clasps her thick, hard old palms together.

"I'm grateful I was there, Reba, when you come along needing your flat tire changed," I say.

"That part was good," she murmurs, as if giving me something I'd long coveted.

We are at the kitchen table inside the house of the photograph, waiting for the pie to cool. The camera belonged to Leonard Prittle, the hired man, who lived in this house once. We don't have a hired man now, we don't have a farm, we live in the house ourselves. Reba encourages Aunt with the photographs. And the Moon-Azures, hey, the damn Moon-Azures think the past belongs to them.

"Want me to whip the cream to go on the pie?" I ask Reba.

I do go down to The Chicken sometimes.

The maples in the photograph are all gone, cut when they widened the road. There is Aunt at the wheel of a Reo truck with her hair bobbed. The knuckles are smooth in the pliant hand. They widened the road, but they didn't straighten it.

Aunt takes another picture and another, she can't stop. She lifts them, the heavy-knuckled fingers precise and careful, her narrow Clew head bent and the pale Clew eyes roving over the images of black suits and ruched sleeves, dead children, horses with braided manes, a storm cloud over the barn. She says, "Leonard Prittle could of been something if he'd of had a chance."

Reba cuts the pie into seeping crimson triangles. Back when she worked she gave kitchen parties to show farm women how to get the most out of their freezers and mixers. Now it's all microwaves and the farm women live in apartments in Concord.

I pretend to look at the picture. The weathervanes point at an east wind. There are picket fences, elm trees, a rooster in the weeds. Hey, I've seen that rooster picture a hundred times.

Time has scraped away the picket fences, and you should hear the snowplow throw its dirty spoutings against the clapboards; it sounds like the plow is coming through the kitchen. The leftover Pugleys, Clews, and the Cuckhorns live in these worn-out houses. Reba was a Cuckhorn.

"Properties break apart," says Aunt, sighing and nipping off the pie point with her fork. We know how quarreling sons sell sections of the place to Boston schoolteachers, those believers that country life makes you good. When they find it does not, they spitefully sell the land again, to Venezuelan millionaires, Raytheon engineers, cocaine dealers, and cold-handed developers.

Reba mumbles, "The more you expect from something, the more you turn on it when it disappoints you."

I suppose she means me.

Aunt and I still own a few acres of the place—the hired man's house, where we live, and the barn. *Atlantic Ocean Farm* is painted on the barn door because my father, standing on the height of land as a young man full of hopeful imagination, thought he saw a shining furrow of sea far to the east between a crack in the mountains.

Reba puts plastic wrap over the uneaten pie, turns up the television sound. I go walk in the driveway before the light's gone. Through the barn window I can see empty cardboard appliance boxes stacked inside, soft and shapeless from years of damp.

You can see how nothing has changed in the barn. A knotted length of baling twine, furry with dust, still stretches from the top of the ladder to a beam. The kite's wooden skeleton, a fragile cross, is still up there.

I could take it down.

There is the thick snoring of a car turning in the driveway. It's not dark enough for the headlights, just the fog lights, set wide apart, yellow. The Moon-Azures. They don't see me by the barn. Mrs. Moon-Azure opens the car door and sticks out her legs as straight as celery stalks.

I go back in the house, let the cat in. Moon-Azure says, "Nice evening, Mason." His eyeglasses reflect like the fog lights. "Thought I'd see if you could give me a hand tomorrow. The old willow went down, and it looks like we need a tug with the tractor."

More like half a day's work.

When I look out the window I can see Yogetsky's trailer with the crossed snowshoes mounted over the door, the black mesh satellite dish in front of the picture window. Yogetsky is an old bachelor. His cranky, shining kitchen is full of saved tin cans, folded plastic bags, magazines piled in four-color pyramids. He sets bread dough to rise on top of the television set.

Across the road from his trailer there's the Beaubiens' place. The oldest son's log truck is parked in the driveway, bigger than the house. A black truck with the word *Scorpion* in curly script. The Beaubiens are invisible, maybe behind the truck, maybe inside the house, eating baked beans out of a can, sharing the fork. They eat quick, afraid of losing time that could be put into work. King Olaf sardines, jelly roll showing the crimson spiral inside the plastic wrap, Habitant pea soup.

Yogetsky moved up from Massachusetts about ten years ago and got two jobs, one to live on, the other to pay his property taxes, he says. His thick nose sticks out of his face like a cork. He says, "This trailer, this land," pointing at the shaved jowl of lawn, "is a investment. Way people are coming in, it'll be worth plenty, year or two."

He owns two acres of Pugley's old cow pasture.

Yogetsky is a reader. He takes *USA Today* and magazines of the type with stories in them about dentists who become fur trappers. His garden is fenced in with sheep wire. The tops of tin cans hang on the fence and stutter in the wind. There's his flagpole.

2

We raised apples. Baldwins, Tolman Sweets, Duchess, Snow Apple, Russet, and Sheep's Nose. The big growers were pushing the McIntosh and the Delicious. I was nervy and sick, but I had to help my father string barbwire around the orchard and down through the woods. A quick, sloppy job. The deer would come in late June, the young deer, and eat the new tender leaves, still crumpled and folded on the Baldwin seedlings. Nobody knew what was wrong with me. Nervy, Aunt said. Growing too fast. The Baldwins, torn and stripped, grew crooked.

The McIntosh apple ruined us. My father ruined us.

He said, "Children, it's a hard way to go to make money on sugar, but there's a good dollar in the Baldwin apple." And sold the maples for timber. And bought five hundred Baldwin seedlings. Your Baldwin apple is a dull, cloudy maroon color. It's got somewhat of a tender rootstock.

People wanted a shiny, red apple. Our fruit went to the juice mills. Now it's the other way around. All those old kinds we couldn't give away. Black Twig. Pinkham Pie. They pay plenty for them now.

Once your sugar bush is gone, it's gone for fifty years or forever.

My father sold pieces of the woodlot. Then pieces of pasture. Pieces of this, pieces of that. None of the Baldwins made it through a hard winter just before the war.

Aunt bites off the end of a raveling thread instead of using scissors.

Dad could make a nice stone wall, but he'd be off on something else before it got to any length. He preferred barbwire, get it over with. Still, he had a feel for stonework, for the chisel, without the dogged concentration you need for that work. He was silly. His excited ways, his easy enthusiasm made Aunt say he was a fool. I never heard anybody laugh like he did, a seesawing, gasping laugh like he was drowning for air. It was the brother that died young that had all the sense, says Aunt.

He let the farm drip through his fingers like water until only an anxious dampness was left in our palms. And his friend Diamond used to pick up first me, then Bootie, my sister, sliding his old dirty paws up between our legs, putting his tobacco-stained mouth at our narrow necks.

"He don't mean nothin' by it," Dad said, "quit your cryin'."

Dad told us, "The farmer's up against it."

You know where the golf course is, the Meadowlark condominiums, them sloping meadows along the river? He sold that land for twenty an acre. Giving it away, even then. I told this to Yogetsky and he moaned, hit his forehead with the heel of his hand, said, "Jesus Christ."

We were up against it. There wasn't the money to find out what was wrong with me, hey, just all kinds of homemade junk. Bootie and I took boiled carrots to school in our lunch pails; the cow's hooves made a thick sucking noise when we drove her across the marshy place and that sound made me feel I didn't have a chance. You get used to it.

The grand name for the farm, the hundreds of no-good trees in the orchard, the heavy, tearing rolls of barbwire strung through the woods were all for nothing.

3

What can I tell you about the Moon-Azures?

They own the original old Clew homestead with its crooked door-frames and worn stairs, Dr. and Mrs. Moon-Azure from Basiltower, Maryland. I was born in that house.

The Moon-Azures come up from Maryland every June and go back in August. They scrape nine layers of paint off the paneling in the parlor, point out to us the things they do to better the place. They clear out the dump, get a backhoe in to cut a wide driveway. They get somebody to sand the floors. They buy a horse. Dr. Moon-Azure's hands get roughed up when he works on the stone wall. He holds them out and says admiringly, "Look at those hands." A faint smell comes from his clothes, the familiar brown odor of the old house. His wall buckles with the first frost heaves.

The Moon-Azures have weekend guests. We see the cars go by, out-of-state license plates on Mercedes and Saabs. When the wind is right we can hear their toneless voices knocking together like sticks of wood, *tot, tot-tot, tot*. The horse gets out and is killed on the road.

Nobody knows what kind of doctor he is. They go to him when some woman from Massachusetts backs over the edge of the gravel pit. Somebody drives to Moon-Azure's and asks him to come, but he won't. "I don't practice," he says. "Call the ambulance." He offers them the use of his phone.

They walk a good deal. You drive somewhere and here come the Moon-Azures, stumbling through the fireweed, their hands full of wilted branches.

Tolman at the garage says Moon-Azure's a semiretired psychiatrist, but Aunt thinks he's a heart surgeon who lost his nerve in the middle of an operation. He's got good teeth.

Moon-Azure says, "I'll never get used to the way you people let these fine old places run down." He's found the pile of broken slates that came off the old roof. It's been a tin roof since around 1925.

With Mrs. Moon-Azure it's information. What direction is west, when to pick blackberries, oh, kerosene lamps burn kerosene oil? She thought, gasoline. Like to see her try it. In the winter when they're in Florida, the porcupines get into the house, leave calling cards on the floor. "Look," she says, "bunny rabbits." She writes it all down. "My book on country living," she laughs.

She says "maple surple" for a joke.

"How's the hay coming along?" says Moon-Azure.

Once they come on a Saturday morning, smiling, ask Reba to clean house for them, but she says, "No." A teacup rings hard on the saucer.

They ask Marie Beaubien. They pay her more for wiping their tables and making their beds than any man gets running a chain saw.

"How's the hay coming, Lucien?" says Moon-Azure.

"Good," says Beaubien.

We could of used the money.

Marie Beaubien tells us, "White telephones, one in every room, and a bathroom all pale blue tiles painted with orchids. They got copper pans cost a hundred dollars for each one and more of them than you can count. Antique baskets hanging all over the walls, carpets everywhere."

It's not my taste.

My taste is simpler.

I like to see bare floor boards.

From the first the Moon-Azures are crazy for old deeds and maps of the farm, they trace Clew genealogy as though they bought our ancestors with the land. They like to think the Clews were farmers. He says, "Mason, looks like a good year for hay."

How the hell would I know?

They go down to the town clerk's office and dig up information on the ear notch patterns Clews used 150 years ago to mark their sheep, try to find out if the early Clews did anything. One time they ask us to write down the kinds of apples. The orchards, black rows of heart-rotted trees, belong to them.

But all of their fascination is with the ancestor Clews; living Clews exist, like the Beaubiens, to be used. Dead Clews belong to the property and the property belongs to the Moon-Azures.

The Moon-Azures hire Lucien to clear out the brush and set up fallen stones. When I take Reba and Aunt for a ride up the road sometimes on the weekends you can see the Moon-Azures and their guests walking away from the cemetery, heads a little down as if they are thinking, not *sic transit gloria mundi*,[1] but *this is mine*.

They post all of the land with big white signs stapled on plywood squares and nailed to posts every hundred feet. They set fence everywhere, along the road, up the drive, around the house, through the woods, all split-rail fence. Not an inch of barbwire. But up in the woods the line of trees shows scars like twisted mouths from the wire we strung to keep the deer out of the orchards.

The Moon-Azures are after us, after the Beaubiens, even after Yogetsky for help with things, getting their car going, clearing out the clogged spring, finding their red-haired dog. They need to know how things happened, what things happened. Every year they go back to the city at the end of the summer. Then that changes.

Mrs. Beaubien polishes her spoon with the paper napkin and sifts sugar into her coffee. "The doctor is retired," she says. "They're goin' to stay up here until Christmas, then go off somewhere hot, then come back up here after mud season. Same thing every year from now on."

Aunt says, "Must be nice to have the jingle in your pockets to just run up and down between the nice weather."

"I never known one of them people to stick it out very long," says Mrs. Beaubien. "Wait till they have to scrape the ice off their own windshield. Lucien don't go up there for that, you bet."

I think, bet he will.

The Moon-Azures keep on walking. What else do they have to do after the first black frosts? In the shortening days their friends don't come to visit, and they have only each other to hear their startled exclamations that fallen leaves have a bitter odor, that the hardening earth throws up rods of cloudy ice. They come at us with their clumsy conversation, wasting our time. Beaubien and his son bring them wood and stack it, the autumn shrivels into November.

A week before Thanksgiving here comes Mrs. Moon-Azure again, walking down the field. She knocks on the window, peers in at Aunt. Cockleburs hang on her ankles. Her clothes are the color of oatmeal. Her eyes are gray. The refrigerator switches on as she starts to speak, and she has to repeat herself in a louder voice. "I said, I hear you have some remarkable photographs!"

---

1 *sic transit gloria mundi:* thus passes away the glory of this world. [Latin]

"Well, they're interesting to us," says Aunt. She has flour on her hands, and dusts it off, slapping her palms against her thighs. She shows some of the pictures, standing them up on edge saying, "Mr. Galloon Heyscape doing the Irish clog, Denman Thompson's oxen, the radio of the two sweethearts, Kiley Druge and his crazy daughter."

"These are important photographs," says Mrs. Moon-Azure in the same way she said, "You ran over my horse," to Clyde Cuckhorn. We see how much she wants them.

Hey, too bad.

"I wonder they don't come right out and ask if we'll sell them," says Aunt after she's gone. "She'd give anything to get her mitts on these pictures. No, these are Clew family photographs taken by a very gifted hired man, and here they stay."

Leonard Prittle, our hired man, took his pictures from under a large black cloak cast off by my great-grandmother, says Aunt.

How does she know.

What Aunt is afraid of is that the Moon-Azures will pass the pictures around among their weekend guests, that they will find their way into books and newspapers, and we will someday see our grandfather's corpse in his homemade coffin resting on two sawhorses, flattened out on the pages of some magazine and labeled with a cruel caption.

4

Maybe Dad never imagined himself doing anything but selling off the land and dreaming useless apple thoughts, but in the worst of it he got a job. And this was a time when there wasn't any jobs, and he wasn't looking for one. It wasn't even stonework.

Dad's friend, Diamond Ward, was one of those hard gray men who ate deer meat in every season and could fix whatever was broken again and again until nothing was left of the original machine but its function. Diamond was in the Grange,[2] knew what was going on, and he was one of the first in the country to get a job through the Rural Electrification Act.[3] He got my father in with him. The Ironworks

---

2 **Grange:** a local branch of an association for promoting agricultural interests.

3 **Rural Electrification Act:** The Rural Electrification Administration was established in 1935 when Franklin Roosevelt was president to lend money at low interest rates to help build power lines. Before REA, only 10 percent of American farms had electricity.

County Electric Power Cooperative. Replaced now by Northern Nuclear. We got the alarm in the kitchen that's supposed to go off if there's an accident down there, everybody evacuate in a hurry.

Where to?

The two of them drove around all day in a dark green truck with a painted circle on the side enclosing the letters ICEPC and three bolts of electricity. Everybody called it "The Icepick." Diamond chewed tobacco, and the door on his side was stained brown. Bootie would get in the closet when she heard Diamond coming up the drive.

The kite's paper is gone, burned up in the seasons of August heat under the cracking barn roof.

There was something in my father that had to blow up whatever he did. He got a certain amount of pleasure seeing himself as The Lone Apple-Grower up against a gang of McIntosh men. Now came a chance to be The One Bringing Light to the Farm. He could fool and laugh with people as much as he wanted.

He'd say, "A five-dollar deposit, the price of a pair of shoes, and we'll put the 'lectricity in. You'll hear the radio, hear Amos and Andy." He'd imitate Amos, laugh. "Get rid of them sad irons,⁴ use them for doorstops. Lights? Get twice the work done because you'll be able to see both ends of the cow. *Hawhaw.*"

He got up a mock funeral at the Grange, spent weeks laughing and talking it up. The men carried a coffin around the hall, then took it out and buried it. It was full of oil lamps and blackened chimneys.

Hey, I'm telling you, this is within our lifetime.

Television wasn't invented until 1938.

He'd list the things electricity was going to do away with. No more stinking privies. No more strained, watery eyes from reading by lamplight. No more lonely evenings for widowers who could turn on a radio and hear plays and music. No more families dead from food poisoning when Ma could keep the potato salad in a chilly white refrigerator. No more heating sad irons on a blazing stove in August. The kids would stay on the farm.

He'd look at somebody with his round, clear eyes, he'd say, "If you put a light on every farm, you put a light in every heart." He

---

4 **sad iron:** a heavy iron which must be heated over a fire before pressing cloth or clothes.

never missed a day in four years, until the afternoon Diamond got killed trying to get a kite out of the lines.

Dad always left the house at five in the morning, carrying his lunch in a humped black lunchbox. A thermos bottle of coffee fit inside the top, held in place by a metal clasp. He and Diamond set poles and strung line to canted, ancient barns and to houses settled down on their foundations like old dogs sleeping on porch steps.

He got the idea they ought to carry a radio around in the truck. A farmer did his own wiring in those days, then called up The Icepick and said he was ready. Sometimes they had a washing machine hid under some burlap bags all set up to go as a birthday present for the wife. But usually just a couple of ceiling fixtures, outlets.

Before they turned on the power, Dad got his radio out of the truck, rubbed it up a little if it was dusty. He'd plug it in. There stood the farmer and his wife and the children, all staring at it.

"This is goin' to change your life," Dad would say.

He'd go to the window and signal Diamond to turn on the juice. As the static-rich sound of a braying announcer or a foxtrot poured into the room, he watched the faces of the family, watched their mouths opening a little as if to swallow the sound. The farmer would shake his hand, the wife would dab at her watery, strained eyes and say, "It's a miracle." It was as if my father had personally given them this wonder. Yet you could tell they despised him, too, for making things easy.

I never saw how anybody could rejoice over the harsh light that came out of them clear nippled bulbs.

After Diamond was killed Dad decided to go into the appliance business. That's what I do out in the barn. I was never able to do anything heavy. We still sell a few washers and electric stoves. Reba helps me get them onto the truck. There's not much in appliances now. It's all sound systems and computers. You can buy your washing machines anywhere.

At noon in summer, if they weren't too far away, Dad and Diamond would come back to the farm, drive up into the field and park the truck under the trees. They took the full hour. They had their favorite place. They'd spread out an old canvas tarp in the shade. There was a spring up there. There was a slab of flat rock. Sometimes Bootie or I would bring them up their dinner. We'd skirt wide around Diamond, he'd make mocking kissing sounds with his stained wet mouth.

Dad would laugh, *"Haw."*

Sometimes Diamond was asleep with his shirt over his face so the flies wouldn't bother him, and Dad would be on his knees, tapping away at the rock with the chisel and the stone hammer for something to do. Bootie and I could hear the *tok, tok-tok* when we walked up the track. He was chiseling in the rock, chiseling out a big bas-relief of himself wearing his lineman's gear. We'd play a kind of hopscotch on his grand design.

"Look, Dad," said Bootie, "I'm standin' on the eyes."

In the winter Dad and Diamond sat in the truck with the engine running.

The old family plot, not used for eighty years or so, is up in the back of the house. Diamond Ward is buried down in the Baptist cemetery in Ironworks. *A Lamb of God Call'd Home, His Soul No More Shall Roam*. Hey, we've seen that verse a hundred times.

His eyes reflected a knowledge of his terrible mistake, my father told us. "He looked straight at me, his mouth opened and I seen what I thought was blood, this dark trickle, come out. But it was tobacco juice. He was dead there on the pole, lookin' at me. I was the last thing he saw."

After Diamond was killed, Bootie and I played at the best game we ever invented. We played it over and over for about two years. Bootie thought up the idea of the molasses.

It wasn't so much a game as a play, and not so much a play as acting out an event that gave us a sharp satisfaction. We'd get some molasses in a cup and go out to the barn where we had our things arranged. Pieced-out binder twine sagged between the ladder to the hayloft and a crossbeam. We argued about who would play Diamond first.

Bootie took her turn.

I'd say, "I'm Dad."

Bootie would say, "I'm Diamond." She would twist her face, hitch at her corduroy pants, kick at the floor.

"Hey, Diamond," I'd say, "there's a kite in the lines."

We'd look up into the dry twittering gloom. A kite hung there, as alert and expectant as a wounded bird.

"I'll get the goddamn thing out of our lines," said Diamond, taking up a long narrow stick. He climbed slowly, the stick hitting against the utility pole, *tok, tok-tok*. At the top Diamond turned and faced the kite.

"Be careful," I said.

The stick extended toward the kite, touched it.

5

A thin dust of snow falls. Visitors' cars rush along the road again, stirring up pale clouds.

"Must be havin' a party," says Aunt.

"Goodbye party, I hope," says Reba.

Mrs. Beaubien's little hungry face bobs into her window every time a car goes past.

Reba and Aunt and I get in the truck and go for a ride, careful to look straight ahead. There are eight coffee cans with dead marigolds on Yogetsky's porch. We can see the Moon-Azures up in the high field where the smooth, sloping granite lies exposed. We can see them among the poplars that have multiplied into a grove since I was a kid. Those trees all drop their leaves on the same day in autumn.

"That's the spring up there. Dad used to go up there at noon with old Diamond," I say. "Under the maple that went down."

"They can't be all that excited about a spring," says Aunt.

We see them bending over, one woman down on her knees with a pad of paper, drawing or writing. Dr. Moon-Azure leans forward from his hips with a camera screwed into his eye.

"They've got a body there," says Aunt. I can smell the faint lemony scent of lotion, the thick warmth of hair. The truck heater is on.

"More like a dead porcupine—probably the first one they ever see," says Reba. We turn around and go home and watch The Secret World of Insects. Our spoons clink and scrape at the cream and Jell-O in the bottom of the pressed glass bowls, the double-diamond pattern. It's just the field and the spring and the rock. Hey, I've been up there a hundred times.

The phone rings.

"What do you think," Marie Beaubien says.

"I think they've found a corpse in the bushes, one of those poor girls who'll take a ride from anybody in a red car," says Aunt.

"No, we would of seen that little skinny man, what's his name, over there in Rose of Sharon, the medical examiner."

"Winwell. Avery Winwell. His mother was a Richardson."

"That's right, Winwell. Yes, and the state police and all them. Whatever they've got there isn't no body."

"Well, I don't know what they could have found."

"Something."

The next day I walk down to Yogetsky's to get away from the sound of the vacuum cleaner. Reba knows it gets on my nerves.

Yogetsky is knocking the dead marigolds out of the coffee cans. Brown humps of dirt lie on the ground. He says, "See your neighbors found a Indian carving." I think at first he means the Beaubiens.

"What carving is that," I say.

"I got it inside in the paper," he says. I follow him into the kitchen. He washes his hands in the clean sink. The paper is folded over the arm of a chair. I look out the window and see our house, the gray clapboards stained with brown streaks from the iron nails, see the sign, CLEW'S APPLIANCES.

Yogetsky shakes out his paper until he finds the right place. He peers through his slipping glasses, his blunt finger traces across the text, and he reads aloud. "It says, 'Complex petroglyphs[5] such as the recently discovered Thunder God pictured here are rare among the eastern woodland tribes.' It says, 'Discovered by the owners of a farm in Ironworks County.'" Yogetsky peers at me. "I didn't know there was no Indians around here."

He shows me the picture in the newspaper. I see my father's self-portrait cut deep into rock. In one stone hand he clenches three bolts of electricity. Around his waist is his lineman's belt. His hair flows back, his eyes fix you from the stone.

"Dad, I'm standin' on the eyes," said Bootie.

In our game the stick touched the kite, inexplicably fell away. Diamond swayed, his balance gone. Falling, his hand grasped the wire. His spine arched, his hand clenched living bolts of lightning. His eyes fixed mine, his mouth opened, and from the corner of his lips spilled the dark molasses, like blood, like uncontrollable tobacco juice.

I laugh, because isn't there something funny about this figure slowly cut into the fieldrock during the long summer noons half a century ago? And how can Yogetsky understand?

---

5 **petroglyph:** a carving or drawing made by a member of a prehistoric people.

QUESTIONS FOR DISCUSSION

1. How have time and place affected the lives of the narrator and his family?

2. What function do the old photos serve in the story?

3. What are the natives' attitudes toward the Moon-Azures, and why?

4. What is ironic about the newspaper article about the discovery of the "petroglyph"?

TOPICS FOR WRITING

1. In an essay, contrast the lives of the Moon-Azures and the Beaubiens, Yogetsky, and the narrator's family. Start with a strong topic sentence, and conclude with a statement that expresses your attitude toward all these people.

2. What do you think lies behind the Moon-Azures's "fascination . . . with the ancestor Clews"? Express your views in a paper.

3. Reflect on how setting has influenced you and your family, and examine the influence in a short paper.

SYNTHESIS QUESTIONS

1. Design a Web page for one of the authors in this chapter. You will be able to find the most information on Thomas King and E. Annie Proulx.

2. If you could live anywhere in the world, where would you live? In a few paragraphs, describe the place (it needn't be a real place) and tell why you would want to live there.

3. Have you ever been in a setting that made you uncomfortable, uneasy, or miserable? If so, describe the place and tell why you were miserable.

4. Write a poem or song lyrics about one of the characters in this chapter.

5. Write the first paragraph of a short story in which you convey a certain atmosphere; it can be scary, oppressive, filled with anxiety, humorous, tranquil, or any other mood that appeals to you.

Chapter Three

Character

To say that someone *is* a character suggests that he or she has a strange or eccentric personality; to say that a person *has* character implies his or her moral uprightness; to say something *about* a person's character involves a discussion of his or her personal values and behavior. As a literary term, however, a ***character*** is a person created for a work of fiction.

CLASSIFYING CHARACTERS

How do literary characters differ? In some cases, they are veiled, autobiographical versions of the author. Often, they are people the author knows or people the author has observed or overheard. While the origin of a character is usually irrelevant, a character's dimensionality and purpose in the story *are* important. Will the character be complex or merely a bystander? Will he or she arouse the reader's sympathy? The author's purpose for the character determines the answers to questions such as these.

Round and Flat Characters

In his discussion of character in *Aspects of the Novel*, E. M. Forster suggests that the degree to which fictional characters are realistic classifies them as *round* or *flat*. To Forster, a **round character** is a three-dimensional character complex enough to be able to surprise the reader without losing credibility. Because such characters exhibit many characteristics, some of which may be contradictory, they have what Forster calls the "incalculability of life." Such characters are said to be fully or well developed. When you finish reading about Willa Cather's Paul, Gish Jen's Callie, or Penelope Lively's Anna, you will know them almost as intimately as you know your best friend. In contrast, a **flat**

character is one whom Forster deems incapable of surprising the reader. Such a two-dimensional character can often be summarized with one or two characteristics—cowardly, for example, or puzzled, or stubborn. Paul's father in "Paul's Case," the father in "The Water-Faucet Vision," and a few of the adults in "The French Exchange," qualify as flat characters. Because of their brevity, short stories typically contain more flat characters than round ones.

Major and Minor Characters

The term *protagonist* refers to the main or central character in fiction. **Protagonist** is an ancient Greek word for the central character of a drama. Traditionally, the title character of a story is the protagonist, as in Willa Cather's "Paul's Case," but there are exceptions.

The protagonist is generally the roundest, most fully developed character in a work of fiction. The protagonist may also be the most *sympathetic* character. Don't be confused by that label. It doesn't mean that the character is capable of the emotion of sympathy. It means that the author has created a protagonist who arouses *your* concern and sympathy—even if you do not understand or like him or her.

As noted in Chapter 1, fiction grows out of conflict—the struggle between opposing forces. Since two of those forces—society and a natural/supernatural force—are not human, it is illogical to identify the protagonist's nonhuman opponent as the **villain.** Rather, a more neutral and accurate word to describe the protagonist's opponent is **antagonist.** Like protagonists, many antagonists will also be round characters, though it is possible for an antagonist to be a flat character. Together, the protagonist and antagonist comprise the **major characters** or forces in fiction.

Characters other than major characters are classified as **minor characters.** Their degree of importance depends on their function. One important minor character often appears in television programs: the **confidant** (or, if a female, the **confidante**)—the person in whom the protagonist confides. In many television programs, the protagonist has a partner or one or two friends. Their conversations enable the audience to discover what the protagonist is thinking or planning. This kind of minor character, often known as a **foil,** typically contrasts physically and/or in personality with the main character. The contrast itself serves to emphasize the protagonist's characteristics. Sometimes, the foil provides comic relief. The foil is often but not necessarily a flat character; in "The Water-Faucet Vision," Patty functions as a foil to the narrator.

A **stereotyped character** represents a category of people. The word *stereotype* comes from printing and refers to a metal mold used to mass produce duplicates of printing type. Stereotyped characters—the dumb athlete, the nagging wife, the absent-minded professor—provide authors with a kind of literary shorthand; since readers readily recognize such flat character types, authors need not use up space describing them. Cather could have stereotyped all the teachers in "Paul's Case" as mean and unfeeling, but by giving the drawing master some depth of insight and character, Cather differentiates this teacher from his colleagues. Stereotyped characters are sometimes referred to as **stock** or **type characters.**

A final category of character might be termed the **piece of furniture character.** In short stories such characters are virtually without personality, but like a chair or a sofa they serve a useful function: they sell the newspaper that contains an item that affects the plot or a character; they drive the cab that carries the antagonist to a confrontation with the protagonist; they serve the meals, rake the leaves, fix the dishwasher. It is the medical personnel in "The Water-Faucet Vision," for example, who mention the idea of a miracle—an idea important to the story—but they are otherwise without personality. Minor characters in fictions are rarely round characters, nor—given the limitations of space—should they be.

Active and Static Characters

Another way of classifying characters is to label them as *active* (or *dynamic*) or *static*. An **active character** is one who changes because of what happens in the plot. **Static characters,** however, remain unchanged; their character is the same at the end of the story as at the beginning.

Just as not all characters in a short story will be round, nor will all be active, or dynamic; in fact, they should not be. Sometimes the fact that a character does *not* change becomes crucial to the meaning of the story.

CHARACTERIZATION

Character creation is the art of **characterization**—what the author does to bring a character to life, to provide the reader with a sense of that character's personality, to make that character unique. Authors can characterize or develop a character directly or indirectly.

Direct Characterization

In **direct characterization,** the narrator or a character summarizes or tells the reader what another character looks like or what kind of person he or she is. In the following examples, the words that represent direct characterization are italicized. In the opening paragraphs of "Paul's Case," the narrator describes Paul's appearance by noting he "was *tall* for his age and very *thin*" and *"there was something of the dandy* about him." In "The French Exchange," the character Jean-Paul directly states, *"I am interest . . . in astronomy, philosophy, and the music of Mozart."* Direct characterization often occurs during the exposition since it conveys background information efficiently, but it can occur throughout the story.

Indirect Characterization

In **indirect characterization,** narrators and characters describe, *without comment,* a character's appearance or dress. In this way they suggest something about the character's personality. A character's repeated gesture or a facial tic, for example, may imply a character's arrogance or nervousness.

A character's own statements are another way of revealing character; diction (choice of words) and grammar may connote a person's educational level or, as in "The French Exchange," convey Jean-Paul's difficulty with English as well as his ironic attitude.

A character's actions—including reactions and mannerisms—are another way to "read" a character. Cather's Paul fills his room at the New York hotel with flowers, an indication of his desire to be surrounded by beauty. Through indirect characterization, a writer *shows* rather than *tells,* allowing the reader to *infer* (draw conclusions about) the nature of a character.

What characters think about themselves, external events, or other people often provides the most telling clue to their personality. In the Cather story, Paul's hostile attitude toward his teachers and his father and his loathing of his life on Cordelia Street allow the reader to formulate a deeper picture of his troubled character. The desire of the young girl in "The Water-Faucet Vision" to perform a miracle leads the reader to infer something about her religious faith.

One problem with looking into a character's thoughts is associated with the *point of view* of a story (see Chapter 4). If the story is told from the point of view of a character in a story, the reader must determine whether or to what degree that character's thoughts are valid or trustworthy. In fiction as in life, characters sometimes lie to themselves.

Assessing Characterization

To assess the success of an author's characterization, keep two principles in mind. First, *the actions of a character should be plausibly motivated*. In literature, **motivations** explain or justify why characters act, talk, or feel as they do. If you find a character's motivation implausible or untruthful, you will judge his or her actions to be psychologically unconvincing, and the story itself will seem weak and contrived.

The second principle to consider in assessing an author's characterization is that *the actions of a character should be consistent*. Throughout most of "Paul's Case," the protagonist consistently feels that he deserves a better, more opulent style of life. His method for achieving that life is clearly, and feloniously, wrong, but—given Cather's detailed characterization—understandable. One way to express the idea of inconsistency is to say that a character's actions or statements are not "in character."

Some authors sacrifice plausibility and consistency to create happy endings. While you may be temporarily gratified by such an ending, in the long run you should also be disappointed. One aim of fiction writers is to reveal the truth about the human condition; contrived happy endings brought about by implausible, inconsistent characters are seldom truthful.

SUMMARY

As you discuss the characters in these stories, remember that they can be classified as either round or flat, active or static, major or minor. Major characters are typically limited to the protagonist or the antagonist, with sympathetic characters generally being limited to protagonists and certain minor characters. Minor characters primarily function as foils, stereotypes, or pieces of furniture. In breathing life into their characters, authors use both direct and indirect characterization. When you are asked to judge the effectiveness of a fictional character, remember the principles of plausibility and consistency. Remember, too, that in serious fiction the elements of plot and character are so closely intertwined that it is often impossible to tell whether events prompt a character's behavior or whether a character's nature influences the events.

THE WATER-FAUCET VISION

GISH JEN (born 1955)

Gish Jen's first name is actually Lillian, a name she hated because she associated it with "a type of librarian who wears orange support hose . . . [and] who blinks more than she talks." When some of her high school friends starting calling her Gish, after the silent screen actress Lillian Gish, Jen says she was "ecstatic."

Jen, who refers to herself as a "writing mom," grew up in Scarsdale, New York, and graduated from Harvard University in 1977. During the 1979–1980 academic year, she attended Stanford University and in 1983 received an M. F. A. from the University of Iowa. In 1986, Jen was a lecturer in fiction writing at Tufts University and, during the 1990–1991 school year, a visiting writer at the University of Massachusetts.

Throughout the 1980s Jen was the recipient of a number of awards and honors, including several foundation awards, a residency at the MacDowell Colony, and various writing awards, including a prestigious Guggenheim fellowship. She has published two novels, *Typical American* (1991), nominated for the National Book Critics' Circle Award, and *Mona in the Promised Land* (1996), a work that features the two sisters in "The Water-Faucet Vision." Jen's work appears in several anthologies: *Best American Short Stories of 1988*, *New Worlds of Literature* (1989), and *Home to Stay: Asian American Women's Fiction* (1990). She has also contributed to such periodicals as *The New Yorker*, *Fiction International*, *Yale Review*, and *Iowa Review*.

Although "The Water-Faucet Vision" portrays an Asian-American family, the characters and their experiences are universal. As you read, ask yourself these questions: What kind of person is the narrator? What has significantly influenced her life?

■

To protect my sister Mona and me from the pains—or, as they pronounced it, the "pins"—of life, my parents did their fighting in Shanghai dialect, which we didn't understand; and when my father one day pitched a brass vase through the kitchen window, my mother told us he had done it by accident.

"By accident?" said Mona.

My mother chopped the foot off a mushroom.

"By accident?" said Mona. "By *accident?*"

Later I tried to explain to her that she shouldn't have persisted like that, but it was hopeless.

"What's the matter with throwing things," she shrugged. "He was *mad.*"

That was the difference between Mona and me: Fighting was just fighting to her. If she worried about anything, it was only that she might turn out too short to become a ballerina, in which case she was going to be a piano player.

I, on the other hand, was going to be a martyr. I was in fifth grade then, and the hyperimaginative sort—the kind of girl who grows morbid in Catholic school, who longs to be chopped or frozen to death but then has nightmares about it from which she wakes up screaming and clutching a stuffed bear. It was not a bear that I clutched, though, but a string of three malachite[1] beads that I had found in the marsh by the old aqueduct one day. Apparently once part of a necklace, they were each wonderfully striated and swirled, and slightly humped toward the center, like a jellyfish; so that if I squeezed one, it would slip smoothly away, with a grace that altogether enthralled and—on those dream-harrowed nights—soothed me, soothed me as nothing had before or has since. Not that I've lacked occasion for soothing: Though it's been four months since my mother died, there are still nights when sleep stands away from me, stiff as a well-paid sentry. But that is another story. Back then I had my malachite beads, and if I worried them long and patiently enough, I was sure to start feeling better, more awake, even a little special—imagining, as I liked to, that my nightmares were communications from the Almighty Himself, preparation for my painful destiny. Discussing them with Patty Creamer, who had also promised her life to God, I called them "almost visions"; and Patty, her mouth wadded with the three or four sticks of doublemint she always seemed to have going at once, said, "I bet you'll be doin' miracleth by seventh grade."

---

1 **malachite:** a green semiprecious stone.

Miracles. Today Patty laughs to think she ever spent good time stewing on such matters, her attention having long turned to rugs, and artwork, and antique Japanese bureaus—things she believes in.

"A good bureau's more than just a bureau," she explained last time we had lunch. "It's a hedge against life. I tell you, if there's one thing I believe, it's that cheap stuff's just money out the window. Nice stuff, on the other hand—now that you can always cash out, if life gets rough. *That* you can count on."

In fifth grade, though, she counted on different things.

"You'll be doing miracles too," I told her, but she shook her shaggy head and looked doleful.

"Na' me," she chomped. "Buzzit's okay. The kin' things I like, prayers work okay on."

"Like?"

"Like you 'member that dreth I liked?"

She meant the yellow one, with the criss-cross straps.

"Well gueth what."

"Your mom got it for you."

She smiled. "And I only jutht prayed for it for a week," she said.

As for myself, though, I definitely wanted to be able to perform a wonder or two. Miracle-working! It was the carrot of carrots: It kept me doing my homework, taking the sacraments; it kept me mournfully on key in music hour, while my classmates hiccuped and squealed their carefree hearts away. Yet I couldn't have said what I wanted such powers *for*, exactly. That is, I thought of them the way one might think of, say, an ornamental sword—as a kind of collectible, which also happened to be a means of defense.

But then Patty's father walked out on her mother, and for the first time, there was a miracle I wanted to do. I wanted it so much I could see it: Mr. Creamer made into a spitball; Mr. Creamer shot through a straw into the sky; Mr. Creamer unrolled and re-plumped, plop back on Patty's doorstep. I would've cleaned out his mind and given him a shave en route. I would've given him a box of peanut fudge, tied up with a ribbon, to present to Patty with a kiss.

But instead all I could do was try to tell her he'd come back.

"He will not, he will not!" she sobbed. "He went on a boat to Rio Deniro.[2] To Rio Deniro!"

---

2 **Rio Deniro:** Patty confuses Rio de Janeiro, a city in Brazil, with the actor Robert De Niro.

I tried to offer her a stick of gum, but she wouldn't take it.

"He said he would rather look at water than at my mom's fat face. He said he would rather look at water than at me." Now she was really wailing, and holding her ribs so tightly that she almost seemed to be hurting herself—so tightly that just looking at her arms wound around her like snakes made my heart feel squeezed.

I patted her on the arm. A one-winged pigeon waddled by.

"He said I wasn't even his kid, he said I came from Uncle Johnny. He said I was garbage, just like my mom and Uncle Johnny. He said I wasn't even his kid, he said I wasn't his Patty, he said I came from Uncle Johnny!"

"From your Uncle Johnny?" I said stupidly.

"From Uncle Johnny," she cried. "From Uncle Johnny!"

"He said that?" I said. Then, wanting to go on, to say *something,* I said, "Oh Patty, don't cry."

She kept crying.

I tried again. "Oh Patty, don't cry," I said. Then I said, "Your dad was a jerk anyway."

The pigeon produced a large runny dropping.

It was a good twenty minutes before Patty was calm enough for me just to run to the girls' room to get her some toilet paper; and by the time I came back she was sobbing again, saying "To Rio Deniro, to Rio Deniro" over and over again, as though the words had stuck in her and couldn't be gotten out. As we had missed the regular bus home and the late bus too, I had to leave her a second time to go call my mother, who was only mad until she heard what had happened. Then she came and picked us up, and bought us each a Fudgsicle.

Some days later, Patty and I started a program to work on getting her father home. It was a serious business. We said extra prayers, and lit votive candles; I tied my malachite beads to my uniform belt, fondling them as though they were a rosary, I a nun. We even took to walking about the school halls with our hands folded—a sight so ludicrous that our wheeze of a principal personally took us aside one day.

"I must tell you," she said, using her nose as a speaking tube, "that there is really no need for such peee-ity."

But we persisted, promising to marry God and praying to every saint we could think of. We gave up gum, then gum and Slim Jims both, then gum and Slim Jims and ice cream—and when even that didn't work, we started on more innovative things. The first was looking at flowers. We held our hands beside our eyes like blinders as we hurried by the violets by the flagpole, the window box full of tulips outside the nurse's office. Next it was looking at boys: Patty gave up angel-eyed Jamie Halloran and I, gymnastic Anthony Rossi. It was hard, but in the end our efforts paid off. Mr. Creamer came back a month later, and though he brought with him nothing but dysentery, he was at least too sick to have all that much to say.

Then, in the course of a fight with my father, my mother somehow fell out of their bedroom window.

Recently—thinking a mountain vacation might cheer me—I sublet my apartment to a handsome but somber newlywed couple, who turned out to be every bit as responsible as I'd hoped. They cleaned out even the eggshell chips I'd sprinkled around the base of my plants as fertilizer, leaving behind only a shiny silverplate cake server and a list of their hopes and goals for the summer. The list, tacked precariously to the back of the kitchen door, began with a fervent appeal to God to help them get their wedding thank-yous written in three weeks or less. (You could see they had originally written "two weeks" but scratched it out—no miracles being demanded here.) It went on:

> *Please help us, Almighty Father in Heaven Above, to get Ann a teaching job within a half-hour drive of here in a nice neighborhood.*
> *Please help us, Almighty Father in Heaven Above, to get John a job doing anything where he won't strain his back and that is within a half-hour drive of here.*
> *Please help us, Almighty Father in Heaven Above, to get us a car.*
> *Please help us, A.F. in H.A., to learn French.*
> *Please help us, A.F. in H.A., to find seven dinner recipes that cost less than 60 cents a serving and can be made in a half-hour. And that don't have tomatoes, since You in Your Heavenly Wisdom made John allergic.*
> *Please help us, A.F. in H.A., to avoid books in this apartment such as You in Your Heavenly Wisdom allowed John, for Your Heavenly Reasons, to find three nights ago (June 2nd).*

Et cetera. In the left-hand margin they kept score of how they had fared with their requests, and it was heartening to see that nearly all of them were marked "Yes! Praise the Lord!" (sometimes shortened to PTL), with the sole exception of learning French, which was mysteriously marked "No! PTL to the Highest."

That note touched me. Strange and familiar both, it seemed like it had been written by some cousin of mine—some cousin who had stayed home to grow up, say, while I went abroad and learned what I had to, though the learning was painful. This, of course, is just a manner of speaking; in fact, I did my growing up at home, like anybody else.

But the learning *was* painful: I never knew exactly how it happened that my mother went hurtling through the air that night years ago, only that the wind had been chopping at the house, and that the argument had started about the state of the roof. Someone had been up to fix it the year before, but it wasn't a roofer, it was some man my father had insisted could do just as good a job for a quarter of the price. And maybe he could have, had he not somehow managed to step through a knot in the wood under the shingles and break his uninsured ankle. Now the shingles were coming loose again, and the attic insulation was mildewing besides, and my father was wanting to sell the house altogether, which he said my mother had wanted to buy so she could send pictures of it home to her family in China.

"The Americans have a saying," he said. "They saying, 'You have to keep up with the Jones family.' I'm saying if the Jones family in Shanghai, you can send any picture you want, *an-y* picture. Go take picture of those rich guys' house. You want to act like rich guys, right? Go take picture of those rich guys' house."

At that point my mother sent Mona and me to wash up, and started speaking Shanghaiese. They argued for some time in the kitchen, while we listened from the top of the stairs, our faces wedged between the bumpy Spanish scrolls of the wrought iron railing. First my mother ranted, then my father, then they both ranted at once until finally there was a thump, followed by a long quiet.

"Do you think they're kissing now?" said Mona. "I bet they're kissing, like this." She pursed her lips like a fish and was about to put them to the railing when we heard my mother locking the back door. We hightailed it into bed; my parents creaked up the stairs. Everything at that point seemed fine. Once in their bedroom, though, they started up again, first softly, then louder and louder, until my mother turned on a radio to try to disguise the noise. A door slammed; they began shouting at one another; another door slammed; a shoe or something banged the wall behind Mona's bed.

"How're we supposed to *sleep?*" said Mona, sitting up.

There was another thud, more yelling in Shanghaiese, and then my mother's voice pierced the wall, in English. "So what you want I should do? Go to work like Theresa Lee?"

My father rumbled something back.

"You think you're big shot because you have job, right? You're big shot, but you never get promotion, you never get raise. All I do is spend money, right? So what do you do, you tell me. So what do you do!"

Something hit the floor so hard that our room shook.

"So kill me," screamed my mother. "You know what you are? You are failure. Failure! You are failure!"

Then there was a sudden, terrific, bursting crash—and after it, as if on a bungled cue, the serene blare of an a cappella[3] soprano, picking her way down a scale.

By the time Mona and I knew to look out the window, a neighbor's pet beagle was already on the scene, sniffing and barking at my mother's body, his tail crazy with excitement; then he was barking at my stunned and trembling father, at the shrieking ambulance, the police, at crying Mona in her bunny-footed pajamas, and at me, barefoot in the cold grass, squeezing her shoulder with one hand and clutching my malachite beads with the other.

My mother wasn't dead, only unconscious, the paramedics figured that out right away, but there was blood everywhere, and though they were reassuring about her head wounds as they strapped her to the stretcher, commenting also on how small she was, how delicate, how light, my father kept saying, "I killed her, I killed her" as the ambulance screeched and screeched headlong, forever, to the hospital. I was afraid to touch her, and glad of the metal rail between us, even though its sturdiness made her seem even frailer than she was; I wished she was bigger, somehow, and noticed, with a pang, that the new red slippers we had given her for Mother's Day had been lost somewhere along the way. How much she seemed to be leaving behind, as we careened along—still not there, still not there—Mona and Dad and the medic and I taking up the whole ambulance, all the room, so there was no room for anything else; no room even for my mother's real self, the one who should have been pinching the color back to my father's gray face, the one who should have been calming Mona's cowlick—the one who should have been bending over us, to help us to be strong, to help us get through, even as we bent over her.

Then suddenly we were there, the glowing square of the emergency room entrance opening like the gates of heaven; and immediately the talk of miracles began. Alive, a miracle. No bones broken, a miracle. A miracle that the hemlocks cushioned her fall, a miracle that they hadn't been trimmed in a year and a half. It was a

---

3 **a cappella:** in vocal music, without instrumental accompaniment. [Italian]

miracle that all that blood, the blood that had seemed that night to be everywhere, was from one shard of glass, a single shard, can you imagine, and as for the gash in her head, the scar would be covered by hair. The next day my mother cheerfully described just how she would part it so that nothing would show at all.

"You're a lucky duck-duck," agreed Mona, helping herself, with a little *pirouette*,[4] to the cherry atop my mother's chocolate pudding.

That wasn't enough for me, though. I was relieved, yes, but what I wanted by then was a real miracle, not for her simply to have survived but for the whole thing never to have happened—for my mother's head never to had to been shaved and bandaged like that, for her high, proud forehead to never have been swollen down over her eyes, for her face and neck and hands never to have been painted so many shades of blue-black, and violet, and chartreuse. I still want those things—for my parents not to have had to live with this affair like a prickle-bush between them, for my father to have been able to look my mother in her swollen eyes and curse the madman, the monster that could have dared done this to the woman he loved. I wanted to be able to touch my mother without shuddering, to be able to console my father, to be able to get that crash out of my head, the sound of that soprano—so many things that I didn't know how to pray for them, that I wouldn't have known where to start even if I had the power to work miracles, right there, right then.

A week later, when my mother was home, and her head beginning to bristle with new hairs, I lost my malachite beads. I had been carrying them in a white cloth pouch that Patty had given me, and was swinging the pouch on my pinky on my way home from school, when I swung just a bit too hard, and it went sailing in a long arc through the air, whooshing like a perfectly thrown basketball through one of those holes of a nearby sewer. There was no chance of fishing it out: I looked and looked, crouching on the sticky pavement until the asphalt had crazed the skin of my hands and knees, but all I could discern was an evil-smelling musk, glassy and smug and impenetrable.

My loss didn't quite hit me until I was home, but then it produced an agony all out of proportion to my string of pretty beads. I hadn't cried at all during my mother's accident, and now I was crying all afternoon, all through dinner, and then after dinner too, crying

---

4 *pirouette:* a movement in which one whirls about on one foot or on the toes, as in dancing. In French, the word means "spinning top."

past the point where I knew what I was crying for, wishing dimly that I had my beads to hold, wishing dimly that I could pray but refusing, refusing, I didn't know why, until I finally fell into an exhausted sleep on the couch, where my parents left me for the night—glad, no doubt, that one of the more tedious of my childhood crises seemed to be finally winding off the reel of life, onto the reel of memory. They covered me, and somehow grew a pillow under my head, and, with uncharacteristic disregard for the living-room rug, left some milk and pecan sandies on the coffee table, in case I woke up hungry. Their thoughtfulness was prescient: I did wake up in the early part of the night; and it was then, amid the unfamiliar sounds and shadows of the living room, that I had what I was sure was a true vision.

Even now what I saw retains an odd clarity: the requisite strange light flooding the room, first orange, and then a bright yellow-green, then a crackling bright burst like a Roman candle going off near the piano. There was a distinct smell of coffee, and a long silence. The room seemed to be getting colder. Nothing. A creak; the light starting to wane, then waxing again, brilliant pink now. Still nothing. Then, as the pink started to go a little purple, a perfectly normal middle-aged man's voice, speaking something very like pig latin, told me quietly not to despair, not to despair, my beads would be returned to me.

That was all. I sat a moment in the dark, then turned on the light, gobbled down the cookies—and in a happy flash understood I was so good, really, so near to being a saint that my malachite beads would come back through the town water system. All I had to do was turn on all the faucets in the house, which I did, one by one, stealing quietly into the bathroom and kitchen and basement. The old spigot by the washing machine was too gunked up to be coaxed very far open, but that didn't matter. The water didn't have to be full blast, I understood that. Then I gathered together my pillow and blanket and trundled up to my bed to sleep.

By the time I woke up in the morning I knew that my beads hadn't shown up, but when I knew it for certain, I was still disappointed; and as if that weren't enough, I had to face my parents and sister, who were all abuzz with the mystery of the faucets. Not knowing what else to do, I, like a puddlebrain, told them the truth. The results were predictably painful.

"Callie had a *vision,*" Mona told everyone at the bus stop. "A vision with lights, and sinks in it!"

Sinks, visions. I got it all day, from my parents, from my classmates, even some sixth and seventh graders. Someone drew a cartoon of me with a halo over my head in one of the girls' room stalls; Anthony Rossi made gurgling noises as he walked on his hands at recess. Only Patty tried not to laugh, though even she was something less than unalloyed understanding.

"I don't think miracles are thupposed to happen in *thewers,*" she said.

Such was the end of my saintly ambitions. It wasn't the end of all holiness; the ideas of purity and goodness still tippled my brain, and over the years I came slowly to grasp of what grit true faith was made. Last night, though, when my father called to say that he couldn't go on living in our old house, that he was going to move to a smaller place, another place, maybe a condo—he didn't know how, or where—I found myself still wistful for the time religion seemed all I wanted it to be. Back then the world was a place that could be set right: One had only to direct the hand of the Almighty and say, just here, Lord, we hurt here—and here, and here, and here.

QUESTIONS FOR DISCUSSION

1. How does Jen vary the simple chronology of her story?

2. Describe and account for the relationship between the narrator's parents.

3. What methods of characterization does the narrator use in conveying the parents' relationship?

4. Which of the parents is more fully developed?

5. In the story, is Patty a foil? Explain the reasons for your answer.

6. Describe the narrator, citing passages from the story to support your description.

7. How does the episode of the newlywed couple relate to the main plot?

8. Why does the narrator discount the miracle of her mother's survival?

9. To the narrator, what do the green beads seem to symbolize?

10. Account for the narrator's vision.

TOPICS FOR WRITING

1. In a journal entry, write about a time when your parents protected you from the "pins" of life.

2. Have you or someone you know ever had a mysterious experience—one that could not be logically explained? Write a personal essay, describing the experience.

3. Write an essay discussing who or what is the most probable antagonist in this story.

4. In an essay, attack or defend this statement: The narrator in this story is a static character.

THE FRENCH EXCHANGE

PENELOPE LIVELY (born 1933)

For the first twelve years of her life, the English writer Penelope Lively lived in Cairo, Egypt, a country then a protectorate administered by the British. In 1945, her parents decided to divorce, and Lively was sent to England to live alternately with her two grandmothers. They agreed she should be sent to a boarding school, which she later condemned as a "barbaric institution" that was "aimed at turning out competent hockey and lacrosse players and did not encourage other activities."

Lively attended Oxford University, receiving her B. A. in modern history in 1954. A sense of time and place and the importance of memory are motifs in all her works. She once said in an interview, "I need to write with a very strong sense of topography and place." Her 1976 nonfiction work, *The Presence of the Past: an Introduction to Landscape History,* explores her beliefs about the importance of place and memory.

Lively began writing in the 1970s, with the publication of such children's books as *The Ghost of Thomas Kempe* (1973) and *The House in Norham Gardens* (1974); to date, she has published nearly twenty children's books. By the close of the 1970s she had also published one adult novel and one collection of short stories: *The Road to Lichfield* (1977) and *Nothing Missing but the Samover and Other Stories* (1978). During the 1980s, she continued to publish both children's and adult fiction. Her works include the novels *Judgement Day* (1980), *Perfect Happiness* (1983), *According to Mark* (1984), and *Cleopatra's Sister* (1993), as well as the short story collection *Pack of Cards* (1986) that includes "The French Exchange." In 1987, she received Britain's most prestigious literary award, the Booker Prize, for her novel *Moon Tiger,* a work about a dying historian's review of her life and one that reflects Lively's memories of wartime Egypt.

In 1994, Lively published *Oleander, Jacaranda,* a personal memoir that discusses "the nature of childhood perception and a view of Egypt in the 1930s and 1940s." Critics have praised her "uncannily accurate and honest recall of what it is like to be a child in a world made for adults." As you read "The French Exchange," think about the narrator's presentation of herself, the French boy, and the adults whom they both observe.

There would be the Kramers, Tony and Sue, in their Volvo and the Brands, Kevin and Lisa, in Lisa's new Sprite. And Dad had decided to take the Renault not the Cortina because the hatchback would be better with the picnic things. And the forecast was good. They would go to this prehistoric fort or whatever, anyway it was a hill with a view, Tony Kramer said it was a gorgeous spot. Sue was bringing some new quiche[1] thing she was frightfully proud of and Lisa of course, inevitably, would be stacked to the eyeballs with her precious home-made sorbets. And Kevin was doing some sort of wine cup.

And oh, her mother went on, voice a notch higher, shouting up the stairs, isn't it a shame, Nick Kramer isn't coming after all. He's in France. On an exchange. The Kramers have got the Exchange so they're bringing him instead. He's your and Nick's age and he's called Jean something. Oh well, we'll just have to be nice.

She stood in front of her mirror. She heard her mother clatter back to the kitchen. It didn't matter about Nick Kramer; he was duff[2] anyway. What did matter was that the new jeans quite definitely made her look fat. She took them off and put on the blue skirt instead but then the stripy T-shirt was wrong so she substituted the pink embroidered top with the low neck and suddenly her collar-bones looked enormous. Deformed. She'd always known there was something wrong with her collar-bones, it didn't matter how much people she confidentially asked swore there wasn't. So the pink top was hopeless. That left the yellow shirt that made her look pasty, which was definitely out, so there was nothing for it but to start all over again with the jeans and the loose cream top that hid her bulge but made her bosom nonexistent. And then her mother was shouting that they were here so in despair she had to stay like that and go down, bulging and bosom-less and discontented, and say hello to them all—Sue Kramer with tight white pants and one of those great baggy shirts and Lisa Brand in a short pink linen jacket and skirt thing and her hair done with silver highlights.

Hello, hello, they were all saying, and her mother was wondering if the barbecue stuff should go in the Volvo not the Renault and her father was showing Kevin Brand the new ice-bucket. Hi there, Anna,

---

1 **quiche:** a cheese custard dish baked in an unsweetened pie crust, usually with bacon.

2 **duff:** silly.

Sue Kramer cried, Jean-Paul here's Mary and Clive Becket, and Anna, and the Brands you've already met, I say Kevin we were pursuing you all the way down the dual carriageway[3] . . .

He wasn't very tall and he wore glasses and had spots. Copious spots. Not even remotely good-looking. Oh well. He inclined his head neatly, five times, and said *"Bonjour."* "English, Jean-Paul," scolded Sue. "You must *try.*" And Jean-Paul said "Good day" and inclined again. But everyone was busy now arguing about who should go in which car and her father was looking at Kevin's this year's *AA Book of the Road*[4] with a new bypass on it.

Eventually it was all sorted out. Jean-Paul would come in the Renault with them and the Kramers would take the barbecue stuff and follow and Kevin and Lisa would go on ahead because Lisa would want to go like the clappers[5] once they were out of the speed limit.

He didn't say much. He got in the back beside her and said *"Pardon"* when their knees bumped and when her mother asked where he lived in France he told her and when her father asked if he was keen on sport he said no, perfectly politely. She took a look at him, sideways, without turning her head. Poor boy—it must be awful being so spotty. She could see half her own face in the driving-mirror; the new eye shadow was good, really good. Her mother was talking about Lisa and how she'd put on weight, did you notice, Anna? And then she remembered Jean-Paul and asked if he had any brothers and sisters and Jean-Paul said yes, he had one sister younger and one brother older, Solange and Stéphan, and that rather finished that off so her mother went back to Lisa and wondered if she'd like a copy of the *F-Plan Diet.*

South London thinned out and became Surrey[6] towns all joined on each other and presently bits of country appeared and villages. Jean-Paul gazed out of the window. Once they passed a church and he turned, watching it recede. He said, *"C'est beau, ça.*[7] It is of when?" "That's a church," said Anna's mother. "Yes," said Jean-Paul." Of what time, I ask." "Oh goodness," said Anna's mother. "I'm no good

---

3 **dual carriageway:** English term for a divided four-lane highway.

4 **AA Book . . . Road:** Automobile Association's road guide.

5 **like the clappers:** fast.

6 **Surrey:** a shire (county) in the south of England.

7 *C'est beau, ça:* That's beautiful. More literally, "It's nice, that." [French]

on that sort of thing." *"Pardon,"* said Jean-Paul. He must be Catholic, Anna thought. She looked down and saw that he had awful shoes on, not the sort of thing people wear at all, but presumably they were French. She felt a bit sorry for him. The next time he looked her way she smiled brightly, to make up for the spots and the awful shoes, and he smiled back. His smile didn't somehow go with the rest of him; it was somehow detached, as though perhaps he didn't realize about the spots, or the shoes, or the peculiar way his hair grew at the back. Oh well.

Another village. A stretch of more open country. Jean-Paul leaned forward and said, "Excuse. I wish the toilet please."

Anna went crimson. How ghastly. Poor thing. Having to ask. If it had been her she'd have died rather, in someone else's car, people you didn't know. Actually Jean-Paul should have died rather, in fact. Waves of embarrassment and irritation came from the back of her parents' heads. Her father said, "Oh . . . Yes . . . Sure thing. Soon as there's a likely spot, right?" And after another minute he pulled in at a lay-by beside a wood and the Kramers' Volvo pulled in behind and Jean-Paul got out and plunged off into the bushes.

Anna's mother sighed."I ask you! I mean, you can't tell a sixteen-year-old he should have been before we started."

Sue Kramer appeared at the window. "Sorry. But there it is—if Nick doesn't get his French O-level[8] he'll have to take it again next year. Jean-Paul's been awfully little trouble, actually." And she began to talk to Anna's mother about the holiday the Kramers were going to have in Portugal and presently Jean-Paul came out of the wood and got into the car and Sue went back to the Volvo and they all set off again.

Anna's cheeks still flamed. She slid a glance at Jean-Paul. He didn't, actually, seem embarrassed at all. He was looking out of the window and when they went through a place with a market square with old-looking houses he opened his mouth as though about to say something and then shut it again and smiled slightly, but to himself. Anna's cheeks went back to normal and she thought about their own holiday which would be in Greece and the awful problem was would she or would she not have lost five pounds by then and be able to feel

---

8 **O-level:** ordinary-level examination. To qualify for a job after secondary school, English teenagers must take and pass two or three O-level examinations. If they hope to go to college, they study only two subjects intensely for two years, then take A- or advanced-level examinations.

absolutely all right in a bikini or would she have to spend all of every day on the beach holding her tummy in. None of the barbecue today, definitely none, and only a sliver of Sue Kramer's quiche.

Jean-Paul was saying something. She abandoned the bikini problem. "Sorry?"

"I say, you should wear a hat of fur. Pretty—with black hair." He gestured, circling her head, an odd, rather stylish gesture.

"A hat?" She stared, perplexed. Actually, her hair was very dark brown, not black.

"Karenina. Anna. For your name."

"Oh." She saw now; there was some Russian novel, the film had been on the telly[9] once. "Well . . ." She laughed, awkwardly. "It would be a bit hot, on a day like this."

Jean-Paul looked at her attentively, and then shrugged "*Tant pis.*"[10] He gazed once more out of the window.

And now they were turning off on to the B-road that would take them to this hill and her mother was saying let's pray the charcoal lights properly, I felt such a fool last time with the Kramers, and oh God did I put the avocado dip in? Down lanes and through a village and round a corner and there was the red Sprite parked on the verge and the Brands sitting beside it on folding chairs like film directors use with LISA and KEVIN stencilled on the backs in big black letters.

There was a lot of shunting of cars to and fro to get them off the road and then a lot of unpacking and arranging of who would carry what and in the middle of it Anna's mother suddenly shrieked and pointed at the front of the Kramers' car.

"Tony! You got it! And we never even noticed!"

So everyone looked and now Anna too saw the number-plate: AJK 45.

"Oh, neat!" said Lisa. "Your age too. I'm green with envy."

"How much did that set you back?" asked Anna's father, and Tony Kramer grinned and said he wasn't telling. Jean-Paul was looking at Tony in a most odd way; he wasn't smiling but you felt he was somehow laughing. Everyone began to fuss round the picnic things and the folding chairs and the barbecue again and Jean-Paul said to Anna, "Why?"

"Why what?"

---

9   **telly:** television.

10   *Tant pis:* Can't be helped; too bad. [French]

He pointed at the number-plate.

He must be a bit slow on the uptake, she thought. "It's his initials. And his age."

"I know," said Jean-Paul. "But why?"

She couldn't think, when it came down to it. "Well, it's a thing people do. There are lists in newspapers. Some of them are terribly expensive." Actually her parents had been looking for ages for MRB or CTB but for some reason she decided not to say so. Jean-Paul gazed thoughtfully at Tony Kramer and said, *"Curieux."*[11]

"You're supposed to talk English," said Anna sternly. He was four months younger than her, it had emerged.

"D'accord,"[12] said Jean-Paul, and grinned. Really, his spots were the worst she'd ever seen.

There was a fuss going on now because Lisa had discovered she'd forgotten her sun-tan lotion and although Sue and Anna's mother had some they were the wrong kinds apparently, Lisa had to use this special one, but eventually she decided she might be able to manage with a hat, and they set off, through the gate and up the hill along a rough track.

Everyone was carrying something: the men quite loaded with chairs and loungers and barbecue equipment, the women more lightly burdened with picnic hampers and coolers and ice-buckets. Anna and Jean-Paul were at the back of the procession. Anna had her mother's basket with paper napkins and plastic cutlery and garlic bread in foil, Jean-Paul bore the bag of barbecue charcoal and Kevin Brand's wicker wine-bottle carrier with four bottles wrapped in tissue paper. He padded along a couple of paces behind her; the rest of them snaked ahead, calling out to each other, Lisa slipping and sliding on high-heeled sandals.

Jean-Paul said, "Very serious—*le pique-nique.*"

She turned to look at him. Was he laughing? No, his expression was perfectly solemn. But something about his voice . . . Anna stared ahead at her laden parents, and their laden friends, at the glitter of chrome and the bright glow of plastic. She said—attack and defense together—"Don't your parents do this kind of thing?"

"Ah yes. Absolutely. Also very serious."

She felt, now, faintly uncomfortable. It was as though you were playing a game with someone you knew was much worse at it than you and suddenly they started doing things they shouldn't be able to.

---

11   *Curieux:* Curious; odd; strange. [French]

12   *D'accord:* Agreed; all right. [French]

"You enjoy yourself?" enquired Jean-Paul.

"Of course," said Anna firmly. After a moment she added, "Aren't you?"

"Bien sûr,"[13] said Jean-Paul. He was, she saw, grinning hugely. He waved a hand at the landscape—"It is beautiful day. The sun shines. All is agreeable."

The track had petered out and they were walking on close-cropped turf up the hillside, which rose ahead of them in a series of bumpy terraces on which sheep grazed and small bright flowers grew. The leading group—Kevin and Lisa and Anna's father—had come to a halt and as the others caught up with them an argument arose about the appropriate point at which to pitch camp. Anna's mother wanted further on, at that flat place; Lisa wanted to be near a tree in case she needed some shade. Everyone disputed. Lisa said, "Oh never mind me, I'll manage somehow, at a pinch I can go back to the car," and Tony Kramer said, "Oh no, we're not having that, love. Right then, the tree has it." Kevin gave him a look that was sort of not quite as friendly as it might be and Anna's parents were telling each other that they needn't be so bossy in that joke-tone that, Anna knew, could topple over into not joking at all. And Sue Kramer wasn't joining in but gazed into the distance and tapped one toe on the grass.

Jean-Paul said to Anna, "They enjoy themself too, do you think?" Anna, ruffled, pretended to be doing up her sandal. She was sweating after the climb and suddenly had the most ghastly feeling she might have forgotten to use any deodorant.

A decision, eventually, was made. Chairs, loungers, barbecue were disposed upon the bright grass. Lisa had loosened the heel of her shoe and Tony Kramer was trying to fix it with his natty miniature pliers on a key-chain and Sue Kramer was wishing loudly he'd get on with the fruit cup—everyone must be parched. Kevin was setting up the barbecue, in silence. Anna's mother was speaking to Anna's father in that bright, high voice that meant trouble.

The barbecue was lit. The fruit cup was made. Kebabs sizzled. Sue Kramer arranged herself on a lounger, gazed skywards and said, "Bliss!" Glasses were filled. Birds sang. The spare ribs and the chicken joined the kebabs. Glasses were refilled. Anna's mother uttered an awful cry—"Oh Christ, I've left the second barbecue sauce at home in the fridge!"

---

13   *Bien sûr:* Sure. [French]

"Oh, for heaven's sake . . ." said Anna's father.

There was a silence. "But there's this delicious-looking one over here," said Sue Kramer.

"But just the one!" cried Anna's mother. "There should be a choice!"

"We'll manage," said Kevin Brand. "Forget it."

"*Quelle horreur . . .*"[14] said Jean-Paul, to the grass, shaking his head.

And now the kebabs were handed round on the gay paper plates, and the spare ribs and the chicken and the one sauce and the bright serviettes,[15] two apiece—for lips and lap. And everyone was saying how brilliant of Tony to know about this gorgeous place.

"We are in the middle of a . . . what is it? . . . a field of battle?" asked Jean-Paul.

They all stared at him. "Some sort of camp, I think," said Tony. "Prehistoric."

"Or thereabouts," said Lisa. There was general laughter. "Now, now," said Tony. "It's not nice to make fun of other people's ignorance." Lisa pulled a face at him and he aimed a spare rib at her, threateningly. "Don't you dare!" cried Lisa. "These pants are sheer hell to wash, I'll have you know."

Jean-Paul watched, without expression. He turned to Anna and remarked, quietly, "There is a tradition, then, of picnic here."

"I suppose so," muttered Anna. She had this feeling that everything was getting out of control—not least, in some odd way, Jean-Paul. There he was, with his spots and his awful shoes, and four months younger than her and yet you had this peculiar sense of him being somehow much older and floating above and beyond the spots and the shoes. She stroked her armpits, surreptitiously; she was sure there were visible sweat-marks on the cream top.

The quiche was being handed round now, and the salad, and the garlic bread, and more wine cup. Everyone was talking at once and Lisa Brand was shouting rather and Kevin was having an argument with Tony Kramer about something to do with the insides of cars, whether Tony's Volvo had a this or a that. Jean-Paul said to Anna, "You interest in cars?"

"Not really," said Anna, after a moment's hesitation.

---

14 *Quelle horreur:* Horrors! Literally, "What a horror!" [French]

15 **serviettes:** table napkins.

"Moi non plus,"[16] said Jean-Paul.

And now they were moving on to the dessert: the mousse and the sorbet and the little biscuity things Sue Kramer had brought. A different lot of gay paper plates; more bright plastic cutlery. There was debris all around now: heaps of plastic and paper and left-over food and bottles and glasses. A little way off a small posse of sheep stood gazing and chewing. "Don't look now," said Lisa, "but we're being watched." Tony Kramer laughed uproariously.

Anna glanced at Jean-Paul, but not so that he would notice. He was looking at some little orange butterflies that danced above the turf, and then his attention switched to a bird that hung in the sky just above the brow of the hill, its wings quivering. And then, as Kevin circulated again with the wine cup and a few drops got spilled on Lisa's white pants, causing distress, he observed that, in just the same grave and attentive way as he watched the butterflies and the bird.

The chatter decreased. Lisa was still dabbing at her pants, scowling. Kevin had wandered off a little distance and was lying on his back on the grass. Anna's mother was saying that of course it was heavenly here but what would be nice now would be a swim.

Jean-Paul rose, stowed his dirty plate, cutlery and napkin neatly in Anna's mother's basket and strolled away over the grass. He squatted down beside a clump of flowers.

Sue Kramer said to Anna, "You are being so frightfully good with him. I'm afraid he's rather a dull boy, but there it is. Anyway, you're sweet."

Anna smiled, embarrassed. Actually she'd never been entirely sure she liked Sue Kramer. Nick Kramer she'd known since he was about three, and he was absolutely hopeless.

"And the acne . . ." said Lisa. "One wants to simply pick them up and plunge them in some enormous vat of disinfectant, boys of that age."

Anna looked towards Jean-Paul who, at that moment, glanced over his shoulder, caught her eye and waved. "Look . . ." he called.

"Be nice, darling," said Anna's mother.

There was a glinting coppery butterfly sitting on a plant, opening and closing its wings. Jean-Paul pointed, without speaking. Anna was at a loss; it was a bit odd, to put it bluntly, for a boy to be going on about a butterfly.

---

16 *Moi non plus:* me neither. Literally, "nor I." [French]

"A butterfly," she said, with slight desperation.

"Yes," said Jean-Paul. "Of what kind?"

"I've no idea."

"You are not interest in nature, either?"

"Well, quite," said Anna (blushing now, curse it).

"I am interest," said Jean-Paul, "in astronomy, philosophy and the music of Mozart."

Anna went rigid. Thank heavens at least the others hadn't heard him; they'd have died laughing. He was perfectly serious, that was the awful thing. What on earth could one say? He was gazing at her, reflectively.

"Tell me," he went on. "Why did your parents embarrass? About I need to go to the toilet from the car."

She didn't know where to look. "l don't know," she muttered.

Jean-Paul laughed. "Perhaps they are people who do not need to go to the toilet, never. *Formidable!*"

She looked back to the picnic group. Kevin Brand was still lying on the grass. Her parents were tidying up. Sue Kramer was sitting a little apart, reading a magazine. Lisa Brand and Tony Kramer were walking up the hill together; you could hear them laughing.

"I'm sorry," said Jean-Paul. "Now I make you embarrass too. I am not very nice. Shall we go for a walk?"

"All right," said Anna. In the car, she remembered, she had smiled brilliantly at him to make up for his spots and his shoes.

They went round the flank of the hill, along the crest of one of the great ridges that lapped it. And Jean-Paul, incredibly, began to sing. She was afraid the others might hear. He sang this cheerful little song, the words of which she could not quite catch, and when they got to a point from which you could see great blue distances of landscape all around he stopped and waved at it and said, *"Pas mal, alors?"*[17] He was, she saw, perfectly happy.

She stared at him in surprise. There he was, this not at all nice-looking boy who wasn't tall enough, spending the day with lots of people he didn't know, most of whom hadn't spoken a word to him, and he was happy. It was ridiculous, really.

She said, "Do you like staying with the Kramers?"

Jean-Paul shrugged. *"Ça va.*[18] They are very kind. I must learn English for my examination."

---

17 *Pas mal, alors:* Not bad, eh? [French]

18 *Ça va:* It's okay. [French]

"Like Nick's got to get his French O-level."

He grinned. "So everybody inconveniences themself a little."

They had reached the brow of the hill. Below them on one side was the picnic site, with Anna's parents and Kevin and Sue Kramer just as they had left them and on the other, sitting on the grass, were Tony Kramer and Lisa. Lisa's laugh floated up to them. And then suddenly she was flapping her hands around her head and there was a shriek and Tony was flapping his hands too and bending over her.

"*La pauvre dame,*"[19] said Jean-Paul. "She is bit, I think. A—how do you say it—*une guêpe.*"

"Wasp," said Anna. She didn't feel all that sorry for Lisa Brand. Actually she thought Lisa had been going on rather, with her precious white pants and her jokes. Lisa and Tony were starting back up the hill now, Lisa with her hand clasped to her shoulder.

"Do you believe in God?" said Jean-Paul.

She looked at him in horror. "I don't know."

"*Moi—non.* Not since I am twelve years old. Because of he makes everything beautiful and then puts in the middle a wasp. Everything is nice and then—pouff!—a bus come and run over your mother."

"Honestly?" said Anna, shocked.

"*Pas actuellement.* But it is what happen. *La souffrance.* So I do not think there can be anyone who make a world like that, or if there is he is bad and he is not God, because God is good. *Pas vrai?*"[20]

Quite frankly, she'd never heard anyone talk like that in her life. You didn't know whether to laugh, or what. I mean, sitting on a hill talking about God. But there he was, doing it as though it were the most normal thing in the world.

Lisa and Tony passed them. Lisa was leaning on Tony's arm still clutching her shoulder. Tony waved and Lisa smiled bravely. Jean-Paul said, "Perhaps that lady does not suffer so terrible. In the Middle Age people are roasting each other on fires and putting in hot oil."

"Don't," said Anna. She was hopeless at history, anyway; it was her worst subject, except maths. And this conversation was quite beyond her, out of control like everything on this stupid picnic. For two pins she'd have gone back to the others, except that in some peculiar way it had now become Jean-Paul who made decisions, not

---

19   *La pauvre dame:* Poor woman. Literally, "The poor lady." [French]

20   *Pas actuellement . . . La souffrance . . . Pas vrai?:* Not really (though, literally, the phrase means "Not now") . . . The suffering . . . Right? [French]

her. Just as, eerily, it was Jean-Paul who seemed at ease in this place, on this hillside in a foreign country, rather than the rest of them.

He said, "When I will be president of the Republic—no, when I will be king—king is more amusing, *tant pis pour la Révolution*[21]— when I will be king there will be no earthquakes and no bad weather and I will give to everyone discs of the music of Mozart." He looked at Anna. "And what will you make, when you are queen?"

It was silly, this, really—I mean, if any of one's friends could hear . . . "No more maths."

"Ah. That is difficult for the banks and the shops and the men of business. Never mind, we arrange."

She didn't know if she liked him or not. But more disconcerting was the fact that, so far as he was concerned, it quite evidently didn't matter. He wasn't bothered, one way or the other. And, maddeningly, it began to matter what he thought of her. Which was absurd . . . a boy like that. She tried to think of something to say that would be funny, or clever; nothing came.

"So that's where you've got to." Her mother appeared suddenly behind them. "Lisa's been stung by a wasp. The most unnecessary commotion, frankly. Tony's gone off to that village we came through to get some antihistamine. And someone left the top off the ice-bucket—wouldn't you know so I can't do the iced tea." She looked round irritably." I said all along we should have gone to the beach."

"Where's Dad?"

"He's got one of his headaches, rather predictably. So Sue and I have been clearing up entirely on our own. Kevin's gone off in a huff." She remembered Jean-Paul and said brightly, "I'm so glad Anna's been looking after you." She gave Anna a conspiratorial glance of sympathy. "Anyway, I thought I'd better start rounding people up."

They walked down the hill. Anna's mother told Jean-Paul that this was a frightfully pretty part of the country and Jean-Paul nodded politely and Anna's mother glanced at his shoes and his haircut and Anna knew what she was thinking. She wished she was somewhere else. She wished, particularly, that Jean-Paul was somewhere else but for her own sake rather than for his.

They reached the picnic place, where Anna's father, Lisa Brand, Kevin Brand and Sue Kramer were all sitting a little apart from each

---

21   *tant pis . . . Révolution:* the heck with the Revolution. Literally, "too bad for the Revolution." [French]

other and not saying anything. Lisa was holding a handkerchief to her neck and Anna's father had his eyes closed. And then Tony Kramer came panting up the hill waving a tube and Lisa cried, "Oh, Tony, bless you—you really are an angel." Kevin Brand picked up a newspaper and began to read it and Sue Kramer said, "Sir Lancelot to the rescue," and laughed in a not particularly amused way.

Anna's mother had just discovered she had trodden in a pile of sheep-muck and was hopping about with one of her new Russell & Bromley sandals off, trying to clean it.

Jean-Paul looked around at them all. He smiled benignly. He said, "I wish to thank for you bring me to this charming place." They all gazed at him in astonishment and he continued to smile benignly and sat down on the grass. "I enjoy myself very much," he said.

For a moment there was silence. Then Tony Kramer exclaimed heartily, "And that goes for everyone, I imagine. Terrific outing. Sort of day that should go on for ever."

"Absolutely," murmured Lisa.

"Quite," said Anna's father. "Though alas we, I'm afraid, will have to push off shortly." He gave Anna's mother one of those looks that was not a look but an instruction and she scowled back and continued to rearrange picnic baskets and barbecue stuff.

They walked in procession down the hill. This time Jean-Paul led the way and was the most heavily burdened, having insisted on carrying the two loungers. Even so, he walked faster than anyone else; he was, Anna could hear, singing that little song again. No one else was saying much except Lisa who was telling Tony Kramer her neck felt heaps better now, entirely thanks to him.

The right possessions were stowed into the right cars. They told each other what a marvellous day it had been. Anna's mother kissed everyone and Sue Kramer kissed everyone except Lisa Brand, and Jean-Paul went round shaking hands. When he got to Anna he said, "When I am king I make you minister of finance, O.K.?" and Anna went scarlet. Jean-Paul got in with the Kramers and Kevin and Lisa got into their Sprite and Anna got into the Renault with her parents. Engines started. Everyone waved.

Anna's mother said, "What on earth was that boy saying?"

"Nothing."

"Did you manage to find something to talk to him about?"

"Sort of," said Anna distantly.

There was a grass-stain on her new jeans and she had eaten not one small slice of quiche but two helpings of everything so she would have put on about three pounds. But all that was the least of it.

They travelled back along the same roads but she did not feel the same at all. Ahead of them was the Kramers' car and through the rear window she could see Jean-Paul's head, and that too was different, uncomfortably different; it spoke now not of spots and a ghastly hair-cut but of small coppery butterflies and conversation that embarrassed, that left you uncertain, as though you had peered through strange windows. Jean-Paul did not turn round and presently the Volvo was lost in traffic.

QUESTIONS FOR DISCUSSION

1. In addition to place names, what details establish that the setting for the story is England?

2. Describe your first impressions of Anna's character.

3. What is Anna's first impression of Jean-Paul? Cite evidence from the story.

4. During the story Anna reacts to Jean-Paul's need for a toilet, his regard of the butterfly, and his statements about God. What do Anna's reactions to these incidents tell us about her?

5. How and why does Anna's initial impression of Jean-Paul change?

6. Characterize Anna's parents and speculate about their relationship.

7. What word best describes the relationship among the three couples?

8. How does the fact that Anna narrates the story affect your opinion of the adults?

9. What chief methods of characterization does Lively use to present Anna?

10. Who is the more active character—Anna or Jean-Paul?

TOPICS FOR WRITING

1. On each of three 3" x 5" cards, describe an American custom that a foreigner might find "curieux." On the back of each card, briefly outline your explanation of the American custom.

2. Jean-Paul is writing to a friend about the English people he has met and his opinion of one of them. In your journal, write a character sketch of one of the minor characters.

3. Both "After the War" (in Chapter 1) and "The French Exchange" deal with similar situations. Compare or contrast the two foreign exchange students.

4. In an essay discuss the ways in which Anna could be considered a stereotyped character.

PAUL'S CASE

WILLA CATHER (1873–1947)

One of the most distinguished women in early twentieth-century fiction, Willa Cather was nine when she and her family moved from Virginia to a ranch near Red Cloud, Nebraska. A tomboy, Cather grew up among the many European immigrants who were settling the Great Plains.

While attending the University of Nebraska, Cather worked as a newspaper correspondent; after graduating in 1895, she moved to Pittsburgh, Pennsylvania, one of the settings of her story "Paul's Case."

In 1903, she published *April Twilights,* a book of poems, and in 1905, *The Troll Garden,* a collection of short stories. Although one critic sniffed, "Miss Cather is not at heart a poet," her short stories were praised, and she was invited to join the staff of *McClure's* magazine. While working at *McClure's,* Cather wrote her first novel, *Alexander's Bridge* (1912). Cather's literary mentor, the writer Sarah Orne Jewett, recognized its promise and urged Cather both to leave the world of journalism and to write about her own Nebraska experiences. The suggestion resulted in three novels: *O Pioneers!* (1912), *The Song of the Lark* (1915), and *My Ántonia* (1918), one of Cather's finest works.

In 1922, her novel *One of Ours* won the Pulitzer Prize for fiction. Her next novel, *The Lost Lady* (1923), was seen by one critic as a reflection of "the social disintegration brought about by the rising tide of commerce" in post-World War I America. Cather so hated the movie Hollywood based on this novel that she stipulated in her will that none of her work could ever again be adapted for the screen, stage, radio, television, or any new medium "which hereafter may be discovered or perfected."

As Cather aged, she grew more and more disdainful of the world around her. Critic Lionel Trilling observed, "Miss Cather shares the American belief in the tonic moral quality of the pioneer's life; with the passing of the frontier she conceives that a great source of fortitude has been lost." *Death Comes for the Archbishop* (1927), which earned Cather a medal from the American Academy and Institute of Arts and Letters, is a historical novel based on the life of Archbishop Lamy, the first appointed bishop in the territory of New Mexico; *Shadows on the Rock* (1931) takes place in seventeenth-century Quebec; and her final novel, *Sapphira and the Slave Girl* (1940), recounts a Civil War event Cather had heard about as a small child in Virginia. As you read "Paul's Case," think about Cather's attitude toward her protagonist; think, too, about the significance of the word *case* in the title.

■

It was Paul's afternoon to appear before the faculty of the Pittsburgh High School to account for his various misdemeanors. He had been suspended a week ago, and his father had called at the Principal's office and confessed his perplexity about his son. Paul entered the faculty room suave and smiling. His clothes were a trifle outgrown and the tan velvet on the collar of his open overcoat was frayed and worn; but for all that there was something of the dandy about him, and he wore an opal pin in his neatly knotted black four-in-hand,[1] and a red carnation in his buttonhole. This latter adornment the faculty somehow felt was not properly significant of the contrite spirit befitting a boy under the ban of suspension.

Paul was tall for his age and very thin, with high, cramped shoulders and a narrow chest. His eyes were remarkable for a certain hysterical brilliancy, and he continually used them in a conscious, theatrical sort of way, peculiarly offensive in a boy. The pupils were abnormally large, as though he were addicted to belladonna,[2] but there was a glassy glitter about them which that drug does not produce.

When questioned by the Principal as to why he was there, Paul stated, politely enough, that he wanted to come back to school. This was a lie, but Paul was quite accustomed to lying; found it, indeed, indispensable for overcoming friction. His teachers were asked to state their respective charges against him, which they did with such a rancor and aggrievedness as evinced that this was not a usual case. Disorder and impertinence were among the offenses named, yet each of his instructors felt that it was scarcely possible to put into words the real cause of the trouble, which lay in a sort of hysterically defiant manner of the boy's; in the contempt which they all knew he felt for them, and which he seemingly made not the least effort to conceal. Once, when he had been making a synopsis of a paragraph at the blackboard, his English teacher had stepped to his side and attempted to guide his hand. Paul had started back with a shudder and thrust his hands violently behind him. The astonished woman could scarcely have been more hurt and embarrassed had he struck at her. The insult was so involuntary and definitely personal as to be unforgettable. In

---

1 **dandy about him . . . four-in-hand:** A dandy is a man who is too careful about his dress and appearance; a four-in-hand is a necktie tied in a slipknot with the ends hanging.

2 **belladonna:** a poisonous plant whose leaves yielded a medicine for stomach aches; taking it, however, dilated the eyes.

one way and another he had made all his teachers, men and women alike, conscious of the same feeling of physical aversion. In one class he habitually sat with his hand shading his eyes; in another he always looked out of the window during the recitation; in another he made a running commentary on the lecture, with humorous intention.

His teachers felt this afternoon that his whole attitude was symbolized by his shrug and his flippantly red carnation flower, and they fell upon him without mercy, his English teacher leading the pack. He stood through it smiling, his pale lips parted over his white teeth. (His lips were continually twitching, and he had a habit of raising his eyebrows that was contemptuous and irritating to the last degree.) Older boys than Paul had broken down and shed tears under that baptism of fire, but his set smile did not once desert him, and his only sign of discomfort was the nervous trembling of the fingers that toyed with the buttons of his overcoat, and an occasional jerking of the other hand that held his hat. Paul was always smiling, always glancing about him, seeming to feel that people might be watching him and trying to detect something. This conscious expression, since it was as far as possible from boyish mirthfulness, was usually attributed to insolence or "smartness."

As the inquisition proceeded, one of his instructors repeated an impertinent remark of the boy's, and the Principal asked him whether he thought that a courteous speech to have made a woman. Paul shrugged his shoulders slightly and his eyebrows twitched.

"I don't know," he replied. "I didn't mean to be polite or impolite, either. I guess it's a sort of way I have of saying things regardless."

The Principal, who was a sympathetic man, asked him whether he didn't think that a way it would be well to get rid of. Paul grinned and said he guessed so. When he was told that he could go, he bowed gracefully and went out. His bow was but a repetition of the scandalous red carnation.

His teachers were in despair, and his drawing master[3] voiced the feeling of them all when he declared there was something about the boy which none of them understood. He added: "I don't really believe that smile of his comes altogether from insolence; there's something sort of haunted about it. The boy is not strong, for one thing. I happen to know that he was born in Colorado, only a few

---

3 **drawing master:** art teacher.

months before his mother died out there of a long illness. There is something wrong about the fellow."

The drawing master had come to realize that, in looking at Paul, one saw only his white teeth and the forced animation of his eyes. One warm afternoon the boy had gone to sleep at his drawing-board, and his master had noted with amazement what a white, blue-veined face it was; drawn and wrinkled like an old man's about the eyes, the lips twitching even in his sleep, and stiff with a nervous tension that drew them back from his teeth.

His teachers left the building dissatisfied and unhappy; humiliated to have felt so vindictive toward a mere boy, to have uttered this feeling in cutting terms, and to have set each other on, as it were, in the gruesome game of intemperate reproach. Some of them remembered having seen a miserable street cat set at bay by a ring of tormentors.

As for Paul, he ran down the hill whistling the Soldiers' Chorus from *Faust*[4] looking wildly behind him now and then to see whether some of his teachers were not there to writhe under his light-heartedness. As it was now late in the afternoon and Paul was on duty that evening as usher at Carnegie Hall,[5] he decided that he would not go home to supper. When he reached the concert hall the doors were not yet open and, as it was chilly outside, he decided to go up into the picture gallery—always deserted at this hour—where there were some of Raffelli's[6] gay studies of Paris streets and an airy blue Venetian scene or two that always exhilarated him. He was delighted to find no one in the gallery but the old guard, who sat in one corner, a newspaper on his knee, a black patch over one eye and the other closed. Paul possessed himself of the place and walked confidently up and down, whistling under his breath. After a while he sat down before a blue Rico[7] and lost himself. When he bethought him to look at his watch, it was after seven o'clock, and he rose with a start and ran downstairs, making a face at Augustus, peering out from the cast-room, and an evil gesture at the Venus de Milo as he passed her on the stairway.

---

4 *Faust:* an opera by French composer Charles Gounod (1818–1893).

5 **Carnegie Hall:** a Pittsburgh music hall within The Carnegie, a cultural institution that also includes the Carnegie Library of Pittsburgh, the Carnegie Museum of National History, and the Carnegie Museum of Art. New York City also boasts a Carnegie Hall.

6 **Raffelli:** probably the Frenchman Jean François Raffaelli (1850–1924)

7 **Rico:** Martin Rico y Ortega (1833–1908), a Spaniard who died in Venice.

When Paul reached the ushers' dressing-room half-a-dozen boys were there already, and he began excitedly to tumble into his uniform. It was one of the few that at all approached fitting, and Paul thought it very becoming—though he knew that the tight, straight coat accentuated his narrow chest, about which he was exceedingly sensitive. He was always considerably excited while he dressed, twanging all over to the tuning of the strings and the preliminary flourishes of the horns in the music-room; but to-night he seemed quite beside himself, and he teased and plagued the boys until, telling him that he was crazy, they put him down on the floor and sat on him.

Somewhat calmed by his suppression, Paul dashed out to the front of the house to seat the early comers. He was a model usher; gracious and smiling he ran up and down the aisles; nothing was too much trouble for him; he carried messages and brought programs as though it were his greatest pleasure in life, and all the people in his section thought him a charming boy, feeling that he remembered and admired them. As the house filled, he grew more and more vivacious and animated, and the color came to his cheeks and lips. It was very much as though this were a great reception and Paul were the host. Just as the musicians came out to take their places, his English teacher arrived with checks for the seats which a prominent manufacturer had taken for the season. She betrayed some embarrassment when she handed Paul the tickets, and a *hauteur*[8] which subsequently made her feel very foolish. Paul was startled for a moment, and had the feeling of wanting to put her out; what business had she here among all these fine people and gay colors? He looked her over and decided that she was not appropriately dressed and must be a fool to sit downstairs in such togs. The tickets had probably been sent her out of kindness, he reflected as he put down a seat for her, and she had about as much right to sit there as he had.

When the symphony began Paul sank into one of the rear seats with a long sigh of relief, and lost himself as he had done before the Rico. It was not that symphonies, as such, meant anything in particular to Paul, but the first sigh of the instruments seemed to free some hilarious and potent spirit within him; something that struggled there like the Genius[9] in the bottle found by the Arab fisherman. He felt a sudden zest of life; the lights danced before his eyes and the concert

---

8 *hauteur:* haughtiness; loftiness. [French]

9 **Genius:** genie.

hall blazed into unimaginable splendor. When the soprano soloist came on, Paul forgot even the nastiness of his teacher's being there and gave himself up to the peculiar stimulus such personages always had for him. The soloist chanced to be a German woman, by no means in her first youth, and the mother of many children;[10] but she wore an elaborate gown and a tiara, and above all she had that indefinable air of achievement, that world-shine upon her, which, in Paul's eyes, made her a veritable queen of Romance.

After a concert was over Paul was always irritable and wretched until he got to sleep, and tonight he was even more than usually restless. He had the feeling of not being able to let down, of its being impossible to give up this delicious excitement which was the only thing that could be called living at all. During the last number he withdrew and, after hastily changing his clothes in the dressing-room, slipped out to the side door where the soprano's carriage stood. Here he began pacing rapidly up and down the walk, waiting to see her come out.

Over yonder the Schenley, in its vacant stretch, loomed big and square through the fine rain, the windows of its twelve stories glowing like those of a lighted cardboard house under a Christmas tree. All the actors and singers of the better class stayed there when they were in the city, and a number of the big manufacturers of the place lived there in the winter. Paul had often hung about the hotel, watching the people go in and out, longing to enter and leave school-masters and dull care behind him forever.

At last the singer came out, accompanied by the conductor, who helped her into her carriage and closed the door with a cordial *auf wiedersehen*[11] which set Paul to wondering whether she were not an old sweetheart of his. Paul followed the carriage over to the hotel, walking so rapidly as not to be far from the entrance when the singer alighted and disappeared behind the swinging glass doors that were opened by a negro in a tall hat and a long coat. In the moment that the door was ajar it seemed to Paul that he, too, entered. He seemed to feel himself go after her up the steps, into the warm, lighted building, into an

---

10 **German woman . . . children:** probably Ernestine Schumann-Heink (1861–1936), a noted opera singer and recitalist. Two of her sons fought in World War i on opposing sides.

11 *auf wiedersehen:* see you later. Literally, "to again see." [German]

exotic, tropical world of shiny, glistening surfaces and basking ease. He reflected upon the mysterious dishes that were brought into the dining-room, the green bottles in buckets of ice, as he had seen them in the supper party pictures of the *Sunday World* supplement. A quick gust of wind brought the rain down with sudden vehemence, and Paul was startled to find that he was still outside in the slush of the gravel driveway; that his boots were letting in the water and his scanty overcoat was clinging wet about him; that the lights in front of the concert hall were out and that the rain was driving in sheets between him and the orange glow of the windows above him. There it was, what he wanted—tangibly before him, like the fairy world of a Christmas pantomime, but mocking spirits stood guard at the doors, and, as the rain beat in his face, Paul wondered whether he were destined always to shiver in the black night outside, looking up at it.

He turned and walked reluctantly toward the car tracks. The end had to come sometime; his father in his night-clothes at the top of the stairs, explanations that did not explain, hastily improvised fictions that were forever tripping him up, his upstairs room and its horrible yellow wallpaper, the creaking bureau with the greasy plush collar-box, and over his painted wooden bed the pictures of George Washington and John Calvin,[12] and the framed motto, "Feed my Lambs," which had been worked in red worsted by his mother.

Half an hour later Paul alighted from his car and went slowly down one of the side streets off the main thoroughfare. It was a highly respectable street, where all the houses were exactly alike, and where businessmen of moderate means begot and reared large families of children, all of whom went to Sabbath-school and learned the shorter catechism, and were interested in arithmetic; all of whom were as exactly alike as their homes, and of a piece with the monotony in which they lived. Paul never went up Cordelia Street without a shudder of loathing. His home was next to the house of the Cumberland minister.[13] He approached it tonight with the nerveless sense of defeat, the hopeless feeling of sinking back forever into ugliness and commonness that he had always had when he came home. The moment he turned

---

12 **John Calvin:** French leader (1509-1564) of the Protestant Reformation at Geneva, Switzerland. The Puritans and the Huguenots followed his teachings.

13 **Cumberland minister:** a minister of a Presbyterian sect formed in 1802 in the Cumberland area of Kentucky and Tennessee. Its revivalist preachers were less well educated than traditional Presbyterian ministers. They also believed in the doctrine of the Elect.

into Cordelia Street he felt the waters close above his head. After each of these orgies of living, he experienced all the physical depression which follows a debauch; the loathing of respectable beds, of common food, of a house penetrated by kitchen odors; a shuddering repulsion for the flavorless, colorless mass of every-day existence; a morbid desire for cool things and soft lights and fresh flowers.

The nearer he approached the house, the more absolutely unequal Paul felt to the sight of it all; his ugly sleeping chamber; the cold bath-room with the grimy zinc tub, the cracked mirror, the dripping spiggots; his father, at the top of the stairs, his hairy legs sticking out from his nightshirt, his feet thrust into carpet slippers. He was so much later than usual that there would certainly be inquiries and reproaches. Paul stopped short before the door. He felt that he could not be accosted by his father tonight; that he could not toss again on that miserable bed. He would not go in. He would tell his father that he had no car fare, and it was raining so hard he had gone home with one of the boys and stayed all night.

Meanwhile, he was wet and cold. He went around to the back of the house and tried one of the basement windows, found it open, raised it cautiously, and scrambled down the cellar wall to the floor. There he stood, holding his breath, terrified by the noise he had made, but the floor above him was silent, and there was no creak on the stairs. He found a soap-box, and carried it over to the soft ring of light that streamed from the furnace door, and sat down. He was horribly afraid of rats, so he did not try to sleep, but sat looking distrustfully at the dark, still terrified lest he might have awakened his father. In such reac-tions, after one of the experiences which made days and nights out of the dreary blanks of the calendar, when his senses were deadened, Paul's head was always singularly clear. Suppose his father had heard him getting in at the window and had come down and shot him for a burglar? Then, again, suppose his father had come down, pistol in hand, and he had cried out in time to save himself, and his father had been horrified to think how nearly he had killed him? Then, again, suppose a day should come when his father would remember that night, and wish there had been no warning cry to stay his hand? With this last supposition Paul entertained himself until daybreak.

The following Sunday was fine; the sodden November chill was broken by the last flash of autumnal summer. In the morning Paul had to go to church and Sabbath-school, as always. On seasonable Sunday afternoons the burghers of Cordelia Street always sat out on their front "stoops," and talked to their neighbors on the next stoop, or called to those across the street in neighborly fashion. The men usually sat on gay cushions placed upon the steps that led down to the sidewalk, while the women, in their Sunday "waists,"[14] sat in rockers on the cramped porches, pretending to be greatly at their ease. The children played in the streets; there were so many of them that the place resembled the recreation grounds of a kindergarten. The men on the steps—all in their shirt sleeves, their vests unbuttoned—sat with their legs well apart, their stomachs comfortably protruding, and talked of the prices of things, or told anecdotes of the sagacity of their various chiefs and overlords. They occasionally looked over the multitude of squabbling children, listened affectionately to their high-pitched, nasal voices, smiling to see their own proclivities reproduced in their offspring, and interspersed their legends of the iron kings with remarks about their sons' progress at school, their grades in arithmetic, and the amounts they had saved in their toy banks.

On this last Sunday of November, Paul sat all the afternoon on the lowest step of his "stoop," staring into the street, while his sisters, in their rockers, were talking to the minister's daughters next door about how many shirt-waists they had made in the last week, and how many waffles someone had eaten at the last church supper. When the weather was warm, and his father was in a particularly jovial frame of mind, the girls made lemonade, which was always brought out in a red-glass pitcher, ornamented with forget-me-nots in blue enamel. This the girls thought very fine, and the neighbors always joked about the suspicious color of the pitcher.

Today Paul's father sat on the top step, talking to a young man who shifted a restless baby from knee to knee. He happened to be the young man who was daily held up to Paul as a model, and after whom it was his father's dearest hope that he would pattern. This young man was of a ruddy complexion, with a compressed, red mouth, and faded, near-sighted eyes, over which he wore thick spectacles, with gold bows that curved about his ears. He was clerk to one of the magnates of a great steel corporation, and was looked upon in Cordelia Street as a young man with a future. There was a story that, some five years ago—he was now barely twenty-six—he had been a trifle dissipated but in order to curb his appetites and save the loss of time and strength that a sowing of wild oats might have entailed, he had taken his chief's advice, oft reiterated to his employees, and at twenty-one

---

14   **"waists"**: blouses.

had married the first woman whom he could persuade to share his fortunes. She happened to be an angular schoolmistress, much older than he, who also wore thick glasses, and who had now borne him four children, all near-sighted, like herself.

The young man was relating how his chief, now cruising in the Mediterranean, kept in touch with all the details of the business, arranging his office hours on his yacht just as though he were at home, and "knocking off work enough to keep two stenographers busy." His father told, in turn, the plan his corporation was considering, of putting in an electric railway plant in Cairo. Paul snapped his teeth; he had an awful apprehension that they might spoil it all before he got there. Yet he rather liked to hear these legends of the iron kings, that were told and retold on Sundays and holidays; these stories of palaces in Venice, yachts on the Mediterranean, and high play at Monte Carlo[15] appealed to his fancy, and he was interested in the triumphs of these cash boys who had become famous, though he had no mind for the cash-boy stage.

After supper was over and he had helped to dry the dishes, Paul nervously asked his father whether he could go to George's to get some help in his geometry, and still more nervously asked for car fare. This latter request he had to repeat, as his father, on principle, did not like to hear requests for money, whether much or little. He asked Paul whether he could not go to some boy who lived nearer, and told him that he ought not to leave his schoolwork until Sunday; but he gave him the dime. He was not a poor man, but he had a worthy ambition to come up in the world. His only reason for allowing Paul to usher was that he thought a boy ought to be earning a little.

Paul bounded upstairs, scrubbed the greasy odor of the dish-water from his hands with the ill-smelling soap he hated, and then shook over his fingers a few drops of violet water from the bottle he kept hidden in his drawer. He left the house with his geometry conspicuously under his arm, and the moment he got out of Cordelia Street and boarded a downtown car, he shook off the lethargy of two deadening days, and began to live again.

The leading juvenile of the permanent stock company[16] which played at one of the downtown theaters was an acquaintance of

---

15 **high play at Monte Carlo:** high-stakes gambling in Monaco's chief city.

16 **leading juvenile . . . company:** A stock company is a theatrical company that performs several plays in one theatre. The juvenile is the male actor who takes youthful parts; his female equvalent is called an *ingenue.*

Paul's, and the boy had been invited to drop in at the Sunday-night rehearsals whenever he could. For more than a year Paul had spent every available moment loitering about Charley Edwards' dressing-room. He had won a place among Edwards' following not only because the young actor, who could not afford to employ a dresser, often found him useful, but because he recognized in Paul something akin to what churchmen term "vocation."

It was at the theater and at Carnegie Hall that Paul really lived; the rest was but a sleep and a forgetting. This was Paul's fairy tale, and it had for him all the allurement of a secret love. The moment he inhaled the gassy, painty, dusty odor behind the scenes, he breathed like a prisoner set free, and felt within him the possibility of doing or saying splendid, brilliant, poetic things. The moment the cracked orchestra beat out the overture from *Martha*, or jerked at the serenade from *Rigoletto*,[17] all stupid and ugly things slid from him, and his senses were deliciously, yet delicately fired.

Perhaps it was because, in Paul's world, the natural nearly always wore the guise of ugliness, that a certain element of artificiality seemed to him necessary in beauty. Perhaps it was because his experience of life elsewhere was so full of Sabbath-school picnics, petty economies, wholesome advice as to how to succeed in life, and the unescapable odors of cooking, that he found this existence so alluring, these smartly clad men and women so attractive, that he was so moved by these starry apple orchards that bloomed perennially under the lime-light.

It would be difficult to put it strongly enough how convincingly the stage entrance of that theater was for Paul the actual portal of Romance. Certainly none of the company ever suspected it, least of all Charley Edwards. It was very like the old stories that used to float about London of fabulously rich Jews, who had subterranean halls there, with palms, and fountains, and soft lamps and richly apparelled women who never saw the disenchanting light of London day. So, in the midst of that smoke-palled city, enamored of figures and grimy toil, Paul had his secret temple, his wishing carpet, his bit of blue-and-white Mediterranean shore bathed in perpetual sunshine.

Several of Paul's teachers had a theory that his imagination had been perverted by garish fiction, but the truth was that he scarcely

---

17 ***Martha ... Rigoletto:*** *Martha* is a romantic opera by Friedrich von Flotow (1812–1883); *Rigoletto,* a tragic opera by Giuseppe Verdi (1813–1901).

ever read at all. The books at home were not such as would either tempt or corrupt a youthful mind, and as for reading the novels that some of his friends urged upon him—well, he got what he wanted much more quickly from music; any sort of music, from an orchestra to a barrel organ. He needed only the spark, the indescribable thrill that made his imagination master of his senses, and he could make plots and pictures enough of his own. It was equally true that he was not stage struck—not, at any rate, in the usual acceptation of that expression. He had no desire to become an actor, any more than he had to become a musician. He felt no necessity to do any of these things; what he wanted was to see, to be in the atmosphere, float on the wave of it, to be carried out, blue league after blue league, away from everything.

After a night behind the scenes Paul found the school-room more than ever repulsive; the bare floors and naked walls; the prosy men who never wore frock coats, or violets in their buttonholes; the women with their dull gowns, shrill voices, and pitiful seriousness about prepositions that govern the dative. He could not bear to have the other pupils think, for a moment, that he took these people seriously; he must convey to them that he considered it all trivial, and was there only by way of a jest, anyway. He had autographed pictures of all the members of the stock company which he showed his classmates, telling them the most incredible stories of his familiarity with these people, of his acquaintance with the soloists who came to Carnegie Hall, his suppers with them and the flowers he sent them. When these stories lost their effect, and his audience grew listless, he became desperate and would bid all the boys good-bye, announcing that he was going to travel for a while; going to Naples, to Venice, to Egypt. Then, next Monday, he would slip back, conscious and nervously smiling; his sister was ill, and he should have to defer his voyage until spring.

Matters went steadily worse with Paul at school. In the itch to let his instructors know how heartily he despised them and their homilies, and how thoroughly he was appreciated elsewhere, he mentioned once or twice that he had no time to fool with theorems; adding—with a twitch of the eyebrows and a touch of that nervous bravado which so perplexed them—that he was helping the people down at the stock company; they were old friends of his.

The upshot of the matter was that the Principal went to Paul's father, and Paul was taken out of school and put to work. The manager at Carnegie Hall was told to get another usher in his stead; the door-keeper at the theater was warned not to admit him to the house; and Charley Edwards remorsefully promised the boy's father not to see him again.

The members of the stock company were vastly amused when some of Paul's stories reached them—especially the women. They were hard-working women, most of them supporting indigent husbands or brothers, and they laughed rather bitterly at having stirred the boy to such fervid and florid inventions. They agreed with the faculty and with his father that Paul's was a bad case.

The east-bound train was plowing through a January snow-storm; the dull dawn was beginning to show gray when the engine whistled a mile out of Newark. Paul started up from the seat where he had lain curled in uneasy slumber, rubbed the breath-misted window glass with his hand, and peered out. The snow was whirling in curling eddies above the white bottom lands, and the drifts lay already deep in the fields and along the fences, while here and there the long dead grass and dried weed stalks protruded black above it. Lights shone from the scattered houses, and a gang of laborers who stood beside the track waved their lanterns.

Paul had slept very little, and he felt grimy and uncomfortable. He had made the all-night journey in a day coach, partly because he was ashamed, dressed as he was, to go into a Pullman, and partly because he was afraid of being seen there by some Pittsburgh businessman, who might have noticed him in Denny & Carson's office. When the whistle awoke him, he clutched quickly at his breast pocket, glancing about him with an uncertain smile. But the little, clay-bespattered Italians were still sleeping, the slatternly women across the aisle were in open-mouthed oblivion, and even the crumby, crying babies were for the nonce stilled. Paul settled back to struggle with his impatience as best he could.

When he arrived at the Jersey City station, he hurried through his breakfast, manifestly ill at ease and keeping a sharp eye about him. After he reached the Twenty-third Street station, he consulted a cab-man, and had himself driven to a men's furnishing establishment that was just opening for the day. He spent upward of two hours there, buying with endless reconsidering and great care. His new street suit he put on in the fitting-room; the frock coat and dress clothes he had bundled into the cab with his linen. Then he drove to a hatter's and a shoe house. His next errand was at Tiffany's, where he selected his silver[18] and a new scarf-pin. He would not wait to have his silver marked, he said. Lastly, he stopped at a trunk shop on Broadway, and had his purchases packed into various traveling bags.

It was a little after one o'clock when he drove up to the Waldorf, and after settling with the cabman, went into the office. He registered from Washington; said his mother and father had been abroad, and that he had come down to await the arrival of their steamer. He told his story plausibly and had no trouble, since he volunteered to pay for them in advance, in engaging his rooms; a sleeping-room, sitting-room, and bath.

Not once, but a hundred times Paul had planned this entry into New York. He had gone over every detail of it with Charley Edwards, and in his scrapbook at home there were pages of description about New York hotels, cut from the Sunday papers. When he was shown to his sitting-room on the eighth floor, he saw at a glance that everything was as it should be; there was but one detail in his mental picture that the place did not realize, so he rang for the bellboy and sent him down for flowers. He moved about nervously until the boy returned, putting away his new linen and fingering it delightedly as he did so. When the flowers came, he put them hastily into water, and then tumbled into a hot bath. Presently he came out of his white bath-room, resplendent in his new silk underwear, and playing with the tassels of his red robe. The snow was whirling so fiercely outside his windows that he could scarcely see across the street, but within the air was deliciously soft and fragrant. He put the violets and jonquils on the taboret[19] beside the couch, and threw himself down, with a long sigh, covering himself with a Roman blanket. He was thoroughly tired; he had been in such haste, he had stood up to such a strain, covered so much ground in the last twenty-four hours, that he wanted to think how it had all come about. Lulled by the sound of the wind, the warm air, and the cool fragrance of the flowers, he sank into deep, drowsy retrospection.

It had been wonderfully simple; when they had shut him out of the theater and concert hall, when they had taken away his bone, the

---

18   **Tiffany's . . . silver:** Rich turn-of-the-century gentlemen generally owned a set of silver-backed, often monogrammed personal care items: military-style hair brushes, a comb, and perhaps a shaving brush, a razor, a shoe horn, and a dresser-top tray. Tiffany's, an elegant New York jewelry store, now has many branch stores.

19   **taboret:** a small, cylindrical stand.

whole thing was virtually determined. The rest was a mere matter of opportunity. The only thing that at all surprised him was his own courage—for he realized well enough that he had always been tormented by fear, a sort of apprehensive dread that, of late years, as the meshes of the lies he had told closed about him, had been pulling the muscles of his body tighter and tighter. Until now, he could not remember the time when he had not been dreading something. Even when he was a little boy, it was always there—behind him, or before, or on either side. There had always been the shadowed corner, the dark place into which he dared not look, but from which something seemed always to be watching him—and Paul had done things that were not pretty to watch, he knew.

But now he had a curious sense of relief, as though he had at last thrown down the gauntlet to the thing in the corner.

Yet it was but a day since he had been sulking in the traces;[20] but yesterday afternoon that he had been sent to the bank with Denny & Carson's deposit, as usual—but this time he was instructed to leave the book to be balanced. There was above two thousand dollars in checks, and nearly a thousand in the bank notes which he had taken from the book and quietly transferred to his pocket. At the bank he had made out a new deposit slip. His nerves had been steady enough to permit of his returning to the office, where he had finished his work and asked for a full day's holiday tomorrow, Saturday, giving a perfectly reasonable pretext. The bankbook, he knew, would not be returned before Monday or Tuesday, and his father would be out of town for the next week. From the time he slipped the bank notes into his pocket until he boarded the night train for New York, he had not known a moment's hesitation. It was not the first time Paul had steered through treacherous waters.

How astonishingly easy it had all been; here he was, the thing done; and this time there would be no awakening, no figure at the top of the stairs. He watched the snowflakes whirling by his window until he fell asleep.

When he awoke, it was three o'clock in the afternoon. He bounded up with a start; half of one of his precious days gone already! He spent more than an hour in dressing, watching every stage of his

---

20 **sulking in the traces:** traces were straps, ropes, or chains by which an animal pulled a wagon or a carriage. Here, the phrase is metaphoric, referring to Paul's sulky attitude toward the bonds of work.

toilet carefully in the mirror. Everything was quite perfect; he was exactly the kind of boy he had always wanted to be.

When he went downstairs, Paul took a carriage and drove up Fifth Avenue toward the Park. The snow had somewhat abated; carriages and tradesmen's wagons were hurrying soundlessly to and fro in the winter twilight; boys in woollen mufflers were shovelling off the doorsteps; the avenue stages made fine spots of color against the white street. Here and there on the corners were stands, with whole flower gardens blooming under glass cases, against the sides of which the snowflakes stuck and melted; violets, roses, carnations, lilies of the valley—somewhat vastly more lovely and alluring that they blossomed thus unnaturally in the snow. The Park itself was a wonderful stage winterpiece.

When he returned, the pause of the twilight had ceased, and the tune of the streets had changed. The snow was falling faster, lights streamed from the hotels that reared their dozen stories fearlessly up into the storm, defying the raging Atlantic winds. A long, black stream of carriages poured down the avenue, intersected here and there by other streams, tending horizontally. There were a score of cabs about the entrance of his hotel, and his driver had to wait. Boys in livery were running in and out of the awning stretched across the sidewalk, up and down the red velvet carpet laid from the door to the street. Above, about, within it all was the rumble and roar, the hurry and toss of thousands of human beings as hot for pleasure as himself, and on every side of him towered the glaring affirmation of the omnipotence of wealth.

The boy set his teeth and drew his shoulders together in a spasm of realization; the plot of all dramas, the text of all romances, the nerve-stuff of all sensations was whirling about him like the snow-flakes. He burnt like a faggot[21] in a tempest.

When Paul went down to dinner, the music of the orchestra came floating up the elevator shaft to greet him. His head whirled as he stepped into the thronged corridor, and he sank back into one of the chairs against the wall to get his breath. The lights, the chatter, the perfumes, the bewildering medley of color—he had, for a moment, the feeling of not being able to stand it. But only for a moment; these were his own people, he told himself. He went slowly about the corridors, through the writing-rooms, smoking-rooms, reception-rooms,

---

21 **faggot:** a bundle of sticks or twigs, tied together for burning.

as though he were exploring the chambers of an enchanted palace, built and peopled for him alone.

When he reached the dining-room he sat down at a table near a window. The flowers, the white linen, the many-colored wine-glasses, the gay toilettes of the women, the low popping of corks, the undulating repetitions of the *Blue Danube* from the orchestra, all flooded Paul's dream with bewildering radiance. When the roseate tinge of his champagne was added—that cold, precious, bubbling stuff that creamed and foamed in his glass—Paul wondered that there were honest men in the world at all. This was what all the world was fighting for, he reflected; this was what all the struggle was about. He doubted the reality of his past. Had he ever known a place called Cordelia Street, a place where fagged-looking businessmen got on the early car; mere rivets in a machine they seemed to Paul—sickening men, with combings of children's hair always hanging to their coats, and the smell of cooking in their clothes. Cordelia Street—Ah! that belonged to another time and country; had he not always been thus, had he not sat here night after night, from as far back as he could remember, looking pensively over just such shimmering textures, and slowly twirling the stem of a glass like this one between his thumb and middle finger? He rather thought he had.

He was not in the least abashed or lonely. He had no especial desire to meet or to know any of these people; all he demanded was the right to look on and conjecture, to watch the pageant. The mere stage properties were all he contended for. Nor was he lonely later in the evening, in his loge at the Metropolitan.[22] He was now entirely rid of his nervous misgivings, of his forced aggressiveness, of the imperative desire to show himself different from his surroundings. He felt now that his surroundings explained him. Nobody questioned the purple; he had only to wear it passively. He had only to glance down at his attire to reassure himself that here it would be impossible for anyone to humiliate him.

He found it hard to leave his beautiful sitting-room to go to bed that night, and sat long watching the raging storm from his turret window. When he went to sleep it was with the lights turned on in his bedroom; partly because of his old timidity, and partly so that, if he should wake in the night, there would be no wretched moment of doubt, no horrible suspicion of yellow wallpaper, or of Washington and Calvin above his bed.

---

22 **loge at the Metropolitan:** a box seat at the Metropolitan Opera House.

Sunday morning the city was practically snow-bound. Paul break-fasted late, and in the afternoon he fell in with a wild San Francisco boy, a freshman at Yale, who said he had run down for a "little flyer" over Sunday. The young man offered to show Paul the night side of the town, and the two boys went out together after dinner, not returning to the hotel until seven o'clock the next morning. They had started out in the confiding warmth of a champagne friendship, but their parting in the elevator was singularly cool. The freshman pulled himself together to make his train, and Paul went to bed. He awoke at two o'clock in the afternoon, very thirsty and dizzy, and rang for ice-water, coffee, and the Pittsburgh papers.

On the part of the hotel management, Paul excited no suspicion. There was this to be said for him, that he wore his spoils with dignity and in no way made himself conspicuous. Even under the glow of his wine he was never boisterous, though he found the stuff like a magician's wand for wonder-building. His chief greediness lay in his ears and eyes, and his excesses were not offensive ones. His dearest pleasures were the gray winter twilights in his sitting-room; his quiet enjoyment of his flowers, his clothes, his wide divan, his cigarette, and his sense of power. He could not remember a time when he had felt so at peace with himself. The mere release from the necessity of petty lying, lying every day and every day, restored his self-respect. He had never lied for pleasure, even at school; but to be noticed and admired, to assert his difference from other Cordelia Street boys; and he felt a good deal more manly, more honest, even, now that he had no need for boastful pretensions, now that he could, as his actor friends used to say, "dress the part." It was characteristic that remorse did not occur to him. His golden days went by without a shadow, and he made each as perfect as he could.

On the eighth day after his arrival in New York, he found the whole affair exploited in the Pittsburgh papers, exploited with a wealth of detail which indicated that local news of a sensational nature was at a low ebb. The firm of Denny & Carson announced that the boy's father had refunded the full amount of the theft, and that they had no intention of prosecuting. The Cumberland minister had been interviewed, and expressed his hope of yet reclaiming the motherless lad, and his Sabbath-school teacher declared that she would spare no effort to that end. The rumor had reached Pittsburgh that the boy had been seen in a New York hotel, and his father had gone East to find him and bring him home.

Paul had just come in to dress for dinner; he sank into a chair, weak to the knees, and clasped his head in his hands. It was to be worse than jail, even; the tepid waters of Cordelia Street were to close over him finally and forever. The gray monotony stretched before him in hopeless, unrelieved years; Sabbath-school, Young People's Meeting, the yellow-papered room, the damp dish-towels; it all rushed back upon him with a sickening vividness. He had the old feeling that the orchestra had suddenly stopped, the sinking sensation that the play was over. The sweat broke out on his face, and he sprang to his feet, looked about him with his white, conscious smile, and winked at himself in the mirror, With something of the old childish belief in miracles with which he had so often gone to class, all his lessons unlearned, Paul dressed and dashed whistling down the corridor to the elevator.

He had no sooner entered the dining-room and caught the measure of the music than his remembrance was lightened by his old elastic power of claiming the moment, mounting with it, and finding it all sufficient. The glare and glitter about him, the mere scenic accessories had again, and for the last time, their old potency. He would show himself that he was game, he would finish the thing splendidly. He doubted, more than ever, the existence of Cordelia Street, and for the first time he drank his wine recklessly. Was he not, after all, one of those fortunate beings born to the purple,[23] was he not still himself and in his own place? He drummed a nervous accompaniment to the Pagliacci[24] music and looked about him, telling himself over and over that it had paid.

He reflected drowsily, to the swell of the music and the chill sweetness of his wine, that he might have done it more wisely. He might have caught an outbound steamer and been well out of their clutches before now. But the other side of the world had seemed too far away and too uncertain then; he could not have waited for it; his need had been too sharp. If he had to choose over again, he would do the same thing tomorrow. He looked affectionately about the dining-room, now gilded with a soft mist. Ah, it had paid indeed!

Paul was awakened next morning by a painful throbbing in his head and feet. He had thrown himself across the bed without undressing, and had slept with his shoes on. His limbs and hands were

---

23 **born to the purple:** a phrase connoting high rank. The Romans limited the wearing of purple cloth to emperors and other royals; subsequent cultures continued to associate purple with high rank. A prince is born to the purple.

24 **Pagliacci:** A tragic opera by Ruggiero Leoncavallo (1858–1919).

lead heavy, and his tongue and throat were parched and burnt. There came upon him one of those fateful attacks of clear-headedness that never occurred except when he was physically exhausted and his nerves hung loose. He lay still and closed his eyes and let the tide of things wash over him.

His father was in New York; "stopping at some joint or other," he told himself. The memory of successive summers on the front stoop fell upon him like a weight of black water. He had not a hundred dollars left; and he knew now, more than ever, that money was everything, the wall that stood between all he loathed and all he wanted. The thing was winding itself up; he had thought of that on his first glorious day in New York, and had even provided a way to snap the thread. It lay on his dressing-table now; he had got it out last night when he came blindly up from dinner, but the shiny metal hurt his eyes, and he disliked the looks of it.

He rose and moved about with a painful effort, succumbing now and again to attacks of nausea. It was the old depression exaggerated; all the world had become Cordelia Street. Yet somehow he was not afraid of anything, was absolutely calm; perhaps because he had looked into the dark corner at last and knew. It was bad enough, what he saw there, but somehow not so bad as his long fear of it had been. He saw everything clearly now. He had a feeling that he had made the best of it, that he had lived the sort of life he was meant to live, and for half an hour he sat staring at the revolver. But he told himself that was not the way, so he went downstairs and took a cab to the ferry.

When Paul arrived in Newark, he got off the train and took another cab, directing the driver to follow the Pennsylvania tracks out of the town. The snow lay heavy on the roadways and had drifted deep in the open fields. Only here and there the dead grass or dried weed stalks projected, singularly black, above it. Once well into the country, Paul dismissed the carriage and walked, floundering along the tracks, his mind a medley of irrelevant things. He seemed to hold in his brain an actual picture of everything he had seen that morning. He remembered every feature of both his drivers, of the toothless old woman from whom he had bought the red flowers in his coat, the agent from whom he had got his ticket, and all of his fellow-passengers on the ferry. His mind, unable to cope with vital matters near at hand, worked feverishly and deftly at sorting and grouping these images. They made for him a part of the ugliness of the world, of the ache in his head, and the bitter burning on his tongue. He stopped and put a handful of snow into his mouth as he walked, but that, too, seemed hot. When he reached a little hillside, where the tracks ran through a cut some twenty feet below him, he stopped and sat down.

The carnations in his coat were drooping with the cold, he noticed; their red glory all over. It occurred to him that all the flowers he had seen in the glass cases that first night must have gone the same way, long before this. It was only one splendid breath they had, in spite of their brave mockery at the winter outside the glass; and it was a losing game in the end, it seemed, this revolt against the homilies by which the world is run. Paul took one of the blossoms carefully from his coat and scooped a little hole in the snow, where he covered it up. Then he dozed a while, from his weak condition, seemingly insensible to the cold.

The sound of an approaching train awoke him, and he started to his feet, remembering only his resolution, and afraid lest he should be too late. He stood watching the approaching locomotive, his teeth chattering, his lips drawn away from them in a frightened smile; once or twice he glanced nervously sidewise, as though he were being watched. When the right moment came, he jumped. As he fell, the folly of his haste occurred to him with merciless clearness, the vastness of what he had left undone. There flashed through his brain, clearer than ever before, the blue of Adriatic water, the yellow of Algerian sands.

He felt something strike his chest, and that his body was being thrown swiftly through the air, on and on, immeasurably far and fast, while his limbs were gently relaxed. Then, because the picture-making mechanism was crushed, the disturbing visions flashed into black, and Paul dropped back into the immense design of things.

QUESTIONS FOR DISCUSSION

1. The story takes place in Pittsburgh and New York during November and January. What might these settings (time and place) signify or foreshadow?

2. Paul has a decided effect on both his father and his teachers. What is it about his character that troubles these people?

3. Paul comes fully to life only at his job as a Carnegie Hall usher and at Charley Edwards's theater. Explain what this tells about Paul.

4. In what way(s) is Paul's lying another key to his character?

5. Why does Cather juxtapose (put side by side) the descriptions of the Schenley Hotel and Paul's home?

6. Is the young man who was "daily held up to Paul as a model" meant to be a foil to Paul or Paul's antagonist?

7. Were you surprised by Paul's crime? Why or why not?

8. Cather often wrote about the difficulties that artists have in a world more dedicated to business than to the arts. Is this idea central to the meaning of the story?

9. In the story what is the function of flowers, especially the red carnations that Paul wears?

TOPICS FOR WRITING

1. In a journal entry, write about an adult who totally misunderstood you or one of your friends. Explain how and/or why this situation occurred.

2. In Paul's bedroom hang pictures of George Washington and John Calvin. Cather could have chosen pictures of many other people. Find out enough about each man to write a paper of analysis discussing what comment on Paul those pictures might be making.

3. When "Paul's Case" was first published, it was subtitled "A Study in Temperament." In an essay explain whether this subtitle helps reveal Cather's intent in writing this story.

4. Cather takes great pains to establish Paul's attraction to various forms of culture. Does she also mock this attraction? In an essay, support your position with quotations from the story.

5. Cather foreshadows the end of the story through her strong characterization of Paul. In an essay, focus on additional ways foreshadowing occurs, such as through images or objects.

SYNTHESIS QUESTIONS

1. Which protagonist in these stories seems the most fully developed or three-dimensional? Cite both reasons and supporting evidence for your answer.

2. Analyze the direct and indirect methods by which one of these authors characterizes a major character.

3. Which character in these stories do you find inconsistent? Explain why.

4. Does any major character seem to be a static character? Explain.

5. Which character is most changed by the events of the story?

6. Considering only the elements of plot, setting, and character, which story do you find the most satisfying? Defend your choice.

Chapter Four

POINT OF VIEW AND TONE

Point of view is the vantage point from which an author tells a story. There are two main points of view: **first person** (*I*) and **third person** (*he, she, they*), but there are variations within these points of view.

FIRST-PERSON POINT OF VIEW

The "I" narrator is not the author. Instead, the author creates a persona or mask through which he or she tells the story. While there may be some or even many autobiographical details in a story, it is never safe to assume this. Rather, it is better to assume that the author has taken some details from his or her own life and from other sources and reworked them. To identify the narrator, ignore all dialogue and look to narrative sections. If there are no "I's," the story is probably told from the third-person point of view.

The "I" narrator may be a character in the story, as in Mark Helprin's "Tamar," Cedric Yamanaka's "The Lemon Tree Billiards House," and Eudora Welty's "Why I Live at the P.O." Alternatively, the "I" narrator may be merely an observer of events and not a character in the story at all. And, if a character, the narrator may be a main character or a minor one. Further, the first-person narrator may or may not fully understand the events in the story: if he or she does not, then the narrator is termed a **naive narrator.**

Charlotte Brontë's novel *Jane Eyre* is told from the first-person point of view and from the viewpoint of a character in the story. Here, the narrator, Jane, writes of the beginning of her journey to become a governess:

151

> A new chapter in a novel is something like a new scene in a
> play; and when I draw up the curtain this time, reader, you must
> fancy you see a room in the George Inn at Millcote, with such large
> figured papering on the walls as inn rooms have; such a carpet, such
> furniture, such ornaments on the mantelpiece, such prints, including a
> portrait of George the Third, and another of the Prince of Wales, and
> a representation of the death of Wolfe. All this is visible to you by the
> light of an oil lamp hanging from the ceiling, and by that of an excel-
> lent fire, near which I sit in my cloak and bonnet. . . .

In Henry James's novel *The Portrait of a Lady,* the "I" is not a
character. He turns up in the narrative on occasion, describes actions,
reports conversations, tells us what some of the characters are thinking, and even interprets events, but he is distant from the scene, as
this paragraph indicates:

> I may not attempt to report in its fulness our young woman's
> response to the deep appeal of Rome, to analyse her feelings as
> she trod the pavement of the Forum or to number her pulsations as
> she crossed the threshold of Saint Peter's. It is enough to say that
> her impression was such as might have been expected of a person
> of her freshness and her eagerness.

If the first-person narrator expresses only unspoken thoughts,
then the technique is called **interior monologue.** The following
excerpt from "The Yellow Wallpaper," a short story by Charlotte
Perkins Gilman, is told entirely through interior monologue:

> I suppose John never was nervous in his life. He laughs at me
> so about this wallpaper!
> At first he meant to repaper the room, but afterward he said
> that I was letting it get the better of me, and that nothing was worse
> for a nervous patient than to give way to such fancies.
> He said that after the wallpaper was changed it would be the
> heavy bedstead, and then the barred windows, and then that gate
> at the head of the stairs, and so on.

THIRD-PERSON POINT OF VIEW

The third-person point of view may be **omniscient;** that is, it may
reveal the thoughts of all or most of the characters. In contrast,
limited omniscient point of view focuses on the thoughts of a single

character, as in R. K. Narayan's "Like the Sun." (The word *omniscient* literally means "all-knowing.")

One type of limited omniscience is the objective point of view, in which the author makes no commentary but records only those details that can be seen and heard, rather as a newspaper reporter does. This point of view is more common in nonfiction—historical accounts, for example—than in fiction.

Long works of fiction are often told from several points of view, but short stories are commonly presented from a single point of view.

TONE

Tone in writing is somewhat like tone of voice in speech. You can tell, for example, how your mother feels about you or your actions from her tone of voice. Similarly, tone in writing is the author's attitude toward the characters, the topic, or the readers, as expressed by the narrator, and it may come across in a number of ways. For example, in "Why I Live at the P.O.," the narrator tells us in the first paragraph that her sister told a falsehood and is spoiled. Then she says she does not "enjoy being referred to as a hussy by my own grandfather." She describes her Uncle Rondo as "a good case of a one-track mind" and wonders aloud whether her sister's child is normal. These comments all point to the author's attitude toward the weirdly assorted characters, made clear through the persona of the narrator. This attitude creates sympathy for the narrator, who can no longer stand to live at home. Welty's tone is best described as gently amused and sympathetic.

Tone in writing can be, among other things, serious, introspective, satirical, sad, ironic, playful, condescending, formal, or informal. Tone is achieved through descriptive details of setting and character, through dialogue, and through a narrator's direct comment. An author's tone is not necessarily the same throughout a work, although in a short story, the same tone is usually maintained throughout.

Tone and Mood

The terms *tone* and *mood* are sometimes confused. While tone conveys the author's attitude, mood refers to the atmosphere in a story. Atmosphere may be mysterious, horror-filled, or serene, for example. The atmosphere in "Why I Live at the P.O." is sometimes turbulent and sometimes full of recrimination. While both the tone and the mood of a story may be the same (both may be sad, for example), it is usually common to distinguish between these two terms. Also, the mood of a story is not necessarily the same throughout. The climax may bring about a change from despair to triumph, or from anxiety to relief, or from any mood to another.

Determining Tone

One way of determining the tone of a story is to decide what effect the story has on you.

Do you feel sympathetic or disgusted with the characters? Does the story make you smile or make you weep? Did you rejoice at the ending or did you shudder? Your response is to all the elements of a story, but it is likely to be similar to the tone. For example, if the author seems sympathetic or hostile to a character, you likely will be too. If the author's tone seems aloof, you may feel a corresponding aloofness. If the author's tone is lightly satirical, the effect on you is likely to be amusement or a sense that the author's satire is well aimed.

SUMMARY

A story may be told from the first-person or the third-person point of view. The "I" narrator may be a main character in the story, a minor character, or someone outside the story. If the narrator does not fully understand the circumstances of a story, he or she is termed a naive narrator. If the narrator's thoughts are unspoken throughout, the author has used interior monologue. The third-person narrator may tell a story from the omniscient, limited omniscient, or objective point of view.

Finally, the tone of a work expresses the author's attitude toward the characters, topic, or audience. Tone is usually distinguished from mood—the atmosphere of a work.

TAMAR

MARK HELPRIN (born 1947)

Mark Helprin wrote short stories as an undergraduate English major at Harvard in the 1960s and had two stories published in *The New Yorker* in 1969, the year he graduated. He has continued to write novels and stories and has won a PEN/Faulkner Award, a National Jewish Book Award, and an American Book Award nomination, all for *Ellis Island and Other Stories* (1981), from which the following story is taken. He has also won a Prix de Rome from the American Academy and Institute of Arts and Letters and was a Guggenheim fellow in 1984.

Helprin was born in New York City, received an M.A. degree in 1972 from Harvard, and did postgraduate study at Oxford in England. He served with the Israeli Infantry and the Israeli Air Force in 1972–1973 and with the British Merchant Navy. *A Dove of the East and Other Stories* (1975) was his first collection of short stories. His novels include *Refiner's Fire: The Life and Adventure of Marshall Pearl, a Foundling* (1977); *Winter's Tale* (1983), an allegory; *A Soldier of the Great War* (1990), about an old Italian soldier; and *Memoir from Antproof Case* (1995). He has also collaborated with illustrator Chris Van Allsburg on three books for children: a retelling of the ballet *Swan Lake* (1989); *A City in Winter* (1996); and *The Veil of Snows* (1997).

Helprin's writing is rich in description of both setting and characters. As you read "Tamar," note what the narrator reveals about himself.

■

Before the War,[1] in London, I was trying to arrange a system whereby the Jews of Germany and Austria could sell their paintings and other works of art without depressing demand. It was very serious business, for our primary aim was to require that twenty-five percent of each sale go into an escape fund to provide transport for those who could not make it on their own. We thought that we could exact this price if we managed to keep market values steady. But all of Europe was on edge about the political situation, and no one was in the mood to buy anything. And then, after *Kristallnacht*,[2] every Jew in Germany came forward, wanting to sell precious objects.

At the time of our greatest hope, my job was to set up fronts for selling what we expected would be a flood of art coming in from Middle Europe. If it had appeared that English collectors were opening their storerooms to take advantage of a favorable market, the excitement might well have pushed values upward. So we tried to get the cooperation of those prominent collectors who had the foresight to see what was about to happen on the Continent and were in sympathy with our cause. Excepting a very few, these were Jews. The others simply were not interested, and, anyway, we did not want to divulge the plan in too many places.

Soon I found myself deeply involved in the high society of Jews in London and in their great houses throughout the countryside. My conviction was then, as it is now, that it is not possible for Jews to be in "society" but that their efforts to be so are (except when immoderate or in bad taste) courageous, for the mechanisms of high social status are encouragements of vulnerability, safe only for those who can afford to lose themselves in pursuits superficial and deep and not fear that their fundamental positions will drop out from under them as a result of their inattention. My attitude toward the Jewish peers[3] and the Jewish upper class in general was mixed, and had complex roots. I admired their bravery while occasionally chafing at their blindness. I knew that, in spite of their learning and culture, they were isolated in such a way as to make me—a young man of thirty-two—far better a

---

1 **the War:** World War II.

2 **Kristallnacht:** literally, the night of broken glass, the nights of November 9th and 10th in 1938 when Nazi storm troopers broke windows of Jewish shops in Germany, burned synagogues, and arrested over 20,000 people.[German]

3 **peers:** in Great Britain and Ireland, a member of one of degrees of nobility (duke, marquis, earl, viscount, baron).

judge of certain things than were they. I had been in the ghetto in Warsaw not a month before, and the people there had confided to me that they felt the end was near. They said, "Tell them, in England, that in Poland they are killing Jews." I had been in Berlin, Munich, Vienna, and Prague. I had passed through Jewish villages from Riga to Bucharest, where I had seen a temple about to fall. How misty and beautiful it was, that autumn. I cannot describe the quiet. It was as if the nineteenth century—indeed, all the past—were in hiding and feared to give itself away. The whole world of the Jews in Central Europe looked outward with the saddest eyes. What could *I* do? I tried my best. I was working for the Jewish Agency, and had just come from two years in Palestine, in the desert, and thought that my responsibility was to save the Jews of Europe. Like all young men, I was full of speeches that I could not deliver. Somehow, I imagined that the art scheme would be everything. I have since forgiven myself.

Visions of the Jews in the forests, in green pine valleys as sharp as chevrons, in villages marked by silent white ribbons of wood smoke, never left me as I undertook to master the intricacies of the London social season. I cannot remember when I have enjoyed myself more. Sometimes I became as lost and trusting as my hosts, and, even when I did not, the contrast between the Eastern European *Heimat*[4] and the drawing rooms of modern London was incalculably enlivening. I was suspended between two dream-worlds.

Just before Christmas, that time in all capitals when the city flares most brightly, I was oppressed with invitations. I had a blue pad upon which I listed my engagements, and one terrible, lovely week it had sixteen entries. I met so many dukes, duchesses, M.P.s,[5] industrialists, and academics that my eyes began to cross. But we had begun to succeed in hammering out a network for art sales, and I was confident and happy.

Then a magical power in the Jewish Agency must have decided that these several score dinners had made me into a diplomat, for I received an invitation to a dinner party on the twenty-first at the house of the most eminent Jew in all the British Empire. Only that summer, I had scrubbed pots, guarded at night, and lived in a tent, in a collective settlement in the Negev.[6] Now I ballooned with pride.

---

4 *Heimat:* home, native land. [German]

5 **M.P.s:** members of Parliament, the legislature of Great Britain.

6 **Negev:** a desert in what is now southern Israel.

The entire seventeenth century could not have produced enough frills to clothe the heavy monster of my pomposity. Sure that all my troubles were over forever, I spent every bit of my money on the most beautiful three-piece suit in London. When the tailor—who was himself a knight—heard where I was going, he set his men to work, and they finished it in three days. London became, for me, the set of a joyous light opera.

On the night of the twentieth, just twenty-four hours before what I assumed would be my apotheosis[7] (it was said that the Prime Minister would be there, and I imagined myself declaring to him a leaden diplomatic précis[8] along the lines of the Magna Carta or the Treaty of Vienna), I had yet another engagement, this one at the house of a Jewish art dealer whom I had recently regarded as a big fish. I was so overconfident that I left my hotel without his address, thinking that I would manage to find it anyway, since I knew its approximate location in Chelsea.

I was due at six-thirty. For an hour and a half I rushed through Chelsea in this direction and that, trying to find the house. Everyone, it seemed, was having a dinner party, and all the buildings looked alike. When, finally, I arrived at the right square, I stood in a little park and stared at the house. It was five stories tall and it was lit like a theater. Through the sparkling windows came firelight, candlelight, and glimpses of enormous chandeliers—while the snow fell as if in time to sad and troubling music. Red and disheveled from running about, I stood in my splendid suit, frightened to go in. In that square, the coal smoke was coiling about like a great menagerie of airborne snakes, and occasionally it caught me and choked me in its unbearable fumes. But I remember it with fondness, because it was the smell of Europe in the winter; and, though it was devilish and foul, it seemed to say that, underneath everything, another world was at work, that the last century was alive in its clumsiness and warmth, signaling that all was well and that great contexts remained unbroken.

I was afraid to go in, because I was so late and because I knew what a fool I had been in judging these people according to the hierarchy in which they believed, and thus underrating them in comparison to the plutocrats of the next night. But I took hold of

---

7 **apotheosis:** elevation to a divine state.

8 **précis:** a summary.

myself and rang their bell. I heard conversation stop. A servant came to the door. Each of his steps shot through the wood like an X-ray. I was taken upstairs to a magnificent room in which were five tables of well-dressed people completely motionless and silent, like a group of deer surprised by a hunter. Every eye was upon me. Though frightened of fainting, I remained upright and seemingly composed. My host stood to greet me. Then he took me about like a roast, and introduced me to each and every guest, all of whom had a particular smile that can be described only as simultaneously benevolent, sadistic, and amused. I don't know why, but I broke into German, though my German was not the best. They must have been thinking, Who is this strange red-faced German who does not speak his own language well? Or perhaps they thought that I was confused as to my whereabouts. I suppose I was.

Then Herr Dennis, as I called him, took me by the arm and explained that, since they had readjusted the seating in my absence, I (who, the next day, would be waltzing with the Prime Minister) would have to sit at the children's table. It was a very great blow, especially since the poor children were bunched up all by themselves in a little ell of the room that led to the kitchen. I was in no position to protest; in fact, I was, by that time, quite numb.

As he led me, in a daze, toward the children's table, I imagined myself sitting with five or ten infants in bibs, staring down at them as if from a high tower, eating sullenly like a god exiled from Olympus. But when we rounded the corner of the ell, I discovered that the children were adolescents; and their charm arose to envelop me. First, there were four red-headed girl cousins, all in white. They were from thirteen to sixteen; they had between them several hundred million freckles; and they were so disturbed by my sudden arrival that they spent the next half hour swallowing, darting their eyes about, clearing their throats, and adjusting fallen locks of hair. They spoke as seriously as very old theologians, but ever so much more delicately; they pieced together their sentences with great care, the way new skaters skate, and when they finished they breathed in relief, not unlike students of a difficult Oriental language, who must recite in class. At the end of these ordeals, they looked at each other with the split-second glances common to people who are very familiar. Then, there was a boy with dark woolly hair and the peculiarly adolescent animal-lost-out-on-the-heath expression common to young men whose abilities greatly exceed their experience. At my appearance, he lowered his horns, knowing that he was going to spend the rest of the evening bashing himself against a castle wall. I admired his courage; I liked him;

I remembered. Next to him was a fat boy who wanted to be an opera singer. He was only fourteen, and when he saw that the threat presented by the woolly-haired boy was neutralized, he went wild with excitement, blooming at the four cousins with a gregariousness of which he had probably never been aware.

I liked these children. They seemed somewhat effete, and sheltered, but I knew that this was because I was used to the adolescents of our collective, who were much older than their years, and that these young people were the products of an ultra-refined system of schooling. I knew that, if protected during this vulnerability, they might emerge with unmatched strength. I had been through the same system, and had seen my schoolmates undergo miraculous transformations. I knew as well that they were destined for a long and terrible war, but, then again, so were we all. Yes, I liked these children, and I enjoyed the fact that I had left those years behind.

I have not described everyone at that table. One remains. She was the daughter of my host, the eldest, the tallest, the most beautiful. Her name was Tamar, and as I had turned the corner she had seemed to rise in the air to meet me, while the others were lost in the dark. Tamar and I had faced one another in a moment of silence that I will not ever forget. Sometimes, on a windy day, crosscurrented waves in the shallows near a beach will spread about, trapped in a caldron of bars and brakes, until two run together face to face and then fall back in shocked tranquillity. So it was with Tamar. It was as if I had run right into her. I was breathless, and I believe that she was, too.

I immediately took command of myself, and did not look at her. In fact, I studied every face before I studied hers—black eyes; black hair; her mouth and eyes showing her youth and strength in the way they were set, in the way they moved, not ever having been tried or defeated or abused. She wore a rich white silk blouse that was wonderfully open at the top, and a string of matched pearls. For a moment, I was convinced that she was in her twenties, but when she smiled I saw a touching thin silver wire across her upper teeth, and I knew that she was probably no more than seventeen. She *was* seventeen, soon to be eighteen, soon to take off the wire, soon (in fact) to become a nurse with the Eighth Army in Egypt. But at that time she was just on the verge of becoming a woman, and she virtually glowed with the fact.

As soon as I saw the wire, I felt as if I could talk with her in a way that could be managed, and I did. Unlike the four red-headed cousins, she was fearless and direct. She laughed out loud without the slightest self-consciousness, and I felt as if in our conversation we were not speaking but dancing. Perhaps it was because she was so clear of voice, so alert, and so straightforward. She was old enough to parry, and she did, extraordinarily well.

"Tamar is going to Brussels next year," volunteered one of the red-haired girls, in the manner of a handmaiden at court, "to study at the Royal Laboratory for Underzek and Verpen."

"No, no, no," said Tamar. "What you're thinking of, Hannah, is called the Koninklijk Laboratorium voor Onderzoek van Voorwerpen van Kunst en Wetenschap, and it's in The Hague." She glided over the minefield of Dutch words without hesitation and in a perfect accent.

"Does Tamar speak Dutch?" I asked, looking right at her.

"Yes," she answered, "Tamar speaks Dutch, because she learnt it at her Dutch grandmother's knee—Daddy's mother. But," she continued, shaking a finger gently at Hannah, though really speaking to me, "I'm going to Brussels, to study restoration at the Institut Central des Beaux-Arts, or, if Fascism flies out the window in Italy between now and next year, to the Istituto Nazionale per il Restauro, in Rome."

When she realized that her recitation of the names of these formidable institutes, each in its own language, might have seemed ostentatious, she blushed.

Emboldened nearly to giddiness, the fat boy interjected, "We went to Rome. We ate shiski ba there, and the streets are made of water."

"That's *Venice, stupid,*" said one of the red-haired girls. "And what is shiski ba?"

"Shiski ba," answered the fat boy, guilelessly, "is roasted meat on a stick. The Turks sell it in the park."

"Bob," I offered, by way of instruction. A silence followed, during which the poor boy looked at me blankly.

"Richard," he said, sending the four cousins (who knew him well) into a fit of hysteria. Tamar tried not to laugh, because she knew that he hung on her every gesture and word.

To change the subject, I challenged Tamar. "Do you really think," I said, "that you will be able to study on the Continent?"

She shrugged her shoulders and smiled in a way that belied her age. "I'll do the best I can," she answered. "Even if there is a war, it will have an end. I'll still be young, and I'll start again."

My eyes opened at this. I don't know exactly why; perhaps it was that I imagined her in the future and became entranced with the possibility that I might encounter her then—in some faraway place where affection could run unrestrained. But I wanted to steer things away from art, war, and love.

So, while constantly fending off the quixotic charges of the woolly-haired boy (without ever really looking at him), I told a long story about Palestine. Because they were children, more or less, I told them anything I wanted to tell them. Until long after the adults had left for the living room, I spoke of impossible battles between Jews and Bedouins, of feats of endurance which made me reel merely in imagining them, of horses that flew, and golden shafts of light, pillars of fire, miracles here and there, the wonders of spoken Hebrew, and the lions that guarded the banks and post offices of Jerusalem—in short, anything which seemed as if it might be believed.

Tamar alternated between belief and disbelief with the satisfying rhythm of a blade turning back and forth over a whetstone. She was weaving soft acceptance and sparkling disdain together in a tapestry which I feared she would throw right over my head. She did this in a most delicate cross-examination, the object of which was to draw out more of the tale for the sake of the children, to satisfy her own curiosity, to mock me gently, and to continue—by entrapment and release—the feeling we had that, though we were still, we were dancing.

"Why," she asked, "did you not get water from the Bedouins that you captured, if you had already gone without it for ten days?"

"Ah!" I said, holding up my finger in the same way she had done with Hannah. "I was only able to capture them because they themselves had run out of water, and were thirstier than I was. And I did not capture them with a gun but by giving a graphic dissertation on European fountains; they were especially taken with my description of the Diana fountain in Bushy Park, and I believe that they would have followed me anywhere after I told them what goes on in the Place de la Concorde."

"What is it like to be a British Jew in Palestine?" asked Hannah, earnestly, and with such *Weltschmerz*[9] that it was as if an alpine storm cloud had rolled over the table.

"What is it like? It's like being an Italian Negro in Ethiopia,[10]

---

9   *Weltschmerz:* feeling of sorrow or pain; world weariness. [German]

10   **an Italian Negro in Ethiopia:** that is, you may seem to fit in because of your ethnic background, but your nationality makes it difficult.

or"—I looked at Tamar—"like living in a continuous production of 'Romeo and Juliet.'" I had meant the allusion to "Romeo and Juliet" to be purely illustrative, but with a life of its own it turned Tamar as red as a throbbing coal, and I, a generation apart, nearly followed suit. I was caught in my own springe, enchanted—yet never really in danger, for not only did her father come to fetch me back into the world of adults but I had run those rapids before, and knew the still and deep water at their end.

I recall exactly how the children were sitting when I left them, poised to explode in gossip as soon as I had disappeared—it is likely that in my absence I was cut to ribbons by the woolly-haired boy, and perhaps deservedly so. As Tamar's father and I climbed a broad staircase to the library, where we would discuss business, I remembered the opera singer with whom I had once fallen in love. Her voice was like liquid or a jewel. I have not since heard such a beautiful voice. But she was, oddly enough, almost unknown. I went to Covent Garden to find out in what productions she would sing. Her name was Erika, and when I inquired of the old man at the ticket office I found that he, too, was in love with her.

"I'm too old," he said, "and you're too young." I knew that this was true, and I must have looked pained, because he grabbed me through the ticket window and said, "Don't you see, it's much better that way!"

"I see nothing," I said. "If that's better, then I'm sorry to be alive."

"Wait," he said, and laughed. "You'll see. It's sweeter, much sweeter."

I went to the opera that season two dozen times just to see and hear Erika of the liquid voice. I wanted, despite the fact that I was fifteen, to marry her immediately, to run away to Brazil or Argentina, to take her with me to the South Seas, etc., etc., etc. It had been unspeakable torture to watch her on a brilliantly lighted stage, singing in a way that fired up all my emotions.

But by the time I met Tamar, I knew that a lighted stage is often best left untouched, and I knew, further, that all connections are temporary, and, therefore, can be enjoyed in their fullness even after the most insubstantial touch—if only one knows how. I was, that night, in a dream within a dream. I was young again in a room of bright colors and laughter; and all the time the dark image of a smoky continent called me away and threatened to tear me apart. I did not know then that there is no contradiction in such contradictions; they are made for one another; without them, we would have nothing to lose and nothing to love.

Tamar was the most lovely girl—and had it not been for that delicate and slim bit of silver wire, I might not have known her as well as I did. Her father agreed to the scheme, but then the scheme collapsed, and the world collapsed soon after. Six years of war. Most of the Jews did not survive. Most of the paintings did. In six years of war, there was probably not a day when I did not think of the time when I had had to sit at the children's table, in a world of vulnerable beauty. Perhaps things are most beautiful when they are not quite real; when you look upon a scene as an outsider, and come to possess it in its entirety and forever; when you live the present with the lucidity and feeling of memory; when, for want of connection, the world deepens and becomes art.

QUESTIONS FOR DISCUSSION

1. What do we learn about the rather complex narrator from what he says about himself?

2. What adjectives would you use to describe the narrator at various points in the story?

3. The narrator says that he admired the bravery of the Jewish upper class in London and chafed at their blindness. What are the reasons for his feelings?

4. The narrator remarks on the contradiction between being in a "room of bright colors and laughter" and the "dark image of a smoky continent." Explain what you think he means by saying that without such contradictions "we would have nothing to lose and nothing to love."

5. What is the tone of the story?

TOPICS FOR WRITING

1. In the next-to-last paragraph of the story, the narrator states, "a lighted stage is often best left untouched." Analyze the meaning of this statement in the context of the story and in relation to your own experience of life. (Note that at one point in the story the narrator describes the house as "lit like a theater.")

2. Analyze the many contrasts in this story, including the contrasts in mood.

3. Briefly, analyze the conflict or conflicts in this story.

4. Have you ever felt instantly attracted to someone? In your journal, write about the attraction and the qualities that drew you to the person you found attractive.

LIKE THE SUN

R. K. NARAYAN (born 1906)

R. K. Narayan was born in Madras, India, and received a degree in 1930 from Maharaja's College, now the University of Mysore. His fiction and essays are written in English, and his novels are set in the fictional village of Malgudi. Among his novels are *The English Teacher* (1945); *The Financial Expert* (1951, 1953); *Waiting for the Mahatma* (1955); *The Guide* (1958), often considered his best novel, in which a former convict is mistaken for a holy man when he arrives in Malgudi; *The Man-Eater of Malgudi* (1961); *The Vendor of Sweets* (1967); *The Painter of Signs* (1976); and *A Tiger for Malgudi* (1983), which is narrated by a tiger. His short story collections include *Gods, Demons, and Others* (1965) and *Under the Banyan Tree and Other Stories* (1985). *My Days* (1974) is a memoir. In 1978, he published a translation of the *Mahabharata*, an Indian epic.

Many of Narayan's stories are gently humorous and focus on ordinary middle-class characters who experience disappointment or failure but who grow in knowledge. The main character in "Like the Sun"—a teacher—is condemned by the headmaster of his school to suffer through an excruciating evening.

■

Truth, Sekhar reflected, is like the sun. I suppose no human being can ever look it straight in the face without blinking or being dazed. He realized that, morning till night, the essence of human relationships consisted in tempering truth so that it might not shock. This day he set apart as a unique day—at least one day in the year we must give and take absolute Truth whatever may happen. Otherwise life is not worth living. The day ahead seemed to him full of possibilities. He told no one of his experiment. It was a quiet resolve, a secret pact between him and eternity.

The very first test came while his wife served him his morning meal. He showed hesitation over a titbit, which she had thought was her culinary masterpiece. She asked, "Why, isn't it good?" At other times he would have said, considering her feelings in the matter, "I feel full-up, that's all." But today he said, "It isn't good. I'm unable to swallow it." He saw her wince and said to himself, Can't be helped. Truth is like the sun.

His next trial was in the common room when one of his colleagues came up and said, "Did you hear of the death of so and so? Don't you think it a pity?" "No," Sekhar answered. "He was such a fine man—" the other began. But Sekhar cut him short with: "Far from it. He always struck me as a mean and selfish brute."

During the last period when he was teaching geography for Third Form A,[1] Sekhar received a note from the headmaster: "Please see me before you go home." Sekhar said to himself: It must be about these horrible test papers. A hundred papers in the boys' scrawls; he had shirked this work for weeks, feeling all the time as if a sword were hanging over his head.

The bell rang and the boys burst out of the class.

Sekhar paused for a moment outside the headmaster's room to button up his coat; that was another subject the headmaster always sermonized about.

He stepped in with a very polite "Good evening, sir."

The headmaster looked up at him in a very friendly manner and asked, "Are you free this evening?"

Sekhar replied, "Just some outing which I have promised the children at home—"

"Well, you can take them out another day. Come home with me now."

---

1 **Third Form A:** a *form* is a grade or class of pupils in a British secondary school.

"Oh . . . yes, sir, certainly . . ." And then he added timidly, "Anything special, sir?"

"Yes," replied the headmaster, smiling to himself . . . "You didn't know my weakness for music?"

"Oh, yes, sir . . ."

"I've been learning and practicing secretly, and now I want you to hear me this evening. I've engaged a drummer and a violinist to accompany me—this is the first time I'm doing it full-dress and I want your opinion. I know it will be valuable."

Sekhar's taste in music was well known. He was one of the most dreaded music critics in the town. But he never anticipated his musical inclinations would lead him to this trial. . . . "Rather a surprise for you, isn't it?" asked the headmaster. "I've spent a fortune on it behind closed doors. . . ." They started for the headmaster's house. "God hasn't given me a child, but at least let him not deny me the consolation of music," the headmaster said, pathetically, as they walked. He incessantly chattered about music: how he began one day out of sheer boredom; how his teacher at first laughed at him, and then gave him hope; how his ambition in life was to forget himself in music.

At home the headmaster proved very ingratiating. He sat Sekhar on a red silk carpet, set before him several dishes of delicacies, and fussed over him as if he were a son-in-law of the house. He even said, "Well, you must listen with a free mind. Don't worry about these test papers." He added half humorously, "I will give you a week's time."

"Make it ten days, sir," Sekhar pleaded.

"All right, granted," the headmaster said generously. Sekhar felt really relieved now—he would attack them at the rate of ten a day and get rid of the nuisance.

The headmaster lighted incense sticks. "Just to create the right atmosphere," he explained. A drummer and a violinist, already seated on a Rangoon mat, were waiting for him. The headmaster sat down between them like a professional at a concert, cleared his throat, and began an alapana,[2] and paused to ask, "Isn't it good Kalyani?" Sekhar pretended not to have heard the question. The headmaster went on to sing a full song composed by Thyagaraja and followed it with two more. All the time the headmaster was singing, Sekhar went on commenting within himself, He croaks like a dozen frogs. He is bellowing like a buffalo. Now he sounds like loose window shutters in a storm.

---

2 **alapana:** in south Indian music, an introduction to a song.

The incense sticks burnt low. Sekhar's head throbbed with the medley of sounds that had assailed his ear-drums for a couple of hours now. He felt half stupefied. The headmaster had gone nearly hoarse, when he paused to ask, "Shall I go on?" Sekhar replied, "Please don't, sir, I think this will do. . . ." The headmaster looked stunned. His face was beaded with perspiration. Sekhar felt the greatest pity for him. But he felt he could not help it. No judge delivering a sentence felt more pained and helpless. Sekhar noticed that the headmaster's wife peeped in from the kitchen, with eager curiosity. The drummer and the violinist put away their burdens with an air of relief. The headmaster removed his spectacles, mopped his brow, and asked, "Now, come out with your opinion."

"Can't I give it tomorrow, sir?" Sekhar asked tentatively.

"No. I want it immediately—your frank opinion. Was it good?"

"No, sir . . ." Sekhar replied.

"Oh! . . . Is there any use continuing my lessons?"

"Absolutely none, sir . . ." Sekhar said with his voice trembling. He felt very unhappy that he could not speak more soothingly. Truth, he reflected, required as much strength to give as to receive.

All the way home he felt worried. He felt that his official life was not going to be smooth sailing hereafter. There were questions of increment and confirmation and so on, all depending upon the headmaster's goodwill. All kinds of worries seemed to be in store for him. . . . Did not Harischandra[3] lose his throne, wife, child, because he would speak nothing less than the absolute Truth whatever happened?

At home his wife served him with a sullen face. He knew she was still angry with him for his remark of the morning. Two casualties for today, Sekhar said to himself. If I practice it for a week, I don't think I shall have a single friend left.

He received a call from the headmaster in his classroom next day. He went up apprehensively.

"Your suggestion was useful. I have paid off the music master. No one would tell me the truth about my music all these days. Why such antics at my age! Thank you. By the way, what about those test papers?"

"You gave me ten days, sir, for correcting them."

---

3 **Harischandra:** (1850–1885), an Indian poet, critic, and journalist.

"Oh, I've reconsidered it. I must positively have them here tomorrow. . . ." A hundred papers in a day! That meant all night's sitting up! "Give me a couple of days, sir . . ."

"No. I must have them tomorrow morning. And remember, every paper must be thoroughly scrutinized."

"Yes, sir," Sekhar said, feeling that sitting up all night with a hundred test papers was a small price to pay for the luxury of practicing Truth.

QUESTIONS FOR DISCUSSION

1. What would be gained or lost if this story had been told from a different point of view?

2. Why does Sekhar ask the headmaster whether he can wait until tomorrow to give his opinion on the headmaster's singing?

3. Sekhar, at the end of the story, feels that practicing Truth is a luxury. Would you agree? Explain.

TOPICS FOR WRITING

1. Keep a journal for several days in which you record times you tempered the truth "so that it might not shock."

2. In a short paragraph analyze the tone of the story.

THE LEMON TREE BILLIARDS HOUSE

CEDRIC YAMANAKA (born 1963)

Cedric Yamanaka was born in Honolulu, Hawaii. As a kid growingup in Kalihi (a working-class neighborhood in Honolulu), he had dreams of being the quarterback for the Dallas Cowboys or a drummer in a rock band. He never had any real dreams of being a writer.

Yamanaka graduated from the University of Hawaii with a B.A. in English in 1986. While at the university, he won the Ernest Hemingway Memorial Award for Crerative Writing. At Boston University, where he received an M.A., he was awarded the Helen Deutsch Fellowship for Creative Writing in 1987. After returning to Hawaii, he worked as a radio journalist and a television news reporter.

His fiction has appeared in a number of publications. In 1992, he won the *Honolulu* magazine fiction contest. In 1996, "The Lemon Tree Billards House" was adapted for film, and Yamanaka wrote the screenplay. The film won the award for Best Hawaiian Film at the prestigious Hawaii International Film Festival.

Yamanaka continues to work on several writing projects, including a novel.

■

The Lemon Tree Billiards[1] House is on the first floor of an old concrete building on King Street, between Aloha Electronics and Uncle Phil's Flowers. The building is old and the pool hall isn't very large—just nine tables, a ceiling fan and a soda machine. No one seems to know how the place got its name. Some say it used to be a Korean Bar. Others say it was a funeral home. But all seem to agree that it has a lousy name for a pool hall. At one point, someone circulated a petition requesting the name be changed. But Mr. Kong, the proud owner, wouldn't budge. He said his pool hall would always be called the Lemon Tree Billiards House.

Mr. Kong keeps his rates very reasonable. For two dollars an hour, you can hit all of the balls you want. One day, I was in there playing eight-ball[2] with a 68-year-old parking attendant. The guy played pretty well—I was squeezing for a while—but he missed a tough slice and left me enough openings to clear the table and sink the eight-ball. I won twenty bucks.

Another guy walked up to me. He had a moustache, baseball cap and a flannel shirt.

"My name Hamilton," he said. "I ain't too good—but what—you like play?"

I ain't too good. *Sure.*

"My name's Mitch," I said. "Let's play."

We agreed on fifty bucks. Hamilton racked the balls. I broke. It was a good one. The sound of the balls cracking against each other was like a hundred glass jars exploding.

As three striped balls—the nine, twelve, and fifteen—shot into three different pockets, I noticed a goodlooking girl in a black dress sitting on a stool in the corner. I don't know if I was imagining it or not but I thought I caught her looking my way. I missed an easy shot on the side pocket. I'd burned my finger cooking *saimin* and couldn't get a good grip on the cue stick.

"Oh, too bad," said Hamilton. "Hard luck! I tot you had me deah . . ." He was what I call "a talker." The kind of guy who can't

1 **billiards:** any of several games played with hard balls that are propelled by a cue stick on a table covered with felt. Pocket billiards, or pool, is played on a table with six pockets.

2 **eight ball:** a game in which one player must pocket all of either the solid-color balls or the striped ones before being permitted to attempt the pocketing of the eight ball, which wins. Before each shot, a player must "call the shot"; that is, he or she identifies the ball and the pocket in which it is to drop.

keep his mouth shut. The kind of guy who treats a game of pool like a radio call-in show.

Anyway, Hamilton hit four balls in but stalled on the fifth. I eventually won the game.

Afterwards, the girl in the black dress walked up to me.

"Hi," she said, smiling.

"Hello," I said.

"You're pretty good," she said.

"Thanks."

"You wanna play my dad?"

"Who's your dad?"

"You wanna play or not?"

"Who is he?"

"He'll give you five hundred bucks if you beat him . . ."

"Let's go."

I'm a pool hustler and the Lemon Tree Billiards House is my turf. You see, I've been playing pool all my life. It's the only thing I know how to do. My dad taught me the game before they threw him in jail. I dropped out of school, left home, and traveled around the country challenging other pool players. I've played the best. Now I'm home.

All right, all right. I'm not a pool hustler. I'm a freshman at the University of Hawaii. And my dad's not in jail. He's an accountant. And I never challenged players around the country. I did play a game in Waipahu[3] once.

I have been playing pool for awhile, though. Sometimes I do real well. Sometimes, I don't. That's how the game is for me. Four things can happen when I pick up a cue stick. One, sometimes I feel like I'll win and I win. Two, sometimes I feel like I'll win and I lose. Three, sometimes, I feel like I'll lose and I'll lose. Four, sometimes I feel like I'll lose and I win.

I'll tell you one thing, though. I could've been a better pool player if I hadn't been cursed. Yes, cursed.

It all happened back when I was seven years old. My dad had taken me to a beach house. I'm not sure where it was. Somewhere near Malaekahana,[4] maybe. I remember walking along the beach and seeing some large boulders. I began climbing on the rocks, trying to get a good look at the ocean and the crashing waves. The view was

3 **Waipahu:** a town on the island of Oahu.

4 **Malaekahana:** a recreation area on the ocean in northern Oahu.

stunning. The water was so blue. And off shore, I thought I spotted some whales playing in the surf.

All of a sudden, my father came running down the beach. "Mitch!" he said. "Get off da rocks! Da rocks sacred! No climb up deah! No good!"

Ever since that day, I've lived with a curse. One day in the eighth grade, I dropped a touchdown pass and we lost a big intramural football game. I smashed my first car three minutes after I drove it off the lot. My first girlfriend left me for a guy in prison she read about in the papers. I'm the kind of guy who will throw down four queens in a poker game, only to watch helplessly as some clown tosses down four kings. If I buy something at the market, it'll go on sale the next day.

It hasn't been easy. The only thing I do okay is play eight-ball. But I could've been better. If it just weren't for this curse.

I don't know why I agreed to play pool with this strange girl's father. Maybe it was because she was so beautiful. The best looking woman I've ever seen. Six feet, two hundred pounds, hairy legs, moustache. Okay. Okay. So she wasn't *that* beautiful. Let's just say she was kind of average.

Anyway, we got into her car and she drove towards the Waianae coast. She had one of those big, black Cadillacs you saw in the seventies. The kind Jack Lord[5] used to drive to Iolani Palace. In about a half hour or so, we wound up at a large beach house with watermills and bronze buddhas in the yard. Everywhere you looked, you saw trees. Mango, avocado, papaya, banana.

"My dad likes to plant things," the girl explained.

We walked past a rock garden and a *koi*[6] pond and she led me into a room with a pool table. There were dozens of cues lined up neatly on the wall, just like at the Lemon Tree Billiards House.

"You can grab a stick," the girl said. "I'll go get my dad."

In a few minutes, I realized why she didn't want to tell me who her father was. I was standing face to face with Locust Cordero. *The* Locust Cordero. All 6–5, 265 pounds of him. Wearing of all things, a purple tuxedo and a red carnation in his lapel. Locust Cordero, who stood trial for the murder-for-hire deaths of three Salt Lake gamblers several years back. I was about to play eight-ball with a hitman.

---

5 **Jack Lord:** (1922–1998) the starring actor in the television series *Hawaii Five-O*, which was filmed in Honolulu from 1968 to 1980 and featured Lord as police investigator Steve McGarrett.

6 *koi:* carp. [Japanese]

"Howzit," he said. "Mahalos[7] fo coming. My name Locust."

What should I say? I know who you are? I've heard of you? I've seen your mug shots on T.V.? Congratulations on your recent acquittal? Nice tuxedo?

"Nice to meet you, sir," I said, settling on the conservative. "I'm Mitch."

We shook hands. He wore a huge jade ring on his finger.

"My daughter says you pretty good . . ."

"I try, sir."

"How you like my tuxedo?" he said.

"Nice," I said.

"Shaka, ah?" he said, running his hands over the material. "Silk, brah. Jus bought 'em. What size you?"

"What?"

"What size you?" he repeated, opening up a closet. I was stunned. There must have been two dozen tuxedos in there. All sizes. All colors. Black, white, maroon, blue, red, pink. "Heah," said Locust, handing me a gold one. "Try put dis beauty on . . ."

"Uh," I said. "How about the black one?"

Again, I was leaning towards the conservative.

"Whatevahs," said Locust, shrugging.

I changed in the bathroom. It took me a while because I'd never worn a tuxedo before. When I walked out, Locust smiled.

"Sharp," he said. "Look at us. Now we really look like pool players . . ."

Locust chalked his cue stick. He was so big, the stick looked like a tooth pick in his hands.

"Break 'em, Mitch."

"Yes, sir."

I walked to the table and broke. I did it real fast. I don't like to think about my shots too long. That always messes me up. *Crack!* Not bad. Two solid balls shot into the right corner pocket.

"Das too bad," said Locust, shaking his head.

"Why's that, sir?" I asked.

"Cause," said Locust. "I hate to lose."

One day, not too long before, I'd visited an exorcist. To get rid of my curse. He was an old Hawaiian man in his late forties or early fifties,

---

7 **Mahalos:** thanks. [Hawaiian]

recommended to me by a friend. When I called for an appointment, he said he couldn't fit me in. There were a lot of folks out there with problems, I guessed. I told him it was an emergency.

"Okay, come ovah," he said. "But hurry up."

I drove to his house. He lived in Palolo Valley. I was very scared. What would happen? I could see it now. As soon as I walked into the room, the man would scream and run away from me. He'd tell me he saw death and destruction written all over my face. The wind would blow papers all over his room and I'd be speaking weird languages I had never heard before and blood and mucous would pour out my mouth.

But nothing like that happened. I walked into his house, expecting to see him chanting or praying. Instead, he was sitting behind a *koa* desk in a Munsingwear shirt and green polyester pants.

"Dis bettah be good," he said. "I went cancel my tee time at da Ala Wai fo you . . ."

I smiled. I told him my plight. I started from the beginning—telling him about the day I climbed on the rocks and the bad luck I've had ever since.

"You ain't cursed," the man said. He bent down to pick something up from the floor. What was it? An ancient amulet? A charm? None of the above. It was a golf club. An eight iron. "Da mind is one very powerful ting," he said, waving the right iron around like a magician waving a wand. "It can make simple tings difficult and difficult tings simple."

"What about the rocks?" I said.

"Tink positive," the man said. "You one negative buggah. Da only curse is in yo mind."

That's it? No reading scripture. No chanting?

"I tell you one ting, brah," the Hawaiian man said. "One day, you going encountah one challenge. If you beat em, da curse going to *pau*.[8] But, if you lose, da rest of yo life going shrivel up like one slug aftah you pour salt on top . . ."

"Anything else?" I said.

"Yeah," said the Hawaiian man. "You owe me twenty bucks."

Locust and I had played ten games. We'd agreed on eleven. I'd won five, he'd won five. In between, his daughter brought us fruit punch and smoked marlin. It was already dark. I had an Oceanography test the next day.

---

8 *pau:* end. [Hawaiian]

On the final game, I hit an incredible shot—the cue ball[9] jumping over Locust's ball like a fullback leaping over a tackler and hitting the seven into the side pocket. This seemed to piss Locust off. He came right back with a beauty of his own—a masse I couldn't believe. In a masse, the cue ball does bizarre things on the table after being hit—like weaving between balls as if it has a mind of its own. Those are the trick shots you see on T.V. Anyway, Locust hit a masse, where the cue ball hit not one, not two, not three, but four of his balls into four different holes. *Come on!* I was convinced Locust could make the cue ball spell his name across the green velvet sky of the pool table.

Pretty soon, it was just me, Locust, and the eight ball. I looked at Locust, real fast, and he stared at me like a starving man sizing up a Diner's chicken *katsu*[10] plate lunch. I took a shot but my arm felt like a lead pipe and I missed everything. Locust took a deep breath, blew his shot, and swore in three different languages. It was my turn.

And then I realized it. This was the moment that would make or break me. The challenge the exorcist guy was talking about. I had to win.

I measured the table, paused, and said the words that would change my life and save me from shrivelling up like a slug with salt poured on it.

"Eight ball. Corner pocket."

I would have to be careful. Gentle. It was a tough slice to the right corner pocket. If I hit the cue ball too hard, it could fall into the wrong pocket. That would be a scratch. I would lose.

I took a deep breath, cocked my stick, and aimed. I hit the cue ball softly. From here, everything seemed to move in slow motion. The cue ball tapped the eight ball and the eight ball seemed to take hours to roll towards the hole. Out of the corner of my eye, I saw Locust's daughter standing up from her seat, her hands covering her mouth.

Clack. *Plop.*

The ball fell into the hole. The curse was lifted. I had won. I would have been a happy man if I hadn't been so damned scared.

Locust walked up to me, shaking his head. He reached into his pocket. Oh, no. Here it comes. He was gonna take out his gun, shoot me, and bury my body at some deserted beach. Goodbye, cruel world. Thanks for the memories . . .

---

9   **cue ball:** the ball struck by the cue, as distinguished from the other balls.

10   *katsu:* breaded, deep-fried cutlet. [Japanese]

"I no can remembah da last time I wen lose," he said, pulling out his wallet and handing me five crispy one hundred dollar bills. "Mahalos fo da game."

Locust asked me to stay and talk for awhile. We sat on straw chairs next to the pool table. The place was dark except for several gas-lit torches, hissing like leaky tires. Hanging on the walls were fishing nets and dried, preserved fish, lobsters, and turtles.

"You must be wond'ring why we wearing dese tuxedos," said Locust.

"Yeah," I said.

"Well, dis whole night, it's kinda one big deal fo me." Locust leaned towards me. "You see, brah, I nevah leave my house in five years . . ."

"Why?" I said. I couldn't believe it.

"All my life, evry'body been scared of me," said Locust, sighing. "Ev'rywheah I go, people look at me funny. Dey whispah behind my back . . ."

"But . . ."

"Lemme tell you someting," he continued. "Dey went try me fo murder coupla times. Both times, da jury said I was innocent. Still, people no like Locust around. Dey no like see me. And das why, I never step foot outta dis place."

"Forgive me for saying so, sir," I said. "But that's kinda sad. That's no way to live . . ."

"Oh, it ain't dat bad," said Locust. "I play pool. I go in da ocean, spear *uhu*.[11] I trow net fo mullet. Once in a while, I go in da mountains behind da house and shoot one pig . . ."

"But don't you ever miss getting out and walking around the city. Experiencing life?"

I was getting nervous again. I mean, here I was, giving advice on how to live to Locust Cordero. After I had just beaten the guy at eight-ball.

"Whasso great about walking around da streets of da city?" said Locust, after awhile. "People shooting and stabbing each othah. Talking stink about each othah. Stealing each othah's husbands and wives. Breaking each othah's hearts . . ."

"You scared?" I said, pressing my luck.

---

11   *uhu:* parrot fish. [Hawaiian]

"Yeah," said Locust, looking me straight in the eye. "I guess I am."

We didn't say anything for awhile. I could hear the waves of the ocean breaking on the beach.

"So," said Locust, shifting in his seat. "Where you went learn fo shoot pool?"

"The Lemon Tree Billiards House," I said.

"Da Lemon Tree Billards House?" Locust said, shaking his head. "What kine name dat? Sound like one funeral home . . ."

"Sir," I said. "I'm sorry. Can I say something?"

"Sure."

"You're living your life like a prisoner. You might as well have been convicted of murder and locked in jail."

Yeah, sometimes it seems I just don't know when to shut up.

"Evah since I was one kid, I had hard luck," said Locust, moving closer to me and whispering. "You see, I'm cursed . . ."

"You're what?" I said, surprised.

"I'm cursed," Locust repeated, raising his voice. "Jeez, fo one young kid, you got lousy hearing, ah? Must be all dat loud music you buggahs listen to nowadays."

"How'd you get cursed?" I said.

"One day, when I was one kid, I was climbing some rocks looking out at da ocean. Down Malaekahana side. All of a sudden, my brud-dah start screaming, 'Get down from deah. No good. Da rocks sacred.' "

I couldn't believe it. Locust and I were cursed by the same rocks. We were curse brothers.

"Da ting's beat me," said Locust, shaking his head.

"You're talking like a loser."

"A what?" said Locust, getting out of his chair.

"Locust," I said, my voice cracking. "I lived with the same curse and I beat it . . ."

"How?" said Locust, sitting back down. "I tried everything. Hawaiian salt. Ti^{12} leaves. Da works . . ."

"You gotta believe in yourself."

"How you do dat?"

"With your mind," I said. "See, the first thing you gotta do is meet a challenge and beat it," I said. "Go outside. Walk the streets. Meet people . . ."

---

12 *Ti:* a tropical, palmlike plant.

"You evah stop fo tink how dangerous da world is?" said Locust. "Tink about it. How many things out deah are ready, waiting, fo screw you up. Death, sickness, corruption, greed, old age . . ."

It was scary. Locust was starting to make sense.

"I don't know," I finally said.

"Tink about it," said Locust. "Tink about it."

One day, several weeks later, I was playing eight-ball at the Lemon Tree Billiards House. Several people were arguing about the source of an unusual smell. Some said it came from a cardboard box filled with rotten *choy sum* outside on the sidewalk in front of the pool hall. Others said it was Kona winds blowing in the pungent smell of *taegu* from Yuni's Bar B-Q. Still others said the peculiar smell came from Old Man Rivera, who sat in a corner eating a lunch he had made at home. Too much *patis*—fish sauce—in his *sari sari.*

"If you like good smell," said Mr. Kong, the owner of the Lemon Tree Billiards House. "Go orchid farm. If you like play pool, come da Lemon Tree Billiards House."

I was on table number three with a young Japanese guy with short hair. He had dark glasses and wore a black suit. He looked like he was in the *yakuza.*[13]

I had already beaten three guys. I was on a roll. It gets like that every now and then. When you know you can't miss.

The Yakuza guy never smiled. And everytime he missed a shot, he swore at himself. Pretty soon, he started to hit the balls very hard— thrusting his cue stick like a samurai spearing an opponent. He was off, though, and I eventually won the game.

"You saw how I beat the *Yakuza* guy?" I said to Mr. Kong, who was now on a stepladder unscrewing a burned-out lightbulb.

"*Yakuza* guy?" said Mr. Kong. "What *yakuza* guy?"

"The Japanese guy in the suit . . ." I said.

"Oh," said Mr. Kong, laughing like crazy. "You talking about Yatsu! Das my neighbor. He ain't no *yakuza*. He one pre-school teachah . . ."

Just then, Locust Cordero walked into the Lemon Tree Billiards House. Mr. Kong stopped laughing. Everyone stopped their games. No one said a word. The only sound you heard was the ticking of a clock on the wall.

---

13 **yakuza:** a criminal organization or someone alleged to be involved in organized
crime. [Japanese]

"Mitch," said Locust. "I went take yo advice. I no like live like one prisonah no moah . . ."

I was speechless.

"You know what dey say," said Locust. "Feel like one five hundred pound bait lifted from my shoulders . . ."

"Weight," I said.

"Fo what?" said Locust, obviously confused.

"No, no," I said. "Five hundred pound *weight*. Not bait . . ."

"Whatevahs," said Locust. "Da curse is gone . . ."

He walked over to Mr. Kong's finest tables, ran his thick fingers over the smooth wood, and looked into the deep pockets like a child staring down a mysterious well.

"Eight-ball?" he asked, turning to me.

"Yeah," I said, smiling. "Yeah, sure."

QUESTIONS FOR DISCUSSION

1. How does the author arouse your interest in the first part of the story?

2. Why do you think the narrator briefly provides a false biography in the story?

3. Why is Mitch a little afraid of beating Locust Cordero at pool?

4. How are the narrator and Cordero alike?

5. When does your attitude toward Cordero begin to change?

6. How do the people the narrator plays pool with help to provide suspense?

TOPICS FOR WRITING

1. Analyze the structure of the story, including the exposition, rising action, climax, falling action, and resolution.

2. In an essay, discuss how the tone of the story might have changed if the story had been told from Cordero's point of view.

3. If you have encountered an unusual person on the street, on a bus, or in another public place, write a character sketch of that person from the first-person point of view. (Alternatively, you could depict that person in a poem.)

WHY I LIVE AT THE P.O.

EUDORA WELTY (born 1909)

Eudora Welty told of the early influences on her writing in her book *One Writer's Beginnings* (1984), the outcome of a series of lectures she gave at Harvard University. The book won an American Book Award and a National Book Critics Circle Award. Born and raised in Jackson, Mississippi, Welty was brought up in a family of readers. She attended Mississippi State College for Women, received a B.A. from the University of Wisconsin in 1929, and attended Columbia University Graduate School of Business.

She worked for the Works Progress Administration (WPA) during the Depression, traveling through Mississippi taking photographs and interviewing all classes of people. Not until 1971 were the results of her work published, however; *One Time, One Place: Mississippi in the Depression; a Snapshot Album* contains many of the photographs and was republished in 1996. Her first collection of stories, *A Curtain of Green,* was published in 1941 and contains some of her most famous stories, including "A Worn Path" and "The Key." *Selected Stories* (1953, 1992) contains all of the stories in *A Curtain of Green* and *The Wide Net, and Other Stories* (1943).

Among her other works are the novels *Delta Wedding* (1946), *The Ponder Heart* (1954), *Losing Battles* (1970), and *The Optimist's Daughter* (1972), which won the Pulitzer Prize in fiction. Welty has won many other awards and received honorary degrees from many universities.

Welty has been praised for her characterizations, her comic vision, and her portrayals of women's lives. "Why I Live at the P.O." was turned down by six magazines before finally finding a publisher. It is the story she has been most often asked to read aloud at gatherings of students and others.

■

Iwas getting along fine with Mama, Papa-Daddy and Uncle Rondo until my sister Stella-Rondo just separated from her husband and came back home again. Mr. Whitaker! Of course I went with Mr. Whitaker first, when he first appeared here in China Grove, taking "Pose Yourself" photos, and Stella-Rondo broke us up. Told him I was one-sided. Bigger on one side than the other, which is a deliberate, calculated falsehood: I'm the same. Stella-Rondo is exactly twelve months to the day younger than I am and for that reason she's spoiled.

She's always had anything in the world she wanted and then she'd throw it away. Papa-Daddy gave her this gorgeous Add-a-Pearl necklace when she was eight years old and she threw it away playing baseball when she was nine, with only two pearls.

So as soon as she got married and moved away from home the first thing she did was separate! From Mr. Whitaker! This photographer with the popeyes she said she trusted. Came home from one of those towns up in Illinois and to our complete surprise brought this child of two.

Mama said she like to made her drop dead for a second. "Here you had this marvelous blonde child and never so much as wrote your mother a word about it," says Mama. "I'm thoroughly ashamed of you." But of course she wasn't.

Stella-Rondo just calmly takes off this *hat,* I wish you could see it. She says, "Why, Mama, Shirley-T.'s adopted, I can prove it."

"How?" says Mama, but all I says was, "H'm!" There I was over the hot stove, trying to stretch two chickens over five people and a completely unexpected child into the bargain, without one moment's notice.

"What do you mean—'H'm!'?" says Stella-Rondo, and Mama says, "I heard that, Sister."

I said that oh, I didn't mean a thing, only that whoever Shirley-T. was, she was the spit-image of Papa-Daddy if he'd cut off his beard, which of course he'd never do in the world. Papa-Daddy's Mama's papa and sulks.

Stella-Rondo got furious! She said, "Sister, I don't need to tell you you got a lot of nerve and always did have and I'll thank you to make no future reference to my adopted child whatsoever."

"Very well," I said. "Very well, very well. Of course I noticed at once she looks like Mr. Whitaker's side too. That frown. She looks like a cross between Mr. Whitaker and Papa-Daddy."

"Well, all I can say is she isn't."

"She looks exactly like Shirley Temple to me," says Mama, but Shirley-T. just ran away from her.

So the first thing Stella-Rondo did at the table was turn Papa-Daddy against me.

"Papa-Daddy," she says. He was trying to cut up his meat. "Papa-Daddy!" I was taken completely by surprise. Papa-Daddy is about a million years old and's got this long-long beard. "Papa-Daddy, Sister says she fails to understand why you don't cut off your beard."

So Papa-Daddy l-a-y-s down his knife and fork! He's real rich. Mama says he is, he says he isn't. So he says, "Have I heard correctly? You don't understand why I don't cut off my beard?"

"Why," I says, "Papa-Daddy, of course I understand, I did not say any such of a thing, the idea!"

He says, "Hussy!"

I says, "Papa-Daddy, you know I wouldn't any more want you to cut off your beard than the man in the moon. It was the farthest thing from my mind! Stella-Rondo sat there and made that up while she was eating breast of chicken."

But he says, "So the postmistress fails to understand why I don't cut off my beard. Which job I got you through my influence with the government. 'Bird's nest'—is that what you call it?"

Not that it isn't the next to smallest P.O. in the entire state of Mississippi.

I says, "Oh, Papa-Daddy," I says, "I didn't say any such of a thing, I never dreamed it was a bird's nest, I have always been grateful though this is the next to smallest P.O. in the state of Mississippi, and I do not enjoy being referred to as a hussy by my own grandfather."

But Stella-Rondo says, "Yes, you did say it too. Anybody in the world could of heard you, that had ears."

"Stop right there," says Mama, looking at *me*.

So I pulled my napkin straight back through the napkin ring and left the table.

As soon as I was out of the room Mama says, "Call her back, or she'll starve to death," but Papa-Daddy says, "This is the beard I started growing on the Coast when I was fifteen years old." He would of gone on till nightfall if Shirley-T. hadn't lost the Milky Way she ate in Cairo.

So Papa-Daddy says, "I am going out and lie in the hammock, and you can all sit here and remember my words: I'll never cut off my beard as long as I live, even one inch, and I don't appreciate it in you at all." Passed right by me in the hall and went straight out and got in the hammock.

It would be a holiday. It wasn't five minutes before Uncle Rondo suddenly appeared in the hall in one of Stella-Rondo's flesh-colored kimonos, all cut on the bias, like something Mr. Whitaker probably thought was gorgeous.

"Uncle Rondo!" I says. "I didn't know who that was! Where are you going?"

"Sister," he says, "get out of my way, I'm poisoned."

"If you're poisoned stay away from Papa-Daddy," I says. "Keep out of the hammock. Papa-Daddy will certainly beat you on the head if you come within forty miles of him. He thinks I deliberately said he ought to cut off his beard after he got me the P.O., and I've told him and told him and told him, and he acts like he just don't hear me. Papa-Daddy must of gone stone deaf."

"He picked a fine day to do it then," says Uncle Rondo, and before you could say "Jack Robinson" flew out in the yard.

What he'd really done, he'd drunk another bottle of that prescription. He does it every single Fourth of July as sure as shooting, and it's horribly expensive. Then he falls over in the hammock and snores. So he insisted on zigzagging right on out to the hammock, looking like a half-wit.

Papa-Daddy woke up with this horrible yell and right there without moving an inch he tried to turn Uncle Rondo against me. I heard every word he said. Oh, he told Uncle Rondo I didn't learn to read till I was eight years old and he didn't see how in the world I ever got the mail put up at the P.O., much less read it all, and he said if Uncle Rondo could only fathom the lengths he had gone to get me that job! And he said on the other hand he thought Stella-Rondo had a brilliant mind and deserved credit for getting out of town. All the time he was just lying there swinging as pretty as you please and looping out his beard, and poor Uncle Rondo was *pleading* with him to slow down the hammock, it was making him as dizzy as a witch to watch it. But that's what Papa-Daddy likes about a hammock. So Uncle Rondo was too dizzy to get turned against me for the time being. He's Mama's only brother and is a good case of a one-track mind. Ask anybody. A certified pharmacist.

Just then I heard Stella-Rondo raising the upstairs window. While she was married she got this peculiar idea that it's cooler with the windows shut and locked. So she has to raise the window before she can make a soul hear her outdoors.

So she raises the window and says, *"Oh!"* You would have thought she was mortally wounded.

Uncle Rondo and Papa-Daddy didn't even look up, but kept right on with what they were doing. I had to laugh.

I flew up the stairs and threw the door open! I says, "What in the wide world's the matter, Stella-Rondo? You mortally wounded?"

"No," she says, "I am not mortally wounded but I wish you would do me the favor of looking out that window there and telling me what you see."

So I shade my eyes and look out the window.

"I see the front yard," I says.

"Don't you see any human beings?" she says.

"I see Uncle Rondo trying to run Papa-Daddy out of the hammock," I says. "Nothing more. Naturally, it's so suffocating-hot in the house, with all the windows shut and locked, everybody who cares to stay in their right mind will have to go out and get in the hammock before the Fourth of July is over."

"Don't you notice anything different about Uncle Rondo?" asks Stella-Rondo.

"Why, no, except he's got on some terrible-looking flesh-colored contraption I wouldn't be found dead in, is all I can see," I says.

"Never mind, you won't be found dead in it, because it happens to be part of my trousseau, and Mr. Whitaker took several dozen photographs of me in it," says Stella-Rondo. "What on earth could Uncle Rondo *mean* by wearing part of my trousseau out in the broad open daylight without saying so much as 'Kiss my foot,' *knowing* I only got home this morning after my separation and hung my negligee up on the bathroom door, just as nervous as I could be?"

"I'm sure I don't know, and what do you expect me to do about it?" I says. "Jump out the window?"

"No, I expect nothing of the kind. I simply declare that Uncle Rondo looks like a fool in it, that's all," she says. "It makes me sick to my stomach."

"Well, he looks as good as he can," I says. "As good as anybody in reason could." I stood up for Uncle Rondo, please remember. And I said to Stella-Rondo, "I think I would do well not to criticize so freely if I were you and came home with a two-year-old child I had never said a word about, and no explanation whatever about my separation."

"I asked you the instant I entered this house not to refer one more time to my adopted child, and you gave me your word of honor you would not," was all Stella-Rondo would say, and started pulling out every one of her eyebrows with some cheap Kress tweezers.

So I merely slammed the door behind me and went down and made some green-tomato pickle. Somebody had to do it. Of course Mama had turned both the niggers loose; she always said no earthly power could hold one anyway on the Fourth of July, so she wouldn't even try. It turned out that Jaypan fell in the lake and came within a very narrow limit of drowning

So Mama trots in. Lifts up the lid and says, "H'm! Not very good for your Uncle Rondo in his precarious condition, I must say. Or poor little adopted Shirley-T. Shame on you!"

That made me tired. I says, "Well, Stella-Rondo had better thank her lucky stars it was her instead of me came trotting in with that very peculiar-looking child. Now if it had been me that trotted in from Illinois and brought a peculiar-looking child of two, I shudder to think of the reception I'd of got, much less controlled the diet of an entire family."

"But you must remember, Sister, that you were never married to Mr. Whitaker in the first place and didn't go up to Illinois to live," says Mama, shaking a spoon in my face. "If you had I would of been just as overjoyed to see you and your little adopted girl as I was to see Stella-Rondo, when you wound up with your separation and came on back home."

"You would not," I says.

"Don't contradict me, I would," says Mama.

But I said she couldn't convince me though she talked till she was blue in the face. Then I said, "Besides, you know as well as I do that that child is not adopted."

"She most certainly is adopted," says Mama, stiff as a poker.

I says, "Why, Mama, Stella-Rondo had her just as sure as anything in this world, and just too stuck up to admit it."

"Why, Sister," said Mama. "Here I thought we were going to have a pleasant Fourth of July, and you start right out not believing a word your own baby sister tells you!"

"Just like Cousin Annie Flo. Went to her grave denying the facts of life," I remind Mama.

"I told you if you ever mentioned Annie Flo's name I'd slap your face," says Mama, and slaps my face.

"All right, you wait and see," I says.

"I," says Mama, "I prefer to take my children's word for anything when it's humanly possible." You ought to see Mama, she weighs two hundred pounds and has real tiny feet.

Just then something perfectly horrible occurred to me

"Mama," I says, "can that child talk?" I simply had to whisper! "Mama, I wonder if that child can be—you know—in any way? Do you realize," I says, "that she hasn't spoken one single, solitary word to a human being up to this minute? This is the way she looks," I says, and I looked like this.

Well, Mama and I just stood there and stared at each other. It was horrible!

"I remember well that Joe Whitaker frequently drank like a fish," says Mama. "I believed to my soul he drank *chemicals*." And without another word she marches to the foot of the stairs and calls Stella-Rondo.

"Stella-Rondo? O-o-o-o-o! Stella-Rondo!"

"What?" says Stella-Rondo from upstairs. Not even the grace to get up off the bed.

"Can that child of yours talk ?" asks Mama.

Stella-Rondo says, "Can she what?"

"Talk! Talk!" says Mama. "Burdyburdyburdyburdy!"

So Stella-Rondo yells back, "Who says she can't talk?"

"Sister says so," says Mama.

"You didn't have to tell me, I know whose word of honor don't mean a thing in this house," says Stella-Rondo.

And in a minute the loudest Yankee voice I ever heard in my life yells out, "OE'm Pop-OE the Sailor-r-r-r Ma-a-an!" and then somebody jumps up and down in the upstairs hall. In another second the house would of fallen down.

"Not only talks, she can tap-dance!" calls Stella-Rondo, "Which is more than some people I won't name can do."

"Why, the little precious darling thing!" Mama says, so surprised. "Just as smart as she can be!" Starts talking baby talk right there. Then she turns on me. "Sister, you ought to be thoroughly ashamed! Run upstairs this instant and apologize to Stella-Rondo and Shirley-T."

"Apologize for what?" I says. "I merely wondered if the child was normal, that's all. Now that she's proved she is, why, I have nothing further to say."

But Mama just turned on her heel and flew out, furious. She ran right upstairs and hugged the baby. She believed it was adopted. Stella-Rondo hadn't done a thing but turn her against me from upstairs while I stood there helpless over the hot stove. So that made Mama, Papa-Daddy and the baby all on Stella-Rondo's side.

Next, Uncle Rondo.

I must say that Uncle Rondo has been marvelous to me at various times in the past and I was completely unprepared to be made to jump out of my skin, the way it turned out. Once Stella-Rondo did something perfectly horrible to him—broke a chain letter from Flanders Field[1]—and he took the radio back he had given her and gave it to me. Stella-Rondo was furious! For six months we all had to call her Stella instead of Stella-Rondo, or she wouldn't answer. I always thought Uncle Rondo had all the brains of the entire family. Another time he sent me to Mammoth Cave, with all expenses paid.

But this would be the day he was drinking that prescription, the Fourth of July.

So at supper Stella-Rondo speaks up and says she thinks Uncle Rondo ought to try to eat a little something. So finally Uncle Rondo said he would try a little cold biscuits and ketchup, but that was all. So *she* brought it to him.

"Do you think it wise to disport with ketchup in Stella-Rondo's flesh-colored kimono?" I says. Trying to be considerate! If Stella-Rondo couldn't watch out for her trousseau, somebody had to.

"Any objections?" asks Uncle Rondo, just about to pour out all the ketchup.

"Don't mind what she says, Uncle Rondo," says Stella-Rondo. "Sister has been devoting this solid afternoon to sneering out my bedroom window at the way you look."

"What's that?" says Uncle Rondo. Uncle Rondo has got the most terrible temper in the world. Anything is liable to make him tear the house down if it comes at the wrong time.

So Stella-Rondo says, "Sister says, 'Uncle Rondo certainly does look like a fool in that pink kimono!' "

Do you remember who it was really said that?

Uncle Rondo spills out all the ketchup and jumps out of his chair and tears off the kimono and throws it down on the dirty floor and puts his foot on it. It had to be sent all the way to Jackson to the cleaners and re-pleated.

"So that's your opinion of your Uncle Rondo, is it?" he says. "I look like a fool, do I? Well, that's the last straw. A whole day in this house with nothing to do, and then to hear you come out with a remark like that behind my back!"

---

1 **Flanders Field:** a region in Belgium and the scene of heavy fighting in World War I. Canadian poet John McCrae wrote a famous poem entitled "In Flanders Fields" about the soldiers buried there.

"I didn't say any such of a thing, Uncle Rondo," I says, "and I'm not saying who did, either. Why, I think you look all right. Just try to take care of yourself and not talk and eat at the same time," I says. "I think you better go lie down."

"Lie down my foot," says Uncle Rondo. I ought to of known by that he was fixing to do something perfectly horrible.

So he didn't do anything that night in the precarious state he was in—just played Casino with Mama and Stella-Rondo and Shirley-T. and gave Shirley-T. a nickel with a head on both sides. It tickled her nearly to death, and she called him "Papa." But at 6:30 A.M. the next morning, he threw a whole five-cent package of some unsold one-inch firecrackers from the store as hard as he could into my bedroom and they every one went off. Not one bad one in the string. Anybody else, there'd be one that wouldn't go off.

Well, I'm just terribly susceptible to noise of any kind, the doctor has always told me I was the most sensitive person he had ever seen in his whole life, and I was simply prostrated. I couldn't eat! People tell me they heard it as far as the cemetery, and old Aunt Jep Patterson, that had been holding her own so good, thought it was Judgment Day and she was going to meet her whole family. It's usually so quiet here.

And I'll tell you it didn't take me any longer than a minute to make up my mind what to do. There I was with the whole entire house on Stella-Rondo's side and turned against me. If I have anything at all I have pride.

So I just decided I'd go straight down to the P.O. There's plenty of room there in the back, I says to myself.

Well! I made no bones about letting the family catch on to what I was up to. I didn't try to conceal it.

The first thing they knew, I marched in where they were all playing Old Maid and pulled the electric oscillating fan out by the plug, and everything got real hot. Next I snatched the pillow I'd done the needlepoint on right off the davenport from behind Papa-Daddy. He went "Ugh!" I beat Stella-Rondo up the stairs and finally found my charm bracelet in her bureau drawer under a picture of Nelson Eddy.

"So that's the way the land lies," says Uncle Rondo. There he was, piecing on the ham. "Well, Sister, I'll be glad to donate my army cot if you got any place to set it up, providing you'll leave right this minute and let me get some peace." Uncle Rondo was in France.[2]

---

2 **Uncle Rondo . . . France:** evidently a reference to his military service in World War I.

"Thank you kindly for the cot and 'peace' is hardly the word I would select if I had to resort to firecrackers at 6:30 A.M. in a young girl's bedroom," I says back to him. "And as to where I intend to go, you seem to forget my position as postmistress of China Grove, Mississippi," I says. "I've always got the P.O."

Well, that made them all sit up and take notice.

I went out front and started digging up some four-o'clocks to plant around the P.O.

"Ah-ah-ah!" says Mama, raising the window. "Those happen to be my four-o'clocks. Everything planted in that star is mine. I've never known you to make anything grow in your life."

"Very well," I says. "But I take the fern. Even you, Mama, can't stand there and deny that I'm the one watered that fern. And I happen to know where I can send in a box top and get a packet of one thousand mixed seeds, no two the same kind, free."

"Oh, where ?" Mama wants to know.

But I says, "Too late. You 'tend to your house, and I'll 'tend to mine. You hear things like that all the time if you know how to listen to the radio. Perfectly marvelous offers. Get anything you want free."

So I hope to tell you I marched in and got that radio, and they could of all bit a nail in two, especially Stella-Rondo, that it used to belong to, and she well knew she couldn't get it back, I'd sue for it like a shot. And I very politely took the sewing-machine motor I helped pay the most on to give Mama for Christmas back in 1929, and a good big calendar, with the first-aid remedies on it. The thermometer and the Hawaiian ukulele certainly were rightfully mine, and I stood on the step-ladder and got all my watermelon-rind preserves and every fruit and vegetable I'd put up, every jar. Then I began to pull the tacks out of the bluebird wall vases on the archway to the dining room.

"Who told you you could have those, Miss Priss?" says Mama, fanning as hard as she could.

"I bought 'em and I'll keep track of 'em," I says. "I'll tack 'em up one on each side the post-office window, and you can see 'em when you come to ask me for your mail, if you're so dead to see 'em."

"Not I! I'll never darken the door to that post office again if I live to be a hundred," Mama says. "Ungrateful child! After all the money we spent on you at the Normal."

"Me either," says Stella-Rondo. "You can just let my mail lie there and *rot,* for all I care. I'll never come and relieve you of a single, solitary piece."

"I should worry," I says. "And who you think's going to sit down and write you all those big fat letters and postcards, by the way?

Mr. Whitaker? Just because he was the only man ever dropped down in China Grove and you got him—unfairly—is he going to sit down and write you a lengthy correspondence after you come home giving no rhyme nor reason whatsoever for your separation and no explanation for the presence of that child? I may not have your brilliant mind, but I fail to see it."

So Mama says, "Sister, I've told you a thousand times that Stella-Rondo simply got homesick, and this child is far too big to be hers," and she says, "Now, why don't you all just sit down and play Casino?"

Then Shirley-T. sticks out her tongue at me in this perfectly horrible way. She has no more manners than the man in the moon. I told her she was going to cross her eyes like that some day and they'd stick.

"It's too late to stop me now," I says. "You should have tried that yesterday. I'm going to the P.O. and the only way you can possibly see me is to visit me there."

So Papa-Daddy says, "You'll never catch me setting foot in that post office even if I should take a notion into my head to write a letter some place." He says, "I won't have you reachin' out of that little old window with a pair of shears and cuttin' off any beard of mine. I'm too smart for you!"

"We all are," says Stella-Rondo.

But I said, "If you're so smart, where's Mr. Whitaker?"

So then Uncle Rondo says, "I'll thank you from now on to stop reading all the orders I get on postcards and telling everybody in China Grove what you think is the matter with them," but I says, "I draw my own conclusions and will continue in the future to draw them." I says, "if people want to write their inmost secrets on penny postcards, there's nothing in the wide world you can do about it, Uncle Rondo."

"And if you think we'll ever *write* another postcard you're sadly mistaken," says Mama.

"Cutting off your nose to spite your face then," I says. "But if you're all determined to have no more to do with the U.S. mail, think of this: What will Stella-Rondo do now, if she wants to tell Mr. Whitaker to come after her?"

"Wah!" says Stella-Rondo. I knew she'd cry. She had a conniption fit right there in the kitchen.

"It will be interesting to see how long she holds out," I says. "And now—I am leaving."

"Good-bye," says Uncle Rondo.

"Oh, I declare," says Mama, "to think that a family of mine should quarrel on the Fourth of July, or the day after, over Stella-

Rondo leaving old Mr. Whitaker and having the sweetest little adopted child! It looks like we'd all be glad!"

"Wah!" says Stella-Rondo, and has a fresh conniption fit.

"*He* left *her*—you mark my words," I says. "That's Mr. Whitaker. I know Mr. Whitaker. After all, I knew him first. I said from the beginning he'd up and leave her. I foretold every single thing that's happened."

"Where did he go?" asks Mama.

"Probably to the North Pole, if he knows what's good for him," I says.

But Stella-Rondo just bawled and wouldn't say another word. She flew to her room and slammed the door.

"Now look what you've gone and done, Sister," says Mama. "You go apologize."

"I haven't got time, I'm leaving," I says

"Well, what are you waiting around for?" asks Uncle Rondo.

So I just picked up the kitchen clock and marched off, without saying "Kiss my foot" or anything, and never did tell Stella-Rondo good-bye.

There was a nigger girl going along on a little wagon right in front.

"Nigger girl," I says, "come help me haul these things down the hill, I'm going to live in the post office."

Took her nine trips in her express wagon. Uncle Rondo came out on the porch and threw her a nickel.

And that's the last I've laid eyes on any of my family or my family laid eyes on me for five solid days and nights. Stella-Rondo may be telling the most horrible tales in the world about Mr. Whitaker, but I haven't heard them. As I tell everybody, I draw my own conclusions.

But oh, I like it here. It's ideal, as I've been saying. You see, I've got everything cater-cornered, the way I like it. Hear the radio? All the war news. Radio, sewing machine, book ends, ironing board and that great big piano lamp—peace, that's what I like. Butter-bean vines planted all along the front where the strings are.

Of course, there's not much mail. My family are naturally the main people in China Grove, and if they prefer to vanish from the face of the earth, for all the mail they get or the mail they write, why, I'm not going to open my mouth. Some of the folks here in town are taking up for me and some turned against me. I know which is which. There are always people who will quit buying stamps just to get on the right side of Papa-Daddy.

But here I am, and here I'll stay. I want the world to know I'm happy.

And if Stella-Rondo should come to me this minute, on bended knees, and *attempt* to explain the incidents of her life with Mr. Whitaker, I'd simply put my fingers in both my ears and refuse to listen.

QUESTIONS FOR DISCUSSION

1. The tone of this story is perhaps the most striking thing about it. How is it achieved?

2. How well do you feel you know the various characters in this story? Which one do you know the best? Who are the round characters? the flat characters?

3. How important is Stella-Rondo's daughter to the story?

4. What are the causes of the narrator's difficulties with each of her relatives?

5. Are the narrator's relatives believable? Why or why not?

TOPICS FOR WRITING

1. Analyze how the narrator makes you sympathize with her.

2. Listen to dialogue in your own family and record it in your journal. Use this dialogue to begin a short story.

SYNTHESIS QUESTIONS

1. Review the opening paragraphs of the stories in this chapter. Which ones do you find most compelling?

2. Which story in this chapter has the most suspense?

3. In which story does the tone seem to be most humorous?

4. Which of the first-person narrators do you find most appealing, and why?

5. With a partner, write an acting scene or a one-act play based on one of the stories in this chapter.

6. If you were awarding a prize for the story in this chapter with the best plot, which one would get the award? Why?

Chapter Five

THEME

The word **theme** denotes the central idea of serious fictional works such as novels, plays, poems, or short stories. Theme is an author's insight or general observation about human nature or the human condition that is conveyed through characters, plot, and imagery. In a story about a naive young politician, for example, the theme might be "Even the most idealistic of politicians must sometimes compromise his or her principles"; in a story about the growth of the protagonist from youth to maturity, the author might suggest that "Disappointment is necessary to the process of maturing." If you examine carefully these two quotations expressing theme, you should deduce two important clues to the nature of a theme statement: first, it is presented in a complete sentence, and second, its content is debatable.

Thesis, the term used to denote the central focus or argument of a nonfiction work, is usually stated explicitly in the opening paragraphs or chapter. In contrast, theme is more often implicit. Because it must be inferred by the reader, theme is therefore more subtle and more open to various interpretations. Indeed, different readers may state a story's theme in differing but equally valid ways.

PARTICULARITY AND UNIVERSALITY

Fiction presents two seemingly contradictory qualities: particularity and universality. **Particularity** refers to the uniqueness or singularity of a work of fiction. Mark Twain's Tom Sawyer, for example, is a specific character who lives in a specific place (Hannibal, Missouri, a Mississippi River town) at a specific time (*c.* 1840); who has friends and relatives (Huckleberry Finn, Becky Thatcher, a black man named Jim, Aunt Polly); and who experiences specific adventures (whitewashing the fence, witnessing a murder, hiding out on an island,

199

finding gold in a cave). These are some of the unique particulars or "facts" of *The Adventures of Tom Sawyer.*

Universality, on the other hand, refers to the relevance or applicability of a fictional work to large groups of people across time and place. That is, Tom Sawyer is not just Twain's idea of an adventuresome adolescent; Tom typifies all young men who look for excitement and who, if they don't find it, create it. Tom Sawyer could be as real to a young William Shakespeare living in England in the 1500s as to a Korean, Brazilian, or Israeli 50 years from now. Books such as *Tom Sawyer* are often termed *classics* because their universality transcends space or time.

THE ROOTS OF THEME

Although the modern short story as a recognized literary form dates from the early 1800s, short fiction goes back to the Egyptians. More than 2,500 years ago the Greek slave Aesop told **fables**—short-short animal tales that illustrate and then state a moral or a lesson about life. You may recall "The Fox and the Grapes."

> Mister Fox was just about famished, and thirsty, too, when he stole into a vineyard where the sun-ripened grapes were hanging up on a trellis in a tempting show, but too high for him to reach. He took a run and a jump, snapping at the nearest bunch, but missed. Again and again he jumped, only to miss the luscious prize. At last, worn out with his efforts, he retreated, muttering: "Well, I never really wanted those grapes anyway. I am sure they are sour, and perhaps wormy in the bargain."
>
> MORAL: Any fool can despise what he cannot get.

Fables, along with parables such as the biblical story of the prodigal son, are considered **didactic literature**—literature whose primary purpose is to teach some moral or philosophical truth.
Because of this heritage, some readers expect all fiction to teach a moral "lesson" or to convey a "message."

Not all fiction has a didactic purpose, however, nor should it have. The detective story, for example, is written almost solely as entertainment or diversion. The same might be said about ghost or horror stories, westerns, science-fiction, adventure stories, or many highly popular romance novels. Literary experts classify these works as escape literature, not serious literature. Why? Because in escape literature *plot,* or what happens, is often more important than *theme,* and the themes tend to be simple clichés that confirm our expectations: "Crime doesn't pay" or "Love conquers all." In discussing serious literature, literary critics and scholars avoid such terms as *moral* or *lesson,* preferring the more neutral word *theme.*

LOCATING THEME

How do you discover the theme of a short story or novel? Unfortunately, there is no sure-fire formula to guarantee success. One approach, however, is to focus first on the elements of each story as you read. Examine those elements closely, rereading as needed. From the factual details of plot (especially conflict), character, and setting (especially imagery), clues to the author's debatable opinion will emerge.

To illustrate how to go about this process, let's examine a widely read work. In Ernest Hemingway's short novel *The Old Man and the Sea,* a poor Cuban fisherman named Santiago has not caught a fish for 87 days. Because the other fishermen are superstitious, they think that Santiago has lost his luck. As a result, the father of Santiago's teenaged helper Manolin forbids the boy to work for Santiago. Alone, Santiago sails into the Gulf Stream, catches some bait, daydreams of lions and his hero Joe Dimaggio, hooks an enormous marlin, and, for three days, is dragged further and further away from shore, fighting exhaustion and physical pain in order to secure the fish to his boat. As Santiago heads for port, marauding sharks attack and eat the marlin. The other fisherman admire the skeleton of the immense marlin and Manolin decides he will fish again with Santiago. The old man trudges up the hill to his house and falls asleep dreaming of the lions. These are a few of the *particulars*—the facts—of the story. With them in mind, what theme statement might you formulate to answer the following question: "What is *The Old Man and the Sea* about?"

Some readers might answer that the theme of Hemingway's short novel is "fishing" or "a Cuban fisherman." While this is true enough, "fishing" is a *topic* and "Cuban fisherman" is the *subject* of the book. Remember: statements of theme go beyond topics and subjects to express an opinion.

Other readers might answer, "Oh, this old has-been fisherman sets out alone, wrestles for three days to land a huge fish, then has to watch sharks eat it before he can get it back to port." This reply is a *plot summary* because it conveys only the facts of the story and does not comment on them.

To pinpoint the theme of a work of fiction, then, active readers must absorb the facts of a story, then ask, "What might these facts signify? In other words, what general or universal truth about human beings is the author suggesting?" For *Old Man* you might reply, "courage," "endurance," or "nature." By choosing these *abstract nouns*, you have recognized important ideas in the book—ideas that will help you formulate a theme statement. In *The Old Man and the Sea* the concepts of courage or endurance or nature would be considered **motifs**. A motif can be an image, word or phrase, action, idea, object, or even a situation. Note that an idea becomes a motif when it is repeated. This repetition serves to draw your attention to and to emphasize the motif.

FORMULATING A THEME STATEMENT

You might come up with the following theme statement:

> Despite extraordinary courage and endurance, Santiago loses his struggle against hostile and powerful natural forces.

This is a complete sentence, but its specific reference to Santiago prevents it from being a general statement about human beings. You can easily make it a more general statement:

> Despite extraordinary courage and endurance, human beings often lose their struggle against more powerful natural forces.

Expressing Theme as Multiple Statements

The statement above suggests that because Santiago's three-day ordeal ends in his losing the fish, the book reflects a pessimistic view of life. You recall that Santiago thought of the sea birds and the fish as his brothers, powerful but not alien. You also recall Santiago's dreams of Joe DiMaggio, the lions, and other images of greatness. Finally, you reread the final paragraphs of the book, often an important clue to the meaning of a work of fiction. There, Manolin watches as Santiago sleeps and dreams of lions. Does this reference to an image of greatness sound pessimistic to you? If not, perhaps you should modify the original theme statement:

> Despite extraordinary courage and endurance, human beings often lose the struggle against more powerful natural forces. Still,

> even a temporary triumph over solitude, age, physical exhaustion, and bad luck enables humans to regain their pride and dignity.

For a complex work, you may need to express statements of theme in several sentences.

Avoiding Excessive Theme Statement

After you formulate a general statement of theme for the Hemingway book, you remember learning in history class about Fidel Castro, head of Cuba's communist state. You check a few facts and come up with the following theme:

> Despite extraordinary courage and endurance, human beings often lose the struggle against hostile and powerful natural forces. Still, even a temporary triumph over solitude, age, physical exhaustion, and bad luck enables humans to regain their pride and dignity unless they are living under a communist regime.

Have you improved the theme statement, making it more encompassing? Absolutely not. Hemingway makes no mention of nor allusion to Castro or communism in the book. He couldn't: *The Old Man and the Sea* was published in 1952, and Castro didn't come to power until 1959. This illustrates the need to formulate statements of theme *only* on the facts contained within the work; going beyond those facts to broaden the theme usually leads to a misrepresentation of the author's insight.

The stories in this chapter are considered serious literature. As you read the Sherman Alexie story, think not only about life and death, but about the title, especially the word *Phoenix*. Is it merely a city, or should you recall the mythical bird? Alice Walker and D. H. Lawrence ask you to consider issues of love and marriage and materialism. As you read each story in this section, think about how you would state its theme. Remember that a theme statement must account for all the major details in a story. Don't ignore a fact just because it contradicts your idea of the theme; that's intellectually dishonest. Statements of theme must accommodate all the details of the story.

SUMMARY

Theme is an opinion statement suggesting the author's central insight or general comment about human nature or the human condition as conveyed through the character, action, and imagery. A nonfiction thesis is explicitly stated; theme is often implicit and therefore subject to differing interpretations. Didactic literature is literature whose primary purpose is to teach some moral or philosophical truth. Instead of using the terms *moral, message,* or *lesson,* however, literary experts prefer the more neutral word *theme.* Serious literature, unlike escape literature, contributes to our knowledge of ourselves and others, or of the conditions in which we live.

Statements of theme are *not* topics, subjects, clichés, plot summaries, or motifs. Theme may need to be stated in several sentences; can be formulated *only* on the facts of the work; can be expressed in various, equally accurate ways; and must accommodate the main details of the story.

THIS IS WHAT IT MEANS TO SAY PHOENIX, ARIZONA

SHERMAN ALEXIE (born 1967)

Spokane-Coeur d'Alene Indian—a term he prefers to that of Native American—Sherman Alexie was born hydrocephalic and given the last rites when it was feared that brain surgery would kill him. Although he had epileptic seizures until he was seven years ago, Alexie survived surgery and grew up in Wellpinit, a town on the Spokane Indian Reservation some 45 miles west of Spokane, Washington. A 1998 *New York Times Magazine* profile reported that Alexie "began reading Superman comics before he was out of diapers and then read all of the Wellpinit School Library by the time he was twelve."

Alexie's parents were alcoholics, though his mother has recovered and now works as a substance abuse counselor. Because of the pressure to succeed, Alexie himself spent 1985–1987 "in an alcoholic haze"at Gonzaga University; he described these years as a time when he was "one of those Indians upholding our stereotype." By age twenty-three, however, he had quit drinking and transferred to Washington State University where he received his B.A. in 1991. Encouraged by his college mentor, the poet and teacher Alex Kuo, Alexie began writing seriously; in 1992, Hanging Loose Press in New York published a collection of his poetry and short stories: *The Business of Fancydancing.*

To date, Alexie has published ten books, including several collections of poems: *First Indian on the Moon, Old Shirts & New Skins* (both 1993), *Water Flowing Home* (1995), and *The Summer of the Black Widow* (1996). *The Lone Ranger and Tonto Fistfight in Heaven* (1993) is a collection of short stories; *Reservation Blues* (1995) and *Indian Killer* (1996) are novels.

In the late 1990s, Alexie produced the film *Smoke Signals,* the first feature film produced, directed, and written by Indians; it is based on "This Is What It Is to Say Phoenix, Arizona," the story that begins this chapter. Alexie next plans to produce and direct *Indian Killer,* based on his novel.

As you read the story, enjoy Alexie's sophisticated plot structure, deft characterization, and dry sense of humor. Then ask yourself what motifs and theme are suggested by the plot, setting, characters, and imagery.

Just after Victor lost his job at the Bureau of Indian Affairs, he also found out that his father had died of a heart attack in Phoenix, Arizona. Victor hadn't seen his father in a few years, had only talked to him on the telephone once or twice, but there still was a genetic pain, which was as real and immediate as a broken bone. Victor didn't have any money. Who does have money on a reservation, except the cigarette and fireworks salespeople? His father had a savings account waiting to be claimed, but Victor needed to find a way to get from Spokane to Phoenix. Victor's mother was just as poor as he was, and the rest of his family didn't have any use at all for him. So Victor called the tribal council.

"Listen," Victor said. "My father just died. I need some money to get to Phoenix to make arrangements."

"Now, Victor," the council said, "you know we're having a difficult time financially."

"But I thought the council had special funds set aside for stuff like this."

"Now, Victor, we do have some money available for the proper return of tribal members' bodies. But I don't think we have enough to bring your father all the way back from Phoenix."

"Well," Victor said. "It ain't going to cost all that much. He had to be cremated. Things were kind of ugly. He died of a heart attack in his trailer and nobody found him for a week. It was really hot, too. You get the picture."

"Now, Victor, we're sorry for your loss and the circumstances. But we can really only afford to give you one hundred dollars."

"That's not even enough for a plane ticket."

"Well, you might consider driving down to Phoenix."

"I don't have a car. Besides, I was going to drive my father's pickup back up here."

"Now, Victor," the council said, "we're sure there is somebody who could drive you to Phoenix. Or could anybody lend you the rest of the money?"

"You know there ain't nobody around with that kind of money."

"Well, we're sorry, Victor, but that's the best we can do."

Victor accepted the tribal council's offer. What else could he do? So he signed the proper papers, picked up his check, and walked over to the Trading Post to cash it.

While Victor stood in line, he watched Thomas Builds-the-Fire standing near the magazine rack talking to himself. Like he always did. Thomas was a storyteller whom nobody wanted to listen to. That's like being a dentist in a town where everybody has false teeth.

Victor and Thomas Builds-the-Fire were the same age, had grown up and played in the dirt together. Ever since Victor could remember, it was Thomas who had always had something to say.

Once, when they were seven years old, when Victor's father still lived with the family, Thomas closed his eyes and told Victor this story: "Your father's heart is weak. He is afraid of his own family. He is afraid of you. Late at night, he sits in the dark. Watches the television until there's nothing but that white noise. Sometimes he feels like he wants to buy a motorcycle and ride away. He wants to run and hide. He doesn't want to be found."

Thomas Builds-the-Fire had known that Victor's father was going to leave, known it before anyone. Now Victor stood in the Trading Post with a one-hundred-dollar check in his hand, wondering if Thomas knew that Victor's father was dead, if he knew what was going to happen next.

Just then, Thomas looked at Victor, smiled, and walked over to him.

"Victor, I'm sorry about your father," Thomas said.

"How did you know about it?" Victor asked.

"I heard it on the wind. I heard it from the birds. I felt it in the sunlight. Also, your mother was just in here crying."

"Oh," Victor said and looked around the Trading Post. All the other Indians stared, surprised that Victor was even talking to Thomas. Nobody talked to Thomas anymore because he told the same damn stories over and over again. Victor was embarrassed, but he thought that Thomas might be able to help him. Victor felt a sudden need for tradition.

"I can lend you the money you need," Thomas said suddenly. "But you have to take me with you."

"I can't take your money," Victor said. "I mean, I haven't hardly talked to you in years. We're not really friends anymore."

"I didn't say we were friends. I said you had to take me with you."

"Let me think about it."

Victor went home with his one hundred dollars and sat at the kitchen table. He held his head in his hands and thought about Thomas Builds-the-Fire, remembered little details, tears and scars, the bicycle they shared for a summer, so many stories.

Thomas Builds-the-Fire sat on the bicycle, waiting in Victor's yard. He was ten years old and skinny. His hair was dirty because it was the Fourth of July.

"Victor," Thomas yelled. "Hurry up. We're going to miss the fireworks."

After a few minutes, Victor ran out of his family's house, vaulted over the porch railing, and landed gracefully on the sidewalk.

Thomas gave him the bike and they headed for the fireworks. It was nearly dark and the fireworks were about to start.

"You know," Thomas said, "it's strange how us Indians celebrate the Fourth of July. It ain't like it was our independence everybody was fighting for."

"You think about things too much," Victor said. "It's just supposed to be fun. Maybe Junior will be there."

"Which Junior? Everybody on this reservation is named Junior."

The fireworks were small, hardly more than a few bottle rockets and a fountain. But it was enough for two Indian boys. Years later, they would need much more.

Afterward, sitting in the dark, fighting off mosquitoes, Victor turned to Thomas Builds-the-Fire.

"Hey," Victor said. "Tell me a story."

Thomas closed his eyes and told this story: "There were these two Indian boys who wanted to be warriors. But it was too late to be warriors in the old way. All the horses were gone. So the two Indian boys stole a car and drove to the city. They parked the stolen car in the front of the police station and then hitchhiked back home to the reservation. When they got back, all their friends cheered and their parents' eyes shone with pride. 'You were very brave,' everybody said to the two Indian boys. 'Very brave.' "

"Ya-hey," Victor said. "That's a good one. I wish I could be a warrior."

"Me too," Thomas said.

Victor sat at his kitchen table. He counted his one hundred dollars again and again. He knew he needed more to make it to Phoenix and back. He knew he needed Thomas Builds-the-Fire. So he put his money in his wallet and opened the front door to find Thomas on the porch.

"Ya-hey, Victor," Thomas said. "I knew you'd call me."

Thomas walked into the living room and sat down in Victor's favorite chair.

"I've got some money saved up," Thomas said. "It's enough to get us down there, but you have to get us back."

"I've got this hundred dollars," Victor said. "And my dad had a savings account I'm going to claim."

"How much in your dad's account?"

"Enough. A few hundred."

"Sounds good. When we leaving?"

When they were fifteen and had long since stopped being friends, Victor and Thomas got into a fistfight. That is, Victor was really drunk and beat Thomas up for no reason at all. All the other Indian boys stood around and watched it happen. Junior was there and so were Lester, Seymour, and a lot of others.

The beating might have gone on until Thomas was dead if Norma Many Horses hadn't come along and stopped it.

"Hey, you boys," Norma yelled and jumped out of her car. "Leave him alone."

If it had been someone else, even another man, the Indian boys would've just ignored the warnings. But Norma was a warrior. She was powerful. She could have picked up any two of the boys and smashed their skulls together. But worse than that, she would have dragged them all over to some tepee and made them listen to some elder tell a dusty old story.

The Indian boys scattered, and Norma walked over to Thomas and picked him up.

"Hey, little man, are you O.K.?" she asked.

Thomas gave her a thumbs-up.

"Why they always picking on you?"

Thomas shook his head, closed his eyes, but no stories came to him, no words or music. He just wanted to go home, to lie in his bed and let his dreams tell the stories for him.

Thomas Builds-the-Fire and Victor sat next to each other in the airplane, coach section. A tiny white woman had the window seat. She was busy twisting her body into pretzels. She was flexible.

"I have to ask," Thomas said, and Victor closed his eyes in embarrassment.

"Don't," Victor said.

"Excuse me, miss," Thomas asked. "Are you a gymnast or something?"

"There's no something about it," she said. "I was first alternate on the 1980 Olympic team."

"Really?" Thomas asked.

"Really. "

"I mean, you used to be a world-class athlete?" Thomas asked.

"My husband thinks I still am."

Thomas Builds-the-Fire smiled. She was a mental gymnast too. She pulled her leg straight up against her body so that she could've kissed her kneecap.

"I wish I could do that," Thomas said.

Victor was ready to jump out of the plane. Thomas, that crazy Indian storyteller with ratty old braids and broken teeth, was flirting with a beautiful Olympic gymnast. Nobody back home on the reservation would ever believe it.

"Well," the gymnast said. "It's easy. Try it."

Thomas grabbed at his leg and tried to pull it up into the same position as the gymnast's. He couldn't even come close, which made Victor and the gymnast laugh.

"Hey," she asked. "You two are Indian, right?"

"Full-blood," Victor said.

"Not me," Thomas said. "I'm half magician on my mother's side and half clown on my father's."

They all laughed.

"What are your names?" she asked.

"Victor and Thomas."

"Mine is Cathy. Pleased to meet you all."

The three of them talked for the duration of the flight. Cathy the gymnast complained about the government, how they screwed the 1980 Olympic team by boycotting the games.[1]

"Sounds like you all got a lot in common with Indians," Thomas said.

Nobody laughed.

After the plane landed in Phoenix and they had all found their way to the terminal, Cathy the gymnast smiled and waved goodbye.

"She was really nice," Thomas said.

"Yeah, but everybody talks to everybody on airplanes," Victor said.

"You always used to tell me I think too much," Thomas said. "Now it sounds like you do."

"Maybe I caught it from you."

"Yeah."

Thomas and Victor rode in a taxi to the trailer where Victor's father had died.

---

1 **boycotting the games**: After Russia invaded Afghanistan in December 1979, President Jimmy Carter, in protest, decreed that American athletes would not be allowed to take part in the 1980 Olympics in Moscow. Fifty other countries also withdrew their athletes from the games.

"Listen," Victor said as they stopped in front of the trailer. "I never told you I was sorry for beating you up that time."

"Oh, it was nothing. We were just kids and you were drunk."

"Yeah, but I'm still sorry."

"That's all right."

Victor paid for the taxi, and the two of them stood in the hot Phoenix summer. They could smell the trailer.

"This ain't going to be nice," Victor said. "You don't have to go in."

"You're going to need help."

Victor walked to the front door and opened it. The stink rolled out and made them both gag. Victor's father had lain in that trailer for a week in hundred-degree temperatures before anyone had found him. And the only reason anyone found him was the smell. They needed dental records to identify him. That's exactly what the coroner said. They needed dental records.

"Oh, man," Victor said. "I don't know if I can do this."

"Well, then don't."

"But there might be something valuable in there."

"I thought his money was in the bank."

"It is. I was talking about pictures and letters and stuff like that."

"Oh," Thomas said as he held his breath and followed Victor into the trailer.

When Victor was twelve, he stepped into an underground wasps' nest. His foot was caught in the hole and no matter how hard he struggled, Victor couldn't pull free. He might have died there, stung a thousand times, if Thomas Builds-the-Fire had not come by.

"Run," Thomas yelled and pulled Victor's foot from the hole. They ran then, hard as they ever had, faster than Billy Mills, faster than Jim Thorpe,[2] faster than the wasps could fly.

Victor and Thomas ran until they couldn't breathe, ran until it was cold and dark outside, ran until they were lost and it took

---

2 **Billy Mills . . . Jim Thorpe:** In a dramatic upset at the Tokyo Olympics in 1964, William Mervin Mills (b. 1938), a part-Sioux, became the first American to win a gold medal in the 10,000-meter race. In 1912, James Francis Thorpe (1888–1953), of Sauk and Fox descent, won both the decathlon and the pentathlon at the Olympic Games in Stockholm. When in 1913 the Amateur Athletic Union learned that he had played semipro baseball in 1909 and 1910, he was deprived of his record achievement and his medals. In 1982, the IOC made Thorpe and the second-place winner "cowinners" of the race; his medals were restored to his family in 1983.

hours to find their way home. All the way back, Victor counted his stings.

"Seven," Victor said. "My lucky number."

Victor didn't find much to keep in the trailer. Only a photo album and a stereo. Everything else had that smell stuck in it or was useless anyway. "I guess this is all," Victor said. "It ain't much."

"Better than nothing," Thomas said.

"Yeah, and I do have the pickup."

"Yeah," Thomas said. "It's in good shape."

"Dad was good about that stuff."

"Yeah, I remember your dad."

"Really?" Victor asked. "What do you remember?"

Thomas Builds-the-Fire closed his eyes and told this story: "I remember when I had this dream that told me to go to Spokane, to stand by the falls in the middle of the city and wait for a sign. I knew I had to go there but I didn't have a car. Didn't have a license. I was only thirteen. So I walked all the way, took me all day, and I finally made it to the falls. I stood there for an hour waiting. Then your dad came walking up. 'What the hell are you doing here?' he asked me. I said, 'Waiting for a vision.' Then your father said, 'All you're going to get here is mugged.' So he drove me over to Denny's, bought me dinner, and then drove me home to the reservation. For a long time, I was mad because I thought my dreams had lied to me. But they hadn't. Your dad was my vision. *Take care of each other* is what my dreams were saying. *Take care of each other.*"

Victor was quiet for a long time. He searched his mind for memories of his father, found the good ones, found a few bad ones, added it all up, and smiled.

"My father never told me about finding you in Spokane," Victor said.

"He said he wouldn't tell anybody. Didn't want me to get in trouble. But he said I had to watch out for you as part of the deal."

"Really?"

"Really. Your father said you would need the help. He was right."

"That's why you came down here with me, isn't it?" Victor asked.

"I came because of your father."

Victor and Thomas climbed into the pickup, drove over to the bank, and claimed the three hundred dollars in the savings account.

Thomas Builds-the-Fire could fly.

Once, he jumped off the roof of the tribal school and flapped his arms like a crazy eagle. And he flew. For a second he hovered, suspended above all the other Indian boys, who were too smart or too scared to jump too.

"He's flying," Junior yelled, and Seymour was busy looking for the trick wires or mirrors. But it was real. As real as the dirt when Thomas lost altitude and crashed to the ground.

He broke his arm in two places.

"He broke his wing, he broke his wing, he broke his wing," all the Indian boys chanted as they ran off, flapping their wings, wishing they could fly too. They hated Thomas for his courage, his brief moment as a bird. Everybody has dreams about flying. Thomas flew.

One of his dreams came true for just a second, just enough to make it real.

Victor's father, his ashes, fit in one wooden box with enough left over to fill a cardboard box.

"He always was a big man," Thomas said.

Victor carried part of his father out to the pickup, and Thomas carried the rest. They set him down carefully behind the seats, put a cowboy hat on the wooden box and a Dodgers cap on the cardboard box. That was the way it was supposed to be.

"Ready to head back home?" Victor asked.

"It's going to be a long drive."

"Yeah, take a couple days, maybe."

'We can take turns," Thomas said.

"O.K.," Victor said, but they didn't take turns. Victor drove for sixteen hours straight north, made it halfway up Nevada toward home before he finally pulled over.

"Hey, Thomas," Victor said. "You got to drive for a while."

"O.K."

Thomas Builds-the-Fire slid behind the wheel and started off down the road. All through Nevada, Thomas and Victor had been amazed at the lack of animal life, at the absence of water, of movement.

"Where is everything?" Victor had asked more than once.

Now, when Thomas was finally driving, they saw the first animal, maybe the only animal in Nevada. It was a long-eared jackrabbit.

"Look," Victor yelled. "It's alive."

Thomas and Victor were busy congratulating themselves on their discovery when the jackrabbit darted out into the road and under the wheels of the pickup.

"Stop the goddamn car," Victor yelled, and Thomas did stop and backed the pickup to the dead jackrabbit.

"Oh, man, he's dead," Victor said as he looked at the squashed animal.

"Really dead."

"The only thing alive in this whole state and we just killed it."

"I don't know," Thomas said. "I think it was suicide."

Victor looked around the desert, sniffed the air, felt the emptiness and loneliness, and nodded his head.

"Yeah," Victor said. "It had to be suicide."

"I can't believe this," Thomas said. "You drive for a thousand miles and there ain't even any bugs smashed on the windshield. I drive for ten seconds and kill the only living thing in Nevada."

"Yeah," Victor said. "Maybe I should drive."

"Maybe you should."

Thomas Builds-the-Fire walked through the corridors of the tribal school by himself. Nobody wanted to be anywhere near him because of all those stories. Story after story.

Thomas closed his eyes and this story came to him: "We are all given one thing by which our lives are measured, one determination. Mine are the stories that can change or not change the world. It doesn't matter which, as long as I continue to tell the stories. My father, he died on Okinawa in World War II, died fighting for this country, which had tried to kill him for years. My mother, she died giving birth to me, died while I was still inside her. She pushed me out into the world with her last breath. I have no brothers or sisters. I have only my stories, which came to me before I even had the words to speak. I learned a thousand stories before I took my first thousand steps. They are all I have. It's all I can do."

Thomas Builds-the-Fire told his stories to all those who would stop and listen. He kept telling them long after people had stopped listening.

Victor and Thomas made it back to the reservation just as the sun was rising. It was the beginning of a new day on earth, but the same old stuff on the reservation.

"Good morning," Thomas said.

"Good morning."

The tribe was waking up, ready for work, eating breakfast, reading the newspaper, just like everybody else does. Willene LeBret was out in her garden, wearing a bathrobe. She waved when Thomas and Victor drove by.

"Crazy Indians made it," she said to herself and went back to her roses.

Victor stopped the pickup in front of Thomas Builds-the-Fire's HUD house.[3] They both yawned, stretched a little, shook dust from their bodies.

"I'm tired," Victor said.

"Of everything," Thomas added.

They both searched for words to end the journey. Victor needed to thank Thomas for his help and for the money, and to make the promise to pay it all back.

"Don't worry about the money," Thomas said. "It don't make any difference anyhow."

"Probably not, enit?"

"Nope."

Victor knew that Thomas would remain the crazy storyteller who talked to dogs and cars, who listened to the wind and pine trees. Victor knew that he couldn't really be friends with Thomas, even after all that had happened. It was cruel but it was real. As real as the ash, as Victor's father, sitting behind the seats.

"I know how it is," Thomas said. "I know you ain't going to treat me any better than you did before. I know your friends would give you too much stuff about it."

Victor was ashamed of himself. Whatever happened to the tribal ties, the sense of community? The only real thing he shared with anybody was a bottle and broken dreams. He owed Thomas something, anything.

"Listen," Victor said and handed Thomas the cardboard box that contained half of his father. "I want you to have this."

Thomas took the ashes and smiled, closed his eyes, and told this story: "I'm going to travel to Spokane Falls one last time and toss these ashes into the water. And your father will rise like a salmon, leap over the bridge, over me, and find his way home. It will be beautiful. His teeth will shine like silver, like a rainbow. He will rise, Victor, he will rise."

---

3 **HUD house:** HUD is an abbreviation for Department of Housing and Urban Development. In the 1960s, this federal department began overseeing the upkeep of houses on reservations. HUD houses, because they had electricity and plumbing, were often superior to other housing.

Victor smiled.

"I was planning on doing the same thing with my half," Victor said. "But I didn't imagine my father looking anything like a salmon. I thought it'd be like cleaning the attic or something. Like letting things go after they've stopped having any use."

"Nothing stops, cousin," Thomas said. "Nothing stops."

Thomas Builds-the-Fire got out of the pickup and walked up his driveway. Victor started the pickup and began the drive home.

"Wait," Thomas yelled suddenly from his porch. "I just got to ask one favor."

Victor stopped the pickup, leaned out the window, and shouted back.

"What do you want?" he asked.

"Just one time when I'm telling a story somewhere, why don't you stop and listen?" Thomas asked.

"Just once?"

"Just once."

Victor waved his arms to let Thomas know that the deal was good. It was a fair trade. That's all Thomas had ever wanted from his whole life. So Victor drove his father's pickup toward home while Thomas went into his house, closed the door behind him, and heard a new story come to him in the silence afterward.

QUESTIONS FOR DISCUSSION

1. How does Thomas-Builds-the-Fire differ from Victor?

2. Describe the relationship between Victor and Thomas, past and present and future.

3. Which of the two major characters do you find the more sympathetic? Explain your response.

4. How would you describe the structure of the plot?

5. Considering the motifs in the story, what is Alexie's theme?

6. How is the structure of the plot related to the meaning of the story?

7. Why does Alexie include the encounter with the gymnast?

8. What might be significant about the place and manner of Victor's father's death?

Topics for Writing

1. Working with a partner, reread the story, looking for evidence that Alexie's story has universality.

2. Do you find the story essentially pessimistic? optimistic? other? In an essay, explain your position.

3. In an essay, explain the title of the story, relating it, if possible, to the theme.

ROSELILY

ALICE WALKER (born 1944)

One of eight children born to a family of sharecroppers, Alice Walker grew up in Eatonton, Georgia. She began writing when she was eight years old after losing one eye, the result of an accident. Because she felt like an outcast, Walker began to record her observations and feelings in a notebook.

After graduating from college in 1965, she became an active participant in the civil rights movement, registering voters in Georgia and working for welfare rights and children's programs in Mississippi. Her first book, *Once: Poems,* was published in 1968. Two years later she published *The Third Life of Grange Copeland* (1970), a novel that traced the attempt of three generations to conquer the emotional slavery brought about by racism, unemployment, and sexism.

During the 1970s, Walker expanded her writing to include short stories: *In Love & Trouble: Stories of Black Women* (1973). She also published a second book of poetry, *Revolutionary Petunias & Other Poems* (1973), and began to write influential essays: "Saving the Life That Is Your Own: The Importance of Models in the Artist's Life" (1976) and "One Child of One's Own" (1979). In 1977, Walker moved to New York City where she completed *Meridian* (1976), a novel about a young woman in the civil rights movement. She also rescued from obscurity the works of black writer Zora Neale Hurston.

Although the 1980s saw the publication of a second collection of short stories, *You Can't Keep a Good Woman Down* (1981), and essays, *In Search of Our Mother's Gardens: Womanist Prose* (1983), it was the publication and later the movie of *The Color Purple* (1982)—which won both an American Book Award and a Pulitzer Prize in 1983—that brought Walker her greatest fame and controversy. She chronicled her reactions to that period in *The Same River Twice* (1996).

Subsequent publications have included two novels, *The Temple of My Familiar* (1989) and *Possessing the Secret of Joy* (1992), and three children's books, *Langston Hughes: American Poet* (1974), *To Hell with Dying* (1988), and *Finding the Green Stone* (1991).

As you read "Roselily," picture the setting and the speaker, and note the connections between the words of the service and the thoughts of the central character. Then formulate a statement of the theme.

■

Dearly Beloved,

She dreams; dragging herself across the world. A small girl in her mother's white robe and veil, knee raised waist high through a bowl of quicksand soup. The man who stands beside her is against this standing on the front porch of her house, being married to the sound of cars whizzing by on highway 61.

we are gathered here

Like cotton to be weighed. Her fingers at the last minute busily removing dry leaves and twigs. Aware it is a superficial sweep. She knows he blames Mississippi for the respectful way the men turn their heads up in the yard, the women stand waiting and knowledgeable, their children held from mischief by teachings from the wrong God. He glares beyond them to the occupants of the cars, white faces glued to promises beyond a country wedding, noses thrust forward like dogs on a track. For him they usurp the wedding.

in the sight of God

Yes, open house. That is what country black folks like. She dreams she does not already have three children. A squeeze around the flowers in her hands chokes off three and four and five years of breath. Instantly she is ashamed and frightened in her superstition. She looks for the first time at the preacher, forces humility into her eyes, as if she believes he is, in fact, a man of God. She can imagine God, a small black boy, timidly pulling the preacher's coattail.

to join this man and this woman

She thinks of ropes, chains, handcuffs, his religion. His place of worship. Where she will be required to sit apart with covered head. In Chicago, a word she hears when thinking of smoke, from his description of what a cinder was, which they never had in Panther Burn. She sees hovering over the heads of the clean neighbors in her front yard black specks falling, clinging, from the sky. But in Chicago. Respect, a chance to build. Her children at last from underneath the detrimental wheel. A chance to be on top. What a relief, she thinks. What a vision, a view, from up so high.

in holy matrimony.

Her fourth child she gave away to the child's father who had some money. Certainly a good job. Had gone to Harvard. Was a good man but weak because good language meant so much to him he could not live with Roselily. Could not abide TV in the living room, five beds in three rooms, no Bach except from four to six on Sunday afternoons. No chess at all. She does not forget to worry about her son among his father's people. She wonders if the New England climate will agree with him. If he will ever come down to Mississippi, as his father did,[1] to try to right the country's wrongs. She wonders if he will be stronger than his father. His father cried off and on throughout her pregnancy. Went to skin and bones. Suffered nightmares, retching and falling out of bed. Tried to kill himself. Later told his wife he found the right baby through friends. Vouched for, the sterling qualities that would make up his character.

It is not her nature to blame. Still, she is not entirely thankful. She supposes New England, the North, to be quite different from what she knows. It seems right somehow to her that people who move there to live return home completely changed. She thinks of the air, the smoke, the cinders. Imagines cinders big as hailstones; heavy, weighing on the people. Wonders how this pressure finds its way into the veins, roping the springs of laughter.

If there's anybody here that knows a reason why

But of course they know no reason why beyond what they daily have come to know. She thinks of the man who will be her husband, feels shut away from him because of the stiff severity of his plain black suit. His religion. A lifetime of black and white. Of veils. Covered head. It is as if her children are already gone from her. Not dead, but exalted on a pedestal, a stalk that has no roots. She wonders how to make new roots. It is beyond her. She wonders what one does with memories in a brand-new life. This had seemed easy, until she thought of it. "The reasons why . . . the people who" . . . she thinks, and does not wonder where the thought is from.

---

1 **come down to Mississippi . . . father did:** During the civil rights movement of the early 1960s, many northerners went to the South to register black voters who, because of poll taxes and other barriers, had been denied the right to vote.

these two should not be joined

She thinks of her mother, who is dead. Dead, but still her mother. Joined. This is confusing. Of her father. A gray old man who sold wild mink, rabbit, fox skins to Sears, Roebuck. He stands in the yard, like a man waiting for a train. Her young sisters stand behind her in smooth green dresses, with flowers in their hands and hair. They giggle, she feels, at the absurdity of the wedding. They are ready for something new. She thinks the man beside her should marry one of them. She feels old. Yoked. An arm seems to reach out from behind her and snatch her backward. She thinks of cemeteries and the long sleep of grandparents mingling in the dirt. She believes that she believes in ghosts. In the soil giving back what it takes.

together,

In the city. He sees her in a new way. This she knows, and is grateful. But is it new enough? She cannot always be a bride and virgin, wearing robes and veil. Even now her body itches to be free of satin and voile, organdy and lily of the valley. Memories crash against her. Memories of being bare to the sun. She wonders what it will be like. Not to have to go to a job. Not to work in a sewing plant. Not to worry about learning to sew straight seams in workingmen's overalls, jeans and dress pants. Her place will be in the home, he has said, repeatedly, promising her rest she had prayed for. But now she wonders. When she is rested, what will she do? They will make babies—she thinks practically about her fine brown body, his strong black one. They will be inevitable. Her hands will be full. Full of what? Babies. She is not comforted.

let him speak

She wishes she had asked him to explain more of what he meant. But she was impatient. Impatient to be done with sewing. With doing everything for three children, alone. Impatient to leave the girls she had known since childhood, their children growing up, their husbands hanging around her, already old, seedy. Nothing about them that she wanted, or needed. The fathers of her children driving by, waving, not waving; reminders of times she would just as soon forget. Impatient to see the South Side, where they would live and build and be respectable and respected and free. Her husband would free her. A romantic hush. Proposal. Promises. A new life! Respectable, reclaimed, renewed. Free! In robe and veil.

or forever hold

She does not even know if she loves him. She loves his sobriety. His refusal to sing just because he knows the tune. She loves his pride. His blackness and his gray car. She loves his understanding of her *condition*. She thinks she loves the effort he will make to redo her into what he truly wants. His love of her makes her completely conscious of how unloved she was before. This is something; though it makes her unbearably sad. Melancholy. She blinks her eyes. Remembers she is finally being married, like other girls. Like other girls, women? Something strains upward behind her eyes. She thinks of the something as a rat trapped, cornered, scurrying to and fro in her head, peering through the windows of her eyes. She wants to live for once. But doesn't know quite what that means. Wonders if she has ever done it. If she ever will. The preacher is odious to her. She wants to strike him out of the way, out of her light, with the back of her hand. It seems to her he has always been standing in front of her, barring her way.

his peace.

The rest she does not hear. She feels a kiss, passionate, rousing, within the general pandemonium. Cars drive up blowing their horns. Firecrackers go off. Dogs come from under the house and begin to yelp and bark. Her husband's hand is like the clasp of an iron gate. People congratulate. Her children press against her. They look with awe and distaste mixed with hope at their new father. He stands curiously apart, in spite of the people crowding about to grasp his free hand. He smiles at them all but his eyes are as if turned inward. He knows they cannot understand that he is not a Christian. He will not explain himself. He feels different, he looks it. The old women thought he was like one of their sons except that he had somehow got away from them. Still a son, not a son. Changed.

She thinks how it will be later in the night in the silvery gray car. How they will spin through the darkness of Mississippi and in the morning be in Chicago, Illinois. She thinks of Lincoln, the president. That is all she knows about the place. She feels ignorant, *wrong*, backward. She presses her worried fingers into his palm. He is standing in front of her. In the crush of well-wishing people, he does not look back.

QUESTIONS FOR DISCUSSION

1. What is the setting (place and time) of the story?

2. Describe Roselily's life prior to the opening of the story.

3. What are the italicized words and what is their purpose in the story?

4. What word or words might best describe Roselily's state of mind? Explain your response.

5. What evidence in the story suggests that Roselily might be marrying more out of gratitude than for love?

6. What is it about Roselily that might have attracted the man to her?

7. Which of the following motifs in the story seems to be the most important: religion, respect, or romance?

8. Formulate a statement of theme for this story.

9. Walker introduces a number of concrete images that contribute to the meaning of the story: "veils," "cotton to be weighed," "ropes, chains, handcuffs," "cinders big as hailstones; heavy, weighing on the people," "exalted on a pedestal, a stalk that has no roots." Choose two of these images and relate them to your statement of theme.

TOPICS FOR WRITING

1. In a 1973 interview Walker described three kinds of black women characters missing from American literature: those who were exploited both physically and emotionally; those who were victims of psychic violence and thus alienated from their own culture; and those who, despite oppression, achieve some wholeness. In which, if any, of these categories does Roselily seem to fit? In an essay, defend your choice.

2. In an essay indicate the clues by which Walker implies that Roselily is marrying a Muslim.

3. What indications does Walker give that Roselily's marriage will or will not be successful? In an essay, support your opinion with quotations or inferences from the story.

THE ROCKING-HORSE WINNER

D. H. LAWRENCE (1885–1930)

David Herbert Lawrence, the fourth child born to a virtually illiterate coal miner and his educated, pious wife, was one of England's most controversial men of letters. He also struggled with health problems throughout his life, dying of tuberculosis at age forty-five.

In 1901, Lawrence left high school to work as a clerk in a factory. After convalescing from pneumonia, he became a pupil-teacher. In 1908, Lawrence began teaching in a London suburb and working on his first novel, *The White Peacock* (1911). In 1912, Lawrence's mother died, he resigned his teaching position, and he fell in love and ran off with Frieda von Richthofen Weekley, the wife of one of his college professors and the sister of the Red Baron, Germany's famed World War I aviator. The following year Lawrence's partly autobiographical novel, *Sons and Lovers* (1913), was published. Praised for its portrait of English mining life, it was also severely criticized for its language and its frank treatment of sexuality. Two years later his novel *The Rainbow* (1915) was seized by the police and suppressed as obscene.

After 1919, in search of a more congenial and healthful environment, Lawrence and Frieda traveled extensively and continuously, visiting Italy, Capri, Sicily, Germany, Ceylon, Australia, New Zealand, Tahiti, the French Riviera, Mexico, and the American southwest. While in Taos, New Mexico, Lawrence wrote the novel *The Plumed Serpent* (1926). In 1925, Lawrence again became ill, and a bronchial hemmorrhage led to a diagnosis of tuberculosis. His last novel, *Lady Chatterly's Lover,* was privately published in 1928; only after lawsuits in America (1959) and England (1960), however, was it freely available.

"The Rocking-Horse Winner" begins like a typical fable, lacking only the "Once upon a time" opening, but the story deals with serious psychological and sociological issues—family relationships, materialism, the nature of love. These motifs appear often in Lawrence's works. As you read, consider these and other motifs before formulating a theme statement.

■

There was a woman who was beautiful, who started with all the advantages, yet she had no luck. She married for love, and the love turned to dust. She had bonny[1] children, yet she felt they had been thrust upon her, and she could not love them. They looked at her coldly, as if they were finding fault with her. And hurriedly she felt she must cover up some fault in herself. Yet what it was that she must cover up she never knew. Nevertheless, when her children were present, she always felt the center of her heart go hard. This troubled her, and in her manner she was all the more gentle and anxious for her children, as if she loved them very much. Only she herself knew that at the center of her heart was a hard little place that could not feel love, no, not for anybody. Everybody else said of her: "She is such a good mother. She adores her children." Only she herself, and her children themselves, knew it was not so. They read it in each other's eyes.

There were a boy and two little girls. They lived in a pleasant house, with a garden, and they had discreet servants, and felt themselves superior to anyone in the neighborhood.

Although they lived in style, they felt always an anxiety in the house. There was never enough money. The mother had a small income,[2] and the father had a small income, but not nearly enough for the social position which they had to keep up. The father went into town to some office. But though he had good prospects, these prospects never materialized. There was always the grinding sense of the shortage of money, though the style was always kept up.

At last the mother said: "I will see if *I* can't make something." But she did not know where to begin. She racked her brains, and tried this thing and the other, but could not find anything successful. The failure made deep lines come into her face. Her children were growing up, they would have to go to school. There must be more money, there must be more money. The father, who was always very handsome and expensive in his tastes, seemed as if he never *would* be able to do anything worth doing. And the mother, who had a great belief in herself, did not succeed any better, and her tastes were just as expensive.

And so the house came to be haunted by the unspoken phrase: *There must be more money! There must be more money!* The children

---

1 **bonny:** fair to see; pretty.

2 **small income:** In England, the word *income* often implies quarterly interest money earned from stocks, bonds, or an inheritance.

could hear it all the time though nobody said it aloud. They heard it at Christmas, when the expensive and splendid toys filled the nursery. Behind the shining modern rocking horse, behind the smart doll's house, a voice would start whispering: "There *must* be more money! There *must* be more money!" And the children would stop playing, to listen for a moment. They would look into each other's eyes, to see if they had all heard. And each one saw in the eyes of the other two that they too had heard. "There *must* be more money! There *must* be more money!"

It came whispering from the springs of the still-swaying rocking horse, and even the horse, bending his wooden, champing head, heard it. The big doll, sitting so pink and smirking in her new pram, could hear it quite plainly, and seemed to be smirking all the more self-consciously because of it. The foolish puppy, too, that took the place of the teddy bear, he was looking so extraordinarily foolish for no other reason but that he heard the secret whisper all over the house: "There *must* be more money!"

Yet nobody ever said it aloud. The whisper was everywhere, and therefore no one spoke it. Just as no one ever says: "We are breathing!" in spite of the fact that breath is coming and going all the time.

"Mother," said the boy Paul one day, "why don't we keep a car of our own? Why do we always use Uncle's, or else a taxi?"

"Because we're the poor members of the family," said the mother.

"But why *are* we, Mother?"

"Well—I suppose," she said slowly and bitterly, "it's because your father has no luck."

The boy was silent for some time.

"Is luck money, Mother?" he asked rather timidly.

"No, Paul. Not quite. It's what causes you to have money."

"Oh!" said Paul vaguely. "I thought when Uncle Oscar said *filthy lucker,* it meant money."

"*Filthy lucre* does mean money," said the mother. "But it's lucre, not luck."

"Oh!" said the boy. "Then what *is* luck, Mother?"

"It's what causes you to have money. If you're lucky you have money. That's why it's better to be born lucky than rich. If you're rich, you may lose your money. But if you're lucky, you will always get more money."

"Oh! Will you? And is Father not lucky?"

"Very unlucky, I should say," she said bitterly.

The boy watched her with unsure eyes.

"Why?" he asked.

"I don't know. Nobody ever knows why one person is lucky and another unlucky."

"Don't they? Nobody at all? Does *nobody* know?"

"Perhaps God. But He never tells."

"He ought to, then. And aren't you lucky either, Mother?"

"I can't be, if I married an unlucky husband."

"But by yourself, aren't you?"

"I used to think I was, before I married. Now I think I am very unlucky indeed."

"Why?"

"Well—never mind! Perhaps I'm not really," she said.

The child looked at her, to see if she meant it. But he saw, by the lines of her mouth, that she was only trying to hide something from him.

"Well, anyhow," he said stoutly, "I'm a lucky person."

"Why?" said his mother, with a sudden laugh.

He stared at her. He didn't even know why he had said it.

"God told me," he asserted, brazening it out.

"I hope He did, dear!" she said, again with a laugh, but rather bitter.

"He did, Mother!"

"Excellent!" said the mother.

The boy saw she did not believe him; or, rather, that she paid no attention to his assertion. This angered him somewhat, and made him want to compel her attention.

He went off by himself, vaguely, in a childish way, seeking for the clue to "luck." Absorbed, taking no heed of other people, he went about with a sort of stealth, seeking inwardly for luck. He wanted luck, he wanted it, he wanted it. When the two girls were playing dolls in the nursery, he would sit on his big rocking horse, charging madly into space, with a frenzy that made the little girls peer at him uneasily. Wildly the horse careered, the waving dark hair of the boy tossed, his eyes had a strange glare in them. The little girls dared not speak to him.

When he had ridden to the end of his mad little journey, he climbed down and stood in front of his rocking horse, staring fixedly into its lowered face. Its red mouth was slightly open, its big eye was wide and glassy-bright.

Now! he could silently command the snorting steed. Now, take me to where there is luck! Now take me!

And he would slash the horse on the neck with the little whip he had asked Uncle Oscar for. He *knew* the horse could take him to where there was luck, if only he forced it. So he would mount again, and start on his furious ride, hoping at last to get there. He knew he could get there.

"You'll break your horse, Paul!" said the nurse.

"He's always riding like that! I wish he'd leave off!" said his elder sister Joan.

But he only glared down on them in silence. Nurse gave him up. She could make nothing of him. Anyhow he was growing beyond her.

One day his mother and his uncle Oscar came in when he was on one of his furious rides. He did not speak to them.

"Hallo, you young jockey! Riding a winner?" said his uncle.

"Aren't you growing too big for a rocking horse? You're not a very little boy any longer, you know," said his mother.

But Paul only gave a blue glare from his big, rather close-set eyes. He would speak to nobody when he was in full tilt. His mother watched him with an anxious expression on her face.

At last he suddenly stopped forcing his horse into the mechanical gallop, and slid down.

"Well, I got there!" he announced fiercely, his blue eyes still flaring, and his sturdy long legs straddling apart.

"Where did you get to?" asked his mother.

"Where I wanted to go," he flared back at her.

"That's right, son!" said Uncle Oscar. "Don't you stop till you get there. What's the horse's name?"

"He doesn't have a name," said the boy.

"Gets on without all right?" asked the uncle.

"Well, he has different names. He was called Sansovino last week."

"Sansovino, eh? Won the Ascot.[3] How did you know his name?"

"He always talks about horse races with Bassett," said Joan.

The uncle was delighted to find that his small nephew was posted with all the racing news. Bassett, the young gardener, who had been wounded in the left foot in the war and had got his present job through Oscar Cresswell, whose batman[4] he had been, was a perfect blade of the "turf." He lived in the racing events, and the small boy lived with him.

---

3 **Ascot:** a famous race course where every June the best English horses run; the English equivalent of the Kentucky Derby.

4 **batman:** an enlisted man assigned as an orderly (assistant) to an officer. [British]

Oscar Cresswell got it all from Bassett.

"Master Paul comes and asks me, so I can't do more than tell him, sir," said Bassett, his face terribly serious, as if he were speaking of religious matters.

"And does he ever put anything on a horse he fancies?"

"Well—I don't want to give him away—he's a young sport, a fine sport, sir. Would you mind asking him himself? He sort of takes a pleasure in it, and perhaps he'd feel I was giving him away, sir, if you don't mind."

Bassett was serious as a church.

The uncle went back to his nephew and took him off for a ride in the car.

"Say, Paul, old man, do you ever put anything on a horse?" the uncle asked.

The boy watched the handsome man closely.

"Why, do you think I oughtn't to?" he parried.

"Not a bit of it! I thought perhaps you might give me a tip for the Lincoln."

The car sped on into the country, going down to Uncle Oscar's place in Hampshire.[5]

"Honor bright?" said the nephew.

"Honor bright, son!" said the uncle.

"Well, then, Daffodil."

"Daffodil! I doubt it, sonny. What about Mirza?"

"I only know the winner," said the boy. "That's Daffodil."

"Daffodil, eh?"

There was a pause. Daffodil was an obscure horse comparatively.

"Uncle!"

"Yes, son?"

"You won't let it go any further, will you? I promised Bassett."

"Bassett be damned, old man! What's he got to do with it?"

"We're partners. We've been partners from the first. Uncle, he lent me my first five shillings, which I lost. I promised him, honor bright, it was only between me and him; only you gave me that ten-shilling note I started winning with, so I thought you were lucky. You won't let it go any further, will you?"

The boy gazed at his uncle from those big, hot, blue eyes, set rather close together. The uncle stirred and laughed uneasily.

---

5 **Hampshire:** a coastal county southwest of London.

"Right you are, son! I'll keep your tip private. Daffodil, eh? How much are you putting on him?"

"All except twenty pounds," said the boy. "I keep that in reserve."

The uncle thought it a good joke.

"You keep twenty pounds in reserve, do you, you young romancer? What are you betting, then?"

"I'm betting three hundred," said the boy gravely. "But it's between you and me, Uncle Oscar! Honor bright?"

The uncle burst into a roar of laughter.

"It's between you and me all right, you young Nat Gould,"[6] he said, laughing. "But where's your three hundred?"

"Bassett keeps it for me. We're partners."

"You are, are you! And what is Bassett putting on Daffodil?"

"He won't go quite as high as I do, I expect. Perhaps he'll go a hundred and fifty."

"What, pennies?" laughed the uncle.

"Pounds," said the child, with a surprised look at his uncle. "Bassett keeps a bigger reserve than I do."

Between wonder and amusement Uncle Oscar was silent. He pursued the matter no further, but he determined to take his nephew with him to the Lincoln races.

"Now, son," he said, "I'm putting twenty on Mirza, and I'll put five for you on any horse you fancy. What's your pick?"

"Daffodil, Uncle."

"No, not the fiver on Daffodil!"

"I should if it was my own fiver," said the child.

"Good! Good! Right you are! A fiver for me and a fiver for you on Daffodil."

The child had never been to a race meeting before, and his eyes were blue fire. He pursed his mouth tight, and watched. A Frenchman just in front had put his money on Lancelot. Wild with excitement, he flailed his arms up and down, yelling *"Lancelot! Lancelot!"* in his French accent.

Daffodil came in first, Lancelot second, Mirza third. The child, flushed and with eyes blazing, was curiously serene. His uncle brought him four five-pound notes, four to one.

"What am I to do with these?" he cried, waving them before the boy's eyes.

---

6 **Nat Gould:** Gould (1857–1919) was a journalist who wrote novels about horse racing.

"I suppose we'll talk to Bassett," said the boy. "I expect I have fifteen hundred now; and twenty in reserve; and this twenty."

His uncle studied him for some moments.

"Look here, son!" he said. "You're not serious about Bassett and that fifteen hundred, are, you?"

"Yes, I am. But it's between you and me, Uncle. Honor bright!"

"Honor bright all right, son! But I must talk to Bassett."

"If you'd like to be a partner, Uncle, with Bassett and me, we could all be partners. Only, you'd have to promise, honor bright, Uncle, not to let it go beyond us three. Bassett and I are lucky, and you must be lucky, because it was your ten shillings I started winning with. . . ."

Uncle Oscar took both Bassett and Paul into Richmond Park[7] for an afternoon, and there they talked.

"It's like this, you see, sir," Bassett said. "Master Paul would get me talking about racing events, spinning yarns, you know, sir. And he was always keen on knowing if I'd made or if I'd lost. It's about a year since, now, that I put five shillings on Blush of Dawn for him—and we lost. Then the luck turned, with that ten shillings he had from you, that we put on Singhalese. And since then, it's been pretty steady, all things considering. What do you say, Master Paul?"

"We're all right when we're sure," said Paul. "It's when we're not quite sure that we go down."

"Oh, but we're careful then," said Bassett.

"But when are you *sure?*" Uncle Oscar smiled.

"It's Master Paul, sir," said Bassett, in a secret, religious voice. "It's as if he had it from heaven. Like Daffodil, now, for the Lincoln. That was as sure as eggs."

"Did you put anything on Daffodil?" asked Oscar Cresswell.

"Yes, sir. I made my bit."

"And my nephew?"

Bassett was obstinately silent, looking at Paul.

"I made twelve hundred, didn't I, Bassett? I told Uncle I was putting three hundred on Daffodil."

"That's right," said Bassett, nodding.

"But where's the money?" asked the uncle.

"I keep it safe locked up, sir. Master Paul he can have it any minute he likes to ask for it."

---

7 **Richmond Park:** a 2,000-acre park, west of central London and south of the Thames.

"What, fifteen hundred pounds?"

"And twenty! And *forty,* that is, with the twenty he made on the course."

"It's amazing!" said the uncle.

"If Master Paul offers you to be partners, sir, I would, if I were you; if you'll excuse me," said Bassett.

Oscar Cresswell thought about it.

"I'll see the money," he said.

They drove home again, and sure enough, Bassett came round to the garden house with fifteen hundred pounds in notes. The twenty pounds reserve was left with Joe Glee, in the Turf Commission deposit.

"You see, it's all right, Uncle, when I'm *sure!* Then we go strong, for all we're worth. Don't we, Bassett?"

"We do that, Master Paul."

"And when are you sure?" said the uncle, laughing.

"Oh, well, sometimes I'm *absolutely* sure, like about Daffodil," said the boy; "and sometimes I have an idea; and sometimes I haven't even an idea, have I, Bassett? Then we're careful, because we mostly go down."

"You do, do you! And when you're sure, like about Daffodil, what makes you sure, sonny?"

"Oh, well, I don't know," said the boy uneasily. "I'm sure, you know, Uncle; that's all."

"It's as if he had it from heaven, sir," Bassett reiterated.

"I should say so!" said the uncle.

But he became a partner. And when the Leger was coming on, Paul was "sure" about Lively Spark, which was a quite inconsiderable horse. The boy insisted on putting a thousand on the horse, Bassett went for five hundred, and Oscar Cresswell two hundred. Lively Spark came in first, and the betting had been ten to one against him. Paul had made ten thousand.

"You see," he said, "I was absolutely sure of him."

Even Oscar Cresswell had cleared two thousand.

"Look here, son," he said, "this sort of thing makes me nervous."

"It needn't, Uncle! Perhaps I shan't be sure again for a long time."

"But what are you going to do with your money?" asked the uncle.

"Of course," said the boy. "I started it for Mother. She said she had no luck, because Father is unlucky, so I thought if *I* was lucky, it might stop whispering."

"What might stop whispering?"

"Our house. I *hate* our house for whispering."

"What does it whisper?"

"Why—why"—the boy fidgeted—"why, I don't know. But it's always short of money, you know, Uncle."

"I know it, son, I know it."

"You know people send Mother writs,[8] don't you, Uncle?"

"I'm afraid I do," said the uncle.

"And then the house whispers, like people laughing at you behind your back. It's awful, that is! I thought if I was lucky. . . ."

"You might stop it," added the uncle.

The boy watched him with big blue eyes, that had an uncanny cold fire in them, and he said never a word.

"Well, then!" said the uncle. "What are we doing?"

"I shouldn't like Mother to know I was lucky," said the boy.

"Why not, son?"

"She'd stop me."

"I don't think she would."

"Oh!"—and the boy writhed in an odd way—"I *don't* want her to know, Uncle."

"All right, son! We'll manage it without her knowing."

They managed it very easily. Paul, at the other's suggestion, handed over five thousand pounds[9] to his uncle, who deposited it with the family lawyer, who was then to inform Paul's mother that a relative had put five thousand pounds into his hands, which sum was to be paid out a thousand pounds at a time, on the mother's birthday, for the next five years.

"So she'll have a birthday present of a thousand pounds for five successive years," said Uncle Oscar. "I hope it won't make it all the harder for her later."

Paul's mother had her birthday in November. The house had been "whispering" worse than ever lately, and, even in spite of his luck, Paul could not bear up against it. He was very anxious to see the effect of the birthday letter, telling his mother about the thousand pounds.

---

8 **writs:** legal documents; here, presumably, dunning notices for money.

9 **five thousand pounds:** In 1926, when the story was written, five thousand pounds were worth about $28,500; in today's buying power, probably $70,000–$90,000.

When there were no visitors, Paul now took his meals with his parents, as he was beyond the nursery control. His mother went into town nearly every day. She had discovered that she had an odd knack of sketching furs and dress materials, so she worked secretly in the studio of a friend who was the chief artist for the leading drapers. She drew the figures of ladies in furs and ladies in silk and sequins for the newspaper advertisements. This young woman artist earned several thousand pounds a year, but Paul's mother only made several hundreds, and she was again dissatisfied. She so wanted to be first in something, and she did not succeed, even in making sketches for drapery advertisements.

She was down to breakfast on the morning of her birthday. Paul watched her face as she read her letters. He knew the lawyer's letter. As his mother read it, her face hardened and became more expressionless. Then a cold, determined look came on her mouth. She hid the letter under the pile of others, and said not a word about it.

"Didn't you have anything nice in the post for your birthday, Mother?" said Paul.

"Quite moderately nice," she said, her voice cold and absent.

She went away to town without saying more.

But in the afternoon Uncle Oscar appeared. He said Paul's mother had had a long interview with the lawyer, asking if the whole five thousand could not be advanced at once, as she was in debt.

"What do you think, Uncle?" said the boy.

"I leave it to you, son."

"Oh, let her have it, then! We can get some more with the other," said the boy.

"A bird in the hand is worth two in the bush, laddie!" said Uncle Oscar.

"But I'm sure to *know* for the Grand National; or the Lincolnshire; or else the Derby.[10] I'm sure to know for *one* of them," said Paul.

So Uncle Oscar signed the agreement, and Paul's mother touched the whole five thousand. Then something very curious happened. The voices in the house suddenly went mad, like a chorus of frogs on a spring evening. There were certain new furnishings, and Paul had a tutor. He was *really* going to Eton,[11] his father's school, in the following

---

10   **Grand National . . . Lincolnshire . . . Derby:** three famous horse races.

11   **Eton:** Founded in 1440 by King Henry VI, Eton College is an elite secondary boys school located west of London near Windsor Castle.

autumn. There were flowers in the winter, and a blossoming of the luxury Paul's mother had been used to. And yet the voices in the house, behind the sprays of mimosa and almond blossom, and from under the piles of iridescent cushions, simply trilled and screamed in a sort of ecstasy: "There *must* be more money! Oh-h-h; there *must* be more money. Oh, now, now-w! Now-w-w—there *must* be more money!— more than ever! More than ever!"

It frightened Paul terribly. He studied away at his Latin and Greek. But his intense hours were spent with Bassett. The Grand National had gone by; he had not "known," and had lost a hundred pounds. Summer was at hand. He was in agony for the Lincoln. But even for the Lincoln he didn't "know," and he lost fifty pounds. He became wild-eyed and strange, as if something were going to explode in him.

"Let it alone, son! Don't you bother about it!" urged Uncle Oscar. But it was as if the boy couldn't really hear what his uncle was saying.

"I've got to know for the Derby! I've got to know for the Derby!" the child reiterated, his big blue eyes blazing with a sort of madness.

His mother noticed how overwrought he was.

"You'd better go to the seaside. Wouldn't you like to go now to the seaside, instead of waiting? I think you'd better," she said, looking down at him anxiously, her heart curiously heavy because of him.

But the child lifted his uncanny blue eyes. "I couldn't possibly go before the Derby, Mother!" he said. "I couldn't possibly!"

"Why not?" she said, her voice becoming heavy when she was opposed. "Why not? You can still go from the seaside to see the Derby with your uncle Oscar, if that's what you wish. No need for you to wait here. Besides, I think you care too much about these races. It's a bad sign. My family has been a gambling family, and you won't know till you grow up how much damage it has done. But it has done damage. I shall have to send Bassett away, and ask Uncle Oscar not to talk racing to you, unless you promise to be reasonable about it; go away to the seaside and forget it. You're all nerves!"

"I'll do what you like, Mother, so long as you don't send me away till after the Derby," the boy said.

"Send you away from where? Just from this house?"

"Yes," he said, gazing at her.

"Why, you curious child, what makes you care about this house so much, suddenly? I never knew you loved it."

He gazed at her without speaking. He had a secret within a secret, something he had not divulged, even to Bassett or to his uncle Oscar.

But his mother, after standing undecided and a little bit sullen for some moments, said:

"Very well, then! Don't go to the seaside till after the Derby, if you don't wish it. But promise me you won't let your nerves go to pieces. Promise you won't think so much about horse racing and *events,* as you call them!"

"Oh, no," said the boy casually. "I won't think much about them, Mother. You needn't worry. I wouldn't worry, Mother, if I were you."

"If you were me and I were you," said his mother, "I wonder what we *should* do!"

"But you know you needn't worry, Mother, don't you?" the boy repeated.

"I should be awfully glad to know it," she said wearily.

"Oh, well you *can,* you know. I mean, you *ought* to know you needn't worry," he insisted.

"Ought I? Then I'll see about it," she said.

Paul's secret of secrets was his wooden horse, that which had no name. Since he was emancipated from a nurse and a nursery governess, he had had his rocking horse removed to his own bedroom at the top of the house.

"Surely, you're too big for a rocking horse!" his mother had remonstrated.

"Well, you see, Mother, till I can have a *real* horse, I like to have *some* sort of animal about," had been his quaint answer.

"Do you feel he keeps you company?" She laughed.

"Oh, yes! He's very good, he always keeps me company, when I'm there," said Paul.

So the horse, rather shabby, stood in an arrested prance in the boy's bedroom.

The Derby was drawing near, and the boy grew more and more tense. He hardly heard what was spoken to him, he was very frail, and his eyes were really uncanny. His mother had sudden strange seizures of uneasiness about him. Sometimes, for half an hour, she would feel a sudden anxiety about him that was almost anguish. She wanted to rush to him at once, and know he was safe.

Two nights before the Derby, she was at a big party in town, when one of her rushes of anxiety about her boy, her firstborn, gripped her heart till she could hardly speak. She fought with the feeling, might and main, for she believed in common sense. But it was too strong. She had to leave the dance and go downstairs to telephone to the country. The children's nursery governess was terribly surprised and startled at being rung up in the night.

"Are the children all right, Miss Wilmot?"

"Oh, yes, they are quite all right."

"Master Paul? Is he all right?"

"He went to bed as right as a trivet. Shall I run up and look at him?"

"No," said Paul's mother reluctantly. "No! Don't trouble. It's all right. Don't sit up. We shall be home fairly soon." She did not want her son's privacy intruded upon.

"Very good," said the governess.

It was about one o'clock when Paul's mother and father drove up to their house. All was still. Paul's mother went to her room and slipped off her white fur cloak. She had told her maid not to wait up for her. She heard her husband downstairs, mixing a whisky and soda.

And then, because of the strange anxiety at her heart, she stole upstairs to her son's room. Noiselessly she went along the upper corridor. Was there a faint noise? What was it?

She stood, with arrested muscles, outside his door, listening. There was a strange, heavy, and yet not loud noise. Her heart stood still. It was a soundless noise, yet rushing and powerful. Something huge, in violent, hushed motion. What was it? What in God's name was it? She ought to know. She felt that she knew the noise. She knew what it was.

Yet she could not place it. She couldn't say what it was. And on and on it went, like a madness.

Softly, frozen with anxiety and fear, she turned the door handle.

The room was dark. Yet in the space near the window, she heard and saw something plunging to and fro. She gazed in fear and amazement.

Then suddenly she switched on the light, and saw her son, in his green pajamas, madly surging on the rocking horse. The blaze of light suddenly lit him up, as he urged the wooden horse, and lit her up, as she stood, blonde, in her dress of pale green and crystal, in the doorway.

"Paul!" she cried. "Whatever are you doing?"

"It's Malabar!" he screamed, in a powerful, strange voice. "It's Malabar!"

His eyes blazed at her for one strange and senseless second, as he ceased urging his wooden horse. Then he fell with a crash to the ground, and she, all her tormented motherhood flooding upon her, rushed to gather him up.

But he was unconscious, and unconscious he remained, with some brain fever. He talked and tossed, and his mother sat stonily by his side.

"Malabar! It's Malabar! Bassett, Bassett, I *know!* It's Malabar!"

So the child cried, trying to get up and urge the rocking horse that gave him his inspiration.

"What does he mean by Malabar?" asked the heart-frozen mother.

"I don't know," said the father stonily.

"What does he mean by Malabar?" she asked her brother Oscar.

"It's one of the horses running for the Derby," was the answer.

And, in spite of himself, Oscar Cresswell spoke to Bassett, and himself put a thousand on Malabar: at fourteen to one.

The third day of the illness was critical: they were waiting for a change. The boy, with his rather long, curly hair, was tossing ceaselessly on the pillow. He never slept nor regained consciousness, and his eyes were like blue stones. His mother sat, feeling her heart had gone, turned actually into a stone.

In the evening, Oscar Cresswell did not come, but Bassett sent a message, saying could he come up for one moment, just one moment? Paul's mother was very angry at the intrusion, but on second thought she agreed. The boy was the same. Perhaps Bassett might bring him to consciousness.

The gardener, a shortish fellow with a little brown mustache, and sharp little brown eyes, tiptoed into the room, touched his imaginary cap to Paul's mother, and stole to the bedside, staring with glittering, smallish eyes at the tossing, dying child.

"Master Paul!" he whispered. "Master Paul! Malabar came in first all right, a clean win. I did as you told me. You've made over seventy thousand pounds, you have; you've got over eighty thousand. Malabar came in all right, Master Paul."

"Malabar! Malabar! Did I say Malabar, Mother? Did I say Malabar? Do you think I'm lucky, Mother? I knew Malabar, didn't I? Over eighty thousand pounds! I call that lucky, don't you, Mother? Over eighty thousand pounds! I knew, didn't I know I knew? Malabar came in all right. If I ride my horse till I'm sure, then I tell you, Bassett, you can go as high as you like. Did you go for all you were worth, Bassett?"

"I went a thousand on it, Master Paul."

"I never told you, Mother, that if I can ride my horse, and *get there,* then I'm absolutely sure—oh, absolutely! Mother, did I ever tell you? I *am* lucky!"

"No, you never did," said the mother.

But the boy died in the night.

And even as he lay dead, his mother heard her brother's voice saying to her: "My God, Hester, you're eighty-odd thousand to the good, and a poor devil of a son to the bad. But, poor devil, poor devil, he's best gone out of a life where he rides his rocking horse to find a winner."

QUESTIONS FOR DISCUSSION

1. Lawrence submitted "The Rocking-Horse Winner" for an anthology titled *The Ghost Book*. What unrealistic elements does it contain?

2. Describe Paul's parents and assess their importance to the plot and theme.

3. What is the thematic significance of the mother's comment: "*Filthy lucre* does mean money"? 4. Why does Lawrence include the character of Uncle Oscar?

5. Of what importance to the plot is Bassett?

6. Relate the mother's reaction to her anonymous birthday gift to one of the motifs of the story.

7. In what way does the point of view contribute to or reinforce the effect of the story?

8. Is Paul's death inevitable? Explain your answer.

TOPICS FOR WRITING

1. Write an essay evaluating Lawrence's choice of Malabar as a name for the winning horse. Consider whether the effect of the ending would differ had the horse been named "Sweet Sue" or "Break-a-Leg."

2. Some critics have suggested that in many of Lawrence's stories, mothers actively attempt to shape their sons into the opposite of their husbands. In an essay, discuss whether this seems to be the case in "The Rocking-Horse Winner."

3. Write an essay supporting or attacking the following statement: "The Rocking-Horse Winner" is more of a sociological than a psychological study."

SYNTHESIS QUESTIONS

1. Which story do you find the most challenging to understand? Explain why.

2. Which of the stories has a theme so universal that students a hundred years from now could read and be affected by it?

3. In which story is the title most critical to your understanding of the story's meaning?

4. Which stories are linked by common motifs or themes?

5. The theme of some stories simply confirms the reader's beliefs. Which story most challenges your assumptions about life?

6. Which of the stories in this chapter would you most recommend to a friend and why?

7. In a well-written story, each element should contribute to the total effect and meaning. Which story most successfully accomplishes that artistic aim?

Chapter Six

STYLE

One of the more difficult literary terms to define precisely is **style**, a writer's characteristic way of saying things. The French naturalist Georges de Buffon observed that "The style is the man himself," thus suggesting a person's literary style reflects his or her character or personality. To those who agree with Buffon, a discussion of style is similar to a psychological profile of the writer. As such, it is subjective.

Writer Jonathan Swift, the author of *Gulliver's Travels,* takes a more objective approach, however. Swift said of style, "Proper words in proper places make the true definition of a style." Those who agree with his definition break a work into its components and then analyze each component. Because it can be partially quantifiable—number of words and sentences, number of words in sentences, length of paragraphs—the component approach to defining style is somewhat more objective.

In Chapter 4 we examined tone as an aspect of style. Indeed, the "proper words" Swift spoke of serve to establish tone. Other components of style grow out of a writer's diction (choice of words), imagery, syntax/variety, and organizational structure.

DICTION

Diction refers to a writer's choice of words. The words chosen can be described as general or specific (*tree* versus *weeping willow*); formal or informal ("How do you do" versus "Hello"); abstract or concrete (*honor* or *brotherhood* versus *desk*); common (*drat*); jargon (any words understood by members of a specialized group such as doctors, teachers, astronauts); Latin-based or Anglo-Saxon words (*make a hotel reservation* versus *book a room*). Whatever the choice, the author's diction needs to be both clear and appropriate. Note, however, that in fiction the author's diction does not need to be grammatical to be clear or appropriate.

Although some consider ethnic dialect politically incorrect, in Chapter 1 of this text Zora Neale Hurston uses dialect in "Sweat." Her choice and spelling of words establish the setting of her story and the nature of its characters. As you read the selections that follow, note that the diction of Sherwood Anderson's "The Egg" is appropriate to the first-person narrator, an adult looking back on his unhappy childhood; however, if the "I" of the story were a ten-year-old boy, the diction would be too sophisticated. Tony Ardizzone, in "Holy Cards," relates a series of episodes in the life of Dominic, an elementary school boy. Because the narrator freely enters Dominic's mind, he conveys young Dominic's world through concrete words appropriate to his language level. Anna Keesey wrote "Bright Winter" in the 1990s, but its events take place in the mid-1800s; the letter writer's formal diction reflects the story's setting and is appropriate to both the epistolary format and the attitude of its main character, the writer of the letters.

IMAGERY AND SYMBOL

Most readers think that **imagery** refers solely to visual pictures, but in literature, where it may be called *sensory imagery,* the term extends to all the senses—sight, taste, smell, touch, and hearing. Sensory imagery can make ideas vivid and stir the emotions of a reader. Imagery is also associated with **figures of speech** such as simile, metaphor, personification, hyperbole, analogy, and others. In this chapter Anderson limits his imagery to sensory images, using no more than one or two figures of speech in the first several paragraphs. Ardizzone, too, emphasizes sensory images since his main character has not yet progressed from literal to figurative language. The stream of consciousness musings of Granny Weatherall, on the other hand, are filled with striking similes and metaphors.

In broad terms, a **symbol** is anything that signifies, or stands for, something else. In literature, a symbol is anything concrete—an object, a place, a character, an action—that stands for or suggests something abstract. Literary symbols are not signs, since a sign such as a red light has only one meaning while a symbol may have many.

Some symbols are universal: spring, summer, autumn, and winter can represent stages in human life; a journey or a voyage often suggests the passage of a life; darkness and light are often associated with good and evil, even life and death; in recent years doves and hawks came to represent people with opposite points of view toward war. Other symbols are specific to a particular work. The great white whale chased by

Captain Ahab in Melville's novel *Moby Dick,* for example, means different things to different members of Ahab's crew—and to the critics who write about the novel.

Both literal and figurative images can be symbols. An egg, for example, is a literal object but it can be seen as a universal symbol of the beginning of life. Is that its meaning in Anderson's story? Ardizzone makes clear what holy cards are, but readers of "Holy Cards" will have to decide whether they are symbols and what they might symbolize in the story. In the Porter story, is Granny's jilting a symbol?

SYNTAX AND VARIETY

A third component of style is the sentence. **Syntax,** or sentence structure, is the pattern or arrangement of individual words and phrases. A young child's sentences tend to be declarative and follow a basic pattern or order: the subject (usually a noun or a pronoun), followed by the predicate (a verb) and, sometimes, a direct object (also a noun or pronoun): "The dog (noun/subject) ate (verb/predicate) the biscuit (noun/direct object)." Children soon learn that interrogative sentences partially reverse this order: "Did the dog eat the biscuit?" Imperative sentences drop the subject: "Eat the biscuit!"

Once children understand these basic sentence patterns, they next learn how to expand sentences and to make their ideas more specific. To do so, they use adjectives and adverbs—either as single words or as prepositional phrases—to add information to nouns and verbs. Conjunctions serve to link two sentence elements (subjects, predicates, modifiers, even entire sentences), while subordinating adverbs create complex sentences in which one element becomes a dependent clause. With these additions to their writing repertoire, children begin to create varied sentences that reflect the increasing complexity of their thoughts.

As you read more widely, you will realize that interesting writers use many methods to achieve variety. The narrative of "The Egg," for example, is primarily told through declarative sentences, but after several paragraphs Anderson varies the pattern with an interrogative sentence. Sometimes, a writer will even choose to write a fragment; in the second paragraph of "Holy Cards," Ardizzone follows a sentence with a single word: "Snow." Variety also results when writers begin a sentence with something other than a subject. For example, each of the writers in this chapter uses such introductory elements as a prepositional phrase, or verbal phrases introduced by a gerund, participle, or an infinitive. A writer may invert the natural order and begin with the direct object, as Keesey's narrator does in his first letter: "The horse you rode I will consider leased by the day." Note, too, how sentences of contrasting lengths also produce variety; in Anderson's second paragraph, for example, a thirty-word sentence is followed by sentences of six, three, and thirteen words. A story such as the "The Egg" is told primarily through narration, but the rest of the authors featured in this chapter achieve variety by alternating narration with dialogue.

Fiction writers must be acutely aware of the age, background, and attitude of their narrator—especially if he or she is a character in the story. In "The Egg," Anderson's first-person narrator is a middle-aged man who claims that his tendency to see "the darker side of life" derives from growing up on a chicken farm. The sentences illustrate the traditional subject-verb-object pattern, but with some variety. The troubled father in Keesey's "Bright Winter" writes formal sentences, varying them somewhat as in the conversation with his wife in the January 27 letter and others, and by alternating long with occasional short sentences or phrases. In Katherine Anne Porter's "The Jilting of Granny Weatherall," the action fluctuates between past and present. As Granny recalls the past, her interior monologue is conveyed in a stream-of-consciousness style—one appropriate to her mental and physical condition.

ORGANIZATIONAL STRUCTURE

The organizational structure of most fiction is chronological: stories typically begin with exposition that establishes the setting, the chief characters, and the situation, including the conflict. They progress through the rising action, the climax, and the falling action to the resolution. The author arranges the incidents of the plot causally; that is, one event causes a second, that causes a third, and so on. Such a plot is linear: it flows in a direct, logical line from beginning to middle to end, as in Anderson's "The Egg."

Some short story writers choose to vary this predictable structure. Ardizzone's "Holy Cards" and Keesey's "Bright Winter" retain a linear chronology but jettison causality. The series of incidents or letters creates an episodic structure and encourages the reader to determine the connections between each episode. Porter's "The Jilting of Granny Weatherall" contains extensive flashbacks, another device to vary the structure. Some authors like to grab your attention by beginning *in media res*—Latin for "in the middle of things." If their story consists of five scenes, the opening scene may chronologically be scene three. Some authors create frame stories—stories within a story—with two narrators, while others choose to alternate narrators, allowing a story to unfold through two or more points of view. Perhaps you recall reading a recent novel that begins at the end of the plot and in successive chapters moves back in time to the beginning, another variation on structure.

SUMMARY

Style is a writer's characteristic way of saying things. It is a product of both the character of the writer as an individual and the choices that he or she makes concerning diction, imagery, syntax and variety, and organizational structure. Diction must be clear and appropriate. Imagery can be based either in sensory language or in figures of speech. Both literal and figurative images can be symbols—objects, places, characters, or action that stand for or suggest something abstract. A writer's style also grows out of the mixture and variety of sentence patterns used in the writing. Finally, the overall organization of the material is another component of style.

HOLY CARDS

TONY ARDIZZONE (born 1949)

In *Taking It Home: Stories from the Neighborhood* (1995), Tony Ardizzone evokes his Italian Catholic boyhood on the North Side of Chicago, Illinois, during the 1950s.

Ardizzone received his B.A. from the University of Illinois in 1971. After two years at Chicago's St. Mary Center for Learning, he earned an M.F.A. at Bowling Green State University (1975). He taught at Bowling Green until 1978 and then at Old Dominion University until 1987. Since then, Ardizzone has taught creative writing at Indiana University.

Ardizzone has published two novels: *In the Name of the Father* (1978) and *Heart of the Order* (1986); his third novel, *In the Garden of Papa Santuzzu,* is scheduled for publication in 1999. His first story collection, *The Evening News* (1986), won the Flannery O'Connor Award for Short Fiction. His second, the interconnected *Larabi's Ox: Stories of Morocco* (1992) received both the Milkweed National Fiction Prize and the Chicago Foundation for Literature Award for Fiction. Ardizzone's other awards include the Pushcart Prize, the Lawrence Foundation Award, and two fellowships in fiction from the National Endowment for the Arts.

The protagonist of "Holy Cards" is Dominic, an elementary school boy who, in trying to make sense of both the secular and the sacred worlds, often confuses the two. As you read, think about how you would describe the structure and the style of the story.

■

THE MILK BOTTLES

"Children," the Sister of Christian Charity called out. "Children, who made us?"

From his fifth-row desk, Dominic stared dreamily out the classroom window. The sky behind the bare trees on Armitage Avenue appeared to be breaking apart. Little pieces of it drifted lazily to the sidewalk. Snow. A bad window, it showed only the sides of things. Dominic lived in the second-floor flat in the corner building on Fullerton and Southport, and from its high bay windows enjoyed a more expansive view. He enjoyed looking down at all the traffic moving out from the busy stop below. He liked watching the different people on the street. He was small and dark, with a swoop of straight black hair that fell across his forehead like a comma. Here in class, he had to look up to see anything.

"Once again, children. Louder. Who made us?"

This one was easy. "God made us," the children singsonged.

At home a service flag[1] hung in the center window, blocking Dominic's way. He'd have to crouch to see under it, or else he'd push it aside. His ma would yell when she caught him pulling on the flag's fringe. It was something special or holy. Sometimes when there were no buses or delivery trucks to look at, his fingertips would trace the outline of the flag's star. Sitting at his desk watching the snow, Dominic reached forward and traced the figure of his father's star.

Sister rapped her wooden yardstick across her desk. An old woman, perhaps in her late sixties, she wore thick glasses and had a large mole on the right side of her nose and a gold front tooth. "And who is God?"

Dominic pictured the blue cover of his *Baltimore Catechism*.[2] When he sat studying in the red stuffed chair across the room from the windows, he'd try to keep his eyes on the letters in the book and away from the sky and the streets. Sometimes when his Aunt Rose came over to visit, she'd help him out and pretend to be his teacher, Sister Mary Justine. Aunt Rose would ask each question and give him hints whenever he got stuck. After he finished his homework and had

---

1 **service flag:** During World War ii, many windows displayed small blue and white banners with red stars in the center denoting the number of family members in the armed services. Gold stars (as well as a black fringe on the flag) indicated a service person had been killed.

2 **Baltimore Catechism:** one of several books containing questions and answers used to instruct young Catholics in the tenets of their faith. The *Baltimore Catechism* (1885) was the result of a series of councils held in Baltimore, Maryland.

thoroughly dusted the front room and the dining room, he could look out the corner windows and play.

"God is the Supreme Being," the children were reciting, "who is infinitely perfect and who made all things and keeps them in existence."

"And why did God make us?" Sister Justine asked.

The snow outside grew thick and furious, swirling and dashing itself against the panes of glass. "God made us to know, love, and serve him and to be happy with him forever in Heaven," the children chanted. Sister then told the class to open their catechisms to the next chapter. Dominic looked in his book, thinking of Heaven and happiness. But there he saw depicted three milk bottles.

The first bottle was dark, as if full of chocolate milk. Sister Justine explained that actually the bottle was empty, symbolizing the soul before baptism, with its absence of sanctifying grace. With the holy sacrament of baptism, Sister explained, the bottle became filled. The second bottle was white, full of milk, and topped by a glowing halo. The third bottle had spots. Sister explained that the spots in its milk were sins.

"Children," she said, "there is nothing more evil than sin. There is no ink on earth black enough to portray its darkness and horror. Not even Satan himself, the Prince of Evil and enemy of baby Jesus, could make an ink so black as to show you how loathsome sin really is."

Dominic stared out the windows into the raging snow. A milk truck was making its daily delivery to the convent across the street. All the nuns who taught at Saint Stephen's lived in the convent. Dominic tried to see if any of the bottles the milkman was carrying were chocolate. Sister Justine asked the class if sin was dreadful and if they would each renounce it for the remainder of their lives. All the children, particularly the girls of row three, shouted out, nodding. The class grew as rowdy as a birthday party. "Yes, Sister!" the children cried. "Oh, yes! Yes!" Dominic wanted to raise his hand to warn Sister about the milkman, but he couldn't see. The snow was too fast and thick. So he turned away from the window and shouted along with the others.

Then Sister told them to be quiet and to take out their number books and pencils, and Dominic forgot about milk bottles and the Prince of Evil and chocolate and spots. Next to a drawing of seven shiny baseballs he wrote a large 7 and then gave each baseball a pair of eyes and a happy smile and a curly handlebar moustache.[3]

---

3 **handlebar moustache:** a thick moustache with a prominent curve like that of bicycle handlebars.

THE HOLY GHOST

Dominic learned more things about God. He learned that there was only one God, and that Heaven lay just above the clouds. For some weeks then while at the bay windows Dominic ignored the buses and trucks and gazed up at the Chicago sky. He did this until his mother yelled at him to stop before he deformed his neck.

Then Sister Justine confused his picture of things by informing her class about the existence of the Holy Trinity. Try as she would to explain it, even by offering analogies to shamrocks and isosceles triangles and 3-in-One Oil, the children simply couldn't fathom how one person could really be three persons at the same time. No matter how you looked at it, Dominic reasoned, it didn't make any sense. From the lessons in his number book he knew that one plus one plus one could never equal anything but three. Finally he gave up trying to understand, thinking he'd wait until he died in the state of sanctifying grace and his eternal soul drifted up just behind the clouds. Then he'd see God's arithmetic for himself.

Heaven gave Dominic problems too. Sister told the class that Heaven consisted mainly of the beatific vision, which was being able to look upon the face, or faces, of God. Dominic understood that looking at a pretty face was pleasurable—he did like to look at Aunt Rose's face and one evening as a test did for as long as he could until she told him to cut it out because he was making her extremely uncomfortable—but he wondered if he could do it for all of eternity. Eternity was a very long time.

He had pictures of God in his missal[4] and on holy cards, which Sister gave the children occasionally as a special reward for doing some difficult thing perfectly, like cleaning the erasers and not getting chalk dust on everything. Each holy card depicted a special moment in a holy person's life, sort of like snapshots in God's family album. Already Dominic had collected Saint Francis of Assisi talking to several chipmunks, a doe, and two doves. He had one of Saint Christopher giving baby Jesus a piggyback ride. He had Christ pointing to his immense and bloody Sacred Heart. He had Our Lady of Fatima standing on a cloud before three children and their lambs. He had Saint Joseph holding his carpenter's tools and a

---

4 **missal:** a book containing the prescribed prayers and liturgical form for celebrating Mass during the year.

white lily.[5] Dominic cherished his holy cards but didn't think he could look at them or at God forever. Did anyone ever look away? he thought. What happened to them when they did? What if they had to go to thebathroom? Or had to sneeze? Wriggling in his seat, Dominic was tempted to ask Sister these questions but was too frightened. He went back to staring at the sky and the bare, intricate branches of trees.

Sister told the children that when they had questions of faith they should pray to the Holy Ghost for strength. He was in charge of all of God's grace, Sister said. She showed the class a picture of the Holy Ghost hovering over the Virgin Mary's head, shooting out tiny rays of grace.

Dominic prayed then to the Holy Ghost. He felt sort of sorry for him because he was just a bird. It seemed unfair since God the Father, with his long white beard and fancy gold chair up in Heaven, and God the Son, with his crown of thorns and crucifix, got to be actual people. Dominic wondered if the Holy Ghost ever felt jealous. Dominic knew he'd be jealous if he were the Holy Ghost.

While at Mass the next Sunday morning with his mother and Aunt Rose, with the priest singing "Dominus vobiscum," and the people singing in response, "Et cum spiritu tuo,"[6] Dominic spied a pigeon flying just below the high, arched ceiling of the church.

"There's the Holy Ghost!" he cried.

Aunt Rose laughed. His ma told him to hush. But Dominic became so excited that he cried out once more. Aunt Rose then leaned over to him and very seriously whispered, "Look, when he flies near the lights, you can see his halo, can't you?" That silenced Dominic for a while. Sure enough it was true, if you squinted your eyes just right. When Mass was over Dominic pulled away from the two women to kneel and wave good-bye.

The next day at morning Mass with his classmates he kept an eye on the ceiling, and then again just after the Offertory everyone in church saw him as he fluttered off the top of one of the lights and

---

5 **Saint Francis . . . Saint Christopher . . . Our Lady of Fatima . . . Saint Joseph:** Francis of Assisi (1181/2–1226), founder of the Franciscan order and patron of animals; Christopher, martyred in the third century, the patron of travelers; Our Lady of Fatima, a vision who appeared five times to three illiterate Portuguese children in 1917; Saint Joseph, the husband of Mary, the mother of Jesus, and the patron of a good death.

6 **"Dominus vobiscum" . . . "Et cum spiritu tuo":** At the beginning of the Mass and elsewhere, the priest says, "The Lord be with you," and the congregation responds, "And also with your spirit." [Latin]

swooped down low over the children's heads, and each of the children looked up. Then for a while he flew back and forth, kind of showing off, while the priest offered the bread and wine. Then everyone saw him fly straight as an arrow into one of the stained-glass windows and, with a smash, break his holy neck. Several of the children screamed. A few of the smaller kids began to cry, undoubtedly overwhelmed by all of the grace invisibly exploding out of the feebly flapping body as it twirled down through the air and then landed with a soft thump on the church's marble floor.

Dominic smiled and prayed feverishly. He knew that the Holy Ghost had been finally fed up with being just a bird and had decided to die like his big brother Jesus. Dominic knew that after three days the Holy Ghost would rise up and be alive again, and that later he'd ascend into Heaven. And, sure enough, three days later when Dominic checked the pews beneath the stained-glass window, the Holy Ghost was no longer there. Dominic was filled with joy because he knew that the Holy Ghost had risen.

"Alleluia, alleluia," Dominic cried. "Alleluia."[7]

MARTYRS

The Chicago sky was as gray as lint clogging a drain. Dominic sat at his desk, head resting on his arms, eyes staring out the windows. He was counting the pink bricks of the convent across the street, grouping them in tens, then twenties. Before him stood Sister Justine, her arms folded beneath the outer robes of her black habit.

"Children," she was saying, "we learn through example." Her gold front tooth glistened wetly in the room's fluorescent light.

She was telling them the story of Saint Stephen, their patron saint.[8] He had been the Church's first martyr. Stoned by the Church's enemies because they were envious of his knowledge and power, Stephen had gained the immediate reward of Heaven. Sister told the children that they must learn to suffer for their faith.

Before Stephen died, he said two things. Sister had asked the class to memorize these last sacred words, as they were recorded in the Acts of the Apostles by one of the apostles who had witnessed Stephen's death.

---

7 **Alleluia:** Latin form of Hallelujah [Hebrew], "praise be Jehovah" (or "the Lord").

8 **patron saint:** saint chosen as the special protector and advocate in heaven of a person, place, organization, or the like.

Dominic was counting the bricks around the hedges. He was up to sixteen. Four more would make another twenty. He stopped, surveyed the back of the kid's head in front of him, shivered in the suddenly chilly classroom, and then slowly raised his hand.

"Yes, Dominic?" Sister said.

He was nervous as he stood in the aisle. He could feel everyone in class looking at him. It was no small thing interrupting a lesson, but if your question was a good one, one that showed attention and thought, you earned extra points toward your next holy card. Slowly he asked, "Sister, why didn't the apostle try to help Saint Stephen?"

"I don't know what you mean," Sister said.

Maybe it was a dumb question, Dominic thought. He looked out the windows at the convent, then rubbed his chin. "I mean, if he was there too when the heathens were killing him, why didn't he fight too?"

Sister Justine gave him the forced smile that meant she was running out of patience. "I still don't understand you," she said. "Why don't you sit back down and allow the class to continue with today's lesson?"

Dominic started to sit, then hesitated. No, he thought, it was a good question. He cleared his throat. "Didn't Saint Stephen fight, Sister?"

"Fight whom?" said the nun.

"The Church's evil heathen enemies, Sister," replied Dominic.

"Good. Now what were the heathens doing to Stephen?"

Dominic thought for a moment. It was yesterday's new word. Finally he said, "Stoning him, Sister."

"Very good. Now what is your question?"

"I'm asking why the apostle didn't help Saint Stephen fight back." Dominic could feel his back beginning to sweat.

"Saint Stephen didn't fight," Sister said. She turned and drew her yardstick from the top of her desk, then brandished it in the air. "Does anyone else here think that Saint Stephen fought?"

When she said "fought," she sounded as if she were spitting. No one in class raised a hand. The girls of row three stared at Dominic with wide eyes, wagging their astonished heads.

"Well, Dominic," Sister said, "as you can see you're the only one in the room who thinks Saint Stephen fought. Now, children, why didn't he?"

The room erupted with raised hands. "Because fighting's wrong," the girls of row three singsonged.

"Yes, girls," Sister said, "that's very good. And why else?"

No one could think of another reason.

"Because it was the will of God," Sister said. The children nodded their heads. Dominic was confused.

"You mean Saint Stephen just let them kill him, Sister?"

A rush of blood colored Sister's face, leaving a pale halo around the mole on the side of her nose. "Yes, Dominic," she said. "Because it was the will of God."

"But Sister, what about the apostle who was watching, who wrote it all down?"

"Dominic," Sister said sharply, "I think you're deliberately trying to waste the class's time by asking these ridiculous questions. You know that time is invaluable and can never be replaced. Very well then, we'll begin our lesson with you. What did Stephen cry out as he was stoned?"

Dominic was flustered. He was trying to figure out how Stephen and the apostle knew it was the will of God. What if they had tried to fight? he thought. Would God have struck them down right then and there because their actions were against his will? The boy thought of Lot's wife, how God had turned her into a pillar of salt. He thought of how God had banned Moses from entering the land of milk and honey.[9] "Sit down," Sister Justine said, "and write out twenty times the last holy words of Saint Stephen." Dominic held back his tears, and she continued the lesson.

Stephen was buried by a man named Gamaliel in the year A.D. 36. Then, decades later, a pious old priest named Lucien discovered Stephen's body, which was miraculously preserved, still warm to the touch, and as white as the purest of snows.

Dominic wasn't listening. He sat sadly at his desk, his left hand pressed down hard against his writing tablet, his tongue sticking out of the corner of his mouth, writing over and over, *"Lord Jesus, receive my spirit."* And just below that: *"Lord, lay not this sin to their charge."*

GOD'S ALL-STARS

Dominic's mother sat in the red stuffed chair near the old cathedral radio.[10] The chair had been her husband's favorite. Against the wall was the matching sofa, worn and pink at its edges, a pair of end tables, and a lamp. Across from her stood the oil heater. That morning she'd

---

9   **pillar of salt . . . milk and honey:** The first biblical reference is found in Genesis: 19:26. Reference is also made in Numbers: 14:30 and in Deuteronomy: 3:27 and 34:4.

10   **cathedral radio:** a radio whose pointed shape and cutwork front resembled a cathedral and/or its windows.

filled it carefully, not spilling a drop. She was good at not spilling things. She was good at numbers, at keeping them straight. In a notebook she figured the month's expenses, drawing her wool sweater more tightly around herself. It was a Wednesday, her day off from the Dixie Diner, where she worked.

Dominic whistled as he washed in the bathroom. He'd just come home from school and had given his mom a big kiss and his day's papers. His cheeks were flushed. He was wearing his new blue Cubs jacket, purchased the night before.

At the busy department store near Lincoln and Belmont, Dominic had made faces in the mirrors and claimed both his arms were broken until his mom consented to the young salesman to let her son try the Cubs jacket on. It was loose, but Dominic pleaded with her to buy it.

"But honey," she said, "it's the wrong size."

"He's sure to grow into it," the salesman said brightly.

"Please," Dominic said. "Pretty please."

"We've got White Sox jackets too," offered the salesman.

Dominic shook his head. He hated the White Sox even though they were the better team. He was a North Sider, and the Cubs were the North Side team. It was that simple.

She heard him open the icebox, then the silverware drawer. He was making his usual after-school snack, peanut-butter Holy Communions. By working the bread with his hands the boy would form the Hosts, which he then topped with peanut butter or, sometimes, marmalade.

"Dominic," she called.

He walked into the front room, the cuffs of his new jacket hanging over his hands and wet from when he'd washed.

"Dominic," she asked, "what's this?"

She held up his religion test. He'd received a 70. Marked with large red checks were the answers DEE FONDY, HANK SAUER, and ERNIE BANKS.[11]

"Dominic," she said again.

His mouth was full of Communion. He chewed slowly and raised one finger to ask her to wait. Then he ran into his bedroom and returned with his cigar box. He opened it before her, sitting by her legs on the floor.

---

11 **DEE FONDY, HANK SAUER and ERNIE BANKS:** Chicago Cubs players who played together from the fall of 1953, when Banks joined the team, through the 1955 season, when Fondy left.

"Look, Ma," he said proudly. Bound neatly with green rubber bands were his holy cards depicting the bloody deaths of martyrs, the miracles of the Virgin and the many saints, and the various faces of God. Mixed with them were his baseball cards. On several Dominic had drawn halos or put crosses on the bats.

"The Cubs are the martyrs," he said, "see?" showing her the various cards listing previous years' National League standings. On nearly all of them the Cubs were listed seventh or eighth, in last place. "And this guy here, Saint Tarcissus, he was a ballplayer too." Dominic showed his mother his Saint Tarcissus holy card. On its back was the story of how the young Roman martyr had played a crude form of baseball with his friends until the afternoon he agreed to secretly carry the Eucharist beneath his cloak to the catacombs to help the early Christians celebrate Mass and was stoned to death because he refused to stop and play a ball game. He died in the arms of a beautiful maiden. Dominic adored Saint Tarcissus because the card said that he fought back viciously.

"But this test," his mother said.

"Sister don't know nothing," Dominic said.

"But she's there to teach you," his mother began, but then stopped when he took her hand and led her into his bedroom.

Smiling, he pointed to the wall above his dresser. There hung his Cubs pennant and his glow-in-the-dark crucifix. Behind the crucifix and a sheaf of palms was a sheet of his writing paper.

THE ALL-STARS

1. GOD THE FATHER FIRST PERSON 1st base
2. GOD THE SON SECOND PERSON 2nd
3. GOD THE HOLY GHOST THIRD PERSON 3rd
4. ERNIE BANKS I DON'T CARE IF HE'S CHOCOLATE shortstop
5. HANK SAUER right field A HOLY MARTYR CUB
6. RALPH KINER left field A HOLY MARTYR CUB
7. SAINT TARCISSUS catcher BUT HE DOESN'T HAVE TO PLAY IF HE DON'T WANT TO
8. FRANK BAUMHOLTZ center ANOTHER HOLY MARTYR CUB
9. OUR LADY OF PERPETUAL HELP[12] the pitcher BECAUSE OF HER BIG GOOD ARMS

12 **Our Lady of Perpetual Help:** one of the many descriptive names for Mary, the mother of Jesus.

Laughing, his mother suggested they move his lineup from behind the crucifix to just beneath the Cubs pennant. Dominic nodded and then ran to the kitchen for a thumbtack.

THE BLEEDING BUREAU

He was certain his nickel was somewhere. Dominic plunged his hands into his pockets, stretching nearly horizontal at his desk. Around him, the other kids who'd received Communion at morning Mass were finishing their breakfasts, their fingernails idly scraping the sides of their waxed milk cartons. The girls of row three were chewing silently, thirty times before swallowing, as Sister Justine instructed. In five bites Dominic had wolfed down his flat egg on toast, always soggy by the time he ate it.

He checked his back pockets. Each was empty, save for lint. Then he remembered that he'd put his nickel in his shirt pocket, for good luck, in the hope that it would put his row over the five-dollar mark and thus allow them this Friday morning to buy and name a pagan baby.

Kenneth, the tall row captain, had already left his seat and stood waiting before the row. He held his hands at his sides, as if at military attention. Dominic smiled at his nickel, then spat on it. Now it was even more lucky. He dropped his lint into his ink-well and looked back at the pagan baby mission board tallies.

ROW ONE	ROW TWO	ROW THREE	ROW FOUR	ROW FIVE	ROW SIX
Gabriel	Pius X	Stephen	Cosmas	Daria	Hippolytus
Achilleus		Justina	Damian	Agapitus	
		Praxedes		Valentine	
		Clare			
		Madeleine Sophie Barat			
		Scholastica			
		Gertrude			
		Bridget			
		Mary Euphrasia Pelletier			

Sister usually helped out with suggestions for the names, but the children of each row voted, democratically, the majority ruling. This year they were buying their pagan babies from an orphanage in a place called Siam.[13] Dominic liked Siam because he knew it was where Siamese cats and twins came from. Every time the good missionary priests received another five dollars, they took an unnamed boy or girl out of its crib and baptized and named it. Then for all eternity the kid owed the everlasting salvation of its soul to the generosity of the good Catholic children in Chicago whose pennies and nickels and dimes enabled the pagan child to be saved.

Something whizzed past Dominic's face. It was a spitball, likely from someone in row two. Dominic turned in his seat and looked for the culprit. Row two made the room's best spitballs: neither too dry nor too wet. A good spitball smacked but wasn't sloppy. It stuck but didn't stay. Row two was famous for shooting spitballs at the classroom's ceiling, where they'd hang for ten or more tantalizing minutes—so long that maybe even the spitball's creator had forgotten he'd shot it up there—until it fell in the middle of the aisle or on some kid's desk or head, disrupting everything, and nobody was the wiser. Dominic tore a scrap of paper off his tablet and worked up some saliva and wet the paper carefully on his tongue, then chewed it into shape. A guy couldn't not defend himself or else he'd become everybody's target. He squeezed the spitball gently between his fingertips. As Sister turned toward the blackboard, Dominic crouched in the aisle and fired. It hit Willie Berger in row one right on the ear.

"Have your money ready now, children," Sister called out.

Kenneth marched down the aisle, firmly gripping the shoulder of each fifth rower until the kid contributed something—at least a penny or two—to his box. He was a good row captain. Running for election earlier that year, Kenneth told the class that his dad was the alderman's right-hand man, so he knew how to make government work. That was the city's slogan: Chicago was the city that worked. Dominic understood enough to know that only a fool didn't drop a couple of coins on an open palm backed up by a hand squeezing your shoulder.

Suddenly, from the middle of row two, Eddie Dymkowycz stood in his seat and made a noise like a stepped-on horse. Out from his

---

13 **Siam:** present-day Thailand.

mouth shot a stream of vomit so solid it splashed the back of Angela Donofrio's long brunette hair. She grasped her barrettes and shrieked. The first three rows emptied faster than a fire drill, fleeing the sight and surprisingly horrible smell: a cross between old cheese and the wettest corner of a flooded basement. They took refuge by the front blackboard as Eddie let loose a second column of vomit that bounced off his desk top and rained on the floor. Rows four, five, and six darted to the side windows.

Sister Justine rapped her yardstick on her desk for order. With the exception of Angela Donofrio, the kids quieted down to a reasonable roar. Sister then ordered one of the girls of row three to fetch the janitor and told gasping Eddie and hysterical Angela to report immediately to Mother Superior's office. The boys of row six jerked open the windows without her having to ask.

Dominic shivered from the sudden cold. He wanted to throw up too. He was sympathetic that way. When people around him cried, he felt like crying too. When others vomited, he too had to vomit. He swallowed back down a mouthful of his egg-and-toast sandwich and tried to get his mind to change the subject. He tried to get his nose to smell the cold, fresh air. Sister started in on something. Dominic focused on her gold tooth.

"As we wait for the custodian, children, let's continue our unit on the Holy Eucharist and perhaps use this event as a lesson. Let me tell you a true story. There once was a boy who received Holy Communion in the state of mortal sin. Too weak to defend his faith, he ate meat one Friday with his Protestant friends. Then he committed the grave sin of pride and thought it didn't matter. Well, it did! After leaving the Communion rail, just like our Edward he vomited. You see, children, Jesus does not like entering an unclean soul, just as you or I would not like going into a dirty house."

The janitor came to the classroom door wheeling before him a bucket and a mop, and carrying a broom and a bag of sawdust.

"Children," Sister continued, "here's another true story I know, about a bad boy who purposely bit into the Host.[14] He was angry at Jesus for some petty reason. Well, his mouth immediately filled with Christ's blood, and in his shame he swallowed much of it. Then he fell sick and vomited, and only after the blessed sacrament of confession was the boy well again."

---

14 **Host:** wafers of unleavened bread used for communion.

As the janitor mopped up what he could, the children shuffled back to their seats.

"A very curious child once walked to the back of the church and spat the Eucharist[15] into his handkerchief and foolishly took it home, then further desecrated it by hiding it in his dresser drawer. What could this boy have been thinking? Did he think he could contain Christ? By dawn the next morning, his bureau drawer overflowed with blood! It got on his hands and face, and when the boy tried to wipe it off it couldn't be removed! The little sinner then tried to staunch its flow, but no tourniquet save the prayers of an anointed priest could stem the flood of blood gushing from the drawer."

The janitor slowly spread the sawdust.

"Now children, I certainly don't intend to say that either Edward or Angela did any of these things, but I do want to impress upon each of you that God is supremely powerful, and that he works in many strange and mysterious ways!"

Dominic swallowed hard as he stared at a spot on his desk top. He pictured his own bureau gushing with blood, his mother's disappointment, the monsignor's angry face, Aunt Rose's sadness. During the next moment, as a spitball plopped on his desk, he imagined the crucified Christ's extraordinary pain and Satan's simultaneous glee. Dominic shuddered. His pants flowed hot and wet.

As soon as he realized what he'd done, he began crying. No one yet noticed the puddle beneath his desk, so he slowly raised his hand.

When Sister moved on to another story—this one about a bad boy who impaled a stolen Host upon a nail—Dominic stood and covered the front of his pants with his hands and made his way down his row, past a kid picking his nose, a girl copying her spelling words in neat Palmer cursive,[16] a boy playing paper-puck hockey with his pencil and inkwell, Kenneth counting the row's nickels and dimes.

"Dominic," Sister called, "return to your seat at once."

He knew that she'd discover his accident in another minute, so he made his way to Mother Superior's office without waiting to be told. He didn't turn. Peeing was bad enough. He didn't want the whole class to see his tears too.

---

15 **Eucharist:** holy communion; sometimes a reference to the communion bread itself.

16 **Palmer cursive:** Cursive writing connects letters with flowing strokes. Widely taught in elementary schools, Palmer's method moved students from printed letters to connected letters.

NATIVITY

The cathedral radio played a medley of church songs.

"Wear two pairs of socks," his mother called. She was untangling a string of Christmas tree lights at the table in the dining room. Around her were the cardboard boxes in which she stored their holiday things. Already she'd unpacked the wooden manger and a few of their glass ornaments. The figure of the lame shepherd boy carrying a lamb across his shoulders lay in a loose fold of tissue paper. The other figures were still in their boxes, waiting for Dominic to unwrap them and put them in place. Since he was old enough to understand Christmas, she let the boy set up their manger. It was a tradition. She believed in traditions. She could hear her son in his bedroom singing along with the radio. Then the boy's singing stopped.

"Everything stinks," he shouted.

"What?" she said. She walked to the radio and turned it down, then tucked her hands under her arms.

Dominic was trying to open his bedroom window. Beyond the glass it was snowing so thickly that he couldn't make out the lights of the tavern directly across the street. On his bed were his good winter clothes.

"Poison gas," Dominic said. He held his neck and coughed.

His mother laughed. "Take the mothballs out of your pockets, smart guy," she said. Dominic laughed too, then carried the heavy jacket into the front room.

"I'll do it out here with the music," he said.

His mother gathered the lights from the table and sat across from him on the sofa. Dominic took his father's chair.

"When I was a girl," his mother said, "we waited and bought our tree on Christmas Eve. We were poor, and trees were cheaper then." She held up the string of multicolored lights.

Dominic held several mothballs. "Ma," he said, "are we poor?"

The woman smiled. "Well," she said, "are you ever hungry? Or cold? Or do you have to wear rags to school?"

"No," he said.

"Do you have a warm place at night to sleep?"

He nodded.

"Then we're not poor."

"Well," he said, "are we rich then?"

"We don't have money to burn, if that's what you mean," his mother said. She was staring at the radio that was between them.

Dominic laughed. He thought that was pretty funny. "You can't burn nickels or dimes," he said. He put the mothballs on the floor in front of the radio and faced his mother and wiped his hands.

His mother laughed too, then gazed down at the rug. "You know, when I was a little girl, once on Christmas day my father gave me three pennies." She turned and plugged in the string of lights. Dominic gasped. The soft glowing lights made her appear so beautiful. "My pa said that one penny was for the old year, one for the new, and the third"—she stared at him for a moment—"the third penny was for something very special." She smiled, brushing back from her face her long auburn hair. "It was a joke, honey. We were very poor. But you and me, we're a different story. Don't we have enough?" She unplugged the lights and stood.

"Sure," Dominic said. "Three cents is enough."

Outside, the large snowflakes veiled even the streetlights. Mounds of snow grew on window ledges and in doorways, gathered heavily on the tops of awnings, covering the green metal hoods over the traffic lights and the street side of the parking meters. The traffic on Fullerton Avenue moved slowly, muffled into near silence by the thick snow. Dominic's mother took big steps. The boy's heart raced in his chest.

They walked west up Fullerton Avenue past Tartaglia's grocery and fresh meats to the vacant lot between the Jewish bakery and Zileski's shoe store. Bright lights were strung from wooden poles. The lot resembled a pine forest. Knots of people warmed themselves around fires in oil-drum garbage cans. Orange sparks flew eagerly into the air. An old man with a cane and a large black dog sat silently inside a dark shed.

"Stay close by me now," Dominic's mother told him.

He held her arm as they looked at the trees and helped her when she pulled one out and inspected it. Most of them, she said, were too expensive or not full enough or had the wrong kind of needles. Dominic filled his nose with their exciting smell.

"We used to get a tree for twenty cents," she said, shaking her head. "And look, they want three dollars."

"Why don't we wait until next week?" Dominic asked. He remembered the story she'd told him. Next week was Christmas Eve.

"Because we don't have to," she said. She shook her head, then led her son to one of the fires. Dominic spread his hands over the warm flames.

"They'd send me because I was the littlest," she said. "You don't remember them, do you?"

Dominic said no. He didn't realize he had grandparents.

"Of course your Aunt Rose would come with me too, to help me carry the tree home, but I had to go into the lot all by myself. You see, Dominic, the men sold them the cheapest to the smallest children."

His mother's face glowed in the fire.

"The children would gather outside the lot, and then, just after midnight, after the church bells rang out, the men would throw them all the leftover trees. You could get hurt if you weren't careful. We did that for a few years, Rose and me, when we didn't have any money, but when we had a few pennies they'd send me into the lot."

"I can do that this year," Dominic said. He really wanted to.

"Oh no," his mother said. She stared at the flames in the can. "Once I saw a boy robbed by three bigger boys after he let on that he had some money. And once a little girl was trampled because she went for the first tree." She looked at her son. "Besides," she winked, "we've got money."

She turned and walked to the shed. The black dog stood and sniffed the hem of her coat.

"I'll give you a dollar for that tree, take it or leave it," she said to the old man inside. She pointed to the three-dollar tree.

The old man spat on the ground. Dominic watched his mother.

"That's a three-dollar tree," the old man said.

"And I'm a Rockefeller,"[17] Dominic's mother said. "I'll give you a dollar fifty."

The old man rubbed the big dog's neck. "Two and a half and it's yours, lady. Come on, I gotta make a buck."

"Not off me."

"Merry Christmas to you, lady."

"You're going to sell all these trees by next week?" She gestured to the scores of trees that filled the lot. "A very merry Christmas to you, sir." She pulled Dominic's hand and turned.

"OK, lady, two dollars even."

"Let's split the difference. A dollar seventy-five."

The old man nodded.

"A dollar seventy-five then," she said. She was smiling.

The old man stood and hobbled to the tree. The dark tip of his cane sunk deep into the snow. The dog followed him, panting a white cloud. The old man tore the tag from the tree and said, "All right, lady, take it."

---

17 **Rockefeller:** John D. Rockefeller (1839–1937) amassed a fortune in creating the Standard Oil Company; the name became synonymous with great wealth.

Dominic's mother handed him a dollar and three quarters. Snowflakes sparkled in her hair. Dominic helped her carry the green tree.

The two were silent as they began the walk home. Then Dominic grinned and began the song he'd heard earlier on the radio. "O little town of Bethlehem," he sang, "how still we see thee lie." His mother joined him singing as they carried the tree between them through the falling snow.

THE CLOCK

Sleet fell as if without end.

Dominic stood at his front windows. When he looked toward the city's horizon, all he could see were streaks. Above the horizon the sky was dirty white, like an old T-shirt. His hand touched the windowpane. He was glad his mom had finally taken down the service flag. The cold rain fell in broad straight lines and splashed upon the street and its slow traffic.

Below, from the left window, lay Fullerton Avenue, a bright and nearly always crowded street. The file of autos from the east cut through the late-afternoon rain with its headlights. They made the rain and ice on his windows glisten. As the cars passed under the streetlights, their roofs gleamed with a clean, shiny splendor. The tires made a sleepy shushing sound.

The tavern at the opposite corner had dark windows lit by neon beer signs. They flashed off and on, night and day. The tavern door was made of strong wood and had a dark little window shaped like a diamond set so high that you had to be tall—grown up—to see through it.

On the sidewalk in front of the tavern was a bearded Jew. He didn't have an umbrella. Dominic could tell that the man was a Jew because the man wore a Jew's skullcap and walked patiently in his long overcoat. Even when it wasn't sleeting, the Jews on Fullerton walked like that.

The Germans had blond hair. Italians had dark, flashing eyes. The Polish looked like Germans but were skinnier. The Irish had big ears and freckles.

The Jew on the street below walked past the currency exchange and then turned north to walk up Southport Avenue. A passing bread truck pulled close to the curb and splashed him.

By turning to his right and looking out the center window, Dominic could see east down Fullerton toward the lake.[18] Now that he was taller, the cars and buses didn't disappear behind the currency exchange. They disappeared behind the big gray building farther down the block. The currency exchange[19] had a green window, in the center of which hung a huge electric clock. Around its edges were orange lights that rolled word by word on and then flashed off for several seconds and started over. The lights said NOW IS THE TIME TO SAVE.

He could walk north up Southport when he went to see his mother at the restaurant. He could walk down Southport when he went to school or to play with his friends. He was not allowed to walk west, up Fullerton, or east, down Fullerton. He could look at Fullerton from his hallway door, but then he had to turn the corner. He could look into the window of the candy store, but only for a minute and never as if he were begging. The woman in the store always wore the same pink dress.

Once, on Fullerton, he saw a man sleeping on the sidewalk. Once he saw three men drink from a paper bag. Once he saw two women in a parked car kissing. Once he saw a gang of older boys throwing matches at an alley cat. Once, a drunken man on their landing pounded on their door shouting over and over, "Let me in there!" They had to call the police. Once, someone threw up on their hallway staircase, and more than once someone urinated. Each time his mother cleaned it up.

Once, on Southport, he saw a rat as big as a cat run across the sidewalk and into a shady gangway. Dominic ran the rest of the way home to tell his mom about that. She told him rats carried polio and rabies. So did squirrels and dogs. If you got rabies you had to get painful shots with a long needle right in the belly button every day for three months. In first grade in Sister Augustine's class there was a girl who had polio. She sat in a wheelchair in the first row by the side blackboard. She stayed at the school for a month and then left.

Once Dominic dreamed that he had polio and couldn't walk. Once he dreamed that he forgot his address and couldn't find his

---

18 **Fullerton toward the lake:** Fullerton Avenue is an east-west street that ends at Lake Michigan on the east.

19 **currency exchange:** in Chicago, a place to cash checks, buy money orders or moneygrams, apply for auto titles or licenses, pay utility bills, and do various other transactions.

house. Then his mother taught him about Chicago, and a nurse came to school and gave everybody polio shots.

Fullerton was 2400 North. The way you said it was twenty-four hundred. Diversey was 2800. Belmont was 3200, and Armitage was 2000. Saint Stephen's was on Armitage. Southport was 1400 West.

His address was 1401 West Fullerton, Chicago, Illinois, USA.

One of the kids at school said that on Clybourn Avenue there were people who owned goats. He said that the goats ate a million tin cans every day, and that if you parked your car near them they'd eat that too.

Aunt Rose said that was no lie, what with all of the city's thieves. She said it was a changing neighborhood. She said that nearly every time she came over to visit. That was why she'd moved north, to Addison Street. Dominic didn't know what number Addison was, but he did know that it was by the ball park. At her house every time they visited, he gazed out her front windows to see it. It was bigger than Saint Stephen's Church, and if you looked up at it from the sidewalk on Waveland Avenue it said CHICAGO CUBS inside a big bright flag.

Sometimes he'd listen to the ball game on the radio. He'd sit in the big armchair with his head down, concentrating, praying for a Chicago Cubs hit. Once he was sitting there when his mother came in the room from the kitchen. She was folding her apron. He could see her out of the corner of his eye, but he didn't look up because there were two strikes on Ransom Jackson and Dominic was afraid he'd jinx him.

Then he heard his mother say, "You're just like your father."

And she was crying. Ransom Jackson took strike three. Dominic felt bad and wondered if he had done something wrong.

Below, by a fire hydrant, he saw several pigeons. He wondered how they felt when they got wet. Why didn't they fly somewhere out of the rain? They pecked the garbage floating past them in the gutter.

Behind him, wind whistled in the oil heater. The sound startled him. He turned and stared at the silent heater until he again felt safe and then turned back to his window, shivering.

Two Poles were crossing Fullerton, holding newspapers up over their heads. His mother had taught him it was wrong to call them polacks. It was wrong to say krauts or micks or spics or dagos. Nearly everybody in the whole world had a bad name. He wished that the devil had never been invented. Dominic looked at a patrol car double-parked in front of the currency exchange. Its dome light flashed in circles.

NOW, the sign said.

A moment later it said NOW IS THE TIME.

He wondered what currency was. He wondered what exchange meant. He wondered why he didn't have a father. Was it because of something he had done? he thought. The patrol car drove away, siren blaring, and the two Poles huddled inside a doorway.

Dominic stared at the clock's rolling message. NOW it said. NOW IS THE TIME TO SAVE.

It was seven-eighteen. He turned to watch the tavern corner His father was dead, that's all. His fingers tapped the windowsill. Soon, the boy thought, at seven-thirty, his ma would be finished working her shift at the restaurant, and he'd be here to watch her walk home.

QUESTIONS FOR DISCUSSION

1. What is the setting of the story, time and place?

2. What can you infer about Dominic's neighborhood and his knowledge of it?

3. How would you describe the plot structure of this story?

4. Can you infer what happened to Dominic's father?

5. Characterize Dominic's mother.

6. What details in the story suggest Dominic's age?

7. What impact does Dominic's age have on the narrative style of the story?

8. When Dominic tries to apply what he is learning about religion to life, what mistakes does he make and why?

TOPICS FOR WRITING

1. Do you think Ardizzone's title is meant symbolically? In a paragraph, discuss the possible meaning holy cards might have in this story.

2. When Dominic shows his mother his All-Star list, she laughs appreciatively. Write a dialogue between the mother and a co-worker at the Dixie Diner in which she retells this incident.

3. In a paper, recall and compare or contrast your elementary school experience with Dominic's.

4. Do you think that Ardizzone's main purpose is to make you feel sorry for Dominic? Explain your answer by referring to the story.

5. Write a persuasive paper in which you discuss the aspect of style—diction, symbol and imagery, syntax, or organization—that makes "Holy Cards" unique. Support your opinion with references to the story.

THE EGG

SHERWOOD ANDERSON (1876–1941)

Awriter whose natural style and everyday speech influenced both Hemingway and Faulkner, Sherwood Anderson was one of seven children born to a day laborer and sometime house painter. From the age of fourteen he worked as a newsboy, assistant house painter, farmhand, and racetrack helper. When he was twenty, he went to Chicago and rolled barrels of apples in a cold-storage warehouse for two years, then joined the army during the Spanish-American War.

After prep school in Springfield, Ohio, he worked for a Chicago advertising agency. By 1906, however, he became dissatisfied with his work—"There were too many lies being told"—and began a dual life as an Elyria, Ohio, manufacturing executive by day and would-be writer by night.

Anderson slowly began contributing verse and short fiction to various Chicago literary magazines. Through the efforts of writer Theodore Dreiser, he was able to publish two novels written before he abandoned his Elyria business: *Windy McPherson's Son* (1916) and *Marching Men* (1917). In 1918, his first volume of poetry, *Mid-American Chants,* was published; it was followed by two others: *A New Testament* (1927) and *Five Poems* (1939).

What established Anderson's reputation as a writer were the interrelated tales and short sketches of *Winesburg, Ohio* (1919). Its first chapter, "The Book of the Grotesque," anticipates the book's many emotionally frustrated characters. Praised more today for his mastery of the short story than the novel, Anderson also published other story collections: *The Triumph of the Egg* (1921), *Horses and Men* (1923), *Alice and the Lost Novel* (1929), and *Death in the Woods and Other Stories* (1933). In the 1920s, he also published two autobiographical works: *A Story Teller's Story* (1924) and *Tar: A Midwest Childhood* (1926). During the 1930s, he wrote several nonfiction works. When Anderson died in 1941, the Elyria, Ohio, newspaper announced his death with this headline: SHERWOOD ANDERSON, FORMER ELYRIA MANUFACTURER, DIES. Anderson would have appreciated the irony.

The first-person narrator of "The Egg" is typical of many of Anderson's narrators: a man recollecting adolescent experiences that he now vaguely perceives as significant, even crucial in his development. As you read, focus on the style and the tone of the story and ask yourself if "The Egg" is comic or tragic.

■

My father was, I am sure, intended by nature to be a cheerful, kindly man. Until he was thirty-four years old he worked as a farmhand for a man named Thomas Butterworth whose place lay near the town of Bidwell, Ohio. He had then a horse of his own, and on Saturday evenings drove into town to spend a few hours in social intercourse with other farmhands. In town he drank several glasses of beer and stood about in Ben Head's saloon—crowded on Saturday evenings with visiting farmhands. Songs were sung and glasses thumped on the bar. At ten o'clock father drove home along a lonely country road, made his horse comfortable for the night, and himself went to bed, quite happy in his position in life. He had at that time no notion of trying to rise in the world.

It was in the spring of his thirty-fifth year that father married my mother, then a country school-teacher, and in the following spring I came wriggling and crying into the world. Something happened to the two people. They became ambitious. The American passion for getting up in the world took possession of them.

It may have been that mother was responsible. Being a school-teacher she had no doubt read books and magazines. She had, I presume, read of how Garfield, Lincoln, and other Americans rose from poverty to fame and greatness, and as I lay beside her—in the days of her lying-in[1]—she may have dreamed that I would some day rule men and cities. At any rate she induced father to give up his place as a farmhand, sell his horse, and embark on an independent enterprise of his own. She was a tall silent woman with a long nose and troubled gray eyes. For herself she wanted nothing. For father and myself she was incurably ambitious.

The first venture into which the two people went turned out badly. They rented ten acres of poor stony land on Grigg's Road, eight miles from Bidwell, and launched into chicken-raising. I grew into boyhood on the place and got my first impressions of life there. From the beginning they were impressions of disaster, and if, in my turn, I am a gloomy man inclined to see the darker side of life, I attribute it to the fact that what should have been for me the happy joyous days of childhood were spent on a chicken farm.

One unversed in such matters can have no notion of the many and tragic things that can happen to a chicken. It is born out of an egg,

---

1 **lying-in:** In the past a woman recovered from giving birth by staying in bed for a period of days or weeks.

lives for a few weeks as a tiny fluffy thing such as you will see pictured on Easter cards, then becomes hideously naked, eats quantities of corn and meal bought by the sweat of your father's brow, gets diseases called pip, cholera,[2] and other names, stands looking with stupid eyes at the sun, becomes sick and dies. A few hens and now and then a rooster, intended to serve God's mysterious ends, struggle through to maturity. The hens lay eggs out of which come other chickens and the dreadful cycle is thus made complete. It is all unbelievably complex. Most philosophers must have been raised on chicken farms. One hopes for so much from a chicken and is so dreadfully disillusioned. Small chickens, just setting out on the journey of life, look so bright and alert and they are in fact so dreadfully stupid. They are so much like people they mix one up in one's judgments of life. If disease does not kill them, they wait until your expectations are thoroughly aroused and then walk under the wheels of a wagon—to go squashed and dead back to their maker. Vermin infest their youth, and fortunes must be spent for curative powders. In later life I have seen how a literature has been built up on the subject of fortunes to be made out of the raising of chickens. It is intended to be read by the gods who have just eaten of the tree of the knowledge of good and evil. It is a hopeful literature and declares that much may be done by simple ambitious people who own a few hens. Do not be led astray by it. It was not written for you. Go hunt for gold on the frozen hills of Alaska, put your faith in the honesty of a politician, believe if you will that the world is daily growing better and that good will triumph over evil, but do not read and believe the literature that is written concerning the hen. It was not written for you.

I, however, digress. My tale does not primarily concern itself with the hen. If correctly told it will center on the egg. For ten years my father and mother struggled to make our chicken farm pay and then they gave up their struggle and began another. They moved into the town of Bidwell, Ohio, and embarked in the restaurant business. After ten years of worry with incubators that did not hatch, and with tiny— and in their own way lovely—balls of fluff that passed on into semi-naked pullethood and from that into dead henhood, we threw all aside and, packing our belongings on a wagon, drove down Grigg's Road toward Bidwell, a tiny caravan of hope looking for a new place from which to start on our upward journey through life.

---

2 **pip, cholera:** contagious diseases, the first limited to poultry and other birds.

We must have been a sad-looking lot, not, I fancy, unlike refugees fleeing from a battlefield. Mother and I walked in the road. The wagon that contained our goods had been borrowed for the day from Mr. Albert Griggs, a neighbor. Out of its side stuck the legs of cheap chairs, and at the back of the pile of beds, tables, and boxes filled with kitchen utensils was a crate of live chickens, and on top of that the baby carriage in which I had been wheeled about in my infancy. Why we stuck to the baby carriage I don't know. It was unlikely other children would be born and the wheels were broken. People who have few possessions cling tightly to those they have. That is one of the facts that make life so discouraging.

Father rode on top of the wagon. He was then a bald-headed man of forty-five, a little fat, and from long association with mother and the chickens he had become habitually silent and discouraged. All during our ten years on the chicken farm he had worked as a laborer on neighboring farms and most of the money he had earned had been spent on remedies to cure chicken diseases, on Wilmer's White Wonder Cholera Cure or Professor Bidlow's Egg Producer or some other preparations that mother found advertised in the poultry papers. There were two little patches of hair on father's head just above his ears. I remember that as a child I used to sit looking at him when he had gone to sleep in a chair before the stove on Sunday afternoons in the winter. I had at that time already begun to read books and have notions of my own, and the bald path that led over the top of his head was, I fancied, something like a broad road, such a road as Caesar might have made on which to lead his legions out of Rome and into the wonders of an unknown world. The tufts of hair that grew above father's ears were, I thought, like forests. I fell into a half-sleeping, half-waking state and dreamed I was a tiny thing going along the road into a far beautiful place where there were no chicken farms and where life was a happy eggless affair.

One might write a book concerning our flight from the chicken farm into town. Mother and I walked the entire eight miles—she to be sure that nothing fell from the wagon and I to see the wonders of the world. On the seat of the wagon beside father was his greatest treasure. I will tell you of that.

On a chicken farm, where hundreds and even thousands of chickens come out of eggs, surprising things sometimes happen. Grotesques are born out of eggs as out of people. The accident does not often occur—perhaps once in a thousand births. A chicken is, you see, born that has four legs, two pairs of wings, two heads, or what not. The things do not live. They go quickly back to the hand of their maker that has for a moment trembled. The fact that the poor little things could not live was one of the tragedies of life to father. He had some sort of notion that if he could but bring into henhood or roosterhood a five-legged hen or a two-headed rooster his fortune would be made. He dreamed of taking the wonder about the county fairs and of growing rich by exhibiting it to other farmhands.

At any rate, he saved all the little monstrous things that had been born on our chicken farm. They were preserved in alcohol and put each in its own glass bottle. These he had carefully put into a box, and on our journey into town it was carried on the wagon seat beside him. He drove the horses with one hand and with the other clung to the box. When we got to our destination, the box was taken down at once and the bottles removed. All during our days as keepers of a restaurant in the town of Bidwell, Ohio, the grotesques in their little glass bottles sat on a shelf back of the counter. Mother sometimes protested, but father was a rock on the subject of his treasure. The grotesques were, he declared, valuable. People, he said, liked to look at strange and wonderful things.

Did I say that we embarked in the restaurant business in the town of Bidwell, Ohio? I exaggerated a little. The town itself lay at the foot of a low hill and on the shore of a small river. The railroad did not run through the town and the station was a mile away to the north at a place called Pickleville. There had been a cider mill and pickle factory at the station, but before the time of our coming they had both gone out of business. In the morning and in the evening buses came down to the station along a road called Turner's Pike from the hotel on the main street of Bidwell. Our going to the out-of-the-way place to embark in the restaurant business was mother's idea. She talked of it for a year and then one day went off and rented an empty store building opposite the railroad station. It was her idea that the restaurant would be profitable. Traveling men, she said, would be always waiting around to take trains out of town and town people would come to the station to await incoming trains. They would come to the restaurant to buy pieces of pie and drink coffee. Now that I am older I know that she had another motive in going. She was ambitious for me. She wanted me to rise in the world, to get into a town school and become a man of the towns.

At Pickleville father and mother worked hard, as they always had done. At first there was the necessity of putting our place into shape to be a restaurant. That took a month. Father built a shelf on which he put tins of vegetables. He painted a sign on which he put his name in large red letters. Below his name was the sharp command—"EAT HERE"— that was so seldom obeyed. A showcase was bought and filled with cigars and tobacco. Mother scrubbed the floors and the walls of the room. I went to school in the town and was glad to be away from the farm, from the presence of the discouraged, sad-looking chickens. Still I was not very joyous. In the evening I walked home from school along Turner's Pike and remembered the children I had seen playing in the town school yard. A troop of little girls had gone hopping about and singing. I tried that. Down along the frozen road I went hopping solemnly on one leg. "Hippity Hop To The Barber Shop," I sang shrilly. Then I stopped and looked doubtfully about. I was afraid of being seen in my gay mood. It must have seemed to me that I was doing a thing that should not be done by one who, like myself, had been raised on a chicken farm where death was a daily visitor.

Mother decided that our restaurant should remain open at night. At ten in the evening a passenger train went north past our door followed by a local freight. The freight crew had switching to do in Pickleville, and when the work was done they came to our restaurant for hot coffee and food. Sometimes one of them ordered a fried egg. In the morning at four they returned north-bound and again visited us. A little trade began to grow up. Mother slept at night and during the day tended the restaurant and fed our boarders[3] while father slept. He slept in the same bed mother had occupied during the night and I went off to the town of Bidwell and to school. During the long nights, while mother and I slept, father cooked meats that were to go into sandwiches for the lunch baskets of our boarders. Then an idea in regard to getting up in the world came into his head. The American spirit took hold of him. He also became ambitious.

In the long nights when there was little to do, father had time to think. That was his undoing. He decided that he had in the past been an unsuccessful man because he had not been cheerful enough and that in the future he would adopt a cheerful outlook on life. In the early morning he came upstairs and got into bed with mother. She woke and the two talked. From my bed in the corner I listened.

It was father's idea that both he and mother should try to entertain the people who came to eat at our restaurant. I cannot now

---

3 **boarders:** People who pay for meals (board), or a room plus meals, usually in a private house.

remember his words, but he gave the impression of one about to become in some obscure way a kind of public entertainer. When people, particularly young people from the town of Bidwell, came into our place, as on very rare occasions they did, bright entertaining conversation was to be made. From father's words I gathered that something of the jolly innkeeper effect was to be sought. Mother must have been doubtful from the first, but she said nothing discouraging. It was father's notion that a passion for the company of himself and mother would spring up in the breasts of the younger people of the town of Bidwell. In the evening bright happy groups would come singing down Turner's Pike. They would troop shouting with joy and laughter into our place. There would be song and festivity. I do not mean to give the impression that father spoke so elaborately of the matter. He was, as I have said, an uncommunicative man. "They want some place to go. I tell you they want some place to go," he said over and over. That was as far as he got. My own imagination has filled in the blanks.

For two or three weeks this notion of father's invaded our house. We did not talk much, but in our daily lives tried earnestly to make smiles take the place of glum looks. Mother smiled at the boarders and I, catching the infection, smiled at our cat. Father became a little feverish in his anxiety to please. There was, no doubt, lurking somewhere in him, a touch of the spirit of the showman. He did not waste much of his ammunition on the railroad men he served at night, but seemed to be waiting for a young man or woman from Bidwell to come in to show what he could do. On the counter in the restaurant there was a wire basket kept always filled with eggs, and it must have been before his eyes when the idea of being entertaining was born in his brain. There was something pre-natal about the way eggs kept themselves connected with the development of his idea. At any rate, an egg ruined his new impulse in life. Late one night I was awakened by a roar of anger coming from father's throat. Both mother and I sat upright in our beds. With trembling hands she lighted a lamp that stood on a table by her head. Downstairs the front door of our restaurant went shut with a bang and in a few minutes father tramped up the stairs. He held an egg in his hand and his hand trembled as though he were having a chill. There was a half-insane light in his eyes. As he stood glaring at us I was sure he intended throwing the egg at either mother or me. Then he laid it gently on the table beside the lamp and dropped on his knees beside mother's bed. He began to cry like a boy, and I, carried away by his grief, cried with him. The two of us filled the little upstairs room with our wailing voices. It is ridiculous, but of the picture we made I can remember only the fact that mother's hand continually stroked the bald path that ran across the top of his head. I have forgotten what mother said to him and how she induced him to tell her of what had happened downstairs. His explanation also has gone out of my mind. I remember only my own grief and fright and the shiny path over father's head glowing in the lamplight as he knelt by the bed.

As to what happened downstairs. For some unexplainable reason I know the story as well as though I had been a witness to my father's discomfiture. One in time gets to know many unexplainable things. On that evening young Joe Kane, son of a merchant of Bidwell, came to Pickleville to meet his father, who was expected on the ten-o'clock evening train from the South. The train was three hours late and Joe came into our place to loaf about and to wait for its arrival. The local freight train came in and the freight crew were fed. Joe was left alone in the restaurant with father.

From the moment he came into our place the Bidwell young man must have been puzzled by my father's actions. It was his notion that father was angry at him for hanging around. He noticed that the restaurant-keeper was apparently disturbed by his presence and he thought of going out. However, it began to rain and he did not fancy the long walk to town and back. He bought a five-cent cigar and ordered a cup of coffee. He had a newspaper in his pocket and took it out and began to read. "I'm waiting for the evening train. It's late," he said apologetically.

For a long time father, whom Joe Kane had never seen before, remained silently gazing at his visitor. He was no doubt suffering from an attack of stage fright. As so often happens in life he had thought so much and so often of the situation that now confronted him that he was somewhat nervous in its presence.

For one thing, he did not know what to do with his hands. He thrust one of them nervously over the counter and shook hands with Joe Kane. "How-de-do," he said. Joe Kane put his newspaper down and stared at him. Father's eyes lighted on the basket of eggs that sat on the counter and he began to talk. "Well," he began hesitatingly, "well, you have heard of Christopher Columbus, eh?" He seemed to be angry. "That Christopher Columbus was a cheat," he declared emphatically. "He talked of making an egg stand on its end. He talked, he did, and then he went and broke the end of the egg."

My father seemed to his visitor to be beside himself at the duplicity of Christopher Columbus. He muttered and swore. He declared it was wrong to teach children that Christopher Columbus was a great man when, after all, he cheated at the critical moment. He had declared he would make an egg stand on end and then, when his bluff had been called, he had done a trick. Still grumbling at Columbus, father took an egg from the basket on the counter and began to walk up and down. He rolled the egg between the palms of his hands. He smiled genially. He began to mumble words regarding the effect to be produced on an egg by the electricity that comes out of the human body. He declared that, without breaking its shell and by virtue of rolling back and forth in his hands, he could stand the egg on its head. He explained that the warmth of his hands and the gentle rolling movement he gave the egg created a new center of gravity, and Joe Kane was mildly interested. "I have handled thousands of eggs," father said. "No one knows more about eggs than I do."

He stood the egg on the counter and it fell on its side. He tried the trick again and again, each time rolling the egg between the palms of his hands and saying the words regarding the wonders of electricity and the laws of gravity. When after a half-hour's effort he did succeed in making the egg stand for a moment, he looked up to find that his visitor was no longer watching. By the time he had succeeded in calling Joe Kane's attention to the success of his effort, the egg had again rolled over and lay on its side.

Afire with the showman's passion and at the same time a good deal disconcerted by the failure of his first effort, father now took the bottles containing the poultry monstrosities down from their place on the shelf and began to show them to his visitor. "How would you like to have seven legs and two heads like this fellow?" he asked, exhibiting the most remarkable of his treasures. A cheerful smile played over his face. He reached over the counter and tried to slap Joe Kane on the shoulder as he had seen men do in Ben Head's saloon when he was a young farmhand and drove to town on Saturday evenings. His visitor was made a little ill by the sight of the body of the terribly deformed bird floating in the alcohol in the bottle and got up to go. Coming from behind the counter, father took hold of the young man's arm and led him back to his seat. He grew a little angry and for a moment had to turn his face away and force himself to smile. Then he put the bottles back on the shelf. In an outburst of generosity he fairly compelled Joe Kane to have a fresh cup of coffee and another cigar at his expense. Then he took a pan and filling it with vinegar, taken from a jug that sat beneath the counter, he declared himself about to do a new trick. "I will heat this egg in this pan of vinegar," he said. "Then I will put it through the neck of a bottle without breaking the shell. When the egg is inside the bottle it will resume its normal shape and the shell will become hard again. Then I will give the bottle with the egg in it to you. You can take it about with you wherever you go. People will want to know how you got the egg in the bottle. Don't tell them. Keep them guessing. That is the way to have fun with this trick."

Father grinned and winked at his visitor. Joe Kane decided that the man who confronted him was mildly insane but harmless. He drank the cup of coffee that had been given him and began to read his paper again. When the egg had been heated in vinegar, father carried it on a spoon to the counter and going into a back room got an empty bottle. He was angry because his visitor did not watch him as he began to do his trick, but nevertheless went cheerfully to work. For a long time he struggled, trying to get the egg to go through the neck of the bottle. He put the pan of vinegar back on the stove, intending to reheat the egg, then picked it up and burned his fingers. After a second bath in the hot vinegar, the shell of the egg had been softened a little, but not enough for his purpose. He worked and worked and a spirit of desperate determination took possession of him. When he thought that at last the trick was about to be consummated, the delayed train came in at the station and Joe Kane started to go nonchalantly out at the door. Father made a last desperate effort to conquer the egg and make it do the thing that would establish his reputation as one who knew how to entertain guests who came into his restaurant. He worried the egg. He attempted to be somewhat rough with it. He swore and the sweat stood out on his forehead. The egg broke under his hand. When the contents spurted over his clothes, Joe Kane, who had stopped at the door, turned and laughed.

A roar of anger rose from my father's throat. He danced and shouted a string of inarticulate words. Grabbing another egg from the basket on the counter, he threw it, just missing the head of the young man as he dodged through the door and escaped.

Father came upstairs to mother and me with an egg in his hand. I do not know what he intended to do. I imagine he had some idea of destroying it, of destroying all eggs, and that he intended to let mother and me see him begin. When, however, he got into the presence of mother, something happened to him. He laid the egg gently on the table and dropped on his knees by the bed as I have already explained. He later decided to close the restaurant for the night and to come upstairs and get into bed. When he did so, he blew out the light and after much muttered conversation both he and mother went to sleep. I suppose I went to sleep also, but my sleep was troubled. I awoke at dawn and for a long time looked at the egg that lay on the table. I wondered why eggs had to be and why from the egg came the hen who again laid the egg. The question got into my blood. It has stayed there, I imagine, because I am the son of my father. At any rate, the problem remains unsolved in my mind. And that, I conclude, is but another evidence of the complete and final triumph of the egg— at least as far as my family is concerned.

QUESTIONS FOR DISCUSSION

1. Describe the narrator's parents.

2. Describe the narrator and the methods by which Anderson characterizes him.

3. What links the parents' business ventures?

4. How does the first-person point of view affect the style?

5. Is the major conflict in the story internal or external?

6. To what extent is the setting an important element?

7. What is the dominant tone of the story?

8. How would you state the theme of the story?

9. List the possible symbolic meanings of eggs in general and in this particular story.

TOPICS FOR WRITING

1. Write a personal essay about something you tried but failed to do. The tone of the essay may be serious or humorous. Provide details to enable the reader to share your experience and your feelings.

2. You have written a short story. Your teacher comments that its style is Andersonesque. What does he or she mean? In a short paper, define the term *Andersonesque*, citing passages from "The Egg" to support your definition.

3. In what way is "The Egg" similar to or different from "Pigeon Feathers"? Write an essay in which you compare and contrast the two stories' themes and styles.

BRIGHT WINTER

ANNA KEESEY (born 1962)

Anna Keesey was born in California but grew up in Oregon. She attended Stanford University in Palo Alto, California, graduating with a B.A. in English and creative writing in 1984. Accepted by the Writing Workshop of the University of Iowa, she earned her M.F.A. in 1994. She has taught English in several high schools on the west coast, writing at Willamette University in Oregon, and, beginning in the fall of 1998, literature at the University of Portland in Oregon.

Keesey has had several stories published. "Bright Winter" first appeared in *Grand Street* and was then selected for publication in *The Best American Short Stories 1996*. Another story, "DoubleTake," was accepted by the West Coast magazine *Zyzzyva*. Keesey has been awarded fellowships from James Michener-The Copernicus Society and from the Fine Arts Work Center in Provincetown, Massachusetts, and a creative writing fellowship from the National Endowment for the Arts. Her story "One Girl's Blues" won the Nimrod/Hardman Katherine Anne Porter Prize. Keesey is presently working on a historical novel, set during the range wars that erupted in central Oregon around the turn of the twentieth century.

"Bright Winter" is an epistolary story; that is, the events are told in the form of letters, or epistles. The events are based on American religious history. William Miller (1782–1849), an ex-officer who had served in the U. S. Army during the War of 1812, founded the Adventists—Protestant Christians who believed that the personal, visible advent of Christ in glory (the Second Coming) was close at hand. Miller's studies convinced him that not only would Christ come sometime between March 21, 1843, and March 21, 1844, but that He would be accompanied by a fiery conflagration that would purify the world. Miller's beliefs attracted many followers, not always to the delight of their families. As you read, note the changing tone of the father's letters to his son as well as the effect of the blue tent on the townspeople.

■

We believe it to be a case of life and death. It is death to remain connected with those bodies that speak lightly of, or oppose, the coming of the Lord. It is life to come out from all human tradition, and stand upon the Word of God . . . We therefore now say to all who are in any way entangled in the yoke of bondage, "Come out from among them, and be ye separate, saith the Lord."
> — *Joshua V. Himes, in the imminent-advent newspaper* The Midnight Cry, *August 29, 1844*

Broadhill,
January 12th

John Ephraim,

If I chose to I could find you and bring you home. I am known in the several towns where you may be lodged, even as far as Grasstown where the mayor once welcomed my money. Favors are owed to me up and down this county. I could employ men to go around the towns and knock on the doors and demand that the landladies array their boarders on the steps. This would flush you out eventually, no matter how you covered your ears and ignored the noise. But why should your foolishness disrupt my day's work? Duty and self-regard forbid me to go snuffing at your footprints. I shall simply write, and make several copies and distribute them around to those you may have dealings with. In this way you may receive a letter and be assured of my feelings in this matter, that is to say, irked, and faintly amused.

The horse you rode I will consider leased by the day. I will determine the schedule of repayment when you have come home.

Your mother is cheerful but weak, and stays abed. She does not know you've gone. I have said you are traveling with Daniel Kimball to hear the concerts at Braxton. A lie.

your Father

Broadhill,
January 16th

John Ephraim,

Perhaps shame has made you shy. But let me say that if you will see your error and come back, we will forget this episode. It will never color our relations in the future. And your mother need never know.

your Father

January 19th

John Ephraim,

I have had no response from you this week. Twice I sent letters to the Congregation men of Braxton, Lewiston, Rocky Ford, Carlisle, and Grasstown. I have of course bound them to discretion, as reputations are not easily repaired in this county. One letter went along in the pocket of James Spencer, who was traveling to Lewiston. His Marie asks after you, he tells me. I was silent, unwilling to lie—a rude man and a bad neighbor. For this I thank you. The other letters I took myself. I gave them to these church men because who knows where your fellows may gather to worship—I know only that some of them have been expelled from their congregations, and that these ministers may be able to name them. So this is what you want. To leave the world of warm society and sensible character. To shame your family into lies.

Not a man has seen you in any town. I made discreet inquiry, saying my son had passed through recently and asking, had he stopped in to pass the time? No? A heedless young man, too thoughtful, too studious, and thus rude. In this way I dressed your disrespect in the clothes of a common flaw. Again and again, I gave a chuckle that hurt my throat.

But no one had seen you. Once I asked myself if you might be hurt, struck down by robbers on a road. But no. We argued, and you have taken yourself off on your own legs for your own fool's vision. Moreover on my travels a corroborating rumor came to my attention. This was in the hatter's shop in Rocky Ford. The hatter had heard of a gathering, an encampment across the river. People of all kinds were wading the ford with their children, he said, even carrying their babies still in skirts. They've come to play at some absurd game, he said, they're bewitched by preachers with loud voices who rattle chains.

And why they chose us, a sensible township, I don't know. Perhaps because they could get space near the river, and so carry water a shorter distance.

I said, Some people will let their fields to any rabble with cash.

You may be among these feverish pilgrims wetting their toes at the ford. Perhaps you wonder if I was tempted to cross and look for you. I was not. My equilibrium is not such that a gadding child can disturb it, and I had business at the bank. My goodbye to the hatter was comfortable. I've known him for years.

Your silence perplexes me, John Ephraim.

your Father

January 24th

John Ephraim,

My hand begins to tire from copying letters. Colleagues at the bank have noticed it shake a bit when I sign my name. They wonder, too, why I send these letters out to Lewiston, Rocky Ford, Carlisle, Grasstown. They may believe I correspond with creditors. Or, perhaps, a woman. They may be saying Josiah Cole has turned from his wife in her illness.

But now I need not copy. I need send only to the minister Gearhart at Rocky Ford, who will find a suitable messenger. I am sure you are there.

For the story of the great blue tent erected at the crook of the river has appeared in the newspapers amid great joking. It's said that wild-eyed unmarried women make up the majority of the congregation, and are given to shouting prayers until they lose strength and must be carried out. Then there are drinkers, crawling babies, servants, and shaking old men who sing. A respectable community, my son! I see that there are many who share your brooding reading of Revelations, many others who have sat in their attics over the last year eschewing decent work and company, totting up numbers from the Bible as though God would speak to us in some heathenish code. There is even a report that your fellows have ordered a hundred bolts of white cloth, that they may sew robes to wear when they ascend. This sewing at least might someday get you respectable employment We've had tailors in the family before this, and you've already shown you don't mind spending time on your knees. Do you sleep on the ground with strangers, John Ephraim?

Pardon my interest. I understand that they are brothers to you, and will live with you when God has annihilated the rest of us in a storm of fire. Well that you should learn their names, I suppose.

I scarcely dare hope that you have sent a letter crossing this, explaining.

your Father

January 25th

John Ephraim,

Let me amend the common saying and tell you that there's no great tomfoolery without some small gain. I had stopped over for supper with Mr. Partle, the new lawyer, and his wife. There was a good roast of pork and a glass of sherry and pleasant talk. The Partle boy is down at college and will begin to learn law in the autumn. Peculiar how many people seem to plan on autumn's actually arriving.

Partle told me of a story he'd heard, that a woman out in Missouri had suckled an elk and raised it as her child. At least, several people had told him it was true. I opined that we were living in a climate of odd gullibility. Of course I did not elaborate. But see how my point was made for me! As I sat with Partle, there was a knock at the door, and on the stoop was a visitor looking for me. I recognized Will Whiting, our hired man years ago when you were a boy. Do you remember him? The one with a face like a shrew, who could not converse with your mother because he was always hiding his teeth.

Will, I said, it's quite a surprise. I thought you were in Indiana with the railroad.

I was, he said, but I've come back with a bad conscience. He took a little parcel from inside his coat. I opened it. Seven dollars in coin.

He said, When I worked for you I stole seven dollars. Now I'm here to settle my accounts. The Lord is coming, he said, and I want to go to meet him free and clear.

And out he goes! Partle and I had a little laugh over him. To think of old Will Whiting taking his soul so seriously. So the advent-near may have seduced my son, but it has at least given me seven dollars. Partle thought he'd write to all his old hired men anonymously and give them a little shove.

your Father

January 27th

John Ephraim,

Naturally I have had to tell your mother. You may not have considered when you left that she would long for you. Last night she listened to my excuse, and lifted her hand off the blanket.

Enough, now, Josiah, she said. Did he become ill traveling? What is there to tell?

I brought her the newspaper and held the lamp to it. She read slowly.

She said, It's the same as he has been saying these ten months. That God will come to us in the springtime.

They seem very confident, I told her.

So there is no use in planting seeds this year? she asked. Nor in other work?

I told her, No. Nor in repairing the barn or training the foals.

No use to send for a French bonnet?

No use to convert the native. No use to marry.

To marry was ever useless, she said. Oh, your mother smiling.

Then she said, He told us we were in danger. The foolish virgins[1] who keep no oil in their lamps will be shut out from the wedding feast. Ah. This was the danger. Our young man gone.

This is beyond a jest. It is time for you to clear your head and come home.

your Father

February 2nd

John Ephraim,

No answer from you so I will not write.

your Father

---

1 **foolish virgins:** A biblical reference to Matthew 25:1–2.

February 3rd

John Ephraim,
    Gearhart writes that he gives my letters to an old man who claims to belong to your blue congregation. He cannot take them himself, as he is too busy with his own alarmed and talkative flock. But he is not sure this fellow, a troubled drinker of spirits, and full of self-praise, tells him the truth. So I do not know if you read my lines and ignore them, or never receive them at all. Do you reject us utterly? I feel perhaps I

February 4th

    I cannot remember what I meant to say, yesterday, so I start again (you see my strict use of paper has not changed). You may be pleased to know that your mother was up today for nearly two hours. I made her a long chair with a few blankets and the pillow from your bed. I brought out another chair and sat with her. It was very warm, and there were birds calling now and then—in February! The skin of her hand is as thin as silk now. I touched it while she slept. So your parents, hopelessly depraved, spent the afternoon. You may think on this.

your Father

February 7th

John Ephraim,
    Today I rode to Rocky Ford myself. Some children on the street directed me out to the bank of the river, to a muddy place marked by hooves, where other people had come to look. The river went sliding along, very deep, so the surface spun slowly. There seemed to be no ice at all. Across, in the field, I saw the blue tent snapping in the warm wind above the winter grasses. The teetering skeleton of a fence encircled it, in some places ten feet high. Young boys were hammering boards and raw branches to the uprights. Under the crosspieces, children ran to and fro. One little girl dragged out a basket as big as a wheelbarrow, and began to pull it toward the water. A slender young man came out—my heart leapt, and fell—and took basket and child back inside. I stood until only a few blue triangles and the crackling blue roof were still visible to me. I turned to go.

Behind me a man stood on a tree stump. He was dressed like a farmer, with clumsy chunks of mud on his boots. He spoke down to me in an angry voice, and struck his own leg with his cap. He said, Who are they to build a bloody ark? As full of sin as the rest, and now living like that. A crime. And children with them. He said, They should be whipped.

It took me a long time to ride back to Broadhill, and Marie Spencer, who was looking after your mother, was late for her supper at home.

your Father

February 15th

John Ephraim,

Today I met James Spencer on the street and lifted my hand and smiled, and he went on past as though I'd been a phantom. I was so shaken. No explanation occurred to me at first. I went in at the feed-store and there was talking that hushed as the bell of the door died away. In the silence I bought twenty pounds of oats and had to pat my coat endlessly before I found money in its usual pocket.

Usually when I walk into the bank in the morning there is a flurry of industry at the desks; one can hear quills snap in earnestness. Today there was quiet, and a peering-round over shoulders. I sat in my chair and drew my papers toward me but I could not see. In a moment Satterwhite, James's clerk, came in to explain his absence. Addressing not me but the sleeve of my coat, he said that young Marie Spencer had left home on foot to go to the encampment at Rocky Ford, and had been gone all night before her parents caught up to her. They'd brought her back between them in the wagon and were seen by early risers. She spoke of your son, the clerk told me softly. So you see, John Ephraim, naturally the town has lunged to this repast of gossip. While you dally by the river, they feed on our good name.

At dusk, I walked over to the Spencers' place. I brooded on what could be done to quell the talk, to make the town forget you. It was one of the strange warm evenings we've been having, and I passed through the thin black trees of the woodlot, squinting into the last orange glint of the sun. Over my shoulder I saw that my shadow was as long as a path. Have you noticed, where you are, that though it is warm there are no new leaves?

Kit Spencer did not want to invite me in, I could see. But James motioned at the window. He offered me my usual chair and cup of tea.

When we had drunk, he said, Well, Josiah, she wants to be his wife in Heaven.

I tried to laugh a bit. He did not join me. He looked into the fire and rubbed his pinched nose. His face looked as it did years ago, when the river came up suddenly and drowned the lambs in their pen.

I have been wrong, he said, to trust his interest in her well-being.

Should I have said to him then what I had long hoped, that one day our children might love one another, and unite my family with that of my closest friend? I could not. I was afraid to see the impatient jerk of his face, the disdain. I stirred my tea.

He said, He has convinced her that the world will end and that he knows the day.

I said, It is the mad fervor of youth. It will pass. James, it must pass.

But his face was set against me.

Then we saw young Marie at the door. Come through, my dear, said her father, and she came through the room without looking at me. If you are concerned for her, I will tell you: she looked much as usual, but tired. Her hair was escaping around her face and her red braid was rough and unruly behind. They have shown her that she must remain at home, James says. Twice, though, she has woken up weeping. She believes she will die by fire. For shame, John Ephraim. For shame.

your Father

February 24th

Dear John Ephraim,

You may have noticed that I have not written for some time. I had thought of remaining silent and letting curiosity bring you out. But I find there is too much to say to you. It is an empty house, with you gone, and your mother lying quietly abed. I find the space filling up with my thoughts. I build a stingy fire and, when your mother is sleeping, go down and deliberate beside it until it fades. I have been to Sunday services but twice since you went, preferring to worship at home with your mother. I'm not so pleased with this new man Wheelwright. He knows any amount of Scripture, but as for shedding light—he preaches hard on the thinnest verses, with much perspiring and waving of the elbows. In my evenings alone I have turned again to my Bible, and, I must say, have found much censure of your flight. The obvious I need not quote. We both know God's first direction to children, that their days might be long on the land.[2] But do you ever chance to refresh your mind among the Psalms, and read: Rid me and deliver me from the hand of strange children, whose mouth speakest vanity, and their right hand is the hand of falsehood, that our sons may be as green plants grown up in their youth and our daughters may be as cornerstones?[3] And Malachi, who writes that the heart of the children shall turn to the fathers lest the earth be smited with a curse.[4] With these plain instructions and what natural love for us you may still bear, why do you stay away?

To be truthful, I have also been reminded that it is not for a father to provoke his son to anger, and I have sat in reverie, considering it. After a week of such thinking I have decided this. That though your disrespect to your father is a clear sin, though your talk is humbug by his standard, though you have fled your family into a squalid delusion and corrupted the mind of a young girl—though these things be true without doubt in my mind, still I think I may have offended in my own small way. The afternoon before you went, when we spoke hotly near the barn, I implied that your mind was not your own. I saw you step back, brush in hand, from the sorrel who stood stamping and rippling her skin, but I continued, as I felt I must. I did believe it was my duty to decide for you what might enrich or endanger your soul—you were my son, and still young, and living in my house. But when I shook your arm, and called you vain and dramatic, this may have hurt you. I acknowledge it.

Your mother requests that I come to you and ask you back. I cannot see my way to it just now. You must extend your own hand. But may this clear the air between us.

your Father

---

2 **that their days . . . on the land:** biblical reference to Exodus 20:12. The quotation follows the opening words of the first commandment: "Honor thy father and mother. . . ."

3 **Rid me and deliver me . . . :** biblical reference to Psalm 144:11–12.

4 **Malachi:** biblical reference to Malachi 4:5.

March 1st

John Ephraim,

For a week I've gone to the bank and concentrated only on that work. My regular hours, my usual dinner in the safety of friends. I've held conversations that never refer to my family. But at my desk I read. In the lectures and letters the papers print I see that there is discussion of the 18th, 19th, and 20th days of this month, and of whether one must measure time by the time of day in Jerusalem. It is also said that in the encampments the people weave baskets in which they may sit and be whisked to heaven. It is the sneering writers who report this, I admit. I should think it general knowledge that if God wanted to take a man up He would not need to be provided with handles. I make these jokes to myself at my desk and then I lift my head and stare out into the street, and my heart pounds. Since James Spencer has given Marie leave to stay with your mother (though oh how coldly), I rode today to Rocky Ford.

The earth is hard under the drying decay of leaves; one can feel the shock of hooves against it. At the side of the road, poor bleached grasses wave. Some trees bear on their trunks a sleeve of grime, where ice was pooled only a few weeks past. The sun comes up strange, I think, with a light that looks very old, sharply yellow, biting at the eye. And yet nothing grows. Perhaps you have come out of your tent and seen this. The hatter says the weather is called a bright winter and, if one accepts the almanac, should precede an icy wet spring. I think of your tattered, disappointed tent, the rain thudding on you after the joyless great day.

The streets of Rocky Ford are also odd nowadays. They are dusty, and cheap newspapers are forever blowing about. The citizenry look furtive and exhausted. Occasionally I see a strange tight group of women moving along the walk. They carry baskets and buy flour and sugar in small supplies. I saw the storekeeper, the old one, sell a bag of sugar to a woman. He said, Let me sell you the ten pounds, since the price will be better, and looked at her with his face expectant. She laughed and said, No, sir, I thank you, but I buy sugar for this week, and next week, and the week after that. Then I'll have no need to sweeten the food on my table. When she went out, another woman, who had stood stock still and watched, went flying up to the old man and scolded him for selling at all to a wretched woman of the blue tent. The old man's hoarse voice followed me out and was audible on the street.

Your mother had asked again that I go to see you. I went as far as the muddy place from which I watched before. Now the wall is high and sturdy. From where I stood I could see no gate. I did not go around to the ford to seek you. I am still waiting for you to make your choice.

your Father

March 2nd

John,

What I did not say yesterday. I heard a conversation that lowered my spirits. I had gone into the inn between Rocky Ford and Broadhill to drink a little wine and some tea. I thought I'd hear the politics, or about a new book to take home to your mother. But the place was crowded with laughing rabble, in for noon dinner. While I sat watching they hooted and slapped each other, and soon one stood up and called in a high, stern voice for all those at his table to be quiet.

Parson, they cried, put down that beer, unseemly fellow!

Their friend shook his finger at them. Look here, you lot of ruined dogs, he said, still in this high voice like a woman's. Here's a prophecy.

The very word prophecy set them howling.

Then he said, I counted the sneezes of my cross-eyed goat and multiplied it by the seeds of a crooked-neck squash, and subtracted the freckles on the neck of my fat little bride! (A roar.)

How long did you count those freckles, sir? said one who wore a red cap.

Two days, said this parson, And carefully. You may be sure I'm in the right.

And what did you learn, brother? sang out another.

Blockhead! he said. The end of the world! Oh, then it was a merry table. One old fellow pushed back from the board and came over near me to rummage among bags on the floor.

The clever herd was clamoring for instruction. When must I be ready for the end? said the red cap.

No need, said the parson. It came and went the day you were born. The world coughed you up and then died.

Why, Parson, said one, soft and sly. That's no prophecy, then. That's history.

The parson looked into his beer and said, It's prophecy in a looking glass.

It's Jesus don't know if he's coming or going, crowed the red cap. Much laughter.

So I been in Hell and never knew the difference, said the sly one.

Here's the richest bit, said the parson. Those as went to Heaven never knew the difference either.

All stopped a minute and drank. The man at the bags stood near me, watching. Suddenly he turned to me and said, That's some bad nonsense, ain't it?

In my surprise I only nodded. He wiped his hands on his pants, and said, This is how you know it's a democracy. When you see fools free to believe in nothing.

And he took up his bags and went out.

While my attention was on him, the table had quieted. The men were at their food. One fellow, who had eyes skewed almost to the sides of his head, said gravely into the silence, I've got a stony soul or two to throw to that boy parson. I can pick them up off the ground, and throw them right to him. Let us see how quick his hands are.

From the table somewhere, Amen.

I confess I was concerned by this. The derision of the newspaper editors has given way to a savage rancor among the people.

Who is this boy parson, John Ephraim?

your Father

March 6th

John Ephraim,

Once I had a little boy, a sturdy gentle fellow, who crouched peering into the nests of grass fowl, and waited for hours at the lairs of small animals, until his knees were locked and painful and I had to work them with my hands. So where is my patient boy in the young man who demands his Lord come now to earth in his own lifetime? I wonder why the brightest young scholar I ever saw hold a slate should abnegate the future?

I have been thinking of you and what you must feel as you wait for the end. It's difficult. If I thought there would be no rough chain of days leading me onward, if I thought that the land I know, weedy, strewn with manure, camped upon by the vengeful obtuse race of man, if I believed it would all soon vanish in one flaming utterance of the holy, I should feel—grief. In your circumstance I could not muster joy. This in case you thought I might perhaps join you under the blue tent.

Marie Spencer has made supper for your mother and has just brought me apples and cheese. I watched her today as she brought water up the hill from the well. One moment she stopped to rest her pail on the ground, and the wind blew and pressed her dress back against her. The cat ran to her, and she picked it up and put it against her shoulder, and took up her pail and walked on. You are giving away forty years of sleep beside this girl. When this fever is off you, and you come back to look around, what will be left? The door is closing. The world and its doors. My son a gateless tabernacle.[5] My wife a room growing darker.

Father

March 9th

John,

I go down the streets now with coat flapping and people stare. Your mother is worse. She is making preparations. How can you not come to her?

I hear her breathing all night. I hear her.

Father

March 14th

John Ephraim,

An ugly scene in Rocky Ford today. I am hardly recovered. I had gone over to the hatter's to hear the news, over those six miles that are so familiar now. The fields are densely matted, the shrubs bare and curling in the heat. Confused birds dart madly before and behind me as I ride. My winter clothes are heavy and I am wet inside them.

The hatter was not there. Business hours, mind you, and a Monday. The door was looped shut with a piece of rope. I could

---

5 **tabernacle:** originally, a temporary dwelling; tent. Here, the father laments the tent in which his son is living.

hardly believe it, but I knew what it meant. This dour and precise little man, this ready scoffer, had abandoned his life. Strange that I should not have seen it coming, but I have overlooked before this what was placed in plain sight. Inside on the floor of the shop, I could see a man's silk hat. The crown was smashed flat. Beyond were others, treated likewise. I withdrew from this scene along the boardwalk, as if from the fatal spill of a runaway wagon. If the hatter is among you now, I beg you do not tell him the hats are ruined. I consider him my friend, and hope to see him soon, back in his shop. I have known him for years, you know.

But it was more than this. As I came back along the street I saw two men standing some twenty feet apart from a woman I thought I knew, looking at her quite rudely. Other people were at their business all along the street, but they moved slow, slower, as though the spin of the earth were winding down like a clock. It was the woman who had bought such a small bag of sugar from the grocer a few weeks ago. She was not as gay, now, turning her shoulder to these men and tucking her chin down. Then—my God!—a stone rang on the iron ground, and skittered along under her skirt. The people listening moved as slowly as lengthening shadows.

I rejoice, said the woman, I rejoice to be persecuted for the sake of the truth.

One rough laugh, a bray, floated down the street. The scene bore no resemblance to civilized life. I hurried into the breach between them, and took off my hat. Gentlemen, I called, look at yourselves.

I might have gone on, but I saw that both victim and perpetrators had faded away. I was left standing alone, while the livid townspeople stumped past me across the baked and splintered storefronts. I still held my hat in my hand. I thought I heard someone breathe, Who does this old beggar think he is?

Were the people this way before you called them lost, John? Was kind company always a deep fraud, and the mild face of the land a harlot mask? The fence you have built has divided us, son from father. You have called us graceless, and we have plucked up that name and wear it.

I went home and sat by your mother; I sit there now as I write. She drinks a little water now and then. I feel severed even from her, by what I cannot describe. I can write only to you, who never respond, and who indeed may never hear me. I am tired now. The world doubles before me.

Father

March 16th

John,

I hurry to write because the post bag is leaving and I've detained the man at my desk. I think I will come to you the morning after. If you are willing, come out of there and down to the water to meet me.

Father

March 17th

Dear John,

Your great day approaches quickly. I have read that all expectations are now for the night of the 19th. Your mother wishes you well. That is all she will say.

Tonight I read to her from the naturalist's book about northern birds. She fell asleep suddenly, with her body twisted round, and I sat there for a moment with my hand in the book, waiting to see if she would stir. Then suddenly I felt strongly that I must write to you. I thought, this is why the Lord is not coming. Not this year. Not the next. I was sure of it. (But why should I feel so urgent to tell you why the end of the world is not coming, if the end of the world is not coming? I should have plenty of time.) It was this of which I thought, a story you may not know the whole of.

Before your mother and I married, I worked at the bank to earn a home for us. She was waiting. But she had left school and was restless; she spent so much time reading books and seeing lectures that she was full of convictions. These led her to do work through her church down at Braxton. There's a house for the insane there, you know. Faithless, reasonless creatures, calling out like animals. I'd seen them. I was, I confess, against it.

But your mother went to them. She was with another girl; they were both eighteen. She sent me letters. In the mornings she washed their faces and bodies, and fed them by hand. The bedding was always foul and had to be washed nearly every day. Once she wrote me mourning for a white shirtwaist she'd made, that had become so torn, and so dirty with food and refuse, that she'd had to throw it away. But it was as though Providence had ruined her blouse, not people. She did not blame the mad, nor even mention them. In the afternoons, she read Scripture to a huddled group; the men were brought in and seated so they could listen. I remember her writing that Saint Francis had had easy work, preaching to birds. Her audience argued with her, or performed strange sudden dances, or repeated her words a half-measure behind until she could hardly understand her own voice. On the terrible afternoon (she told me when I went down to fetch her) she was reading Psalms—some of the congregation were even asleep in their chairs—and one great sad boy stood up and began singing, and came forward and caught your mother up in his hands. He held her above his head, and she could see the floor turning and the cowering mad women crying. Then he threw her to the ground. Her back was hurt. That is why she has walked so poorly. And perhaps why she is sick now, still a woman in her prime.

I mean just that when I saw your mother sleeping in that twisted way, I think of what she gave, in pain and lost time, in lost work and sickness, to bring God to a place where there was no God. In hope that when she had worked to make earth holy, then God would see his place prepared, and return to us. But John Ephraim! You say God never blinked his distant white eye! That his vision is overcrusted with secret plans, and he will come to earth when it shall suit him, regardless of the extent of goodness, the number of saved. At his whim he will raze our land and purify it for his dwelling—a finer earth will suit him to dwell in, not the one he made long ago, a novice. No. Everything in me rebels at this, a Lord who averts his face from the like of your mother, who wraps his head in a cloak.

For years I have stood at evening on the rise next to Spencer's woodlot and heard every sound and smelled it all, and though the light fades, my eyes are wider and wider open. Then I know a deer has come nosing among the brambles. I do not see her move but feel her there, her wiry fear and unconscious beauty. And by her that landscape is graced. Transformed by that black delicate hoof, the bone shin against which she rubs her face. So the landscape is more graceful for the work we may do, and God sees it. When we have brought all the deer out of the woods to stand in dark-eyed calm, then he will walk among us and feed us from his hand.

You may think I am too selfish an old fellow to speak of such progress. I am sure that I am selfish. But the finer earth must be partly of our making, John. I am sure of this also.

Father

Later. I find I cannot seal this letter without saying it. You have my love. My little boy.

Broadhill,
March 22nd

Dear Reverend Gearhart,

I thank you for your note of March 19th, and the uncollected letter. I am not surprised our letter carrier did not visit you as usual. As you know, it was a difficult morning for many people. I will tell you what I saw, if it will add anything for those who suffered. I went to the camp very early, while it was still night. I won't say I didn't watch the sky as I rode. The stars were weak up there. The nail holes in the tin of my lantern made more light. That night the cold descended—this bright weather has broken all over the state, I hear. It was a queer pleasure to see the deep frost form in the ditches, and the usual fingers of ice extend from the bank of the river. My horse slipped sharply once at the ford, and I had to get down and walk her. When I arrived at the camp, I looked back across the stream and saw the advancing day as a grayness among the trees.

A few people were camped under their wagons, asleep. Beyond them the enclosure looked huge and dark, but above it the tent could be seen, and a little light paled its blue roof. Inside the people were singing. The sound was melodious and brave but very soft. I wondered if some were dozing while others kept the watch, or if all were awake and the gray dawn was striking them, one by one, silent with despair. I stood listening, and my heart was turning inside me.

In the trees across the clearing there was motion. I peered, stopped, blew on my hands, widened my eyes again, but could gather little light. I went over to my horse and put my hands under her blanket to warm them. In retrospect, I believe I saw the ruffians who started the fire. They must have crept up from the south side and there set the brush burning. They must have muffled their lanterns with cloths. If I had seen a glow I might have investigated. But how strange that I should have seen *no* light, that they should have been that stealthy.

The flames came quickly in the vegetation, dry under its frost. Those lying under wagons woke, ran to a small door in the wall, and began pounding upon it. I followed them, and pounded with my frozen hands. The singing separated into individual voices, then ceased. Behind me, my horse reared and tore at her reins. In a few moments the fire drove me back to her. I set her loose. She thumped into the ford, and I followed her, and others were on either side of me, carrying things—a gun, a bag of potatoes. They had abandoned their wagons. The fire was running along the ground, and twigs and branches were jerking and popping as though inspirited. The fence had turned a sweating dark brown, and the uprights were blackening. When the sun came up, that yellow light swallowed the flame, so it appeared simply that the air between us and the enclosure was deforming and wrinkling. I heard shouts and, somewhere, the ringing of an axe on wood. We stood dumbly across the water.

Well, it's as you know. Most came out through the new-cut door and scattered toward us, wailing, through the north-side trees. Eighteen were burned. A few went into the deep curve of the river and were lost.

My son was not among the living or the dead. Late in the day I walked on the smoldering site of the tent, which had burned and floated away in dark feathers that caught on the trees. I looked under the blankets at the wizened black figures. They had held their hands up at the approach of the fire, and still held them there in postures of fear, or praise. None were my boy. I walked along the river and found nothing. The ice had by then made a deep opaque ruffle along the bank. I suppose we will know little until the next thaw. There are others missing. Mine is not the only one. We may yet have peace of mind.

Thank you for asking after Nell. She continues. This, at least. But I look across a threshold always, into the place where I will live as a man alone. And you will be surprised to know of whom I am thinking, Reverend. It is the letter carrier who fills my mind. Yes, I know I have never met him.

You said he was about my age, perhaps older. I will be fifty soon. He was whiskered, and either drunk or longing to be drunk. But he always put the letters under his coat and touched his forehead respectfully. I can imagine him walking up to John Ephraim in the camp, saying, Here's another, and John opening it with his thin hands, and reading. I do not see his face, of course. To recollect the whole face is hard. I have only the feeling the face gave me. He puts the letters carefully between the leaves of his Bible. My letters make that Bible bristly and awkward to handle.

But if John were never there, or if this old man were a liar? Do you see what I am saying, Gearhart? The man takes the letters back to some room, and opens them with his yellow fingers. But the poor fellow cannot read. What was sent in faith he receives with confusion. Plea, argument, and lament are alike unintelligible to him. He touches the hieroglyphs with his fingers. He puzzles over my words in that high far room, he rubs the page against his sunken cheek and smears the ink. It falls from his hand. Already he has forgotten it. He goes to his window across a floor ankle-deep in letters. He treads on every undeciphered word.

If you have the time, Gearhart, I would like to come and see you. I would like to hear your voice.

Josiah Cole

QUESTIONS FOR DISCUSSION

1. What are the advantages and disadvantages of the author's point of view?

2. Identify and discuss the basis (or bases) for the major external conflict in the story.

3. Describe and characterize Josiah Cole, the author of the letters.

4. From the letters, what picture do you get of John Ephraim?

5. How does Keesey prepare you for the destruction of the tent? Is that destruction ironic?

6. At the end, what does the image of the letter carrier tell you about the father's state of mind?

TOPICS FOR WRITING

1. In a literary work, a quotation preceding the opening of a story is called an epigraph. In a paper discuss Keesey's epigraph and relate it to the story.

2. What do you think happened to John Ephraim? In a short essay, express your opinion.

3. Part of the genesis of this story grew out of the burning of the Branch Davidian compound in Waco, Texas, in 1993—the result, in Keesey's view, of "collisions of belief." Have students research similar late twentieth-century collisions and compare their impact to that of Waco.

4. In a paper, discuss the significance of the story's title.

THE JILTING OF GRANNY WEATHERALL

KATHERINE ANNE PORTER (1890–1980)

Born Callie Russell Porter in the town of Indian Creek, Texas, Katherine Anne Porter was only two years old when her mother died and she was sent to live with an aunt. As a young woman she was interested in writing, but her education at boarding schools and an Ursuline convent halted abruptly when she eloped at the age of sixteen.

As a young, divorced woman in need of work, Porter worked on newspapers in Denver and in Chicago, where she also worked as a bit-part film actress. In 1920, she went to Mexico to study Aztec and Mayan art. In Mexico, her "much-loved second country," she became sufficiently confident of her writing style to begin writing fiction, but it was not until she was forty that she published her first short story collection. *Flowering Judas* (1930; enlarged, 1935) contained twelve finely crafted stories, including "The Jilting of Granny Weatherall."

In 1931, as Porter sailed from Vera Cruz, Mexico, to Germany, she conceived the idea of writing a novel about a group of passengers on a long sea voyage. *Ship of Fools* (1962), Porter's only novel, became a "moral allegory about the voyage of life and, according to the author, the way in which 'evil is always done with the collusion of good.'"

Although she also published *The Never-Ending Wrong* (1970), a nonfiction work about the Sacco-Vanzetti case of the 1920s, and *The Days Before* (1952; augmented, 1970), a collection of essays, articles, and book reviews, Porter's reputation rests on her short stories. In her second collection, *Pale Horse, Pale Rider* (1939), the title story is about the end of a youthful romance when a young man dies in the influenza epidemic of 1919. Porter wrote from personal experience; not only did influenza kill a man she loved, but she herself nearly died of it. Some of the stories in her third collection, *The Leaning Tower* (1944), grew out of impressions of time spent in Germany during the rise of Hitler. In 1965, Porter's *Collected Stories* was published; in 1966, it won both the National Book Award and the Pulitzer Prize for fiction.

Asked about her methods, Porter once confided, "I always write my last line, my last paragraphs, my last page first." As you read about Granny Weatherall's final days, note the depth of Granny's characterization in small details, Porter's judicious use of figurative language and the stream of consciousness technique.

She flicked her wrist neatly out of Doctor Harry's pudgy careful fingers and pulled the sheet up to her chin. The brat ought to be in knee breeches. Doctoring around the country with spectacles on his nose! "Get along now, take your schoolbooks and go. There's nothing wrong with me."

Doctor Harry spread a warm paw like a cushion on her forehead where the forked green vein danced and made her eyelids twitch. "Now, now, be a good girl, and we'll have you up in no time."

"That's no way to speak to a woman nearly eighty years old just because she's down. I'd have you respect your elders, young man."

"Well, Missy, excuse me." Doctor Harry patted her cheek. "But I've got to warn you, haven't I? You're a marvel, but you must be careful or you're going to be good and sorry."

"Don't tell me what I'm going to be. I'm on my feet now, morally speaking. It's Cornelia. I had to go to bed to get rid of her."

Her bones felt loose, and floated around in her skin, and Doctor Harry floated like a balloon around the foot of the bed. He floated and pulled down his waistcoat and swung his glasses on a cord. "Well, stay where you are, it certainly can't hurt you."

"Get along and doctor your sick," said Granny Weatherall. "Leave a well woman alone. I'll call for you when I want you. . . . Where were you forty years ago when I pulled through milk-leg[1] and double pneumonia? You weren't even born. Don't let Cornelia lead you on," she shouted, because Doctor Harry appeared to float up to the ceiling and out. "I pay my own bills, and I don't throw my money away on nonsense!"

She meant to wave good-by, but it was too much trouble. Her eyes closed of themselves, it was like a dark curtain drawn around the bed. The pillow rose and floated under her, pleasant as a hammock in a light wind. She listened to the leaves rustling outside the window. No, somebody was swishing newspapers: no, Cornelia and Doctor Harry were whispering together. She leaped broad awake, thinking they whispered in her ear.

"She was never like this, *never* like this!" "Well, what can we expect?" "Yes, eighty years old. . . ."

Well, and what if she was? She still had ears. It was like Cornelia to whisper around doors. She always kept things secret in such a public way. She was always being tactful and kind. Cornelia was dutiful; that

---

1 **milk-leg:** a swelling that occasionally follows pregnancy.

was the trouble with her. Dutiful and good: "So good and dutiful," said Granny, "that I'd like to spank her." She saw herself spanking Cornelia and making a fine job of it.

"What'd you say, Mother?"

Granny felt her face tying up in hard knots.

"Can't a body think, I'd like to know?"

"I thought you might want something."

"I do. I want a lot of things. First off, go away and don't whisper."

She lay and drowsed, hoping in her sleep that the children would keep out and let her rest a minute. It had been a long day. Not that she was tired. It was always pleasant to snatch a minute now and then. There was always so much to be done, let me see: tomorrow.

Tomorrow was far away and there was nothing to trouble about. Things were finished somehow when the time came; thank God there was always a little margin over for peace: then a person could spread out the plan of life and tuck in the edges orderly. It was good to have everything clean and folded away, with the hair brushes and tonic bottles sitting straight on the white embroidered linen: the day started without fuss and the pantry shelves laid out with rows of jelly glasses and brown jugs and white stone-china jars with blue whirligigs and words painted on them: coffee, tea, sugar, ginger, cinnamon, allspice: and the bronze clock with the lion on top nicely dusted off. The dust that lion could collect in twenty-four hours! The box in the attic with all those letters tied up, well, she'd have to go through that tomorrow. All those letters—George's letters and John's letters and her letters to them both—lying around for the children to find afterwards made her uneasy. Yes, that would be tomorrow's business. No use to let them know how silly she had been once.

While she was rummaging around she found death in her mind and it felt clammy and unfamiliar. She had spent so much time preparing for death there was no need for bringing it up again. Let it take care of itself now. When she was sixty she had felt very old, finished, and went around making farewell trips to see her children and grandchildren, with a secret in her mind: This is the very last of your mother, children! Then she made her will and came down with a long fever. That was all just a notion like a lot of other things, but it was lucky too, for she had once for all[2] got over the idea of dying for a

---

2 **once for all:** Sometimes "once and for all" means "certainly" or "definitely."

long time. Now she couldn't be worried. She hoped she had better sense now. Her father had lived to be one hundred and two years old and had drunk a noggin of strong hot toddy[3] on his last birthday. He told the reporters it was his daily habit, and he owed his long life to that. He had made quite a scandal and was very pleased about it. She believed she'd just plague Cornelia a little.

"Cornelia! Cornelia!" No footsteps, but a sudden hand on her cheek. "Bless you, where have you been?"

"Here, Mother."

"Well, Cornelia, I want a noggin of hot toddy."

"Are you cold, darling?"

"I'm chilly, Cornelia. Lying in bed stops the circulation. I must have told you that a thousand times."

Well, she could just hear Cornelia telling her husband that Mother was getting a little childish and they'd have to humor her. The thing that most annoyed her was that Cornelia thought she was deaf, dumb, and blind. Little hasty glances and tiny gestures tossed around her and over her head saying, "Don't cross her, let her have her way, she's eighty years old," and she sitting there as if she lived in a thin glass cage. Sometimes Granny almost made up her mind to pack up and move back to her own house where nobody could remind her every minute that she was old. Wait, wait, Cornelia, till your own children whisper behind your back!

In her day she had kept a better house and had got more work done. She wasn't too old yet for Lydia to be driving eighty miles for advice when one of the children jumped the track, and Jimmy still dropped in and talked things over: "Now, Mammy, you've a good business head, I want to know what you think of this? . . ." Old. Cornelia couldn't change the furniture around without asking. Little things, little things! They had been so sweet when they were little. Granny wished the old days were back again with the children young and everything to be done over. It had been a hard pull, but not too much for her. When she thought of all the food she had cooked, and all the clothes she had cut and sewed, and all the gardens she had made—well, the children showed it. There they were, made out of her, and they couldn't get away from that. Sometimes she wanted to

---

3 **noggin of strong hot toddy:** A *noggin* is a small cup containing about four ounces; a *hot toddy* is a drink of liquor (whiskey, brandy, or rum), hot water, sugar, and spices.

see John again and point to them and say, Well, I didn't do so badly, did I? But that would have to wait. That was for tomorrow. She used to think of him as a man, but now all the children were older than their father, and he would be a child beside her if she saw him now. It seemed strange and there was something wrong in the idea. Why, he couldn't possibly recognize her. She had fenced in a hundred acres once, digging the post holes herself and clamping the wires with just a negro boy to help. That changed a woman. John would be looking for a young woman with the peaked Spanish comb in her hair and the painted fan. Digging post holes changed a woman. Riding country roads in the winter when women had their babies was another thing: sitting up nights with sick horses and sick negroes and sick children and hardly ever losing one. John, I hardly ever lost one of them! John would see that in a minute, that would be something he could understand, she wouldn't have to explain anything!

It made her feel like rolling up her sleeves and putting the whole place to rights again. No matter if Cornelia was determined to be everywhere at once, there were a great many things left undone on this place. She would start tomorrow and do them. It was good to be strong enough for everything, even if all you made melted and changed and slipped under your hands, so that by the time you finished you almost forgot what you were working for. What was it I set out to do? she asked herself intently, but she could not remember. A fog rose over the valley, she saw it marching across the creek swallowing the trees and moving up the hill like an army of ghosts. Soon it would be at the near edge of the orchard, and then it was time to go in and light the lamps. Come in, children, don't stay out in the night air.

Lighting the lamps had been beautiful. The children huddled up to her and breathed like little calves waiting at the bars in the twilight. Their eyes followed the match and watched the flame rise and settle in a blue curve, then they moved away from her. The lamp was lit, they didn't have to be scared and hang on to mother any more. Never, never, never more. God, for all my life I thank Thee. Without Thee, my God, I could never have done it. Hail, Mary, full of grace.

I want you to pick all the fruit this year and see that nothing is wasted. There's always someone who can use it. Don't let good things rot for want of using. You waste life when you waste good food. Don't let things get lost. It's bitter to lose things. Now, don't let me get to thinking, not when I am tired and taking a little nap before supper. . . .

The pillow rose about her shoulders and pressed against her heart and the memory was being squeezed out of it: oh, push down the pillow, somebody: it would smother her if she tried to hold it. Such a fresh breeze blowing and such a green day with no threats in it. But he had not come, just the same. What does a woman do when she has put on the white veil and set out the white cake for a man and he doesn't come? She tried to remember. No, I swear he never harmed me but in that. He never harmed me but in that . . . and what if he did? There was the day, the day, but a whirl of dark smoke rose and covered it, crept up and over into the bright field where everything was planted so carefully in orderly rows. That was hell, she knew hell when she saw it. For sixty years she had prayed against remembering him and against losing her soul in the deep pit of hell, and now the two things were mingled in one and the thought of him was a smoky cloud from hell that moved and crept in her head when she had just got rid of Doctor Harry and was trying to rest a minute. Wounded vanity, Ellen, said a sharp voice in the top of her mind. Don't let your wounded vanity get the upper hand of you. Plenty of girls get jilted. You were jilted, weren't you? Then stand up to it. Her eyelids wavered and let in streamers of blue-gray light like tissue paper over her eyes. She must get up and pull the shades down or she'd never sleep. She was in bed again and the shades were not down. How could that happen? Better turn over, hide from the light, sleeping in the light gave you nightmares. "Mother, how do you feel now?" and a stinging wetness on her forehead. But I don't like having my face washed in cold water!

Hapsy? George? Lydia? Jimmy? No, Cornelia, and her features were swollen and full of little puddles. "They're coming, darling, they'll all be here soon." Go wash your face, child, you look funny.

Instead of obeying, Cornelia knelt down and put her head on the pillow. She seemed to be talking but there was no sound. "Well, are you tongue-tied? Whose birthday is it? Are you going to give a party?"

Cornelia's mouth moved urgently in strange shapes. "Don't do that, you bother me, daughter."

"Oh, no, Mother. Oh, no. . . ."

Nonsense. It was strange about children. They disputed your every word. "No what, Cornelia?"

"Here's Doctor Harry."

"I won't see that boy again. He just left five minutes ago."

"That was this morning, Mother. It's night now. Here's the nurse."

"This is Doctor Harry, Mrs. Weatherall. I never saw you look so young and happy!"

"Ah, I'll never be young again—but I'd be happy if they'd let me lie in peace and get rested."

She thought she spoke up loudly, but no one answered. A warm weight on her forehead, a warm bracelet on her wrist, and a breeze went on whispering, trying to tell her something. A shuffle of leaves in the everlasting hand of God, He blew on them and they danced and rattled. "Mother, don't mind, we're going to give you a little hypodermic." "Look here, daughter, how do ants get in this bed? I saw sugar ants yesterday." Did you send for Hapsy too?

It was Hapsy she really wanted. She had to go a long way back through a great many rooms to find Hapsy standing with a baby on her arm. She seemed to herself to be Hapsy also, and the baby on Hapsy's arm was Hapsy and himself and herself, all at once, and there was no surprise in the meeting. Then Hapsy melted from within and turned flimsy as gray gauze and the baby was a gauzy shadow, and Hapsy came up close and said, "I thought you'd never come," and looked at her very searchingly and said, "You haven't changed a bit!" They leaned forward to kiss, when Cornelia began whispering from a long way off, "Oh, is there anything you want to tell me? Is there anything I can do for you?"

Yes, she had changed her mind after sixty years and she would like to see George. I want you to find George. Find him and be sure to tell him I forgot him. I want him to know I had my husband just the same and my children and my house like any other woman. A good house too and a good husband that I loved and fine children out of him. Better than I hoped for even. Tell him I was given back everything he took away and more. Oh, no, oh, God, no, there was something else besides the house and the man and the children. Oh, surely they were not all? What was it? Something not given back. . . . Her breath crowded down under her ribs and grew into a monstrous frightening shape with cutting edges; it bored up into her head, and the agony was unbelievable: Yes, John, get the Doctor now, no more talk, my time has come.

When this one was born it should be the last. The last. It should have been born first, for it was the one she had truly wanted. Everything came in good time. Nothing left out, left over. She was strong, in three days she would be as well as ever. Better. A woman needed milk in her to have her full health.

"Mother, do you hear me?"

"I've been telling you—"

"Mother, Father Connolly's here."

"I went to Holy Communion only last week. Tell him I'm not so sinful as all that."

"Father just wants to speak to you."

He could speak as much as he pleased. It was like him to drop in and inquire about her soul as if it were a teething baby, and then stay on for a cup of tea and a round of cards and gossip. He always had a funny story of some sort, usually about an Irishman who made his little mistakes and confessed them, and the point lay in some absurd thing he would blurt out in the confessional showing his struggles between native piety and original sin. Granny felt easy about her soul. Cornelia, where are your manners? Give Father Connolly a chair. She had her secret comfortable understanding with a few favorite saints who cleared a straight road to God for her. All as surely signed and sealed as the papers for the new Forty Acres. Forever . . . heirs and assigns forever. Since the day the wedding cake was not cut, but thrown out and wasted. The whole bottom dropped out of the world, and there she was blind and sweating with nothing under her feet and the walls falling away. His hand had caught her under the breast, she had not fallen, there was the freshly polished floor with the green rug on it, just as before. He had cursed like a sailor's parrot and said, "I'll kill him for you." Don't lay a hand on him, for my sake leave something to God. "Now, Ellen, you must believe what I tell you. . . ."

So there was nothing, nothing to worry about any more, except sometimes in the night one of the children screamed in a nightmare, and they both hustled out shaking and hunting for the matches and calling, "There, wait a minute, here we are!" John, get the doctor now, Hapsy's time has come. But there was Hapsy standing by the bed in a white cap. "Cornelia, tell Hapsy to take off her cap. I can't see her plain."

Her eyes opened very wide and the room stood out like a picture she had seen somewhere. Dark colors with the shadows rising towards the ceiling in long angles. The tall black dresser gleamed with nothing on it but John's picture, enlarged from a little one, with John's eyes very black when they should have been blue. You never saw him, so how do you know how he looked? But the man insisted the copy was perfect, it was very rich and handsome. For a picture, yes, but it's not my husband. The table by the bed had a linen cover and a candle and a crucifix. The light was blue from Cornelia's silk lampshades. No sort of light at all, just frippery. You had to live forty years with kerosene lamps to appreciate honest electricity. She felt very strong and she saw Doctor Harry with a rosy nimbus around him.

"You look like a saint, Doctor Harry, and I vow that's as near as you'll ever come to it."

"She's saying something."

"I heard you, Cornelia. What's all this carrying-on?"

"Father Connolly's saying—"

Cornelia's voice staggered and bumped like a cart in a bad road. It rounded corners and turned back again and arrived nowhere. Granny stepped up in the cart very lightly and reached for the reins, but a man sat beside her and she knew him by his hands, driving the cart. She did not look in his face, for she knew without seeing, but looked instead down the road where the trees leaned over and bowed to each other and a thousand birds were singing a Mass. She felt like singing too, but she put her hand in the bosom of her dress and pulled out a rosary, and Father Connolly murmured Latin in a very solemn voice and tickled her feet.[4] My God, will you stop that nonsense? I'm a married woman. What if he did run away and leave me to face the priest by myself? I found another a whole world better. I wouldn't have exchanged my husband for anybody except St. Michael himself, and you may tell him that for me with a thank you in the bargain.

Light flashed on her closed eyelids, and a deep roaring shook her. Cornelia, is that lightning? I hear thunder. There's going to be a storm. Close all the windows. Call the children in. . . . "Mother, here we are, all of us." "Is that you, Hapsy?" "Oh, no, I'm Lydia. We drove as fast as we could." Their faces drifted above her, drifted away. The rosary fell out of her hands and Lydia put it back. Jimmy tried to help, their hands fumbled together, and Granny closed two fingers around Jimmy's thumb. Beads wouldn't do, it must be something alive. She was so amazed her thoughts ran round and round. So, my dear Lord, this is my death and I wasn't even thinking about it. My children have come to see me die. But I can't, it's not time. Oh, I always hated surprises. I wanted to give Cornelia the amethyst set— Cornelia, you're to have the amethyst set, but Hapsy's to wear it when she wants, and, Doctor Harry, do shut up. Nobody sent for you. Oh, my dear Lord, do wait a minute. I meant to do something about the Forty Acres, Jimmy doesn't need it and Lydia will later on,

---

4 **Father Connolly . . . tickled her feet:** As part of the sacrament for the dying, the priest anoints the feet with oil.

with that worthless husband of hers. I meant to finish the altar cloth and send six bottles of wine to Sister Borgia for her dyspepsia.[5] I want to send six bottles of wine to Sister Borgia, Father Connolly, now don't let me forget.

Cornelia's voice made short turns and tilted over and crashed. "Oh, Mother, oh, Mother, oh, Mother. . . ."

"I'm not going, Cornelia. I'm taken by surprise. I can't go."

You'll see Hapsy again. What about her? "I thought you'd never come." Granny made a long journey outward, looking for Hapsy. What if I don't find her? What then? Her heart sank down and down, there was no bottom to death, she couldn't come to the end of it. The blue light from Cornelia's lampshade drew into a tiny point in the center of her brain, it flickered and winked like an eye, quietly it fluttered and dwindled. Granny lay curled down within herself, amazed and watchful, staring at the point of light that was herself; her body was now only a deeper mass of shadow in an endless darkness and this darkness would curl around the light and swallow it up. God, give a sign!

For the second time there was no sign. Again no bridegroom and the priest in the house. She could not remember any other sorrow because this grief wiped them all away. Oh, no, there's nothing more cruel than this—I'll never forgive it. She stretched herself with a deep breath and blew out the light.

---

5 **dyspepsia:** indigestion.

QUESTIONS FOR DISCUSSION

1. Describe the situation as the story begins.

2. What kind of life has Granny led?

3. How might her life explain Granny's irritation with her daughter Cornelia?

4. Granny reacts to what is occurring around her but sometimes without understanding what those occurrences are. Explain what events prompt the following images or thoughts: (a) "Doctor Harry floated like a balloon around the foot of the bed"; (b) "The pillow rose and floated under her, pleasant as a hammock in a light wind"; (c) "'Mother, how do you feel now?' and a stinging wetness on her forehead. But I don't like having my face washed in cold water!"
(d) "Cornelia's voice made short turns and tilted over and crashed. 'Oh, Mother, oh, Mother, oh, Mother. . . .'"

5. Discuss the point of view of the story and its effectiveness in conveying Granny's character and state of mind.

6. How is the style appropriate to the content of the story?

7. What is the significance of the jilting emphasized in the title?

8. Discuss Granny's complicated attitude toward George.

TOPICS FOR WRITING

1. Write about an incident that happened long ago but still troubles you.

2. In a paragraph discuss the appropriateness of the name *Weatherall*.

3. Porter ends the story with the words "and blew out the light." Are readers to interpret these words literally or figuratively? In a paper discuss the symbolic meaning of this action and any others in the story that imply the same meaning.

4. In literature and on film, death scenes are often sentimental and maudlin. In a paper discuss how Porter prevents Granny's death from becoming so.

SYNTHESIS QUESTIONS

1. Religion is either a major or minor motif in three of the stories in this chapter: "Holy Cards," "Bright Winter," and "The Jilting of Granny Weatherall." Discuss the role religion plays in the lives of two characters in the stories.

2. Which story in this unit do you find the most optimistic? the most pessimistic? Explain your reasons.

3. Discuss the first-person narrator you find the most intriguing. Explain your reasons.

4. Each of the authors in this unit has a distinct style—one that you may or may not find inviting. If you were asked to read three additional stories by one of these authors, which would you choose and why?

5. Anna Keesey's "Bright Winter" is based on a historical occurrence and was prompted by a recent event that paralleled it. Discuss the advantages and disadvantages of using factual, historical events as the basis for fiction.

6. William Wordsworth once wrote: "The child is father to the man." Many of the stories in this unit illustrate that statement in their focus on the effect of parents and/or childhood experiences in forming character. Which character in your opinion has had the most beneficial experiences? which, the least? Give reasons for your opinion.

7. Which story has the most powerful symbol? Explain the reasons for your choice.

8. Working in a group, choose one of the stories in this chapter and analyze the contribution made by each of the four aspects of style.

9. Debate the effectiveness of an episodic story versus a causally developed story.

Chapter Seven

POPULAR FICTION

Some fiction is categorized by types, such as detective, mystery, western, science fiction, ghost, horror, romance, or fantasy. This fiction is sometimes called **genre fiction** (because it exists as types or genres) or **popular fiction** (because it is often read by mass audiences for entertainment and relaxation). Although some critics have made distinctions between popular fiction and "serious"—usually realistic—fiction, the distinctions are partly academic since many so-called serious writers have written popular fiction, and many popular stories are serious fiction. Popular fiction is also sometimes referred to as **formula fiction**, because it tends to adhere to standard characters and plot devices. However, the term formula fiction does not imply that all works within a particular genre are the same. As John Cawelti observes in *Adventure, Mystery, and Romance: Formula Stories as Art and Popular Culture*, "The power to employ stereotypical characters and situations in such a way as to breathe new life and interest into them is particularly crucial to formulaic art of high quality since the creator of a western or detective story cannot risk departing very far from the typical characters and situations his audience has come to expect."

In the United States, formula stories owe much of their early existence to dime novels and pulp magazines, inexpensive publications printed on pulpwood paper, the cheapest kind. Famous pulp magazines included *Black Mask* (founded 1919), which published hard-boiled detective fiction of writers such as Dashiell Hammett and Raymond Chandler; *Amazing Stories* (begun in 1926) and *Astounding Stories of Super-Science* (founded in 1929), both of which

315

published early science-fiction; and *Western Story* (founded in 1919). These magazines were eagerly read by thousands of readers; in 1920, the circulation of *Western Story*, for example, was 300,000 copies an issue. There were many pulp magazines over the years, some short-lived, some metamorphosed into different titles, and most of them gone completely by the 1950s. *Spicy Detective, Thrilling Western, The Shadow,* and *Weird Tales,* to name only a few astounding titles, have vanished, as have dime novels, which died in the 1920s. Who were the readers? Nearly everyone, from shopkeepers to bankers, from farmers to company presidents.

The cadre of short-story writers who wrote for one- or one-and-a-half-cents a word had to work quickly to keep up with publication dates, and most of them wrote thousands of words a week to survive, a figure that explains why some sort of formula was necessary. Most authors wrote under several pseudonyms, and sometimes several writers wrote under the same pseudonym. Walter B. Gibson wrote the Shadow series as Maxwell Grant, for example, but for a while a writer named Theodore Tinsley wrote some Shadow stories under the same pseudonym. Some writers, such as Edgar Rice Burroughs, Max Brand, Sax Rohmer, Erle Stanley Gardner, Raymond Chandler, and Robert A. Heinlein, all of whom published in the pulps, are well-known names. Other writers are virtually unknown today, either because they published only a few stories or because the exhausting pace drove them to other pursuits.

The genres haven't vanished, however. The eight stories in this chapter exhibit the resilience of these types of popular fiction. They are organized into four sections: Westerns; Detective and Mystery; Fantasy and Science Fiction; and Ghost and Horror.

SECTION ONE

WESTERNS

The **western** is a genre of popular fiction typically set in the American West of the 1800s. Western stories and novels usually deal with an archetypal hero, an independent male on the move, often on horseback. The plots are formulaic: a lawman tries to restore order to the lawless territory; cattle rustlers feud with settlers; Indians raid wagon trains and homesteads. The setting is the prairie or desert of the frequently inhospitable American frontier west of the Mississippi River. The stories are told from the first- or third-person point of view, sometimes by an anonymous onlooker.

The western story is a unique genre because the American frontier was a unique setting. Full of danger, hardship, beauty, and the promise of wealth (or at least one's own plot of land), the frontier meant the opportunity to achieve genuine independence. It meant a chance to see what lay ahead on this vast continent and an opportunity to start life over. The frontier was also an ideal setting for adventure.

Unfortunately, for the people already there, conflict followed, and many western stories deal with that conflict. In early westerns, Indians were frequently antagonists in both novels and short stories. According to Daryl Jones, writing in *The Dime Novel Western*, "Throughout the 1860s and into the early years of the following decade, the Indian hater continued to be a common protagonist in the dime novel." Occasionally a "good" Native American appeared, but he or she was often acting outside the perceived social habits of his or her tribe.

With some exceptions, writers of westerns have been men. Women appear in westerns, but not until fairly recently have they had star status, usually in stories written by women. Westering was often harder for women than for men, and life on the frontier meant that wives and mothers dealt with the same mundane responsibilities they had back East but under more difficult and unglamorous conditions. In most early westerns, women are merely decorative adjuncts to the chief members of the cast—marshals, gunslingers, gamblers, cowboys, gold-seekers, homesteaders, Indians, horses, cactus, and tumbleweed. In more recent western fiction and movies, however, women (good and bad) have assumed a greater role and the archetypal formulas have acquired new dimensions.

Western novels and stories have a long tradition in American literature. Probably the earliest and certainly the best-known author to write about the frontier was James Fenimore Cooper (1780–1851). Cooper wrote about a frontier that was somewhere in western New York State: but by the time he was writing, the frontier had moved west of there. His five novels, known as the Leatherstocking Tales, are *The Pioneers* (1823), *The Last of the Mohicans* (1826), *The Prairie* (1827), *The Pathfinder* (1840), and *The Deerslayer* (1841). The journals of Lewis and Clark were source material for *The Prairie*. Natty Bumppo, who is known by several names in the books (Leatherstocking, Hawkeye, Deerslayer, and Pathfinder), is the chief character, and his companion is Chingachgook, a Mohican. A fugitive from civilization, Bumppo prefers the wilderness and a simple way of life.

Although the Leatherstocking Tales were in some ways the prototypes for frontier literature—and much mediocre frontier literature followed—the novel that first defined the Western genre was *The Virginian*: *A Horseman of the Plains* (1902) by Owen Wister (1860–1938). Set in Wyoming, Wister's novel is about the hatred between the hero, known only as "the Virginian," and a bad man named Trampas. The unnamed hero finally defeats Trampas in a shoot-out and marries a New England schoolteacher newly arrived on the stagecoach. If the story sounds familiar, it is. Filmed several times, the 1929 black-and-white film starred Gary Cooper and Walter Huston, and the story has been emulated countless times on television. There is much truth in the assertion that the mythic West was created by writers.

Mark Twain, Bret Harte, Hamlin Garland, Stephen Crane, and Conrad Richter wrote about the West, although they are not usually known as writers of westerns. It is rather Zane Grey (1872–1939) who did more than anyone to popularize the western story. Born in Zanesville, Ohio, Grey was a dentist in New York City before traveling in the West between 1907 and 1918. *Riders of the Purple Sage* (1912) was perhaps the most popular of his more than 60 novels, and more than 100 films have been based on his stories.

Another prolific early writer was Frederick Faust (1892–1944), who wrote over 300 western novels under the name Max Brand, and in the 1920s was a regular contributor to *Western Story* magazine. His most famous novel is *Destry Rides Again* (1930). He also wrote detective and spy stories. He was killed during World War II in Italy, where he had gone as a war correspondent. Other famous writers of westerns include Ernest Haycox, J. Frank Dobie, A. B. Guthrie, Jr., whose novel *The Way West* won a Pulitzer Prize for fiction in 1950, Jack Schaefer (author of *Shane*), and Louis L'Amour. The Western Writers of America, founded in 1952 and whose membership includes authors, publishers, and editors, awards Spur Awards (formerly Golden Spur Awards) annually to outstanding western fiction.

Writers of westerns are obviously limited to a specific setting. Although the frontier has gone, and with it, the adventurous men and women who traveled to and settled in territories new to them, the romance of the West is nevertheless alluring for readers both here and abroad. Perhaps the fascination lies in the depiction of untamed and unpolluted wilderness, perhaps in the appeal of men and women forging a way of life unfettered by custom or class, perhaps in the dream that success lies just ahead, if one is willing to search for it.

THE MAN WHO SHOT LIBERTY VALANCE

DOROTHY M. JOHNSON (1905–1984)

Dorothy Johnson was born in Iowa but grew up in Montana. After receiving a B.A. from the University of Montana, she went to New York, where she worked as a magazine editor for fifteen years. The West lured her back, however, and she returned to Montana, where from 1950 to 1952 she was news editor of the *Whitefish Pilot* in the small town of Whitefish and from 1952 to 1967 was Assistant Professor of Journalism at the University of Montana.

Johnson was one of the first western writers to portray Native Americans sympathetically, and she was made an honorary member of the Blackfeet tribe in Montana. One of her most famous works is *The Hanging Tree* (1957), which is set in a Montana gold-mining camp and was filmed in 1958. The movie starred Gary Cooper, Maria Schell, and George C. Scott.

Her other works include a short-story collection, *Flame on the Frontier* (1967); *Warrior for a Lost Nation: A Biography of Sitting Bull* (1969); and *Buffalo Woman* (1977), runner-up for the best Western historical novel of 1977 from the Western Writers of America.

She received a Spur Award from the Western Writers of America in 1956, an honorary Litt. D. from the University of Montana in 1973; a Levi Strauss Golden Saddleman Award in 1976; and a Western Heritage Wrangler Award in 1978. Her stories have been widely translated and have appeared in German, Spanish, Indonesian, Urdu, Polish, and Russian.

"The Man Who Shot Liberty Valance" first appeared in *Cosmopolitan* and was later collected, along with ten other stories, in *Indian Country* (1953). A 1962 film of the same name was loosely based on the story. (For some unaccountable reason, the town named Twotrees in the story was changed to Shin Bone!) Directed by John Ford, it starred James Stewart as Ranse, John Wayne as Bert (although the fictional name is changed in the movie), Vera Miles as Hallie, and Lee Marvin as Liberty Valance.

∎

Bert Barricune died in 1910. Not more than a dozen persons showed up for his funeral. Among them was an earnest young reporter who hoped for a human-interest story; there were legends that the old man had been something of a gunfighter in the early days. A few aging men tiptoed in, singly or in pairs, scowling and edgy, clutching their battered hats—men who had been Bert's companions at drinking or penny ante while the world passed them by. One woman came, wearing a heavy veil that concealed her face. White and yellow streaks showed in her black-dyed hair. The reporter made a mental note: Old friend from the old District. But no story there—can't mention that.

One by one they filed past the casket, looking into the still face of old Bert Barricune, who had been nobody. His stubbly hair was white, and his lined face was as empty in death as his life had been. But death had added dignity.

One great spray of flowers spread behind the casket. The card read, "Senator and Mrs. Ransome Foster." There were no other flowers except, almost unnoticed, a few pale, leafless, pink and yellow blossoms scattered on the carpeted step. The reporter, squinting, finally identified them: son of a gun! Blossoms of the prickly pear. Cactus flowers. Seems suitable for the old man—flowers that grow on prairie wasteland. Well, they're free if you want to pick 'em, and Barricune's friends don't look prosperous. But how come the Senator sends a bouquet?

There was a delay, and the funeral director fidgeted a little, waiting. The reporter sat up straighter when he saw the last two mourners enter.

Senator Foster—sure, there's the crippled arm—and that must be his wife. Congress is still in session; he came all the way from Washington. Why would he bother, for an old wreck like Bert Barricune?

After the funeral was decently over, the reporter asked him. The Senator almost told the truth, but he caught himself in time. He said, "Bert Barricune was my friend for more than thirty years."

He could not give the true answer: He was my enemy; he was my conscience; he made me whatever I am.

Ransome Foster had been in the Territory for seven months when he ran into Liberty Valance. He had been afoot on the prairie for two days when he met Bert Barricune. Up to that time, Ranse Foster had been nobody in particular—a dude from the East, quietly inquisitive, moving from one shack town to another; just another tenderfoot with his own reasons for being there and no aim in life at all.

When Barricune found him on the prairie, Foster was indeed a tenderfoot. In his boots there was a warm, damp squidging where his feet had blistered, and the blisters had broken to bleed. He was bruised, sunburned, and filthy. He had been crawling, but when he saw Barricune riding toward him, he sat up. He had no horse, no saddle, and, by that time, no pride.

Barricune looked down at him, not saying anything. Finally Ranse Foster asked, "Water?"

Barricune shook his head. "I don't carry none, but we can go where it is."

He stepped down from the saddle, a casual Samaritan, and with one heave pulled Foster upright.

"Git you in the saddle, can you stay there?" he inquired.

"If I can't," Foster answered through swollen lips, "shoot me."

Bert said amiably, "All right," and pulled the horse around. By twisting its ear, he held the animal quiet long enough to help the anguished stranger to the saddle. Then, on foot—and like any cowboy Bert Barricune hated walking—he led the horse five miles to the river. He let Foster lie where he fell in the cottonwood grove and brought him a hat full of water.

After that, Foster made three attempts to stand up. After the third failure, Barricune asked, grinning, "Want me to shoot you after all?"

"No," Foster answered. "There's something I want to do first."

Barricune looked at the bruises and commented, "Well, I should think so." He got on his horse and rode away. After an hour he returned with bedding and grub and asked, "Ain't you dead yet?"

The bruised and battered man opened his uninjured eye and said, "Not yet, but soon." Bert was amused. He brought a bucket of water and set up camp—a bedroll on a tarp, an armload of wood for a fire. He crouched on his heels while the tenderfoot, with cautious movements that told of pain, got his clothes off and splashed water on his body. No gunshot wounds, Barricune observed, but marks of kicks, and a couple that must have been made with a quirt.

After a while he asked, not inquisitively, but as one who has a right to know how matters stood, "Anybody looking for you?"

Foster rubbed dust from his clothes, being too full of pain to shake them.

"No," he said. "But I'm looking for somebody."

"I ain't going to help you look," Bert informed him. "Town's over that way, two miles, when you get ready to come. Cache the stuff when you leave. I'll pick it up."

Three days later they met in the town marshal's office. They glanced at each other but did not speak. This time it was Bert Barricune who was bruised, though not much. The marshal was just letting him out of the one-cell jail when Foster limped into the office. Nobody said anything until Barricune, blinking and walking not quite steadily, had left. Foster saw him stop in front of the next building to speak to a girl. They walked away together, and it looked as if the young man were being scolded.

The marshal cleared his throat. "You wanted something, Mister?"

Foster answered, "Three men set me afoot on the prairie. Is that an offense against the law around here?"

The marshal eased himself and his stomach into a chair and frowned judiciously. "It ain't customary," he admitted. "Who was they?"

"The boss was a big man with black hair, dark eyes, and two gold teeth in front. The other two—"

"I know. Liberty Valance and a couple of his boys. Just what's your complaint, now?" Foster began to understand that no help was going to come from the marshal.

"They rob you?" the marshal asked.

"They didn't search me."

"Take your gun?"

"I didn't have one."

"Steal your horse?"

"Gave him a crack with a quirt, and he left."

"Saddle on him?"

"No. I left it out there."

The marshal shook his head. "Can't see you got any legal complaint," he said with relief. "Where was this?"

"On a road in the woods, by a creek. Two days' walk from here."

The marshal got to his feet. "You don't even know what jurisdiction it was in. They knocked you around; well, that could happen. Man gets in a fight—could happen to anybody."

Foster said dryly, "Thanks a lot."

The marshal stopped him as he reached the door. "There's a reward for Liberty Valance."

"I still haven't got a gun," Foster said. "Does he come here often?"

"Nope. Nothing he'd want in Twotrees. Hard man to find." The marshal looked Foster up and down. "He won't come after you here." It was as if he had added, *Sonny!* "Beat you up once, he won't come again for that."

And I, Foster realized, am not man enough to go after him.

"Fact is," the marshal added, "I can't think of any bait that would bring him in. Pretty quiet here. Yes sir." He put his thumbs in his galluses and looked out the window, taking credit for the quietness.

Bait, Foster thought. He went out thinking about it. For the first time in a couple of years he had an ambition—not a laudable one, but something to aim at. He was going to be the bait for Liberty Valance and, as far as he could be, the trap as well.

At the Elite Cafe he stood meekly in the doorway, hat in hand, like a man who expects and deserves to be refused anything he might ask for. Clearing his throat, he asked, "Could I work for a meal?"

The girl who was filling sugar bowls looked up and pitied him. "Why, I should think so. Mr. Anderson!" She was the girl who had walked away with Barricune, scolding him.

The proprietor came from the kitchen, and Ranse Foster repeated his question, cringing, but with a suggestion of a sneer.

"Go around back and split some wood," Anderson answered, turning back to the kitchen.

"He could just as well eat first," the waitress suggested. "I'll dish up some stew to begin with."

Ranse ate fast, as if he expected the plate to be snatched away. He knew the girl glanced at him several times, and he hated her for it. He had not counted on anyone's pitying him in his new role of sneering humility, but he knew he might as well get used to it.

When she brought his pie, she said, "If you was looking for a job . . ."

He forced himself to look at her suspiciously. "Yes?"

"You could try the Prairie Belle. I heard they needed a swamper."

Bert Barricune, riding out to the river camp for his bedroll, hardly knew the man he met there. Ranse Foster was haughty, condescending, and cringing all at once. He spoke with a faint sneer, and stood as if he expected to be kicked.

"I assumed you'd be back for your belongings," he said. "I realized that you would change your mind."

Barricune, strapping up his bedroll, looked blank. "Never changed it," he disagreed. "Doing just what I planned. I never give you my bedroll."

"Of course not, of course not," the new Ranse Foster agreed with sneering humility. "It's yours. You have every right to reclaim it."

Barricune looked at him narrowly and hoisted the bedroll to sling it up behind his saddle. "I should have left you for the buzzards," he remarked.

Foster agreed, with a smile that should have got him a fist in the teeth. "Thank you, my friend," he said with no gratitude. "Thank you for all your kindness, which I have done nothing to deserve and shall do nothing to repay."

Barricune rode off, scowling, with the memory of his good deed irritating him like lice. The new Foster followed, far behind, on foot.

Sometimes in later life Ranse Foster thought of the several men he had been through the years. He did not admire any of them very much. He was by no means ashamed of the man he finally became, except that he owed too much to other people. One man he had been when he was young, a serious student, gullible and quick-tempered. Another man had been reckless and without an aim; he went West, with two thousand dollars of his own, after a quarrel with the executor of his father's estate. That man did not last long. Liberty Valance had whipped him with a quirt and kicked him into unconsciousness, for no reason except that Liberty, meeting him and knowing him for a tenderfoot, was able to do so. That man died on the prairie. After that, there was the man who set out to be the bait that would bring Liberty Valance into Twotrees.

Ranse Foster had never hated anyone before he met Liberty Valance, but Liberty was not the last man he learned to hate. He hated the man he himself had been while he waited to meet Liberty again.

The swamper's job at the Prairie Belle was not disgraceful until Ranse Foster made it so. When he swept floors, he was so obviously contemptuous of the work and of himself for doing it that other men saw him as contemptible. He watched the customers with a curled lip as if they were beneath him. But when a poker player threw a white chip on the floor, the swamper looked at him with half-veiled hatred—and picked up the chip. They talked about him at the Prairie Belle, because he could not be ignored.

At the end of the first month, he bought a Colt .45 from a drunken cowboy who needed money worse than he needed two guns. After that, Ranse went without part of his sleep in order to walk out, seven mornings a week, to where his first camp had been and practice target shooting. And the second time he overslept from exhaustion, Joe Mosten of the Prairie Belle fired him.

"Here's your pay," Joe growled, and dropped the money on the floor.

A week passed before he got another job. He ate his meals frugally in the Elite Cafe and let himself be seen stealing scraps off plates that other diners had left. Lillian, the older of the two waitresses, yelled her disgust, but Hallie, who was young, pitied him.

"Come to the back door when it's dark," she murmured, "and I'll give you a bite. There's plenty to spare."

The second evening he went to the back door, Bert Barricune was there ahead of him. He said gently, "Hallie is my girl."

"No offense intended," Foster answered. "The young lady offered me food, and I have come to get it."

"A dog eats where it can," young Barricune drawled.

Ranse's muscles tensed and rage mounted in his throat, but he caught himself in time and shrugged. Bert said something then that scared him: "If you wanted to get talked about, it's working fine. They're talking clean over in Dunbar."

"What they do or say in Dunbar," Foster answered, "is nothing to me."

"It's where Liberty Valance hangs out," the other man said casually. "In case you care."

Ranse almost confided then, but instead said stiffly, "I do not quite appreciate your strange interest in my affairs."

Barricune pushed back his hat and scratched his head. "I don't understand it myself. But leave my girl alone."

"As charming as Miss Hallie may be," Ranse told him, "I am interested only in keeping my stomach filled."

"Then why don't you work for a living? The clerk at Dowitts' quit this afternoon."

Jake Dowitt hired him as a clerk because nobody else wanted the job.

"Read and write, do you?" Dowitt asked. "Work with figures?"

Foster drew himself up. "Sir, whatever may be said against me, I believe I may lay claim to being a scholar. That much I claim, if nothing more. I have read law."

"Maybe the job ain't good enough for you," Dowitt suggested.

Foster became humble again. "Any job is good enough for me. I will also sweep the floor."

"You will also keep up the fire in the stove," Dowitt told him. "Seven in the morning till nine at night. Got a place to live?"

"I sleep in the livery stable in return for keeping it shoveled out."

Dowitt had intended to house his clerk in a small room over the store, but he changed his mind. "Got a shed out back you can bunk in," he offered, "You'll have to clean it out first. Used to keep chickens there."

"There is one thing," Foster said. "I want two half-days off a week."

Dowitt looked over the top of his spectacles. "Now what would you do with time off? Never mind. You can have it—for less pay. I give you a discount on what you buy in the store."

The only purchase Foster made consisted of four boxes of cartridges a week.

In the store, he weighed salt pork as if it were low stuff but himself still lower, humbly measured lengths of dress goods for the women customers. He added vanity to his other unpleasantnesses and let customers discover him combing his hair admiringly before a small mirror. He let himself be seen reading a small black book, which aroused curiosity.

It was while he worked at the store that he started Twotrees' first school. Hallie was responsible for that. Handing him a plate heaped higher than other customers got at the café, she said gently, "You're a learned man, they say, Mr. Foster."

With Hallie he could no longer sneer or pretend humility, for Hallie was herself humble, as well as gentle and kind. He protected himself from her by not speaking unless he had to.

He answered, "I have had advantages, Miss Hallie, before fate brought me here."

"That book you read," she asked wistfully, "what's it about?"

"It was written by a man named Plato," Ranse told her stiffly. "It was written in Greek."

She brought him a cup of coffee, hesitated for a moment, and then asked, "You can read and write American, too, can't you?"

"English, Miss Hallie," he corrected. "English is our mother tongue. I am quite familiar with English."

She put her red hands on the café counter. "Mr. Foster," she whispered, "will you teach me to read?"

He was too startled to think of an answer she could not defeat.

"Bert wouldn't like it," he said. "You're a grown woman besides. It wouldn't look right for you to be learning to read now."

She shook her head. "I can't learn any younger." She sighed. "I always wanted to know how to read and write." She walked away toward the kitchen, and Ranse Foster was struck with an emotion he knew he could not afford. He was swept with pity. He called her back.

"Miss Hallie. Not you alone—people would talk about you. But if you brought Bert—"

"Bert can already read some. He don't care about it. But there's some kids in town." Her face was so lighted that Ranse looked away.

He still tried to escape. "Won't you be ashamed, learning with children?"

"Why, I'll be proud to learn any way at all," she said.

He had three little girls, two restless little boys, and Hallie in Twotrees' first school sessions—one hour each afternoon, in Dowitt's storeroom. Dowitt did not dock his pay for the time spent, but he puzzled a great deal. So did the children's parents. The children themselves were puzzled at some of the things he read aloud, but they were patient. After all, lessons lasted only an hour.

"When you are older, you will understand this," he promised, not looking at Hallie, and then he read Shakespeare's sonnet that begins:

> *No longer mourn for me when I am dead*
> *Than you shall hear the surly sullen bell*

and ends:

> *Do not so much as my poor name rehearse,*
> *But let your love even with my life decay,*
> *Lest the wise world should look into your moan*
> *And mock you with me after I am gone.*

Hallie understood the warning, he knew. He read another sonnet, too:

> *When in disgrace with Fortune and men's eyes,*
> *I all alone beweep my outcast state,*

and carefully did not look up at her as he finished it:

> *For thy sweet love rememb'red such wealth brings*
> *That then I scorn to change my state with kings.*

Her earnestness in learning was distasteful to him—the anxious way she grasped a pencil and formed letters, the little gasp with which she always began to read aloud. Twice he made her cry, but she never missed a lesson.

He wished he had a teacher for his own learning, but he could not trust anyone, and so he did his lessons alone. Bert Barricune caught him at it on one of those free afternoons when Foster, on a horse from a livery stable, had ridden miles out of town to a secluded spot.

Ranse Foster had an empty gun in his hand when Barricune stepped out from behind a sandstone column and remarked, "I've seen better."

Foster whirled, and Barricune added, "I could have been somebody else—and your gun's empty."

"When I see somebody else, it won't be," Foster promised.

"If you'd asked me," Barricune mused, "I could've helped you. But you didn't want no helping. A man shouldn't be ashamed to ask somebody that knows better than him." His gun was suddenly in his hand, and five shots cracked their echoes around the skull-white sandstone pillars. Half an inch above each of five cards that Ranse had tacked to a dead tree, at the level of a man's waist, a splintered hole appeared in the wood. "Didn't want to spoil your targets," Barricune explained.

"I'm not ashamed to ask you," Foster told him angrily, "since you know so much. I shoot straight but slow. I'm asking you now."

Barricune, reloading his gun, shook his head. "It's kind of late for that. I come out to tell you that Liberty Valance is in town. He's interested in the dude that anybody can kick around—this here tenderfoot that boasts how he can read Greek."

"Well," said Foster softly. "Well, so the time has come."

"Don't figure you're riding into town with me," Bert warned. "You're coming all by yourself."

Ranse rode into town with his gun belt buckled on. Always before, he had carried it wrapped in a slicker. In town, he allowed himself the luxury of one last vanity. He went to the barbershop, neither sneering nor cringing, and said sharply, "Cut my hair. Short."

The barber was nervous, but he worked understandably fast.

"Thought you was partial to that long wavy hair of yourn," he remarked.

"I don't know why you thought so," Foster said coldly.

Out in the street again, he realized that he did not know how to go about the job. He did not know where Liberty Valance was, and he was determined not to be caught like a rat. He intended to look for Liberty.

Joe Mosten's right-hand man was lounging at the door of the Prairie Belle. He moved over to bar the way.

"Not in there, Foster," he said gently. It was the first time in months that Ranse Foster had heard another man address him respectfully. His presence was recognized—as a menace to the fixtures of the Prairie Belle.

When I die, sometime today, he thought, they won't say I was a coward. They may say I was a damn fool, but I won't care by that time.

"Where is he?" Ranse asked.

"I couldn't tell you that," the man said apologetically. "I'm young and healthy, and where he is is none of my business. Joe'd be obliged if you stay out of the bar, that's all."

Ranse looked across toward Dowitt's store. The padlock was on the door. He glanced north, toward the marshal's office.

"That's closed, too," the saloon man told him courteously. "Marshal was called out of town an hour ago."

Ranse threw back his head and laughed. The sound echoed back from the false-fronted buildings across the street. There was nobody walking in the street; there were not even any horses tied to the hitching racks.

"Send Liberty word," he ordered in the tone of one who has a right to command. "Tell him the tenderfoot wants to see him again."

The saloon man cleared his throat. "Guess it won't be necessary. That's him coming down at the end of the street, wouldn't you say?"

Ranse looked, knowing the saloon man was watching him curiously.

"I'd say it is," he agreed. "Yes, I'd say that was Liberty Valance."

"I'll be going inside now," the other man remarked apologetically. "Well, take care of yourself." He was gone without a sound.

This is the classic situation, Ranse realized. Two enemies walking to meet each other along the dusty, waiting street of a Western town. What reasons other men have had, I will never know. There are so many things I have never learned! And now there is no time left.

He was an actor who knew the end of the scene but had forgotten the lines and never knew the cue for them. One of us ought to say something, he realized. I should have planned this all out in advance. But all I ever saw was the end of it.

Liberty Valance, burly and broad-shouldered, walked stiff-legged, with his elbows bent.

When he is close enough for me to see whether he is smiling, Ranse Foster thought, somebody's got to speak.

He looked into his own mind and realized, This man is afraid, this Ransome Foster. But nobody else knows it. He walks and is afraid, but he is no coward. Let them remember that. Let Hallie remember that.

Liberty Valance gave the cue. "Looking for me?" he called between his teeth. He was grinning.

Ranse was almost grateful to him; it was as if Liberty had said, The time is now!

"I owe you something," Ranse answered. "I want to pay my debt."

Liberty's hand flashed with his own. The gun in Foster's hand exploded, and so did the whole world.

Two shots to my one, he thought—his last thought for a while.

He looked up at a strange, unsteady ceiling and a face that wavered like a reflection in water. The bed beneath him swung even after he closed his eyes. Far away someone said, "Shove some more cloth in the wound. It slows the bleeding."

He knew with certain agony where the wound was—in his right shoulder. When they touched it, he heard himself cry out.

The face that wavered above him was a new one, Bert Barricune's.

"He's dead," Barricune said.

Foster answered from far away, "I am not."

Barricune said, "I didn't mean you."

Ranse turned his head away from the pain, and the face that had shivered above him before was Hallie's, white and big-eyed. She put a hesitant hand on his, and he was annoyed to see that hers was trembling.

"Are you shaking," he asked, "because there's blood on my hands?"

"No," she answered. "It's because they might have been getting cold."

He was aware then that other people were in the room; they stirred and moved aside as the doctor entered.

"Maybe you're gonna keep that arm," the doctor told him at last. "But it's never gonna be much use to you."

The trial was held three weeks after the shooting, in the hotel room where Ranse lay in bed. The charge was disturbing the peace; he pleaded guilty and was fined ten dollars.

When the others had gone, he told Bert Barricune, "There was a reward, I heard. That would pay the doctor and the hotel."

"You ain't going to collect it," Bert informed him. "It'd make you too big for your britches." Barricune sat looking at him for a moment and then remarked, "You didn't kill Liberty."

Foster frowned. "They buried him."

"Liberty fired once. You fired once and missed. I fired once, and I don't generally miss. I ain't going to collect the reward, neither. Hallie don't hold with violence."

Foster said thoughtfully, "That was all I had to be proud of."

"You faced him," Barricune said. "You went to meet him. If you got to be proud of something, you can remember that. It's a fact you ain't got much else."

Ranse looked at him with narrowed eyes. "Bert, are you a friend of mine?"

Bert smiled without humor. "You know I ain't. I picked you up off the prairie, but I'd do that for the lowest scum that crawls. I wisht I hadn't."

"Then why—"

Bert looked at the toe of his boot. "Hallie likes you. I'm a friend of Hallie's. That's all I ever will be, long as you're around."

Ranse said, "Then I shot Liberty Valance." That was the nearest he ever dared come to saying "Thank you." And that was when Bert Barricune started being his conscience, his Nemesis, his lifelong enemy and the man who made him great.

"Would she be happy living back East?" Foster asked. "There's money waiting for me there if I go back."

Bert answered, "What do you think?" He stood up and stretched. "You got quite a problem, ain't you? You could solve it easy by just going back alone. There ain't much a man can do here with a crippled arm."

He went out and shut the door behind him.

There is always a way out, Foster thought, if a man wants to take it. Bert had been his way out when he met Liberty on the street of Twotrees. To go home was the way out of this.

I learned to live without pride, he told himself. I could learn to forget about Hallie.

When she came, between the dinner dishes and setting the tables for supper at the café, he told her.

She did not cry. Sitting in the chair beside his bed, she winced and jerked one hand in protest when he said, "As soon as I can travel, I'll be going back where I came from."

She did not argue. She said only, "I wish you good luck, Ransome. Bert and me, we'll look after you long as you stay. And remember you after you're gone."

"How will you remember me?" he demanded harshly.

As his student she had been humble, but as a woman she had her pride. "Don't ask that," she said, and got up from the chair.

"Hallie, Hallie," he pleaded, "how can I stay? How can I earn a living?"

She said indignantly, as if someone else had insulted him, "Ranse Foster, I just guess you could do anything you wanted to."

"Hallie," he said gently, "sit down."

He never really wanted to be outstanding. He had two aims in life: to make Hallie happy and to keep Bert Barricune out of trouble.

He defended Bert on charges ranging from drunkenness to stealing cattle, and Bert served time twice.

Ranse Foster did not want to run for judge, but Bert remarked, "I think Hallie would kind of like it if you was His Honor." Hallie was pleased but not surprised when he was elected. Ranse was surprised but not pleased.

He was not eager to run for the legislature—that was after the Territory became a state—but there was Bert Barricune in the background, never urging, never advising, but watching with half-closed, bloodshot eyes. Bert Barricune, who never amounted to anything, but never intruded, was a living, silent reminder of three debts: a hat full of water under the cottonwoods, gunfire in a dusty street, and Hallie, quietly sewing beside a lamp in the parlor. And the Fosters had four sons.

All the things the opposition said about Ranse Foster when he ran for the state legislature were true, except one. He had been a lowly swamper in a frontier saloon; he had been a dead beat, accepting handouts at the alley entrance of a café; he had been despicable and despised. But the accusation that lost him the election was false. He had not killed Liberty Valance. He never served in the state legislature.

When there was talk of his running for governor, he refused. Handy Strong, who knew politics, tried to persuade him.

"That shooting, we'll get around that. 'The Honorable Ransome Foster walked down a street in broad daylight to meet an enemy of society. He shot him down in a fair fight, of necessity, the way you'd shoot a mad dog—but Liberty Valance could shoot back, and he did. Ranse Foster carries the mark of that encounter today in a crippled right arm. He is still paying the price for protecting law-abiding citizens. And he was the first teacher west of Rosy Buttes. He served without pay.' You've come a long way, Ranse, and you're going further."

"A long way," Foster agreed, "for a man who never wanted to go anywhere. I don't want to be governor."

When Handy had gone, Bert Barricune sagged in, unwashed, unshaven. He sat down stiffly. At the age of fifty, he was an old man, an unwanted relic of the frontier that was gone, a legacy to more civilized times that had no place for him. He filled his pipe deliberately. After a while he remarked. "The other side is gonna say you ain't fitten to be governor. Because your wife ain't fancy enough. They're gonna say Hallie didn't even learn to read till she was growed up."

Ranse was on his feet, white with fury. "Then I'm going to win this election if it kills me."

"I don't reckon it'll kill you," Bert drawled. "Liberty Valance couldn't."

"I could have got rid of the weight of that affair long ago," Ranse reminded him, "by telling the truth."

"You could yet," Bert answered. "Why don't you?"

Ranse said bitterly, "Because I owe you too much. . . . I don't think Hallie wants to be the governor's lady. She's shy."

"Hallie don't never want nothing for herself. She wants things for you. The way I feel, I wouldn't mourn at your funeral. But what Hallie wants, I'm gonna try to see she gets."

"So am I," Ranse promised grimly.

"Then I don't mind telling you," Bert admitted, "that it was me reminded the opposition to dig up that matter of how she couldn't read."

As the Senator and his wife rode out to the airport after old Bert Barricune's barren funeral, Hallie sighed. "Bert never had much of anything. I guess he never wanted much."

He wanted you to be happy, Ranse Foster thought, and he did the best he knew how.

"I wonder where those prickly-pear blossoms came from," he mused.

Hallie glanced up at him, smiling. "From me," she said.

QUESTIONS FOR DISCUSSION

1. Why did Ranse Foster go west?

2. What is Bert Barricune's chief role in the story?

3. What can you infer about the marshal?

4. How many characters are there in this story, and which characters would you label round and flat?

5. In your opinion, are Ranse Foster's and Bert Barricune's actions well motivated?

6. What methods does the author use to characterize Liberty Valance? How do these methods add to the suspense?

TOPICS FOR WRITING

1. Suppose that Hallie had kept a diary (after she learned to write) while living in Twotrees. What would she have written about Ranse Foster at any time in her meetings with him? Write her thoughts.

2. What aspects of the story are formulaic in your opinion? What aspects—if any—are not? Write a paper in which you discuss these questions.

SNOWBLIND

EVAN HUNTER (born 1926)

E van Hunter is better known for his police novels than for his westerns, but he is an extremely versatile writer, as his many published works prove.

Hunter was born in New York to Charles and Marie Lombino and received a B.A. from Hunter College in 1950. He was 28 when his first major book, *The Blackboard Jungle*, was published in 1954; however, he had been writing detective stories for the pulps for several years before that. The book was a result of his short career as a teacher at two vocational high schools in New York City, and Hunter was praised for his depiction of a young male teacher facing the realities of trying to teach indifferent, inner-city students.

As Ed McBain, Hunter has written over forty novels in the 87th Precinct Series, in which the main characters are a group of New York City police. A 1960 television series of the same name was based on the books. *Gladly the Cross-Eyed Bear* (1996) and *The Last Best Hope* (1998) are recent titles in the series.

Other Evan Hunter novels include *Strangers When We Meet* (1958), *Mothers and Daughters* (1961), *Last Summer* (1968), and *The Chisholms: A Novel of the Journey West* (1976). *Happy New Year, Herbie, and Other Stories* (1963) is a story collection. Hunter has also written stage and screenplays, and several of his novels have been made into movies. In 1986, he received a Grand Master Award from the Mystery Writers of America for lifetime achievement.

■

He rode the big roan stiffly, the collar of his heavy mackinaw pulled high on his neck. His battered Stetson was tilted over his forehead, crammed down against his ears. Still, the snow seeped in, trailing icy fingers across the back of his neck.

His fingers inside the right-hand mitten were stiff and cold, and he held the reins lightly, his left hand jammed into his pocket. Carefully, he guided the horse over the snow-covered trail, talking gently to him. He held a hand up in front of his eyes, palm outward to ward off the stinging snow, peered into the whirling whiteness ahead of him.

The roan lifted its head, ears back. Quickly, he dropped his hand to the horse's neck, patted him soothingly.

He felt the penetrating cold attacking his naked hand, withdrew it quickly and stuffed it into the pocket again, clenching it into a tight fist, trying to wrench whatever warmth he could from the inside of the pocket.

"Damnfool kid," he mumbled. "Picks a night like this."

The roan plodded on over the slippery, graded surface, unsure of its footing. Gary kept staring ahead into the whiteness, looking for the cabin, waiting for it to appear big and brown against the smoke-gray sky.

His brows and lashes were interlaced with white now, and a fine sifting of snow caked in the ridges alongside his eyes, lodged in the seams swinging down from his nose flaps. His mouth was pressed into a tight, weary line. He kept thinking of the cabin, and a fire. And a cup of coffee, and a smoke.

It was the smoke that had started it all, he supposed. He shook his head sadly, bewildered by the thought that a simple thing like a cigarette could send a kid kiting away from home. Hell, Bobby was too young to be smoking, and he'd deserved the wallop he'd gotten.

He thought about it again now, his head pressed against the sharp wind. He'd been unsaddling Spark, a frisky sorrel if ever there was one, when he saw the wisp of smoke curling up from behind the barn. At first, he thought it was a fire. He swung the saddle up over the rail and took off at a trot, out of breath when he rounded the barn's corner.

Bobby had been sitting there, his legs crossed, gun belt slung low on his faded jeans, calm as could be. And puffing on a cigarette.

"Well, hello," Gary'd said in surprise.

Bobby jumped to his feet and ground the cigarette out under his heel. "Hello, Dad," he said soberly. Gary remembered wondering why the boy's face had expressed no guilt, no remorse.

His eyes stared down at the shredded tobacco near the boy's boot. "Having a party?" he asked.

"Why, no."

"Figured you might be. See you're wearing your guns, and smoking and all. Figured you as having a little party for yourself."

"I was headin' into town, Dad. Feller has to wear guns in town, you know that."

Gary stroked his jaw. "That right?"

"Ain't safe otherwise."

Gary's mouth tightened then, and his eyes grew hard. "Feller has to smoke in town, too, I suppose."

"Well, Dad . . ."

"Take off them guns!"

Bobby's eyes widened, startling blue against his tanned features. He ran lean fingers through his sun-bleached hair and said, "But I'm goin' to town. I just told . . ."

"You ain't goin' nowheres. Take off them guns."

"Dad . . ."

"No damn kid of mine's goin' to tote guns before he's cut his eyeteeth! And smoking! Who in holy hell do you think you are? Behaving like a gun slick and smoking fit to . . ."

Bobby's voice was firm. "I'm seventeen. I don't have to take this kind of . . ."

Gary's hand lashed out suddenly, open, catching the boy on the side of his cheek. He pulled his hand back rapidly, sorry he'd struck his son, but unwilling to acknowledge his error. Bobby's own hand moved to his cheek, touched the bruise that was forming under the skin.

"Now get inside and take them guns off," Gary said.

Bobby didn't answer. He turned his back on his father and walked toward the house.

The snow started at about five, and when Gary called his son for supper at six, the boy's room was empty. The peg from which his guns usually hung, the guns Gary'd said he could wear when he was twenty-one, was bare. With a slight twinge of panic, Gary had run down to the barn to find the boy's brown mare gone.

Quickly, he'd saddled the roan and started tracking him. The tracks were fresh in the new snow, and before long Gary realized the boy was heading for the old cabin in the hills back of the spread.

He cursed now as the roan slipped again. Damned if he wasn't going to give that boy the beating of his life. Seventeen years old! Anxious to start smoking and frisking around, anxious to wrap his finger around a trigger. It would have been different if Meg . . .

He caught himself abruptly, the old pain stabbing deep inside him again, the pain that thoughts of her always brought. He bit his lip against the cold and against the memory, clamped his jaws tight as if capping the unwanted emotions that threatened to overflow his consciousness again.

This was a rough land, a land unfriendly to women. For the thousandth time he told himself he should never have brought her here. He'd made a big mistake with Meg, perhaps the biggest mistake of his life. He'd surrendered her to a wild, relentless land, and he was left now with nothing but a memory and a tombstone. And Bobby. He would not make the same mistake with Bobby.

How long ago had it been? he asked himself. *How long?*

Was Bobby really seventeen, had it really been that long?

"All right, mister," the voice said.

He lifted his hand, tried to shield his eyes. The snow whirled before them, danced crazily in the knifing wind. Through the snow, he made out the shadowy bulk of three men sitting their horses. His hand automatically dropped to the rifle hanging in the leather scabbard on his saddle.

"I wouldn't, mister," the same voice said.

He squinted into the snow, still unable to make out the faces of the three riders. "What's this all about, fellers?" he asked, trying to keep his voice calm. Through the snow, he could see that two of the riders were holding drawn guns.

"What's it all about, he wants to know," one of the men said.

There was a flurry of movement and the rider in the middle spurred his horse forward, reining in beside Gary's roan.

"Suppose you tell *us* what it's all about, mister."

Gary's eyes dropped inadvertently to the holster strapped outside his mackinaw, the gun butt pointing up toward his pocket.

"Don't know what you mean, fellers."

"He don't know what we mean, Sam."

The rider close to Gary snickered. "What you doin' on this trail?" His breath left white pockmarks on the air. Gary stared hard at his face, at the bristle covering his chin, at the shaggy black brows and hard eyes. He didn't recognize the man.

"I'm lookin' for a stray," Gary said, thinking again of Bobby somewhere on the trail ahead.

"In this weather?" Sam scoffed. "Who you kiddin', mister?"

Another of the riders pulled close to the pair, staring hard at Gary. "He's poster-happy, I think," he said.

"Shut up, Moss," Sam commanded.

The third rider sat his horse in the distance, his hands in his pockets, his head tucked low inside his upturned collar. "Moss is right, Sam. The old geezer's seen our pictures and . . ."

"I said shut up!" Sam repeated.

"Hell, ain't nobody chases strays in a storm," the third rider protested.

Sam lifted the rifle from Gary's scabbard, then took the .44 from the holster at his hip. Gary looked down at the empty holster, raised his eyes again.

"Ain't no need for this," he said. "I'm lookin' for a stray. Wandered off before the storm started, and I'm anxious to get him back 'fore he freezes board-stiff."

"Sure," Sam said, "you're lookin' for a stray. Maybe you're lookin' for *three* strays, huh?"

"I don't know what you're talking about," Gary said. "You feel like throwing your weight around, all right. You're three and I'm one, and I ain't goin' to argue. But I still don't know what you're talking about."

"We gonna freeze out here while this bird gives us lawyer talk?" Moss asked.

The third rider said, "You know of a cabin up here, mister?"

"What?" Gary asked.

"You deaf or some . . ."

"Rufe gets impatient," Sam interrupted. "Specially when he's cold. We heard there was a cabin up here somewheres. You know where?"

"No," Gary said quickly.

"He's poster-happy," Moss insisted. "What the hell're we wastin' time talking for?" He pulled back the hammer of his pistol, and the click sounded loud and deadly beneath the murmur of the wind.

Gary combed his memory, trying to visualize the "wanted" posters he'd seen. It wasn't often that he went to town, and he didn't pay much attention to such things when he did ride in. He silently cursed his memory, realizing at the same time that it didn't matter one way or the other. He didn't know why these men were wanted, or just what they were running from. But he sure as hell knew they *were* wanted. The important thing was to keep them away from Bobby, away from the cabin up ahead.

"Seems I do remember a cabin," he said.

"Yeah? Where is it?"

Gary pointed down the trail, away from the cabin. "That way, I think."

"We can't afford thinkin'," Rufe said. "And we can't afford headin' back toward town either, mister."

"That ain't the way to town," Gary said softly.

"We just come from there," Sam said. He yanked his reins, pulling his horse around. "I think we'll go up this way, mister. Stay behind him, Moss."

Rufe, up the trail a ways, turned his horse and started pushing against the snow, Sam close behind him. Gary kept the roan headed into the wind, and behind him he could hear the labored breathing of Moss's horse.

"We'll have to hole up for tonight," Rufe said over his shoulder.

"Yeah, if we can find that damn cabin," Sam agreed.

"We'll find it. The old geezer ain't a very good liar."

They rode into the wind, their heads bent low. Gary's eyes stayed on the trail, searching for signs beneath the tracks of the lead horse. Bobby had sure as hell been heading for the cabin. Suppose he was there already? The boy was wearing his guns, and would probably be fool enough to try shooting it out with these killers. Maybe they weren't killers, either. Maybe they were just three strangers who weren't taking any chances. Then why had the one called Moss kept harping on posters, and why had Rufe mentioned pictures of the trio? *Stop kidding yourself*, Gary thought. *They'd as soon shoot you as look at you.*

"Well, now ain't that funny!" Rufe shouted back. "Looks like the cabin was up this way after all, mister."

Gary raised his eyes, squinted at the squat log formation ahead on the trail. The ground levelled off a bit, and they walked the horses forward, pulling up just outside the front door. Sam dismounted and looped his reins over the rail outside. Gary felt the sharp thrust of a gun in his back.

"Come on," Moss said.

Gary swung off his saddle, patting the roan on its rump. "These animals will freeze out here," he said.

"You can bring out some blankets," Sam said. Together, he and Rufe kicked open the door of the cabin, their guns level. Gary's heart gave a lurch as he waited for sound from within.

" 'Pears to be empty," Rufe said.

"Ummm. Come on, Moss. Bring the old man in."

They stomped into the cabin, closing the door against the biting wind outside. Sam struck a match, fumbled around in the darkness for a lantern. There was the sound of a scraping chair, the sudden thud of bone against wood.

"Damnit!" Sam bellowed.

Gary waited in the darkness, the hard bore of Moss's pistol in his back. The wick of the lantern flared brightly, faded as Sam lowered it.

"Right nice," Rufe commented.

"Better get a fire going," Sam said.

Rufe crossed the room to the stone fireplace, heaped twigs and papers into the grate, methodically placed the heavier pieces of wood over these. He struck a match, held it to the paper, watched the flames curl upward as the twigs caught.

"There," he said. He shrugged out of his leather jacket. "This ought to be real comfy."

"There's some blankets on the bunk," Sam said. "Take 'em out and cover the horses, mister."

Gary walked to the bunk, filled his arms with the blankets, and started toward the door. Just inside the door, he stopped, waiting.

Moss shrugged out of his mackinaw. "Go on," he told Gary. "We'll watch you from here. Too damn cold out there."

Gary opened the door, ducked his head against the wind, and ran toward the horses. He dropped the blankets, gave one quick look at the door, and then swung up onto the roan's saddle.

"You want a hole in your back?" Sam's voice came from the window.

Gary didn't answer. He kept sitting the horse, staring down at the blankets he'd dropped in the snow.

"Now cover them horses and get back in here," Sam said. "And no more funny business."

Gary dropped from the saddle wearily. Gently, he covered all the horses, feeling the animals shiver against the slashing wind and snow. He was grateful that Bobby hadn't been in the cabin, but he was beginning to wonder now if the boy hadn't been lost in this storm. The thought was a disturbing one. He finished with the horses and headed back for the cabin. Moss pulled open the door for him, slamming it shut behind him as soon as he'd entered.

"Get out of those clothes," Sam said, "and sit over there by the table. One more fool stunt like that last one, and you're a dead man."

Gary walked over to the table, folding his mackinaw over the back of a chair. Rufe was sitting in a chair opposite him, his feet on the table, the chair thrust back at a wild angle.

Gary sat down, his eyes dropping to Rufe's hanging gun.

"Wonder how long this'll last," Sam said from the window.

"Who cares?" Moss said. He was poking around in the cupboard. " 'Nough food here to last a couple of weeks."

"Still, we should be moving on."

"You know," Rufe drawled, "maybe we shoulda split up."

"What the hell brought that on?" Sam asked impatiently.

"Just thinkin'. They'll be lookin' for three men. They won't be expectin' single riders."

"That's what the old man's for," Sam said, smiling.

"I don't follow."

"They won't be expectin' *four* riders, either. The old man's coming with us when we leave."

"The hell I am," Gary said loudly.

"The hell you *are*," Sam repeated.

Gary looked at the gun in Sam's hand. He made a slight movement forward, as if he would rise from his chair, and then he slumped back again. They were treating him like a kid, like a simple, addle-brained . . . He caught his thoughts abruptly. He suddenly knew how Bobby must have felt when he'd slapped him this afternoon.

Sam walked away from the window, stood warming the seat of his pants at the fireplace.

"Four riders," he said. "A respectable old man and his three sons." He looked at Gary and chuckled noisily.

He was still chuckling when the front door was kicked open. Gary turned his head swiftly, his eyes widening at the sight of the white-encrusted figure in the doorway. The figure held two guns, and they gleamed menacingly in the firelight.

Sam clawed at his pistol, and a shot erupted in the stillness of the cabin. The gun came free, and Sam brought it up as the second shot slammed into his chest. He clutched at the stone mantel, swung around, his legs suddenly swiveling from under him. He dropped down near the fire, his hand falling into it in a cascade of sparks.

The men in the room seemed to freeze. Moss with his back to the cupboard, Rufe with his feet propped up on the table, the figure standing in the doorframe with smoking guns.

Gary looked at the figure, trying to understand that this was Bobby, that this was his son standing there, his son who had just shot a man.

And suddenly, action returned to the men in the room. Moss pushed himself away from the cupboard in a double-handed draw. At the same instant, Rufe began to swing his legs off the table.

Gary kicked out, sending the chair flying out from under Rufe. From the doorway, Bobby's guns exploded again and Moss staggered back against the glass-paned cupboard, his shoulders shattering the doors. Bobby kept shooting, and Moss collapsed in a shower of glass shards. Rufe sprawled to the floor, tried to untangle himself from the chair as Gary reached down and yanked the gun from his holster, backing away from the table quickly. Rufe crouched on the floor for an instant, then viciously threw the chair aside and reached for his remaining gun. Gary blinked as he saw flame lance out from the gun in his fist. The bullet took Rufe between the eyes, and he clung to life for an instant longer before he fell to the floor, his gun unfired.

Bobby came into the cabin, hatless, his hair a patchwork of snow.

"I figured you were trailin' me," he said. "I swung around the cabin, trying to lose you."

"Lucky you did," Gary said softly. He stood staring at his son. For a moment, their eyes met, and Bobby turned away.

"I ain't goin' back with you, Dad," he said. "A . . . a man's got to do things his own way. A man can't have . . ."

"Suppose we talk about it later, Bob," Gary said.

He saw his son's eyes widen. He'd never called him anything but Bobby until this moment.

Gary smiled. "Suppose we talk about it later," he repeated. "After we've had a cup of coffee." And then, though it was extremely difficult, he added, "And a smoke together."

QUESTIONS FOR DISCUSSION

1. Who or what are the antagonists in the story?

2. The specific setting of this story is not disclosed. What makes it a western story in your opinion?

3. Compare and contrast the way the plots are constructed in this story and in the previous one.

4. How does the author account for the fact that there are no women in this story?

TOPIC FOR WRITING

Make a list of all the characters' names in "Snowblind" and "The Man Who Shot Liberty Valance." Beside each name, jot down some assumptions you would make about each character if you hadn't read the stories. Then in one or two paragraphs, analyze the names in relation to the stories.

SECTION TWO

MYSTERY AND DETECTIVE

Fiction that involves the unraveling of some puzzle or secret or crime is called a **mystery**. A mystery may have spies, ghosts, vampires, visitors from outer space, or criminals. It will certainly have a character or characters confronting an unexplained event or solving a puzzle. It may also have a detective, making it therefore a detective story, a type of mystery.

The classic **detective story** involves a police, private, or amateur detective who investigates a crime and through observations, questioning, and deduction identifies the motive and the criminal from among a limited group of suspects. Detective fiction is further divided into categories such as the "hard-boiled" story, in which a tough, cynical private investigator works in a violent urban setting; the "procedural," in which a detective, often a police detective, methodically examines witnesses, suspects, and clues provided by forensics experts; and the "cozy," in which an amateur, usually a woman in a more-or-less domestic setting, solves a crime. The point of view may be that of an associate of the detective (who is frequently as baffled as the reader), one of the suspects, or the detective, particularly if he or she is a private eye.

A detective story may be set in any place or period—ancient Egypt, early Rome, medieval England, Victorian America, or any modern-day city in the world; for example, Tony Hillerman's books are set on the Navajo reservation, and Colin Dexter sets his books in Oxford, England. However, the immediate setting must be enough circumscribed that the number of suspects is limited. An English setting might be limited to Buckingham Palace, a country house, or a theatrical troupe, for example; a setting in Rome might be limited to members of the Senate; or a New York setting might be limited to a brokerage house. Cruise ships, monasteries, inns, opera houses, cathedrals, and publishing houses have all been used as settings.

The most cardinal rule of detective fiction is that the author must play fair. That is, the detective cannot make fantastic leaps in logic that the reader has not been prepared for, the reader must be privy to most of the same facts that the detective has, and the solution to the crime cannot rest on improbable coincidence. Detective story writers must tread a fine line between making the outcome so apparent that the reader is ahead of the detective in solving the crime (and thus bored) and making it so perplexing that the reader can't participate in solving the crime. While it is often the least-likely suspect who is guilty, there have been variations on this formula. Occasionally the criminal is known from the beginning, but the puzzle involves determining how or why a crime was committed.

In recent years, much detective fiction has tended to focus on the emotional relationships among the characters and the psychology of the detective as much as, or more than, the mystery itself, a trend begun by Dorothy Sayers and continued by Elizabeth George, Martha Grimes, P. D. James, and others. This focus is just one more way of altering the detective story formula.

Although the world's literature has often dealt with crime, in the 1800s, society began to focus on a rational and scientific approach to social problems, including crime. The Sûreté in Paris was the first criminal investigation department. Prior to the Sûreté, a sort of rough justice prevailed in metropolitan areas. Alleged criminals might be hunted down by individuals or groups of citizens, but there was scant attempt to determine whether in fact the person caught, and sometimes hanged, was really guilty. In fact, many crimes went unpunished or undetected. The Sûreté in Paris and Scotland Yard in London were founded to rectify these matters, and detective fiction followed.

The first detective short story was "The Murders in the Rue Morgue" (1841) by Edgar Allan Poe. Set in Paris, the story's amateur detective is C. Auguste Dupin, who solves a crime—a double murder—that bewilders police. Dupin's unnamed companion narrates the story. The first detective novels are usually attributed to the English writer Wilkie Collins, whose most successful works were *The Woman in White* (1860) and *The Moonstone* (1868). But it was with Arthur Conan Doyle's Sherlock Holmes stories and novels in the late 1800s that the detective story really came into its own. Doyle was an unsucessful eye-doctor who decided to try to increase his income by writing. Literature soon prevailed over medicine. His fictional creation, Sherlock Holmes, was so popular that when Doyle tried to kill him off, readers demanded that the detective be resurrected and Doyle reluctantly did so. The narrator of all but a few of the stories is Dr. Watson, Holmes's dim but amiable friend, always willing to assist the great detective but not always certain of what Holmes is up to. *The Hound of the Baskervilles* (1902) is Doyle's most successful detective novel, but his best detective fiction is to be found in the short stories involving Holmes and Watson.

Critics have labeled the 1920s and 1930s the Golden Age of detective fiction, although many of the writers popular then continued to write well beyond those years. A partial list of writers and, in parentheses, some of their more famous detectives follows: Agatha Christie (Hercule Poirot and Jane Marple), Dorothy Sayers (Lord Peter Wimsey), Margery Allingham (Albert Campion), Josephine Tey (Inspector Alan Grant), Ngaio Marsh (Chief Inspector Roderick Alleyn), C. Day Lewis, writing as Nicholas Blake, (Nigel Strangeways), Michael Innes (Inspector John Appleby), G. K. Chesterton (Father Brown), E. C. Bentley (Philip Trent), and John Dickson Carr, also writing as Carter Dickson, (Dr. Gideon Fell). All wrote too many books to list here.

In the United States, hard-boiled detective fiction emerged with writers Dashiell Hammett (Sam Spade), Raymond Chandler (Philip Marlowe), Mickey Spillane, and later Ross Macdonald (Lew Archer) and John D. McDonald (Travis McGee). Spade, Marlowe, and Archer all worked in southern California; McGee, in Florida. Other popular writers of the 1930s to the 1970s include Erle Stanley Gardner, whose stories and novels about detective Perry Mason were read by thousands of people and seen by millions on a long-running television series; Rex Stout (Nero Wolfe), Frederic Dannay and Manfred B. Lee writing as Ellery Queen, and the French writer Georges Simenon (Inspector Maigret).

More recent writers include Harry Kemelman (Rabbi David Small), Colin Dexter (Inspector Morse), Arthur Upfield (Inspector Napoleon Bonaparte), H. R. F. Keating (Inspector Ghote), P. D. James (Adam Dalgleish), Sue Grafton (Kinsey Millhone), Eleanor Taylor Bland (Marti MacAlister), Tony Hillerman (Jim Chee), Sara Paretsky (V. I. Warshawski), and William X. Kienzle (Father Koestler). These lists are by no means exhaustive, but they do give some idea of the immense popularity of detective fiction.

The Mystery Writers of America (MWA), founded in 1945, bestows Edgar Allan Poe Awards (Edgars) annually on authors of various types of mystery fiction. It also presents a Grand Master Award to recognize an outstanding author of mystery, crime, and suspense. The more recently formed Malice Domestic gives Agatha Awards annually. Works by many of the writers listed here have been adapted for film, television, and the stage, and MWA recognizes excellence in those fields.

In *Detective Fiction: A Collection of Critical Essays,* Robin Winks suggests that "Detective fiction . . . becomes a mirror to society.

Through it we may see society's fears made most explicit; for some, those fears are exorcised by the fiction." The reader and viewer of mysteries and detective stories also enjoys the puzzle, as well as the illusion that all will be well in London, or the Bronx, or Miami, or Los Angeles, if only the right detectives are there to vanquish evil.

THE MISTS OF BALLYCLOUGH

BARBARA CALLAHAN (born 1934)

A Philadelphia native, Barbara Callahan now lives in New Jersey, where she is a prolific writer of mystery stories. Married, the mother of five and grandmother of four, Callahan has been a high school French and English teacher and a technical writer and editor for McGraw Hill Publishing Company. She graduated from Chestnut Hill College in Philadelphia with a B.A. degree in 1956.

In 1978, she received a Scroll from the Mystery Writers of America for one of the five best mystery short stories of the year. She has published in *Ellery Queen's Mystery Magazine* and *Alfred Hitchcock's Mystery Magazine*. Many of her stories have been anthologized; one has been adapted for Italian radio; "Meeting Kathleen Casey," was adapted for radio by the BBC in England; and "Hidden Springs" was included in *Best Detective Stories 1980*. "The Mists of Ballyclough" first appeared in the December 1994 issue of *Ellery Queen's Mystery Magazine*.

Receiving a newspaper clipping about an acquaintance who has achieved celebrity status can either brighten the day or darken it, depending on one's feelings for the person in his pre-fame days. When I opened the envelope postmarked Ballyclough, Republic of Ireland, and read the article inside it, my day darkened. The clipping was sent to me by Margaret Loughlin, a policewoman I had met sixteen years ago when I was twelve years old and summered in Ireland with my Aunt Ellen and cousin Mairead. Featured on the first page of the literary supplement of the *Monitor* was Desmond O'Connor, author of the bestselling novel *Dreams of the Druid*. I met Desmond the same summer I met Margaret. I have never forgotten him. Neither has Margaret.

Desmond was staying at the next house over from Aunt Ellen's bed-and-breakfast in Ballyclough in the west of Ireland. His hosts, an elderly couple named Flynn, encouraged their fourteen-year-old guest to spend time with the young people at Aunt Ellen's house. Before I arrived from the States for my summer visit, Desmond had practically become a member of the family, calling himself "cousin by adoption" to Mairead, who wrote me about him.

"Mother says that Desmond is startlingly handsome. I'm not sure I agree with her. He's got black hair and black eyes and I prefer redheads. Mother also says that he looks like the reincarnation of one of Grace O'Malley's pirates.[1] She hopes Desmond doesn't have the black heart of a pirate, though. I don't think he does. He's very funny."

It seems fitting that Desmond became a novelist. That summer in Ballyclough he made up stories about everyone—passersby on the road leading to the strand, folk singers at the Cliffs of Mohr, and the monk who founded St. Theobald's Abbey. Vividly, I remember him nudging me when an old turf farmer, Seamus Brennan, approached us on the road past Aunt Ellen's bed-and-breakfast.

Desmond whispered, "He's a defrocked[2] priest, you know. He consorted with witches at midnight on the eve of Allhallows[3] in the ruins of St. Theobald's Abbey. The bishop found out because one of

---

1 **Grace O'Malley's pirates:** Grace O'Malley (c. 1530–c.1600) was an Irish clan leader and the daughter of a family of seafarers, considered by some to be pirates, on the Western coast of the region of Connacht. She led raiding parties and had a major role in the Irish struggle against English authority.

2 **defrocked:** stripped of priestly functions and privileges.

3 **eve of Allhallows:** Allhallows is All Saints Day, November 1. The eve of Allhallows is Halloween, which is a shortened form of "All Hallows Even[ing]." *Hallow* comes from an Old English word meaning "holy."

the witches, Bridey Maguire, later confessed to him. Witching is a sin that can only be forgiven by a bishop. Of course, Bridey had to name names and she named Seamus Brennan as the chief consorter. Consorting is a desperate bad sin, especially for a priest, so he was immediately defrocked."

Although Aunt Ellen had warned us about Desmond's "storifying," as she put it, we wide-eyed kids shivered delightedly as Desmond tipped his cap at Seamus Brennan and wished him good day. Consorting sounded like one of the sins that made Sister Aurelia blush when she taught catechism. Hearing the word flow so glibly from Desmond's lips deepened our awe of him. It never occurred to us to ask Desmond, who was as new to the region as I was, to reveal his sources.

Desmond storified me on our first meeting at Shannon Airport when he accompanied Aunt Ellen to pick me up. Exhilarated by my first flight and anticipating the two-month stay in Ireland with my widowed aunt and a cousin the same age as I, whom I had met two years before in the States, I tried hard to keep my American-Irish skin from betraying my excitement. The flush, however, the bane of red-heads, flared up in spite of my efforts. Aunt Ellen hugged me warmly and so did Mairead, my elder by three days.

When they introduced Desmond, he stepped back and bowed. "Greetings, Deirdre from America, namesake of our famous mythological character, Deirdre of the Sorrows.[4] But I don't see you as a wretched being weighed down by sorrows. No, I see you as an astronaut, hurtling through space, always searching for the joys of the future, always looking to the morrow. Yes, you are definitely Deirdre of the Morrows."

Instead of blushing more deeply, I felt my skin cool down. Desmond's analysis of me had the calming effect of a fortuneteller's prediction of good things. Instantly, I was under his spell. He was not a pirate but a gypsy empowered to read silent thoughts. I secretly dreamed I would be a pioneer female space traveler. It was not until the end of the summer when I had slipped away from Desmond's thrall that I learned he had read my earnest letters to Mairead, filled with my fascination with NASA's activities.

After Desmond's greeting, Aunt Ellen rolled her eyes and grinned at me. "Desmond, love, please get us a trolley[5] so we can put

---

4 **Deirdre of the Sorrows:** a legendary princess of Ulster who killed herself after the king, who wanted to marry her, murdered her lover.

5 **trolley:** luggage cart.

Deirdre's bags in the car." As Desmond hastened to perform that mundane task, Aunt Ellen filled me in. "He's not really a relative of ours, but Mairead kind of adopted him because he's the great-great-nephew of the Flynns who live the next farm over. They're in their eighties now, God love them, a wee bit dotty, and glad for the company. Since Mairead has always called the Flynns Auntie and Uncle, that made Desmond an unofficial cousin. I don't know all the details that brought Desmond into our lives, but according to him, his parents are both actors touring Australia this summer."

"I wonder why he didn't go with them," I said.

"Oh, I can tell you that," Mairead answered. In a Desmond-like voice, she intoned, "I didn't want to go down under with the folks because I'm keen on doing historical research, and what better place to do it than at the ruins of St. Theobald's Abbey, dating back to eleven nineteen A.D. and only one kilometer away from the Flynns'."

"That will do, Mairead," Aunt Ellen chided, but with a smile tugging at her lips. Mairead's Desmond imitation was really quite good. "We do, however, have another visitor who's staying with us this summer, Deirdre," she said. "I didn't want to write your mother about him because I was afraid she wouldn't let you come, thinking we'd be too crowded, which we're not. His name is Finbar and he's just turned thirteen."

Something was not quite right about the way Aunt Ellen mentioned the other visitor. Her voice quivered a bit and she looked away. Mairead took my arm and chatted about my letters as Desmond opened the car doors for us.

"I believe I heard you mention Finbar, Aunt Ellen," Desmond commented as she maneuvered the car out of the airport car park. "Have you told Deirdre about the wee tragic lad?"

"No, Desmond," Aunt Ellen snapped. "That can wait."

It waited until after lunch, at which the mysterious Finbar was not present, when Aunt Ellen shooed me upstairs for a rest. As I closed the door to my room, Desmond jumped in front of me, putting a finger to his lips.

"Shh, Deirdre, don't make any noise. I have to tell you something. Aunt Ellen can't talk about Finbar yet without getting desperately weepy. But you must know about him before you meet him. Here, sit on the bed and I'll take the chair."

Desmond commanded obedience, and I sat meekly on the bed.

"It's a sad story, love, but I think you can bear it."

I nodded my resolve.

"Finbar came down here a month ago. Practically speechless, he was. Barely could say hello. Traumatized, he was."

"Traumatized?"

"It's a word, love, that means he saw something so horrible that he went out of his senses. He went catatonic for a few days, too."

"Catatonic?"

"Oh, sorry. Catatonic means what he saw made him climb inside himself. Didn't respond to any outside prodding. Could stick a pin in his toes, you could, and he wouldn't even move."

I shivered. "What happened to make him traumatized and catatonic?"

"Arms and legs, Deirdre. Arms and legs shooting up in the air. Blood showering down from the skies and spattering his face. Brains gushing onto his jacket. Arms, legs, blood, and brains of people he was queued next to waiting for the bus in Belfast."

Desmond added a few more details that I blocked out to keep from losing my lunch. "What happened?" I finally croaked.

He gave me his patented Desmond look, the first of many I received that summer: arched left eyebrow, flicker of a smile, stark pity for one so uninformed.

"Maybe it hasn't been on the American telly, Deirdre, or if it has maybe you've been busy watching other things. But there's terrible troubles up in the north of Ireland. Those that want to stay with England and those that don't are having a go at each other. First it was just marches and rock-throwing, and bombing statues and power stations, but lately it's been bombs where people are. A car carrying a bomb exploded directly next to the bus queue where Finbar stood."

"Oh," I said quietly, visualizing arms and legs torn from their owners, leaving torsos bouncing on the ground until they and heads exploded into fragments of flesh and bone. Aunt Ellen's potato and leek soup churned in my stomach.

Desmond tilted his head back, rather enjoying, I thought, my discomfort. I tried hard to look unaffected, but beads of sweat formed over my upper lip.

Having delivered me the shock of my young lifetime, Desmond grinned, patted my shoulder, then climbed out the window and leapt two stories into the soft dirt of the yard. It was an exit worthy of Errol Flynn, my mother's favorite swashbuckling movie star. I lay sleepless on the bed, projecting the terrible images of dismembered bodies onto the wall. Suddenly I bolted upright. Could Desmond have been lying? Could he have been storifying Finbar as Aunt Ellen had warned?

When I met Finbar at afternoon tea, I knew Desmond had told the truth. His skin was gray, the gray of Play-Doh when you mix all the colors together. His body was soft and pudgy, like an oversized toddler's, but his face, though unwrinkled, was old, like the death masks on the effigies I later saw in St. Theobald's Abbey.

Finbar came to Aunt Ellen's because his parents were also in the bus queue that day, a detail most likely related to me by Desmond when my mind had ceased to absorb more horror. When a police-woman came to him, Mairead told me, Finbar was sitting on the curb, clasping the severed arm of his mother. Finbar's mother was Aunt Ellen's best friend, a Catholic like her, who had left Ballyclough to marry a Protestant and settle in Northern Ireland. Her family disowned her, but they welcomed the orphan after the death of their daughter. Finbar's psychiatrist, however, believed the boy would do better for a time with Aunt Ellen, who had kept in touch with Finbar and his mother throughout the years.

After my first week at Ballyclough, I joined in the routine of the household because my mother had made it clear to Aunt Ellen and me that I was not to be treated like one of the guests at the B & B. Like Mairead, I helped with the chores, which were clearing the breakfast dishes and washing and drying them, and hoovering[6] the guest rooms.

Finbar also had chores, but they were animal-based. He had to feed the russet setter, occasionally groom him, and also escort back home the cows that frequently strayed from Gallaher's pasture. Mairead and I could never tell from his face if he liked these chores, but we thought he did because we often found him outside sitting with the dog, deriving some kind of comfort from stroking its fur. Each weekday morning about nine his Uncle Brendan came to the B & B and drove Finbar to a psychiatrist in Kilmeath.

Mairead's and my communication with Finbar was limited to polite queries, such as, "Isn't it a nice day today, Finbar?" To which he solemnly answered yes without meeting our eyes. Mairead and I vowed that we'd make him smile before the summer was done, but Desmond beat us to it.

Every afternoon after Finbar's Uncle Brendan dropped him off, Desmond appeared, bringing treats for the dog, who had collapsed in

---

6 **hoovering:** vacuuming. The word is derived from the name of the Hoover company that makes electric sweepers or vacuum cleaners.

the yard from the exertion of wildly welcoming Finbar home. Finbar settled on the grass beside the dog, waiting dutifully, it seemed, for the arrival of Desmond the Dramatic. Sometimes Desmond entered the yard by the low stone wall that separated the B & B from the Flynns', carrying a pole and mimicking a tipsy trapeze artist. Sometimes he snatched a towel from Aunt Ellen's clothesline. Appropriately caped, he feinted and lunged on the imaginary parapet of the stone wall, dueling and triumphing over invisible opponents.

Mairead and I were his best audience. We laughed and applauded at all the right places. Finbar watched silently but did respond to Desmond's post-performance greetings, delivered in the dialect *du jour*. To "Och, mon, how goes it?", Finbar replied, "Fine, thank you." To *"Bonjour, Monsieur Finbar, comment ça va?"* Finbar replied "Fine, thank you." Undaunted by Finbar's reticence, Desmond plopped down beside him on the grass and addressed Shamrock, the Irish setter.

Narrowing his eyes, Desmond stared accusingly at the beast. "Reprobate! Cur! I know who you are. You have passed through many lifetimes. Your sorry mother helped you, Sham O'Rock, to betray kings! You were there, at Clontarf on Dublin Bay in the year of Our Lord ten fourteen when the forces of Brian Boru,[7] King of Munster, battled the Danes for control of Ireland. Too frail to lead battle, Brian lay in his tent, awaiting news with you there as his watch-dog. When the Dane Brodar approached his tent, you properly growled until the nefarious Brodar slipped you something, something for which you forfeited your duty and abetted the journey of Brian Boru to his eternal reward!"

During the tirade, Shamrock's head sank lower and lower until it rested on the damp earth in as clear a posture of shame as I have ever seen.

"He understands you," I squealed.

"Of course he does. And now, Finbar, you may ask what Brodar the Nefarious gave to Sham O'Rock."

"But I know what Brodar gave Shamrock, Desmond," Finbar said, his eyes coming alive for the first time since I'd met him.

"And pray, what is that, friend of the treacherous Sham O'Rock?"

"Well, Brodar was a Dane, so it must have been Danish pastry."

Mairead and I howled with laughter at Finbar's answer and howled even louder when we saw Desmond's face set in the forlorn

---

7 **Brian Boru:** (926–1014) an Irish king who fought the Danes and the Norse.

expression of the one-upped. Finbar looked pleased, then worried. Obviously he didn't want to offend Desmond. Sighing, Desmond patted his shoulder and said, "Touché, my man." Later in the day, Desmond told us that he would have accepted any answer from "the wee tragic lad who badly needed a win."

The Sham O'Rock incident gave Finbar a lift. Since he could hold his own with Desmond, he agreed to accompany us on afternoon excursions planned by Desmond as long as Shamrock came along. Aunt Ellen and Finbar's Uncle Brendan were very pleased. Our first outing was to a beehive hut of corbeled stone,[8] set on a hill midway between the B & B and the Cliffs of Dun Maurgis. Although the climb was steep, Finbar gamely followed the leader, stopping occasionally to admonish Shamrock for barking at the sheep that dotted the hill. When we reached the hut, Desmond extended his arm, signaling us to stop.

Frightened, I clutched Mairead as I wondered if a mad old hermit would come out of the hut, long white hair and beard flowing, calling down deprecations from heaven for our intrusion into his solitude. From his pocket, Desmond pulled out a piece of soda bread and a juice glass filled with salt. Solemnly, he broke the bread into smaller pieces and gave us each a chunk.

"Within this hut," he intoned, "dwelled Jeremiah the Just, holy recluse of Ballyclough, who spent his days in prayer within this mortarless dwelling, fashioned by his own hands. Constantly besieged by devils to leave this holy place and tempted to consort by lady devils wearing no clothes, Jeremiah refused and prayed only harder. He remained here until the age of ninety-seven, and was lovingly carried down this hill by the monks of St. Theobald's Abbey to be buried there."

"Then why the bread, Desmond?" asked Mairead. "If Jeremiah the Just is gone, who needs it? Henry the Hungry?"

Finbar and I smiled weakly, worried that Mairead's sarcasm would somehow call forth lingering devils.

Desmond frowned. "Do not mock, Mairead. Since Jeremiah's departure, evil spirits have squatted here, waiting for souls less worthy to enter. I have carefully researched spirit infestation in medieval tomes and learned how to ward them off. Our ancestors developed a

---

8 **beehive hut of corbeled stone:** a hut in the shape of a beehive, possibly prehistoric; corbelling is an overlapping arrangement of stones.

simple ritual to be followed before entering hovel or castle. Take a piece of this bread and dip it into this container of salt, then eat it."

As we obediently ate the salted bread, Desmond plucked four blades of grass and arranged them in his hand.

"A variation on choosing straws," he said. "The person who picks the shortest blade goes into the beehive hut first."

I shivered. The exterior of the hut with its lichen-covered stones appeared not out of place atop a hillside bearing masses of eons-old rock. Several wildflowers growing out of mortarless niches gave the hut an almost homey look. But the sun-deprived interior, entered by a small opening in the rocks, could offer only dungeonlike hospitality.

When none of us approached Desmond's outstretched hand, he tossed the blades of grass into the air and looked at us with contempt. "I'll be the first, then, as usual," he announced. Before he could move toward the hut, Finbar pushed him aside. "No, Desmond. I will be the first."

Mairead and I exchanged surprised glances. Desmond, however, slapped him on the shoulder—a man-to-man gesture, the lieutenant congratulating the timid recruit turned volunteer. As Finbar made his way up the slight incline leading to the hut, Shamrock tugged at the cuffs of his pants. Finbar gently shook him off.

"Be gone, Sham O'Rock. Your master is not the cowardly cur that you are," thundered Desmond.

Finbar looked so proud. He straightened his shoulders and continued his march to the door of the hut. As he stopped to enter it, he turned and grinned at us. I think he sensed that Mairead and I were afraid for him. At that moment, I understood that Finbar had come to realize that nothing he encountered in the hut could be as horrible as what he had experienced in the Belfast queue. Fear was no longer his master.

It seemed like an hour before Finbar came out of the hut, but I'm sure it was only a few minutes. Bearing trophies, he crawled outside, a dead bat perched jauntily on his tweed cap, an empty pint of Guinness in one hand, and a half dozen Fry candy wrappers in the other.

"Ah, my fellow pilgrims," he shouted, "I had to fight twenty devils themselves for these relics, but I won, I won!"

Ah yes, you won, Finbar. You completed your rite of passage from darkness into light. You won Desmond's respect and Mairead's and my deepest affection. We were no longer afraid of you or for you. Your Play-Doh complexion turned into that rosy Irish glow, your boyhood returned, at least for a while.

Finbar's visits to the doctor in Kilmeath dwindled to once a week, a session most likely devoted to his relating tales from "The Adventures of the Four Cousins," Desmond's Holmesian title for our excursions. Some of our adventures occurred on the Aran Islands,[9] where Desmond marched us over the rock-strewn terrain as "defenders of the fort of Dun Aengus once again under siege." Our ascent in double time to the fort almost dislodged many of the tourists, who descended the narrow path at a leisurely pace, unaware of the "struggles" above.

We scrambled up the Cliffs of Mohr in great haste before edging ourselves out to the farthest rocks where we could blend in with the German tourists who sat in silent wonder at the sea lapping gently at the limestone cliffs.

"Sorry, cousins, that I had to rush you up the cliffs but I spotted potential trouble."

"What kind of trouble?" I asked.

"Spurned lovers' revenge."

Feeling a story coming on, Finbar grinned and lay back on the rocks. Mairead and I smirked, but gave Desmond our full attention. Spurned lovers were welcome additions to Desmond's repertoire.

Desmond told us that the two young women, one playing a small accordion and the other a guitar, at the foot of the path leading to the cliffs, did not come there each week for the coins tossed into their box by tourists. Maeve and Fiona, their names somehow known by Desmond, came to the cliffs looking for their lovers who had met two American girls and subsequently emigrated. Maeve and Fiona knew, however, that the treacherous lads would return one day to gaze longingly at the Cliffs of Mohr. When that occurred, the two had devised a plan to toss the men over the cliffs.

"So what made you think Maeve and Fiona will send their lads flying today?" asked Mairead.

"Elementary, my dear Mairead. I noticed that their rendition of 'The Fields of Athenry' became quite agitato when the two young men in front of us passed by them."

Finbar rolled over on his stomach and squinted at Desmond. "My dear Holmes," he said, "could it be that the agitato came from the fact that the two lads winked at them and pointed to their watches,

---

9 **Aran Islands:** three islands off the western coast of Ireland; they have many prehistoric and early Christian remains.

which I deduced meant that they wanted to know what time Maeve and Fiona would finish playing so that they could have a date?"

At Finbar's riposte, Desmond turned glacial. How dare the peasant poach on the territory of the master! Abruptly, he left the rock and swept regally down the path, never looking backwards at us or sidewards at the two musicians. Finbar turned pale and chewed on his lip. Mairead and I wanted to console him, but we were not quite sure what Finbar's offense was. The sin of upstaging the star was something we were not acquainted with.

All the way home in the motor coach, Desmond stared out the window. Certain that Desmond had checked out of our lives, Mairead whispered to me, "It's going to be bleak without him."

During the next two days, unrelenting rain added to the bleakness. Finbar, Mairead, and I had just about exhausted Aunt Ellen's supply of games when we heard a tap on the parlor window.

Finbar's face when he saw Desmond at the window warmed us more than the return of the sun. "I knew he'd come back," he yelled as he dashed to the front door. Finbar must have sensed that the life of a star without an audience was even bleaker than ours.

"Sorry to have been out of touch," Desmond said, "but I've been indentured for the past two days."

"How so?" asked Mairead as Finbar stood by beaming like a child whose punishment has been mercifully remitted.

"The Flynns, those dotty old dears, have finally sold their dress shop in Kilmeath. The buyer is going to turn it into a betting parlor so he's got no need for the mirrors, curtains, mannequins, hangers, and all the other accoutrements of the former Fashions de Beauté. For some reason, auld lang syne, I suppose, the Flynns had me fill up their spare room with the junk. For two days, I've been desperately wet, hauling cargo in the mud like a wretched convict at Botany Bay."[10]

"I would have helped you, Desmond," said Finbar.

"Of course you would have, lad, and the girls too, but the Flynns are very noblesse oblige and all that."

Noblesse oblige, whatever that meant, I didn't care. What mattered was that Mairead, Finbar, and I had received mass absolution. Finbar had been forgiven for de-storifying Desmond's "Tale of the Two Jilted Musicians" and Mairead and I pardoned for not shunning

---

10 **Botany Bay:** an inlet of the Tasman Sea south of Sydney, Australia, to which convicts were once sent from England.

the sinner. Having been fully reinstated into Desmond's good graces, we were now ready for our next adventure.

"It's about time we investigated St. Theobald's Abbey," Desmond announced. "Legend has it that the place is haunted."

Finbar and I shivered delightedly, but Mairead bit her lip to hold back a smile. Later she told me that there had never been a local legend that St. Theobald's was haunted, but she didn't want to be guilty of de-storification and incur the displeasure of Desmond.

The ruin of St. Theobald's Abbey was one of the area's most interesting but least visited attractions because of its location atop a rock-strewn hill accessible only by a steep footpath. We set out to visit it on a drizzly summer afternoon in weather that the Irish call "soft." A roofless limestone chapel in various stages of decay remained standing. It had once been quite beautiful and still retained some semblance of loveliness. As we came close to the ruin, Desmond assumed the role of tour guide.

"In eleven nineteen, Eammon of Ennisbowden, descendant on his mother's side from the Viking, Olaf the Unruly, fled to this very spot to avoid being drawn and quartered for his many crimes. Though a noble by birth, Eammon was a scoundrel by choice. He changed his name to Theobald because he was on the run for being a poacher, a horse thief, a despoiler of virgins, a part-time pirate, and most heinously of all, a necromancer."

Pausing more for effect than to catch his breath like the rest of us, Desmond waited until Finbar asked the proper question.

"What's a necromancer, Des?"

Desmond timed his response to coincide with our arrival at a scattering of Celtic crosses almost obscured by high weeds and grasses that marked the burial places of St. Theobald's monks. "A necromancer is a sorcerer who predicts the future by communicating with the dead."

As Desmond led the way to the east wall of the chapel, Mairead whispered, "Blarney. St. Theobald's was founded by a saintly monk named Theobald, a nobleman who gave most of his riches to the poor and saved just enough to pay the stonemasons to build the abbey. Only the chapel remains now."

Although the roof of the chapel had disappeared, the four walls remained intact. As I walked under the Romanesque arch into the nave of the building, the sense of having entered a holy place overwhelmed me. As Mairead, Finbar, and Desmond scampered over the stones of the floor, their native Irishness making them more familiar with the venerable, I made the sign of the cross before reverently touching the stone wall. I had never touched workmanship that was centuries old.

For several minutes, I tried to absorb the sense of the place, to visualize long-dead abbots and priests seated on the chipped sedilia[11] during mass, to hear the sounds of the "Dies Irae"[12] being sung as the abbot's coffin, also long gone, was placed into the empty sarcophagus on whose sides were carved ribbonlike spirals, symbols of eternity. When Mairead began to play her tin whistle, I fully believed that I had willed the music of centuries to sound once more just for us. The plaintive notes from her simple instrument sent a sweet greeting to the monks and their benefactors who were interred within the chapel. I felt connected to everyone, living and dead.

"In a trance, are you, Deirdre?" shouted Desmond.

His voice shattered the moment. "Come look at this, will you?" He stood high above us on a narrow stone walk. "I'm up here in the scriptorium, the place where the monks did their homework, copied books and all that."

We climbed up crumbling steps, made for smaller feet than ours, onto the remains of the scriptorium, and inched over the west wall. I was so careful of my footing that I hadn't noticed Finbar's pallor until we reached Desmond.

"Seen the ghost of Eammon of Ennisbowden, Finbar?" asked Desmond. "Or is it the height that's made you go ashy?"

"Neither one," I snapped. "He's just naturally pale."

Desmond smiled, then pointed to the arch over the niche in the wall.

"There are the heads," he said, "of the stonemasons who built this chapel. They always carved likenesses of themselves somewhere in the edifices they built. Here's my favorite."

The face that he chose leered at us. Unlike the other small jovial heads that could have graced jesters' wands, Desmond's favorite, with its full lips and dilated nostrils, could have decorated the lintel of a brothel.

"O, stonemason of yesteryear, where are you now?" he intoned. "In hell, with the other despoilers, I should guess. Sizzling for your sins, I suppose, you despoiler of all despoilers. Are you roasting with Eammon of Ennisbowden, who built this place so he wouldn't be hanged?"

---

11   **sedilia:** one of a set of seats for the clergy in some Roman Catholic and Anglican churches.

12   **Dies Irae:** a medieval Latin hymn used in some masses for the dead.

"Desmond, shh," Mairead urged. "This is a holy place."

"Afraid I'll call up the demons, are you, love? And well you should be, because demons historically lurk around chapels, peddling temptations to the pure. Demons of Ballyclough, unite!"

"Blasphemy, Desmond," cried Mairead as she crossed herself and climbed down from the scriptorium. Finbar and I followed. The sacred mood broken, we went outside and started down the hill. Finbar kept turning around, looking for Desmond, torn between adulation of the older boy and his ingrained piety. When Desmond caught up with us, full of penitent phrases, Finbar instantly forgave him. Mairead and I made him work for our forgiveness, not participating in his capers for two days.

We gave in after Finbar begged us to come to the Flynns' backyard. On his knees on the low stone wall, Desmond bowed low, then raised his head so we could see the ashes smeared across his face and the sackcloth wrapped around his neck.

"Father O'Reilly says I must soil me face and put the cloth around me neck till I receive the pardon of two fair maidens."

The two fair maidens burst into laughter as the penitent crossed his eyes in the telling.

"Actually, I only got three Our Fathers and three Hail Marys, so how blasphemous could I have been?"

If Father O'Reilly absolved him, how could we not forgive him? The four of us resumed our adventures, but limited them to the strand. Much of the time it was too cold to swim, but not too cold to listen to the pirate tales that Desmond made up. Finbar never got bored with the stories, but Mairead and I finally did. We frequently went off by ourselves to St. Theobald's, where we confessed to each other that we were afraid of Desmond ever since he had invoked the demons.

It was in the middle of August that the foursome really split up. At first, Finbar asked us politely to join Desmond and him on a Desmond-inspired treasure hunt, an imaginary archaeological dig, or a real ride in a curragh[13] with a local fisherman. Whenever we declined, he never seemed disappointed. We knew he liked having Desmond to himself.

The adults in our lives that summer, Aunt Ellen and Finbar's Uncle Brendan, radiated joy at Finbar's recovery. His Uncle Brendan

---

13   **curragh** (kur´ə): a small, light, wicker-frame boat that is covered in skins or tarred canvas.

practically glowed the day he told Aunt Ellen that Finbar's psychiatrist thought the boy didn't need him anymore and that he'd be able to attend school in Kilmeath in September.

"I understand that Desmond will be going to school with him," Aunt Ellen said. "He told me today that his parents are off to South America with their theater troupe and he'll stay here for at least a term."

"It will be good for the boys to be together," Finbar's Uncle Brendan said. "In fact, if you don't mind, we'd like Finbar to finish the summer with you so as not to disrupt his friendships with Mairead and Deirdre, and, of course, Desmond, with him being the next farm over."

"Of course," answered Aunt Ellen. "We love having him."

The prospect of attending school with Desmond thrilled Finbar. He started riding Aunt Ellen's old bike to strengthen his legs so he could ride with Desmond the four miles to school in Kilmeath. When he had mastered the bike, he planned a trial ride to Kilmeath. Aunt Ellen didn't want him to go, but Mairead and I coaxed her into approving.

The Finbar that returned three hours later was so subdued that Mairead and I were sure that he'd run over someone's pet or knocked over an outdoor fruit stand. When we asked him how his ride went, he answered not very convincingly, "Lovely." Strapped to the bike's handlebars was a packet of newspapers, and some more were piled in a basket in back. Before we could ask him about the papers, Desmond appeared.

"Hail to the conquering hero. You made it. And what have you here? The newspapers took your picture, did they?"

Finbar brushed Desmond's hand away from the basket and smiled shyly. "No, it's just that the *Monitor* has some pictures of soccer players that I want to send to my friends in Belfast."

"The Flynns get the *Monitor*, don't they, Desmond?" Mairead asked. "Maybe you could give the paper to Finbar when they've finished."

"Would love to, but dotty Mrs. Flynn wrapped fish in it before I could even read my horoscope. Heaven knows what will befall me today because I surely don't."

Finbar excused himself and carried the newspapers up to his room. When he refused my offer to help, I was relieved because I felt achy and feverish. Aunt Ellen had come outside to welcome Finbar home, but focused more on my flushed cheeks.

"The summer flu, the very worst kind. To bed with you now, and I'll bring you up my remedies."

Fever dreams are the worst. I dreamed I was drowning in a tureen of tomato soup and just when I thought I was done for the soup turned into newspapers. While I was trying to climb out of the newspapers, President Kennedy and his brother Robert, looking exactly like the picture on the wall in Aunt Ellen's dining room, hoisted me out of the paper ocean and sat me on the window sill of my first-floor bedroom where I heard a really eerie, dream conversation.

Somebody was telling somebody that tonight was Sorcerer's Solstice, the one night in the year when the necromancer, Eammon of Ennisbowden, allows one soul to return from the dead to visit with a living relative. But the relative had to be brave enough to go by himself to a burial place like, say, St. Theobald's Abbey, at midnight, armed only with a flashlight, and stand before the sarcophagus in the chapel. If he followed those instructions, his worthiness would be assured and the deceased would visit him.

The tomato soup washed over me again, then stained the walls of my bedroom. After another dose of Aunt Ellen's remedies, the redness disappeared and so did the voice in the yard. I slept soundly until I heard different voices, voices shrill with panic—Aunt Ellen's and Finbar's Uncle Brendan's. I heard Aunt Ellen say that Finbar wasn't in his room, that he must have gone out during the night.

At noon they called the *garda*. A pretty young policewoman, Margaret Loughlin, came to the house and took his description. She tried to soothe Aunt Ellen, who kept pacing back and forth until she saw me in the hall and apologized for not checking on my condition.

"I'm okay, Aunt Ellen," I reassured her, "my fever's gone. But I had the strangest dream. And maybe Finbar had it too. In the dream a voice said it was time to go to St. Theobald's Abbey to speak to a dead relative. Maybe Finbar didn't realize it was only a dream and went there, maybe to see his mother."

"Dear saints in heaven," Aunt Ellen moaned, "maybe the lad did go there. Maybe he hasn't been as well as we thought."

"We'll check the abbey, miss," Margaret said.

Finbar's Uncle Brendan carried him back to our house, thinking perhaps the sight of familiar faces would revive him, but it didn't. Uncle Brendan and Margaret found Finbar lying motionless on the stones of the chapel in front of the empty sarcophagus. He had been there quite awhile and was not only catatonic, but suffering from exposure to the cool night air. His face looked as if a stonemason had chiseled it into a permanent expression of horror. When Desmond came in to see Finbar before the ambulance came, he wept.

"The poor lad," Desmond sobbed. "What could have possessed him to go off in the night to the abbey?"

No one had an answer to his question, except me, and I was too embarrassed to say, "The Sorcerer's Solstice possessed him," because after all, it was only a dream, and a fever dream at that. And my fever might not have been fully gone because when I looked at Desmond as he held the door for the paramedics, I saw that his face had assumed the characteristics of the leering stonemason at St. Theobald's chapel.

During the first week, we clung to the hope that Finbar would awaken from his paralyzed state, but he didn't. On her own time, Margaret Loughlin visited us, probing gently into our lives that summer, trying to penetrate the mist that shrouded the night Finbar went to the abbey. No foul play had been determined, she assured us. The *garda* had concluded that an excitable, vulnerable boy for reasons unknown had gone to a deserted place late at night and become terrified at being there.

"Had you ever made a dare with each other," Margaret asked Mairead and me, "to go to the mysterious abbey at night?" We truthfully answered no. Margaret also wondered about my dream. She told me there were instances of people having the same dream, like I thought Finbar and I might have had, but they were extremely rare. Could I have heard a real conversation? she wondered. I smiled sadly.

"Since the Kennedy brothers were in my dream too, I don't think I heard a real voice talking about St. Theobald's."

On her afternoon off on my last week in Ireland, Margaret cycled by to say goodbye. As she walked through the front gate, she met Uncle Brendan, who was carrying Finbar's clothes to the car. I was behind him loaded down with all the newspapers Finbar had bought in Kilmeath. When Margaret asked about them, I explained that Finbar was going to send pictures of soccer players to his friends and I wanted Uncle Brendan to have them to give to Finbar when he woke up.

"I don't think he'll need them, love," Uncle Brendan said gently. "The doctors say he won't come out of this one."

"When did he buy the papers?" Margaret asked.

"On the day he went ill," I told her.

Before I put the papers in the trash, Margaret took the one on top. It wasn't until ten years later when I was doing graduate work in psychology at the university in Galway, that I found out what was in the newspaper. When I learned that Margaret was lecturing in forensics at the university, I looked her up, and we've been friends ever since, united by our concern for Finbar.

"There were no pictures of soccer players in the newspaper that day," she told me, "but there was a feature article on the front page about people who had informed on the activities of the I.R.A. and been executed by them. The photograph of a very handsome man caught my eye, as it must have Finbar's when he was in Kilmeath. The man, who had been shot three months before the article had appeared, was an older version of Desmond and was also named Desmond O'Connor."

"Desmond's father," I exclaimed, "was an informer!"

"Yes."

"Then his father was never an actor in Australia and South America like Desmond told us. But what about his mother?"

"I did some checking and learned that she died when Desmond was three. After his father's death, Desmond was spared life in an orphanage when he remembered the Flynns and contacted them. They became his legal guardians."

"So Finbar found out the truth about Desmond when he cycled to Kilmeath and bought a newspaper."

"Yes, and I think Desmond believed that Finbar was going to circulate the newspapers in school and ruin his standing with his classmates," Margaret added, "because even in the Republic, no one loves an informer or his kin."

But Finbar wouldn't have done that, I told Margaret. He idolized Desmond. So why, I wondered, did he buy all those papers?

"Oh, I think I know," Margaret said sadly. "He bought the newspapers in the futile hope that he could keep potential classmates from seeing the article and remembering the photo when Desmond arrived. After all, it was only two weeks until school started. Finbar bought the newspapers to protect Desmond."

Margaret and I lingered over tea for quite a while, each of us parting the curtain of memory to face once again the pain of that summer. Margaret had been a policewoman less than a year when she met us. Finbar had been the first child victim she had encountered and he moved her deeply. She had never been satisfied with the conclusion that no foul play had occurred. Over the years, just like Mairead and I had, she checked on Finbar's condition, which never changed.

"If only he could have told us what happened," I mused.

"Oh, I think I know what happened," Margaret said.

I put my scone down slowly and stared at her. The cafeteria, almost empty, had become quiet except for the rain beating against the windows. Margaret looked away from me toward the windows, but I knew she was not checking the weather. She was gathering strength to relate the horrible.

"From the start, your dream of Eammon of Ennisbowden and the abbey disturbed me. I didn't think it was a dream. I thought you overheard a real conversation involving Finbar and someone encouraging him to go to the abbey. After talking to your Aunt Ellen and learning how Finbar worshiped Desmond, I was convinced that Finbar would only go to the abbey at midnight if someone he trusted like Desmond told him to. Desmond was desperately afraid that Finbar was going to pass the newspapers around school and he contrived a plan to stop him."

Her eyes narrowed. "And the little beast almost succeeded."

"What was the plan, Margaret?"

"Quite simply, Desmond intended to scare him to death. Finbar didn't die, but Desmond was satisfied because catatonia, a living death, essentially eliminated Finbar as an imagined threat."

Outside, the wind keened for Finbar.

"What happened at the abbey, Margaret?"

"To find out, I walked circles around the abbey whenever I had a chance that fall. And I found two things that showed me what Desmond had done, but I could never prove they triggered the catatonia."

"What were they?"

"An arm and a paper wrapper."

I shivered. "An arm?"

"A mannequin's arm. I found it about a quarter mile from the abbey in a thicket of gorse. The wrapper I found inside the chapel in a holy water font. It had covered a firecracker and Desmond must have forgotten to retrieve it. The arm he dropped on his way home."

"What did Desmond do with them?"

"He used them to restage the event that had initially traumatized Finbar, the bombing death of his parents. Here's what I think happened. Desmond went to the chapel ahead of Finbar and climbed into the sarcophagus and concealed himself. When he heard Finbar, he tossed a firecracker up in the air to simulate the light and noise of a bomb. Then he threw out the items he had placed on top of himself, the body parts of a dismembered mannequin."

"Oh, my God."

"And Finbar once again saw his mother mutilated by the bomb, just as he had in the bus queue."

For several minutes we sat in silence until, for sanity's sake, my mind shifted from the horrible scene to the technical details of the crime.

"The mannequin. The Flynns had sold their dress shop and Desmond helped bring the contents of the store, which included mannequins, to their house. Did you ever question the Flynns?"

"Oh, yes, but by the time I discovered the arm and found out from your Aunt Ellen what the Flynns' business was, Desmond had convinced the old couple to sell everything to a junk dealer, so there was no way I could check for a mannequin with a missing arm. As for firecrackers, they could be bought in Kilmeath. I asked storekeepers there but no one remembered a lad matching Desmond's description buying them. The firecrackers could have been at the Flynns' before he came there."

For two years, Margaret followed Desmond's career. He did well at the school in Kilmeath, acting in school plays and graduating at the top of his class. To Margaret's knowledge, no one at the school held his father's past against him, which would certainly have pleased Finbar. After high school, he moved on to Trinity College and from there, Margaret lost his trail.

Until two weeks ago. On a Sunday afternoon, Margaret opened the *Monitor*'s literary section and saw Desmond proudly signing copies of his book in a shop on Grafton Street in Dublin. The buyer of the book, a young woman, looked adoringly at the author, who was movie-star handsome. Margaret sent me the article, with a paragraph highlighted in yellow marker that noted that Desmond would be in New York at the Benton Book Store on Madison Avenue on November 5th, a week from the day I received the article. She had attached a Post-it to the piece that read, "World at his feet, eh?"

I went to Benton's Book Store and stood in line with about one hundred other purchasers of *Dreams of the Druid,* almost all women, who offered him the kind of irrational attention usually reserved for rock stars. Whenever Desmond finished signing and smiled at the recipient of his largesse, a collective squeal erupted from the line. When I got close to him, I studied his face for signs that some of life's events, particularly his crime against Finbar, had caused him anguish, but nothing registered on that flawless face but the sheen of self-love. I knew I could change that.

When I reached the front of the line, I said, "Please sign the book, 'To Deirdre of the Morrows.' "

He began to write, then slapped his wrist against his forehead and clasped my hand. The line went wild with envy.

"Oh my God, it's you. The American cousin. How long has it been? Fifteen, sixteen years. Why, you've turned into a beauty. Married, of course?"

"No, I'm married to my work."

He kissed my hand. "And what might that be, fair lady?"

"Psychology, I'm a research psychologist."

"And vat is it that vomen vant?" he said, puffing on an imaginary cigar.

"Just autographs."

I handed him another copy of his book.

"Please sign this, 'To Finbar.' "

A flicker of anxiety, but just a flicker, crossed those beautiful features.

"You don't mean our Finbar, do you, the wee tragic lad?"

"Yes, I do."

"But the poor lad's irreversibly catatonic. I used to inquire regularly about him."

I smiled beatifically. "In the past few years great strides have been made. New medications and therapy have done wonders. Because of personal and professional interest, I've kept in touch with his condition. He might be completely cured within the year and his memory will return. He's been transferred to a hospital in the States. I don't know where. Isn't that wonderful?"

"Oh, it's lovely, quite lovely," Desmond said.

Quickly, he scribbled "To Finbar" on my book, then wiped beads of perspiration from his forehead.

"Not feeling too well," he told the store manager as he lurched from the desk and made his way past the disappointed crowd into the street. I followed him out and watched as he headed for the nearest bar. The world might be at his feet, as Margaret said, but the past was thudding against his head. It wouldn't do at all for the world to know the truth about its latest darling when the wee tragic lad came to and told his story.

But the wee tragic lad will never tell his story. He died six months ago in Ireland. I made up the part about his apparent recovery and sojourn in a hospital in the States. Since I am sure that Desmond will go looking for Finbar, I wanted to give the famous author the vast expanse of this country for his futile search. The deception won't bring Finbar back, but perhaps a crease or two might furrow the brow of the Bard of Ballyclough.

QUESTIONS FOR DISCUSSION

1. Although there is a policewoman in the story, most of the story has nothing to do with detecting. What is the purpose of the extended rising action?

2. What makes Finbar susceptible to Desmond's moods and wishes?

3. Analyze Desmond from a psychological point of view.

4. Is Finbar's accident foreshadowed in any way? If so, how?

5. Is this a story about "the perfect crime"? Why or why not?

TOPICS FOR WRITING

1. In a paper, discuss the importance of setting in this story.

2. Make a list showing the following: the victim, the accident, the alleged perpetrator, relevant clues that point to the perpetrator, and the motive for the crime, if crime there was. Then tell in one or two paragraphs why no one was arrested.

INSPECTOR WEXFORD AND THE WINCHURCH AFFAIR

RUTH RENDELL (born 1930)

Ruth Rendell was awarded the 1997 Grand Master award by the Mystery Writers of America, a tribute to this Englishwoman's immense talent and popularity. Born in London, the daughter of parents who were teachers, she was educated in Essex, England. She has also won the Edgar Allan Poe Award several times for stories, story collections, and novels, the Gold Dagger Award from the Crime Writers Association, and a British National Book Award.

She introduced Chief Inspector Reginald Wexford of Kingsmarkham, Sussex, England, in her first novel, *From Doon with Death* (1964), and Wexford has, along with his associate, Inspector Michael Burden, been investigating an unusual number of crimes in this town in many short stories and novels.

The Wexford stories and novels are chiefly police procedurals, but Rendell's other books are mysteries that involve abnormal psychology and often verge on horror. She also publishes novels under the name Barbara Vine, including *A Dark-Adapted Eye* (1985), *A Fatal Inversion* (1987), *Gallowglass* (1990), *The Brimstone Wedding* (1996), and *The Chimney Sweeper's Boy* (1998). Her stories are collected in *Blood Lines: Long and Short Stories* (1996) and in some earlier volumes.

In this story Chief Inspector Wexford is what is commonly called an armchair detective. That is, his discoveries are made entirely from a chair in his living room, an often much longed-for place for this busy, middle-aged, very married man.

■

"Matrimony," said Chief Inspector Wexford, "begins with dearly beloved and ends with amazement."

His wife, sitting beside him on the bridegroom's side of the church, whispered, "What did you say?"

He repeated it. She steadied the large floral hat which her husband had called becoming but not exactly conducive to *sotto voce*[1] intimacies. "What on earth makes you say that?"

"Thomas Hardy. He said it first. But look in your Prayer Book."

The bridegroom waited, hangdog, with his best man. Michael Burden—Inspector Michael Burden, Wexford's assistant—was very much in love, was entering this second marriage with someone admirably suited to him, had agreed with his fiancée that nothing but a religious ceremony would do for them, yet at forty-four was a little superannuated[2] for what Wexford called "all this white wedding gubbins." There were two hundred people in the church. Burden, his best man, and his ushers were in morning dress. Madonna lilies and stephanotis and syringa decorated the pews, the pulpit, and the chancel steps. It was the kind of thing that is properly designed for someone twenty years younger. Burden had been through it before when he *was* twenty years younger.

Wexford chuckled silently, looking at Burden's pale anxious face above the high white collar. But as Dora, leafing through the marriage service, said, "Oh, I *see*," the organist went from voluntaries into the opening bars of the Lohengrin march, and Jenny Ireland appeared at the church door on her father's arm.

A beautiful bride, of course. Seven years younger than Burden, blonde, gentle, low-voiced and given to radiant smiles. The Rector of St. Peter's began: "Dearly beloved, we are gathered together . . ."

While Burden and Miss Ireland were being informed that marriage was not for the satisfaction of their carnal instincts and that they must bring up their children in a Christian manner, Wexford quenched his boredom by studying the congregation. In front of himself and Dora sat Burden's sister-in-law Grace whom everyone had thought he would marry after the death of his first wife, her only sister. But Burden had found consolation with a red-headed woman, wild and sweet and strange, gone now God knew where, and Grace had married someone else. Two little boys now sat between Grace

1 *sotto voce:* in soft tones; literally "under voice." [Italian]

2 **superannuated:** elderly.

and that someone else, giving their parents a full-time job keeping them quiet.

Burden's parents were dead. Wexford thought he recognized, from one meeting a dozen years before, an aged aunt. Beside her sat Dr. Crocker and his wife, beyond them and behind was a crowd he knew either only by sight or not at all. Next to Wexford was his older daughter and her sons, a little senior to Grace's children, then Neil her husband, at the central aisle end his younger daughter, the actress, Sheila Wexford of the Royal Shakespeare Company, who on her entry had commanded nudges, whispers, every gaze.

"I, Michael George, take thee, Janina, to be my wedded wife, to have and to hold from this day forward . . ."

Janina. *Janina?* Wexford had supposed her name was Jennifer. What sort of parents called a daughter Janina? Fans of Dumas?[3] He turned to have a good look at these philonomatous progenitors. They looked ordinary enough—Mr. Ireland, apparently exhausted from the effort of giving the bride away, Jenny's mother already making use of the lace handkerchief provided for the specific purpose of crying into it those tears of joy and loss. What romantic streak had led them to dismiss names like Elizabeth and Susan and Anne in favor of—Janina?

"Those whom God hath joined together, let no man put asunder. Forasmuch as Michael George and Janina have consented together in holy wedlock . . ."

Had they been as adventurous in the naming of their son? All Wexford could see of him was a broad back, a bit of profile, and now a hand. The hand was passing a large white handkerchief to his mother, her own being saturated. Wexford found himself suddenly yanked to his feet to sing a hymn.

"O, Perfect Love, all human thought transcending,

Lowly we kneel in prayer before Thy throne . . ."

These words had the effect of evoking from Mrs. Ireland audible sobs. Her son—hadn't Burden said he was in publishing?—looked embarrassed, turning his head. A young woman, strangely dressed in black with an orange hat, edged past the publisher to put a consoling arm round his mother.

"O Lord, save Thy servant and Thy handmaid."

"Who put their trust in Thee," said Dora and most of the rest of the congregation.

---

3 **Dumas:** Alexandre Dumas (1802–1870), French novelist and dramatist.

"O Lord, send them help from Thy holy place."

Wexford, to show team spirit, said, "Amen," and when everyone else said, "And evermore defend them," decided to keep quiet in the future.

Mrs. Ireland had stopped crying. Wexford's gaze drifted to his own daughters, Sheila singing lustily, Sylvia, the Women's Liberationist, with less assurance as if she doubted the ethics of lending her support to so archaic and sexist a ceremony.

"Almighty God, who at the beginning did create our first parents, Adam and Eve . . ."

Dear Mike, thought Wexford with the flash of sentimentality that came to him perhaps once every ten years, you'll be okay now. No more lusts conflicting with a puritan conscience, no more loneliness, no more worrying about those selfish kids of yours, no more temptation-of-St.-Anthony stuff.[4]

"For after this manner in the old time the holy women who trusted in God . . ."

He was quite surprised that they were using the ancient form. Still, the bride had promised to obey. He couldn't resist glancing at Sylvia.

". . . being in subjection to their own husbands . . . "

Her face was a study in incredulous dismay as she mouthed at Neil "unbelievable" and "antique."

"Even as Sarah obeyed Abraham, calling him Lord, whose daughters ye are as long as ye do well, and are not afraid with any amazement."

It was over. Wexford grinned at his wife. "There you are!" The principal players went off into the vestry.

At the Olive and Dove Hotel there was a reception line to greet guests, Mrs. Ireland smiling, re-rouged and restored, Burden looking like someone who has had an operation and been told the prognosis is excellent, Jenny smiling and serene as a bride should be.

Dry sherry and white wine on trays. No champagne.

Wexford remembered that there was a younger Ireland daughter, absent with her husband in some far-off place—Botswana? Lesotho?

---

4 **temptation-of-St.-Anthony stuff:** St. Anthony, or Antony (251–356?), was born near Memphis in Egypt, and engaged in struggles with the devil and temptations that are legendary. In 272, he became a hermit in a tomb in a cemetery, living on bread and water, but later emerged to found several monasteries.

No doubt all the champagne funds had been expended on her. It was a buffet lunch, but a good one—smoked salmon and duck and strawberries. Nobody, he said to himself, has ever really thought of anything better to eat than smoked salmon and duck and strawberries unless it might be caviar and grouse and syllabub.[5] He was weighing the two menus against one another, must without knowing it have been thinking aloud, for a voice said, "Asparagus, trout, apple pie."

"Well, maybe," said Wexford, "but I do like meat. Trout's a bit insipid. You're Jenny's brother. I'm sorry I don't remember your name. How d'you do?"

"How d'you do? I know who you are. Mike told me. I'm Amyas Ireland."

So that funny old pair hadn't had a single indulgence when they had named Janina. Wexford's face must have shown what he was thinking.

"Okay, I know," said Ireland. "But how about my other sister? She's called Cunegonde.[6] Her husband calls her Queenie. Look, I'd like to talk to you. Could we get together a minute away from all this crush? Mike was going to help me out but I can't ask him now, not when he's off on his honeymoon. It's about a book we're publishing."

The girl in black and orange, Burden's nephews, Sheila Wexford, Burden's best man, and a gaggle of children, all carrying plates, passed between them at this point. It was at least a minute before Wexford could ask "Who's we?" and another half minute before Amyas Ireland understood what he meant.

"Carlyon Brent," he said, his mouth full of duck. "I work for Carlyon Brent."

One of the largest and most distinguished of publishing houses and still independent. Wexford was impressed. "You published the Vandrian, didn't you, and the de Coverly books?"

Ireland nodded. "Mike said you were a great reader. That's good. Can I get you some more duck? No? I'm going to. I won't be a minute." Enviously Wexford watched him shovel fat-rimmed slices of duck breast onto his plate, take a brioche, have a second thought and take another. The man was thin as a rail too, positively emaciated. He

---

5 **syllabub:** a drink made with sweetened milk or cream and wine or spirits; also a cold dessert made with sweetened cream, gelatin, and wine or fruit juice.

6 **Cunegonde:** a character in Voltaire's novel *Candide*.

sat down again and said, "I look after the crime list. As I said, Mike half promised . . . This isn't fiction, it's fact. It happened here in Kingsmarkham, although a long time ago. The Winchurch case?"

"Ah."

"I know it's a bit of a nerve asking, but would you read a manuscript for me?"

Wexford took a cup of coffee from a passing tray. "What for?"

"Well, in the interests of truth. Mike was going to tell me what he thought." Wexford looked at him dubiously. He had the highest respect and the deepest affection for Inspector Burden but he was one of the last people he would have considered as a literary critic. "To tell me if he thought it was accurate," the publisher said. "You see, it's worrying me. The author has discovered some new facts and they more or less prove Mrs. Winchurch's innocence." He hesitated. "Have you ever heard of a writer named Kenneth Gandolph?"

Wexford was saved from answering by the pounding of a gavel on the top table and the beginning of the speeches. A great many toasts had been drunk, several dozen telegrams read out, and the bride and groom had departed to change their clothes before he had an opportunity to reply to Ireland's question. And he was glad of the respite, for what he knew of Gandolph, though based on hearsay, was not flattering.

"Doesn't he write crime novels?" Wexford asked when the inquiry was repeated. "And the occasional examination of a real-life crime?"

Nodding, Ireland said, "It's good, this manuscript of his. We want to do it for next spring's list. It's about an eighty-year-old murder, sure, but people are still fascinated by it. I think this new version could cause quite a sensation."

"Florence Winchurch was hanged," said Wexford, "yet there was always some margin of doubt about her guilt. Where does Gandolph get his fresh facts from?"

"May I send you a copy of the typescript? You'll find all that in the introduction."

Wexford shrugged, then smiled. "I suppose so. You do realize I can't do more than maybe spot a mistake in forensics? I did say 'maybe,' mind." But his interest had already been caught. It made him say, "Florence was married here at St. Peter's, you know, and she also had her wedding reception here."

"And spent part of her honeymoon in Greece. It's all in Ken's book."

Burden and Jenny had come back into the room, he in a gray lounge suit, she in pale blue sprigged muslin. Wexford felt an absurd impulse of tenderness toward his assistant. It was partly caused by Jenny's hat which she would never wear again, would never have occasion to wear, would remove the minute they got into the car. But Burden was the sort of man who could never be happy with a woman who didn't have a hat as part of her "going-away" costume. Burden's own suit was eminently unsuitable for flying to Crete in June. They both looked very happy and embarrassed.

Mrs. Ireland seized her daughter in a crushing embrace.

"It's not forever, Mother," said Jenny. "It's only for two weeks."

"Well, in a way," said Burden. He shook hands gravely with his own son, down from Reading University for the weekend, and planted a kiss on his daughter's forehead. Must have been reading novels, Wexford thought, grinning to himself.

"Good luck, Mike," he said.

The bride took his hand and put a soft cool kiss onto the corner of his mouth. Say I'm growing old but add, Jenny kissed me.[7] He didn't say that aloud. He nodded and smiled and took his wife's arm and frowned at Sylvia's naughty boys like the patriarch he was. Burden and Jenny went out to the car which had *Just Married* written in lipstick on the rear window and a shoe tied on the back.

There was a clicking of handbag clasps, a flurry of hands, and then a tempest of confetti broke over them.

The house stood isolated, some twenty yards back from the Myfleet Road. Plumb in the center of its façade was a plaque bearing the date 1896. Wexford had often thought that there seemed to have been positive intent on the part of late-Victorian builders to design and erect houses that were not only ugly, complex, and inconvenient, but also distinctly sinister in appearance. The Limes, though well maintained and set in a garden as multicolored, cushiony, and floral as a quilt, nevertheless kept this sinister quality.

Without being able to define exactly how, Wexford could see that, in relation to the walls, the proportions of the sash windows were wrong. A turret grew out of each of the front corners, and each of these turrets was topped by a conical roof, giving the place the look of a cross between Balmoral Castle and a hotel in Kitzbühel. The lime

---

7 **Say . . . Jenny kissed me:** a reference to a famous poem by Leigh Hunt (1784–1859) that begins "Jenny kissed me when we met, . . . " and ends with the lines quoted by Wexford.

trees which gave the house its name had been lopped so many times since their planting at the turn of the century that now they were squat and misshapen.

In the days of the Winchurches it had been called Paraleash House. But this name, of historical significance for its relation to the ancient manor of Paraleash, had been changed specifically on account of the murder of Edward Winchurch. Even so, the house had stood empty for ten years. Then it had found a buyer a year or so before the First World War, a man who was killed in that war. Its present owner had occupied it for half a dozen years, and in the time intervening between then and 1918 it had been variously a nursing home, the annex of an agricultural college, and a private school, before reverting to the purpose for which it had been built, a dwelling house. The owner was a retired brigadier. As he emerged from the front door with two sealyhams[8] on a lead, Wexford retreated to his car and drove home.

It was Monday evening and Burden's marriage was two days old. Monday was also the evening of Dora's pottery class, the fruits of which, bruised-looking and not invariably symmetrical, were scattered haphazardly about the room like windfalls. Hunting along his book-shelves for F. Tennyson Jesse's *When the Summer is Shed* and *The Trial of Florence Winchurch* in the Notable British Trials Series, he nearly knocked over one of these rotund yet lopsided objects. With a sigh of relief that it was unharmed, he set about refreshing his memory with the help of Miss Jesse's classic.

Florence May Anstruther had been nineteen at the time of her marriage to Edward Winchurch and he forty-seven. She was a good-looking fair-haired girl, rather tall and Junoesque, the daughter of a Kingsmarkham chemist—that is, a pharmacist, for her father had kept a shop on High Street. In 1895 this damned her as of no account in the social hierarchy, and few people would have bet much on her chances of marrying well. But she did.

Winchurch was a barrister who, at this stage of his life, practiced law more from inclination than need. His father, a Sussex landowner, had died some three years before and had left him what for the last decade of the nineteenth century was an enormous fortune—£200,000. Presumably, he had been attracted to Florence by her

---

8 **sealyham:** a terrier bred in Wales. It has a white coat with brown markings on the head and ears.

youth, her looks, and her ladylike ways. She had been given the best education, including six months at a finishing school, that the chemist could afford. Winchurch's attraction for Florence was generally supposed to have been solely his money.

They were married in June 1895 at the parish church of St. Peter's, Kingsmarkham, and went on a six-months' honeymoon, touring Italy, Greece, and the Swiss Alps. When they returned home, Winchurch took a lease of Sewingbury Priory while building began on Paraleash House, and it may have been that those conical roofs on those turrets were inspired directly by what Florence had seen on her Alpine travels. They moved into the new house, which was lavishly furnished, in May 1896, and Florence settled down to the life of a Victorian lady with a wealthy husband and a staff of indoor and outdoor servants—a vapid life at best, even if alleviated by a brood of children. But Florence was to have no children.

Once or twice a week Edward Winchurch went up to London by the train from Kingsmarkham as commuters had done before and have been doing ever since. Florence gave orders to her cook, arranged the flowers, paid and received calls, read novels, and devoted a good many hours a day to her face, her hair, and her dress. Local opinion of the couple at that time seemed to have been that they were as happy as most people, that Florence had done very well for herself and knew it, and Edward not so badly as had been predicted.

In the autumn of 1897 a young doctor of medicine bought a practice in Kingsmarkham and came to live there with his unmarried sister. Their name was Fenton. Frank Fenton was an extremely handsome man, twenty-six years old, six feet tall, with jet-black hair, a Byronic eye, and an arrogant lift to his chin. The sister was called Ada, and she was neither good-looking nor arrogant, being partly crippled by poliomyelitis which had left her with one leg badly wasted and paralyzed.

It was ostensibly to befriend Ada Fenton that Florence first began calling at the Fentons' house on Queen Street. Florence professed great affection for Ada, took her about in her carriage, and offered her the use of it whenever she had to go any distance. From this it was an obvious step to persuade Edward that Frank Fenton should become the Winchurches' doctor. Within another few months young Mrs. Winchurch had become the doctor's mistress.

It was probable that Ada knew nothing, or next to nothing, about it. In the 1890s a young girl could be, and usually was, very innocent. At the trial it was stated by Florence's coachman that he would be sent to the Fentons' house several times a week to take Miss Fenton driving, while Ada's housemaid said that Mrs. Winchurch would arrive on foot soon after Miss Fenton had gone out and be admitted through a French door by the doctor himself.

During the winter of 1898 it seemed likely that Frank Fenton had performed an abortion on Florence Winchurch, and for some months afterward they met only at social gatherings and occasionally when Florence was visiting Ada. But their feelings for each other were too strong for them to bear separation and by the following summer they were again meeting at Fenton's house while Ada was out, and now also at Paraleash House on the days when Edward had departed for the law courts.

Divorce was difficult but by no means impossible or unheard-of in 1899. At the trial Frank Fenton said he wanted Mrs. Winchurch to ask her husband for a divorce. He would have married her in spite of the disastrous effect on his career. It was she, he said, who refused to consider it on the grounds that she did not think she could bear the fearful disgrace.

In January 1900 Florence went to London for the day and, among other purchases, bought at a grocer's two cans of herring fillets marinaded in a white wine sauce. It was rare for canned food to appear in the Winchurch household, and when Florence suggested that these herring fillets should be used in the preparation of a dish called *Filets de hareng marinés à la Rosette,* the recipe for which she had been given by Ada Fenton, the cook, Mrs. Eliza Holmes, protested that she could prepare it from fresh fish. Florence, however, insisted, one of the cans was used, and the dish was made and served to Florence and Edward at dinner. It was brought in by the parlor-maid, Alice Evans, as a savory or final course to a four-course meal. Although Florence had shown so much enthusiasm about the dish, she took none of it. Edward ate a moderate amount and the rest was removed to the kitchen where it was shared among Mrs. Holmes, Alice Evans, and the housemaid, Violet Stedman. No one suffered any ill effects. The date was January 30th, 1900.

Five weeks later, on March 6th, Florence asked Mrs. Holmes to make the dish again, using the remaining can, as her husband had liked it so much. This time Florence too partook of the herring dish, but when the remains of it were about to be removed by Alice to the kitchen, Florence advised her to tell the others not to eat it as she "thought it had a strange taste and was perhaps not quite fresh." However, although Mrs. Holmes and Alice abstained, Violet Stedman ate a larger quantity than had either Florence or Edward.

Florence, as was her habit, left Edward to drink his port alone. Within a few minutes a strangled shout was heard from the dining room and a sound as of furniture breaking. Florence and Alice Evans and Mrs. Holmes went into the room and found Edward Winchurch lying on the floor, a chair with one leg wrenched from its socket tipped over beside him and an overturned glass of port on the table. Florence approached him and he went into a violent convulsion, arching his back and baring his teeth, his hands grasping the chair in apparent agony.

John Barstow, the coachman, was sent to fetch Dr. Fenton. By this time Florence was complaining of stomach pains and seemed unable to stand. Fenton arrived, had Edward and Florence removed upstairs, and asked Mrs. Holmes what they had eaten. She showed him the empty herring-fillets can, and he recognized the brand as that by which a patient of a colleague of his had recently been infected with botulism, a virulent and usually fatal form of food poisoning. Fenton immediately assumed that it was *bacillus botulinus* which had attacked the Winchurches, and such is the power of suggestion that Violet Stedman now said she felt sick and faint.

Botulism causes paralysis, difficulty in breathing, and a disturbance of the vision. Florence appeared to be partly paralyzed and said she had double vision. Edward's symptoms were different. He continued to have spasms, was totally relaxed between spasms, and although he had difficulty in breathing and other symptoms of botulism, the onset had been exceptionally rapid for any form of food poisoning. Fenton, however, had never seen a case of botulism, and he supposed that the symptoms would vary greatly from person to person. He gave jalap and cream of tartar as a purgative and, in the absence of any known relatives of Edward Winchurch, he sent for Florence's father, Thomas Anstruther.

Edward's condition was steadily worsening, but Frank Fenton continued to insist that his illness and Florence's were due to botulism. If he was less innocent than was supposed, he had made a mistake in sending for Anstruther, for Florence's father insisted on a second opinion, and at ten o'clock went himself to the home of that very colleague of Fenton's who had recently witnessed a known case of botulism. This was Dr. Maurice Waterfield, twice Fenton's age, a popular man with a large practice in Stowerton. He looked at Edward Winchurch, at the agonized grin which overspread his features, and as Edward went into his last convulsive seizure, pronounced that he had been poisoned not by *bacillus botulinus* but by strychnine.

Edward died a few minutes afterward. Dr. Waterfield told Fenton that there was nothing physically wrong with either Florence or Violet

Stedman. The former was suffering from shock or "neurasthenia," the latter from indigestion brought on by overeating. The police were informed, an inquest took place, and after it Florence was immediately arrested and charged with murdering her husband by administering to him a noxious substance, to wit *strychnos nux vomica,* in a decanter of port wine.

Florence's trial took place in London at the Central Criminal Court. She was twenty-four years old, a beautiful woman, and was by now known to have been having a love affair with the young and handsome Dr. Fenton. As such, she and her case attracted national attention. Fenton had by then lost his practice, lost all hope of succeeding with another in the British Isles, and even before the trial his name had become a byword, and scurrilous doggerel was being sung about him and Florence in the music halls. But far from increasing his loyalty to Florence, this seemed to make him the more determined to dissociate himself from her. He appeared as the prosecution's principal witness, and it was his evidence which sent Florence to the gallows.

Fenton admitted his relationship with Florence but said that he had told her it must end. The only possible alternative was divorce and ultimately marriage to himself. In early January 1900 Florence had been calling on his sister Ada, and he had come in to find them looking through a book of recipes. One of the recipes called for the use of herring fillets marinaded in white wine sauce, the mention of which had caused him to tell them about a case of botulism which a patient of Dr. Waterfield's was believed to have contracted from eating the contents of a can of just such fillets. He had named the brand and advised his sister not to buy any of that kind.

When, some six or seven weeks later, he was called to the dying Edward Winchurch, the cook had shown him an empty can of that very brand. In his opinion, Mrs. Winchurch herself was not ill at all, was not even ill from "nerves" but was shamming. The judge said that he was not there to give his opinion, but the warning came too late. The point had already been made to the jury.

Asked if he was aware that strychnine had therapeutic uses in small quantities, Fenton said he was but that he kept none in his dispensary. In any case, his dispensary was kept locked and the cupboards inside it were also locked, so it would have been impossible for Florence to have entered the room or to have appropriated anything while on a visit to Ada. Ada Fenton was not called as a witness. She was ill, suffering from what her doctor, Dr. Waterfield, called "brain fever."

The prosecution's case was that, in order to inherit Edward's fortune and marry Dr. Fenton, Florence Winchurch had attempted to poison her husband with infected fish, or fish she had good reason to suppose might be infected. When this failed she saw to it that the dish was provided again, and herself added strychnine to the port decanter. It was postulated that she obtained the strychnine from her father's pharmacy, without his knowledge, where it was kept in stock for the destruction of rats and moles. After her husband was taken ill, she herself simulated symptoms of botulism in the hope that the convulsions of strychnine poisoning would be confused with the paralysis and impeded breathing caused by the bacillus.

The defense tried to shift the blame to Frank Fenton, at least to suggest a conspiracy between him and Florence, but it was no use. The jury was out for forty minutes. They pronounced her guilty, the judge sentenced her to death, and she was hanged twenty-three days later.

After the execution Frank and Ada Fenton emigrated to the United States and settled in New England. Fenton's reputation had gone before him. He was never again able to practice as a doctor but worked as a traveling salesman for a firm of pharmaceutical manufacturers until his death in 1932. He never married. Ada, on the other hand, surprisingly enough, did. Ephraim Hurst fell in love with her in spite of her sickly constitution and withered leg. They were married in the summer of 1902 and by the spring of 1903 Ada Hurst was dead in childbirth.

By then Paraleash House had been renamed The Limes and lime trees planted to help conceal its forbidding yet fascinating façade from the curious passer-by . . .

The parcel from Carlyon Brent, the publisher, arrived in the morning with a polite covering letter from Amyas Ireland, grateful in anticipation. Wexford had never before seen a book in this embryo stage. The typescript, about 100,000 words long, was bound in red, and through a window in its cover appeared the provisional title: *Poison at Paraleash. A Reappraisal of the Winchurch Case* by Kenneth Gandolph.

"Remember all that fuss about Gandolph?" Wexford said to Dora across the coffee pot. "About four years ago?"

"Somebody confessed a murder to him, didn't they?"

"Well, maybe. While a prison visitor, he spent some time talking to Paxton, the bank robber, in Wormwood Scrubs. Paxton died a few months later, and Gandolph then published an article in a newspaper in which he said that during the course of their conversations Paxton had confessed to him that he was the perpetrator of the Conyngford murder in 1962. Paxton's widow protested, there was a heated correspondence, MPs wanting the libel laws extended to libeling the dead, Gandolph shouting about the power of truth. Finally, the by then retired Detective Chief Superintendent Warren of Scotland Yard ended all further controversy by issuing a statement to the press. He said Paxton couldn't have killed James Conyngford because on the day of Conyngford's death in Brighton, Warren's sergeant and a constable had Paxton under constant surveillance in London. In other words, he was never out of their sight."

"Why would Gandolph invent such a story, Reg?" said Dora.

"Perhaps he didn't. Paxton may have spun him all sorts of tales as a way of passing a boring afternoon. Who knows? On the other hand, Gandolph does rather set himself up as the elucidator of unsolved crimes. Years ago I believe he did find a satisfactory and quite reasonable solution to some murder in Scotland, and maybe it went to his head. Marshall, Groves and Folliott used to be his publishers. I wonder if they've refused this one because of the Paxton business, if it was offered to them first and they turned it down."

"But Mr. Ireland's people have taken it," Dora pointed out.

"Mm-mm. But they're not falling over themselves with enthusiasm, are they? They're scared. Ireland hasn't sent me this so I can check up on the police procedural part. What the hell do I know about police procedure in 1900? He's sent it to me in the hope that if Gandolph's been up to his old tricks I'll spot what they are."

The working day presented no opportunity for a look at *Poison at Paraleash,* but at eight o'clock that night Wexford opened the package and read Gandolph's long introduction. He found himself growing interested, then deeply fascinated. Gandolph began by writing that, as a criminologist, he had always been aware of the Winchurch case and of the doubt which many felt about Florence Winchurch's guilt. Therefore, when he was staying with friends in Boston, Massachusetts, some two years before and they spoke to him of an acquaintance of theirs who was the niece of one of the principals in the case, he had asked to be introduced to her. The niece was Ada Hurst's daughter Lina, still Miss Hurst, seventy-four years old and suffering from a terminal illness.

Miss Hurst showed no particular interest in the case. She had been brought up by her father and his second wife and had hardly known her uncle. All her mother's property had come into her possession, including the diary which Ada Fenton Hurst had kept for three years prior to Edward Winchurch's death. Lina Hurst told Gandolph she had kept the diary for sentimental reasons but that he might borrow it and after her death she would see he got it.

Within weeks Lina Hurst did die and her stepbrother, who was her executor, had the diary sent to Gandolph. He had read it carefully and had been enormously excited by certain entries because, in his view, they incriminated Frank Fenton and exonerated Florence Winchurch. Here Wexford turned back a few pages and noted the author's dedication: *In memory of Miss Lina Hurst, of Cambridge, Massachusetts, without whose help this reappraisal would have been impossible.*

More than this he had no time to read that evening, but he returned to it on the following day. The diary, it appeared, was a five-year one. At the top of each page was the date—for example, April 1—and beneath that five spaces each, headed 18 . . . There was room for the diarist to write perhaps forty or fifty words in each space. On the January 1 page, in the number of the year, the 8 had been crossed out and a 9 substituted, and so it went on for every subsequent entry until March 6, after which no more entries were made until the diarist resumed in December 1900 by which time she and her brother were in Boston.

Wexford proceeded to Gandolph's first chapters. The story he had to tell was substantially the same as F. Tennyson Jesse's, and it was not until he came to chapter five and the weeks preceding the crime that he began to concentrate on the character of Frank Fenton. He suggested that Fenton wanted Mrs. Winchurch for the money and property she would inherit on her husband's death. Far from encouraging Florence to seek a divorce, he urged her never to let her husband suspect her preference for another man. Divorce would have left Florence penniless and homeless and have ruined his career. Fenton had known that it was only by making away with Winchurch and so arranging things that the death appeared natural, that he could have Florence, the money, and his career.

There was only his word for it, said Gandolph, that he had spoken to Florence of botulism and had warned her against those particular canned herrings. Of course he had never seriously expected those cans to infect Winchurch, but that the fish should be eaten by him was necessary to his plans. On the night before Winchurch's death, after dining with his sister at Paraleash House, he had introduced strychnine into the port decanter. He had also, Gandolph suggested, contrived to bring the conversation round to a discussion of food and to fish dishes of which he would have said he was fond. From that it would have been a short step to get Winchurch to admit how much he had enjoyed *Filets de hareng marinés à la Rosette* and ask Florence to have them served again on the following day.

Wexford paused here, questioning the writer's assumptions. He didn't think it would have been a short step; to him it seemed that the difficulties of making a man put such a remote and haphazard request were nearly insuperable. But perhaps Gandolph was implying that Edward Winchurch, a mild and not very strong-willed man, had been easily led, and within a few more pages he understood that this was the implication. Edward, apparently, would have been highly likely to take his doctor's advice even when in health, even on such a matter as what he should eat for the fourth course of his dinner, while Edward's wife did everything her lover, if not her husband, told her to do.

It was no surprise to Frank Fenton to be called out on the following evening to a man whose spasms only he would recognize as symptomatic of having swallowed strychnine. The arrival of Dr. Waterfield was an unlooked-for circumstance. Once Winchurch's symptoms had been defined as arising from strychnine poisoning, there was nothing left for Fenton to do but shift the blame to his mistress. Gandolph suggested that Fenton attributed the source of the strychnine to Anstruther's chemist's shop out of revenge on Anstruther for calling in Waterfield and thus frustrating his own hopes.

And what grounds had Gandolph for believing all this? Certain entries in Ada Hurst's diary. Wexford read them slowly and carefully.

For February 27, 1900, she had written, filling the entire small space: *Very cold. Leg painful again today. FW sent round the carriage and had John drive me to Pomfret. Compton says rats in the cellars and old stables. Dined at home with F. F says rats carry leptospiral jaundice, must be got rid of.*

February 28: *Drove in FW's carriage to call on old Mrs. Paget. FW still there, having tea with F when I returned. I hope there is no harm in it. Dare I warn F?*

February 29: *F destroyed twenty rats with strychnine from his dispensary. What a relief!*

March 1: *Heard poor old Mrs. Paget passed away in the night. A merciful release. Compton complained about the rats again. Warmer this evening and raining.*

There was no entry for March 2.

March 3: *Annie gave notice, she is getting married. Shall be sorry to lose her. Would not go out in carriage for fear of leaving FW too much alone with F. To bed early as leg most painful.*

March 4: *My birthday. 26 today and an old maid now, I think. FW drove over, brought me beautiful Indian shawl. She is always kind. Invited F and me to dine tomorrow.*

There was no entry for March 5, and the last entry for nine months was the one for March 6: *Dined last night at Paraleash House, six guests besides ourselves and the W's. F left cigar case in the dining room, went back after seeing me home. I hope and pray there is no harm.*

Gandolph was evidently basing his case on the entries for February 29th and March 6th. In telling the court he had no strychnine in his dispensary, Fenton had told a lie. He had had an obvious opportunity for the introduction of strychnine into the decanter when he returned to Paraleash House to retrieve his cigar case, and when he no doubt took care that he entered the dining room alone.

The next day Wexford carefully reread the chapters in which the new information was contained and he studied with concentration the chapters concerning the diary. But unless Gandolph was simply lying about the existence of the diary and, or, of those two entries—something which he would hardly dare to do—there seemed no reason to differ from his inference. Florence Winchurch was innocent, Frank Fenton was the murderer of Edward. But Wexford wished Burden were there so that they might have one of their often acrimonious but always fruitful discussions. Somehow, with old Mike to argue against him and put up opposition, he felt things might have been better clarified.

And the morning brought news of Burden, if not of the inspector himself, in the form of a postcard from Agios Nikolaios. The blue Aegean, a rocky escarpment, green pines. Who but Burden, as Wexford remarked to Dora, would send postcards while on his honeymoon? The post also brought a parcel from Carlyon Brent. It contained books, a selection from the publishing house's current list as a present for Wexford, and on a compliments slip accompanying them, a note from Amyas Ireland. *I shall be in Kingsmarkham with my people at the weekend. Can we meet? AI*

The books were the latest novel about Regency London—*The Golden Reticule,* by Camilla Barnet; *Put Money in Thy Purse,* the biography of Vassili Vandrian, the financier; the memoirs of Sofya Bolkonska, Bolshoi ballerina; an omnibus version of three novels of farming life by Giles de Coverley; the *Cosmos Book of Stars and Calendars;* and Vernon Trevor's short stories, *Raise Me Up, Samuel.* Wexford wondered if he would ever have time to read them, but he enjoyed looking at them, their handsome glossy jackets, and smelling the civilized, aromatic, slightly acrid print smell of them. At ten he phoned Amyas Ireland, thanked him for the present, and said he felt reasonably—well, thoroughly really—satisfied about Gandolph's book.

"But we can talk about it?"

"Sure. I'll be here all Saturday and Sunday."

"Let me take you and Mrs. Wexford out to dinner on Saturday night," said Ireland.

But Dora refused. She would be an embarrassment to both of them, she said; they could have their talk much better without her, and she could spend the evening at home having a shot at making a coil pot on her own. So Wexford went alone to meet Ireland in the bar of the Olive and Dove.

"I suppose," Wexford said, accepting a glass of Moselle, "that we can dispense with the fiction that you wanted me to read *Poison at Paraleash* to check on police methods and court procedure? Not to put too fine a point on it, you were afraid that Gandolph might be up to his old tricks again."

"Oh, well now, come," said Ireland. He seemed thinner than ever. He looked about him, he looked at Wexford, made a face, wrinkling up nose and mouth. "Well, if you must put it like that—yes."

"There may not have been any tricks, though, may there? Paxton couldn't have murdered James Conyngford, but that doesn't mean he didn't tell Gandolph he did murder him. Certainly the people who give Gandolph information seem to die very conveniently afterwards. He picks on the dying—first Paxton, then Lina Hurst. I suppose you've seen this diary?"

"Oh, yes. We shall be using reproductions of the two relevant pages."

"No possibility of forgery?"

Ireland looked unhappy. "Ada Hurst wrote a very stylized hand, what's called a *Ronde* hand,[9] which she had obviously taught herself. It would be easy to forge. Shall I submit it to a handwriting expert?"

"I think it's genuine." As Ireland's face grew less anxious, Wexford continued to comfort him. "I take it that it was not unusual for Ada Hurst to leave blanks as she did for March second and March fifth?"

---

9 *Ronde* **hand:** *Ronde* is French for "round"; that is, the letters in the handwriting
   are rounded rather than spiky.

Ireland nodded. "Quite usual. Every month there were half a dozen days on which she made no entries." A waiter came up to them with two large menus. "I'll have the *bouillabaisse* and the lamb *en croûte* and the *médaillon* potatoes and French beans," said Ireland.

"*Consommé* and then the Parma ham," said Wexford austerely. When the waiter had gone he grinned at Ireland. "Pity they don't do *Filets de hareng à la Rosette*. It might have provided us with the authentic atmosphere." He was silent for a moment, savoring the delicate tangy wine. "I take it," he said, "that you've checked that 1900 genuinely was a Leap Year?"

"All first years of a century are."

Wexford considered, thought about it. "Yes, of course, all years divisible by four are Leap Years."

"I must say it's a great relief to me you're so happy about it."

"I wouldn't quite say that," said Wexford.

They went into the dining room and were shown, at Ireland's request, to a sheltered corner table. A waiter brought a bottle of Château de Portets 1973. Wexford looked at the basket of rolls, croissants, little plump brioches, miniature wholemeal loaves, and Italian sticks; he swallowed his desire and refused with an abrupt shake of the head. Ireland took two croissants.

"What exactly do you mean?" he said.

"It strikes me as being odd," said the chief inspector, "that in the entry for February twenty-ninth Ada Hurst says that her brother destroyed twenty rats with strychnine, yet in the entry for March first that Compton, whom I take to be the gardener, is still complaining about the rats. Why wasn't he told how effective the strychnine had been? Hadn't he been taken into Fenton's confidence about the poisoning? Or was twenty only a very small percentage of the horde of rats which infested the place?"

"Right. It is odd. What else?"

"I don't know why, on March sixth, she mentions Fenton's returning for the cigar case. It wasn't interesting and she was limited for space. She doesn't record the name of a single guest at the dinner party, doesn't say what any of the women wore, but she carefully notes that her brother had left his cigar case in the Paraleash House dining room and had to go back for it. Why did she write that?"

"Oh, surely because by now she was nervous whenever Frank was alone with Florence."

"But he wouldn't have been alone with Florence. Winchurch would have been there." Wexford put forward his objection about Fenton's alleged manipulation of Winchurch to have the herring dish served to him on March 6th, and Ireland said he would mention this to Gandolph. They discussed the typescript throughout the meal, and later pored over it, Ireland with his brandy, Wexford with coffee. But the outcome was that the new facts were really new and, moreover, were sound, and that Carlyon Brent could safely publish the book in the spring.

Wexford got home to find Dora sitting with a wobbly looking half-finished coil pot beside her, and deep in the *Cosmos Book of Stars and Calendars.*

"Reg, did you know that for the Greeks the year began on Midsummer Day? And that the Chinese and Jewish calendars have twelve months in some years and thirteen in others?"

"I can't say I did."

"We avoid that, you see, by using the Gregorian Calendar and correct the error by making every fourth year a Leap Year. You really must read this book, it's fascinating."

But Wexford's preference was for the Vassili Vandrian and the farming trilogy, though with little time to read he hadn't completed a single one of these works by the time Burden returned on the following Monday week. Burden had a fine even tan but for his nose which had peeled.

"Have a good time?" said Wexford with automatic politeness.

"What a question," said the inspector, "to ask a man who has just come back from his honeymoon. Of course I had a good time." He cautiously scratched his nose. "What have you been up to?"

"Seeing something of your brother-in-law. He got me to read a typescript."

"Ha!" said Burden. "I know what that was. He said something about it, but he knew Gandolph'd get short shrift from me. A devious liar if ever there was one. It beats me what sort of satisfaction a man can get out of the kind of fame that comes from foisting on the public stories he *knows* aren't true. All that about Paxton was a pack of lies, and I've no doubt he bases his new version of the Winchurch case on another pack of lies. He's not interested in the truth, he's only interested in being known as the great criminologist and the man who shows the police up for fools."

"Come on, Mike," said Wexford, "that's a bit sweeping. I told Ireland I thought it would be okay to go ahead and publish."

Burden's face wore an expression that was almost a caricature of sophisticated, scathing knowingness. "Well, of course I haven't seen it, so I can't say. I'm basing my objection to Gandolph on the Paxton affair. Paxton never confessed to any murder and Gandolph knows it."

"You can't say that for sure."

Burden sat down. He tapped his fist lightly on the corner of the desk. "I *can* say. I knew Paxton, you see. I knew him well."

"I didn't know that."

"No, it was years back, before I came here. In Eastbourne it was, when Paxton was with the Garfield gang. In the force down there we knew it was useless ever trying to get Paxton to talk. He *never* talked. I don't mean he just didn't give away any info, I mean he didn't answer when you spoke to him. Various times when we tried to interrogate him he just maintained this total silence.

"A mate of his told me years ago he'd made it a rule not to talk to policemen or social workers or lawyers or any what you might call establishment people, and he never had. He talked to his wife and his kids and his mates all right. But I remember once he was in the dock at Lewes Assizes and the judge addressed him. He just didn't answer, he wouldn't, and the judge—it was old Clydesdale—sent him down for contempt. So don't tell me Paxton made any sort of confession to Kenneth Gandolph, not *Paxton*."

The effect of all this was to reawaken all Wexford's former doubts. He trusted Burden, he had a high opinion of his opinion. It looked as if Gandolph had chosen Paxton as the Conyngford murderer because he knew the old lag never talked, never would defend himself, and was dying anyway. Had he chosen to falsify Ada Fenton Hurst's diary because Lina Hurst also hadn't long to live?

Wexford began to wish he had advised Ireland to have tests made to determine the age of the ink used in the February 29th and March 6th entries, or to have the writing examined by a handwriting expert. Yet if Ada Hurst had had a stylized hand self-taught in adulthood . . . what good were handwriting experts anyway? Not much, in his experience. And of course Ireland couldn't suggest to Gandolph that the ink be tested without offending the man to such an extent that he would refuse publication of *Poison at Paraleash* at Carlyon Brent.

But Wexford was suddenly certain that those two entries were false and that Gandolph had forged them. Very subtly and cunningly he had forged them, having judged and judged correctly, that the addition to the diary of just thirty-four words would alter the whole balance of the Winchurch case and shift the guilt from Florence to her lover.

Thirty-four words. Wexford had made a copy of the diary entries and now he looked at them again. February 29: *F destroyed twenty rats with strychnine from his dispensary. What a relief!* March 6: *F left cigar case in the dining room, went back after seeing me home. I hope and pray there is no harm.* There were no anachronisms—men certainly used cigar cases in 1900—no divergence from Ada's usual style. He could see no permissible way of proving forgery, so he tried to put the Winchurch case out of his mind and concentrate on *Put Money in Thy Purse.* The phone rang as he was getting into the last chapter. It was Jenny Burden. Would he and Dora come to dinner on Saturday? Her parents would be there, and her brother.

Wexford said Dora was out to her pottery class, but, yes, they would love to, and had she had a nice time in Crete?

"How *sweet* of you to ask," said the bride. "No one else has. Thank you, we had a lovely time."

He had meant it when he had said they would love to, but still he didn't feel very happy about meeting Amyas Ireland again. He had a feeling that once the book was published some as yet unimagined Warren or Burden would turn up and denounce it. When he saw Ireland again he ought to say, "Don't do it, don't take the risk. Publish and be damned can have another meaning than the popular one." But how to give such a warning with no sound reason for giving it, with nothing but one of those vague feelings, this time of foreboding, which had so assisted him yet run him into so much trouble in the past?

No, there was nothing he could do. He sighed, finished the last chapter of the Vandrian book, and moved on to the farmer's fictionalized memoirs.

Afterward Wexford was in the habit of saying that he got more reading done that week than he had in years. Perhaps it had been a way of escape from fretful thought. But certainly he had passed a freakishly slack week, getting home most nights by six. He even read Miss Camilla Barnet's *The Golden Reticule.* And by Friday night there was nothing left but the *Cosmos Book of Stars and Calendars.*

It was a large party, Mr. and Mrs. Ireland and their son, Burden's daughter Pat, his sister-in-law from his first marriage and her husband, and of course the Burdens themselves. Jenny's face glowed with happiness and Aegean sunshine. She welcomed the Wexfords with kisses and brought them drinks served in their own wedding present to her.

The meeting with Amyas Ireland wasn't the embarrassment Wexford had feared it would be—had feared, that is, up till a few minutes before he and Dora had left home. And now he knew that he couldn't contain himself till after dinner, till the morning, or perhaps worse than that—a phone call on Monday morning. He asked his hostess if she would think him very rude to want to speak to her brother alone for five minutes.

She laughed. "Not rude at all. I think you must have got the world's most wonderful idea for a crime novel and Ammy's going to publish it. But I don't know where to put you unless it's the kitchen. And you," she said to her brother, "are not to eat anything, mind."

"I couldn't wait," Wexford said as they found themselves stowed away into the kitchen where every surface was necessarily loaded with the constituents of dinner for ten people. "I only found out this evening at the last minute before we were due to come here."

"It's something about the Winchurch book?"

Wexford said eagerly, "It's not too late, is it? I was worried it might be too late."

"Good God, no. We hadn't planned to start printing for a month." Ireland, who had seemed about to disobey his sister and help himself to a macaroon from a silver dish, suddenly lost his appetite. "This is serious?"

"Wait till you hear. I was waiting for my wife to finish dressing." Wexford grinned. "You should make it a rule to read your own books, you know. That's what I was doing, reading one of those books you sent me, and that's where I found it. You won't be able to publish *Poison at Paraleash*."

Wexford's smile went and he looked almost fierce. "I've no hesitation in saying that Kenneth Gandolph is a forger and a cheat and you'd be advised to have nothing to do with him in the future."

Ireland's eyes narrowed. "Better know it now than later. What did he do and how do you know?"

From his jacket pocket Wexford took the copy he had made of the diary entries. "I can't prove that the last entry, the one for March sixth that says, *F left his cigar case in the dining room, went back for it after seeing me home*—I can't prove that's forged. I only think it is. What I know for certain is that the entry for February twenty-ninth—that is a forgery."

"Isn't that the one about the strychnine?"

"*F destroyed twenty rats with strychnine from his dispensary. What a relief!*"

"How do you know it's forged?"

"Because the day itself didn't occur," said Wexford. "In 1900 there was no February twenty-ninth. It wasn't a Leap Year."

"Oh, yes, it was. We've been through all that before." Ireland's voice sounded both relieved and impatient. "All years divisible by four are Leap Years. All century years are divisible by four and 1900 was a century year. 1897 was the year she began the diary, following 1896 which was a Leap Year. Needless to say, there was no February twenty-ninth in 1897, 1898, or 1899—so there must have been one in 1900."

"It wasn't a Leap Year," said Wexford. "Didn't I tell you I found this out through that book of yours, the *Cosmos Book of Stars and Calendars*? There's a lot of useful information in there, and one of the bits of information is about how Pope Gregory composed a new civil calendar to correct the errors of the Julian Calendar. One of his rulings was that every fourth year should be a Leap Year except in certain cases—"

Ireland interrupted him. "I don't believe it!" he said with the voice of someone who knows he believes every word.

Wexford shrugged. He went on, "Century years were not Leap Years unless they were divisible not by four but by four hundred. Therefore, 1600 would have been a Leap Year if the Gregorian Calendar had by then been adopted, and 2000 will be a Leap Year, but 1800 was not and 1900 was not. So in 1900 there was February twenty-ninth and Ada Hurst left the space on the blank for the very good reason that the day following February twenty-eighth was March first. Unluckily for him, Gandolph, you and me and most people, didn't know this—otherwise he would surely have inserted his strychnine entry into the blank space March second and his forgery might never have been discovered."

Ireland slowly shook his head at man's ingenuity or perhaps chicanery. "I'm very grateful to you. We should have looked, shouldn't we?"

"I'm glad Florence wasn't hanged in error," Wexford said as he went back to join the others. "Her marriage didn't begin with dearly beloved, but if she was afraid at the end it can't have been with amazement."

QUESTIONS FOR DISCUSSION

1. How does Wexford get involved in the Winchurch affair?

2. This is an intricate story about two crimes, and, in a sense, two detectives—one real and one, who calls himself a criminologist, deliberately false. Explain how the two crimes are linked.

3. In a detective story, the climax must be plausibly postponed until the detective has worked through the clues that point to a possible crime, or to the uncovering of the criminal. In a small group, discuss your reactions to the rising action in this story.

4. Did the author "play fair"? That is, did the author give you enough clues so that you could begin to see how the story would be resolved? Or were you totally surprised by the ending?

TOPICS FOR WRITING

1. In an essay, tell how the motif of marriage, marriage vows, and divorce runs through this story.

2. Using what you know about methods of criminal investigation today, tell how the Winchurch Affair would have been investigated had it happened last year.

SECTION THREE

FANTASY AND SCIENCE FICTION

Stories involving other worlds and other forms of life reach back to a time before writing, when the way people transmitted history and culture was through the spoken word only. Folktales, myths, and ballads, all recited from memory and later written down, contain accounts of underworlds and other worlds, people who could fly, beings who were transformed, either from human to animal or animal to human, animals who could talk, and other creatures unknown in the real world. All fiction is imaginary, but some of it does not bear much resemblance to the world as we know it. That is where fantasy and science fiction come in.

Fantasy and science fiction can both be set in this world or in other worlds in any time. Both can, and often do, have social and political meaning. Fantasy has elements of the supernatural or magic. Science fiction, as its name suggests, is rooted in scientific and technological truths or in the possibility of scientific advancements based on what is known. Thus *Alice's Adventures in Wonderland* (1865) by Lewis Carroll is fantasy, and H. G. Wells's *The War of the Worlds* (1898), in which the world is invaded by Martians, is science fiction. Or, as Thomas M. Disch writes in *The Dreams Our Stuff Is Made Of: How Science Fiction Conquered the World*, "Rocket ships are sf and magic carpets are fantasy, even though those who ride them might be similarly costumed and having almost the same adventures."

The fantasy stories of the 1800s and early 1900s owe many of their settings, themes, and effects to the Gothic novels of the 1700s. Gothic novels emphasized mysterious settings, brooding atmosphere, and supernatural events. However, modern geographic and scientific knowledge also influenced fantasy.

Edgar Allan Poe and Mary Shelley are often regarded as two of the most significant writers of fantasy in the 1800s, partly because they introduced something new into their fiction, something that made their work early *science* fiction, although the term wasn't used when they were writing. Shelley's *Frankenstein or the Modern Prometheus* (1818) is the story of Victor Frankenstein, who creates a living human out of body parts.

In France, Jules Verne was writing novels that combined fantasy with scientific possibilities in books such as *The Journey to the Center of the Earth* (1864) and *Twenty-thousand Leagues under the Sea* (1869). Other writers of the late 1800s who wrote popular adventure tales that included scientific elements are Samuel Butler, H. Rider Haggard, Robert Louis Stevenson (*The Strange Case of Dr. Jekyll and Mr. Hyde*, 1886), and Mark Twain (*A Connecticut Yankee in King Arthur's Court*, 1889).

Two of the most famous fantasies of the early 1900s enjoyed by children and adults alike were L. Frank Baum's *The Wonderful Wizard of Oz* (1900) and Kenneth Grahame's *The Wind in the Willows* (1908). (Legend has it that Baum, searching for a name for Dorothy's destination, happened to spot a file drawer with the alphabetical label O–Z.)

As the detective story begins with Arthur Conan Doyle, so science fiction as a popular form starts with the novels and short stories of H. G. Wells (1866–1946). Wells, whose brilliant fictional works were called scientific romances by critics of his day, was an English writer who studied biology at the Normal School of Science in London. There he came under the influence of T. H. Huxley, a strong believer in Charles Darwin's theories. Wells's novel *The Time Machine* (1895) is set far in the future and depicts a society divided into two classes, one of which serves as food for the other. *The Island of Dr. Moreau* (1896) is about a scientist who surgically transforms animals into human beings. *The Invisible Man* (1897) describes how a scientist discovers, to his downfall, how to become invisible. In *The First Men in the Moon* (1901), Wells wrote of a trip to the moon 68 years before the Apollo 11 lunar landing.

In the United States, the pulp magazines published both fantasy and science fiction, and Edgar Rice Burroughs was a writer who could provide both. In 1912, *All-Story* magazine published serially his "Under the Moons of Mars" (published in 1917 in book form as *A Princess of Mars*) and *Tarzan of the Apes*. Both books had many sequels published in several magazines and made Burroughs, whose writing focused on action and setting rather than characterization or theme, a wealthy and famous man. His hometown in California was renamed Tarzana.

Although Burroughs was sometimes called a one-plot writer, many pulp writers tried to emulate his successes. Jungle stories, barbarian stories, such as Robert Howard's Conan stories in the 1930s, and stories of lost worlds all followed, as well as the stories of Buck Rogers, an intrepid space adventurer, by Philip Francis Nowlan, introduced in 1928 in *Amazing* magazine.

Burroughs, and others, were actually writing science fiction before it was called science fiction. Hugo Gernsback, publisher of *Amazing Stories,* first used the term in 1929. (He initially called such stories scientifiction.) During the late 1930s and early 1940s, many of the most famous writers of science fiction began to publish in science-fiction magazines: James Blish, Arthur C. Clarke, Isaac Asimov, Robert A. Heinlein, and Theodore Sturgeon, to name a few.

Notable science fiction novels and stories throughout the years include Olaf Stapledon's *Last and First Men: A Story of the Near and Far Future* (1930); Aldous Huxley's *Brave New World* (1932); Isaac Asimov's "Strange Playfellow" (1940), the first story in his Robot series, "Nightfall" (1941), possibly the most famous science fiction story ever written, and "Foundation" (1942), the first story in his Foundation series; John Wyndham's *The Day of the Triffids* (1951); Ray Bradbury's *Martian Chronicles* (1951) and *Fahrenheit 451* (1953); Robert A. Heinlein's *Double Star* (1956); James Blish's *The Frozen Year* (1957); and Walter M. Miller's *A Canticle for Leibowitz* (1960). Readers of science fiction can easily complete this list for themselves.

In later years, popular fantasies include J. R. R. Tolkien's *The Hobbit* (1937), *The Lord of the Rings* (1954–56), and *The Silmarillion* (1977); T. H. White's tetralogy, *The Once and Future King*, based on the stories of King Arthur; Ursula Le Guin's books for young people, *A Wizard of Earthsea* (1968) and *The Farthest Shore* (1973), which won a National Book Award; and Richard Adams's *Watership Down* (1972). These books are set in various places and times.

The number of writers writing science fiction, fantasy, or both has ballooned in recent years. (The categories often overlap and sometimes merge into the genre of horror fiction.) Among the many popular science fiction and fantasy writers, both living and dead, are Isaac Asimov, Ray Bradbury, Marion Zimmer Bradley, Octavia Butler, Philip K. Dick, Thomas Disch, Harlan Ellison, Samuel L. Delany, Philip José Farmer, Frank Herbert, Damon Knight, Ursula Le Guin, Anne McCaffrey, Kim Stanley Robinson, Frederik Pohl, Clifford Simak, and Theodore Sturgeon. (The list is by no means exhaustive.) New topics and themes appeared in the 1980s and 1990s. Computers, genetic engineering, virtual reality, and artificial intelligence all figure in today's science fiction and have somewhat overshadowed robots, spaceships, and androids.

The stories and novels of magic realists have emerged as a kind of fantasy. **Magic realism**, originally descriptive of some modern Latin

American fiction, is a type of literature that describes magical or fantastical events within ordinary, real-world settings. These events do not particularly worry or astonish the characters, who accept that there are many unexplained happenings in everyday life. "The Very Old Man with Enormous Wings" by Gabriel García Márquez and Isabel Allende's *The House of the Spirits* are two examples of magic realism. Angela Carter, whose story is included in this chapter, is also sometimes known as a magic realist.

The World Science Fiction Society gives Hugo Awards (established in honor of Hugo Gernsback) to recognize outstanding achievement in science fiction or fantasy. The Science Fiction and Fantasy Writers of America, Inc. gives the Nebula Award annually and also bestows the Grand Master Award to recognize lifetime contributions to the field of science fiction.

Although critics quibble over definitions of fantasy and science fiction, and about which genre particular works belong to, most readers are less concerned with labels and judge science fiction and fantasy as they judge any literature. Is the story compelling? Is it inventive? Can I believe, at least while I'm reading the story, that the world the writer creates is plausible?

THE COURTSHIP OF MR. LYON

ANGELA CARTER (1940–1992)

Angela Carter was born in London, educated at the University of Bristol, where she received a B.A. in 1965. Her first novel, a tale of murder entitled *Shadow Dance*, appeared in 1966. (It was republished in the United States in 1967 as *Honeybuzzard*.) Among her subsequent books are *Several Perceptions* (1968, 1969), which won the Somerset Maugham Award and is about a young man who tries and fails to commit suicide; and *Heroes and Villains* (1969, 1970), set in a barbaric future world. *The Magic Toyshop* (1967), a fantasy book for young adults, won the John Llewelyn Rhys Memorial Prize. Her last novel, *Wise Children* (1992) concerns two siblings (twins) who have earned a living in both vaudeville and Hollywood.

Carter wrote radio scripts, poetry, and nonfiction and edited several anthologies. She also published three collections of short stories, including *The Bloody Chamber and Other Stories* (1979), in which "The Courtship of Mr. Lyon" appears. The book won the Cheltenham Festival Literary Prize.

Myth, fairy tale, fantasy, feminism, and social commentary are all present in Carter's work, much of which puzzled and annoyed some critics. The following story is based on an old tale.

■

Outside her kitchen window, the hedgerow glistened as if the snow possessed a light of its own; when the sky darkened towards evening, an unearthly, reflected pallor remained behind upon the winter's landscape, while still the soft flakes floated down. This lovely girl, whose skin possesses that same, inner light so you would have thought she, too, was made all of snow, pauses in her chores in the mean kitchen to look out at the country road. Nothing has passed that way all day; the road is white and unmarked as a spilled bolt of bridal satin.

Father said he would be home before nightfall.

The snow brought down all the telephone wires; he couldn't have called, even with the best of news.

The roads are bad. I hope he'll be safe.

But the old car, stuck fast in a rut, wouldn't budge an inch; the engine whirred, coughed, and died and he was far from home. Ruined, once; then ruined again, as he had learnt from his lawyers that very morning; at the conclusion of the lengthy, slow attempt to restore his fortunes, he had turned out his pockets to find the cash for petrol to take him home. And not even enough money left over to buy his Beauty, his girl-child, his pet, the one white rose she said she wanted; the only gift she wanted, no matter how the case went, how rich he might once again be. She had asked for so little and he had not been able to give it to her. He cursed the useless car, the last straw that broke his spirit; then, nothing for it but to fasten his old sheepskin coat around him, abandon the heap of metal and set off down the snow-filled lane to look for help.

Behind wrought-iron gates, a short, snowy drive performed a reticent flourish before a miniature, perfect Palladian[1] house that seemed to hide itself shyly behind snow-laden skirts of an antique cypress. It was almost night; that house, with its sweet, retiring, melancholy grace, would have seemed deserted but for a light that flickered in an upstairs window, so vague it might have been the reflection of a star, if any stars could have penetrated the snow that whirled yet more thickly. Chilled through, he pressed the latch of the gate and saw, with a pang, how, on the withered ghost of a tangle of thorns, there clung, still, the faded rag of a white rose.

---

1 **Palladian:** in the style of Italian architect Andrea Palladio, who lived in the 1500s.

The gate clanged loudly shut behind him; too loudly. For an instant, that reverberating clang seemed final, emphatic, ominous as if the gate, now closed, barred all within it from the world outside the walled, wintry garden. And, from a distance, though from what distance he could not tell, he heard the most singular sound in the world: a great roaring, as of a beast of prey.

In too much need to allow himself to be intimidated, he squared up to the mahogany door. This door was equipped with a knocker in the shape of a lion's head, with a ring through the nose; as he raised his hand towards it, it came to him this lion's head was not, as he had thought at first, made of brass, but, instead, of gold. Before, however, he could announce his presence, the door swung silently inward on well-oiled hinges and he saw a white hall where the candles of a great chandelier cast their benign light upon so many, many flowers in great, free-standing jars of crystal that it seemed the whole of spring drew him into its warmth with a profound intake of perfumed breath. Yet there was no living person in the hall.

The door behind him closed as silently as it had opened, yet, this time, he felt no fear although he knew by the pervasive atmosphere of a suspension of reality that he had entered a place of privilege where all the laws of the world he knew need not necessarily apply, for the very rich are often very eccentric and the house was plainly that of an exceedingly wealthy man. As it was, when nobody came to help him with his coat, he took it off himself. At that, the crystals of the chandelier tinkled a little, as if emitting a pleased chuckle, and the door of a cloakroom opened of its own accord. There were, however, no clothes at all in this cloakroom, not even the statutory[2] country-garden mackintosh to greet his own squirearchal sheepskin, but, when he emerged again into the hall, he found a greeting waiting for him at last—there was, of all things, a liver and white King Charles spaniel crouched with head intelligently cocked, on the kelim runner.[3] It gave him further, comforting proof of his unseen host's wealth and eccentricity to see the dog wore, in place of a collar, a diamond necklace.

The dog sprang to its feet in welcome and busily shepherded him (how amusing!) to a snug little leather-panelled study on the first floor, where a low table was drawn up to a roaring log fire. On the

---

2 **statutory:** required by a statute or law; here, so common as to seem necessary.

3 **kelim runner:** a woven carpet made in Turkey, Kurdistan, and elsewhere. It is often spelled Kilim.

table, a silver tray; round the neck of the whisky decanter, a silver tag with the legend: *Drink me,* while the cover of the silver dish was engraved with the exhortation: *Eat me,* in a flowing hand. This dish contained sandwiches of thick-cut roast beef, still bloody. He drank the one with soda and ate the other with some excellent mustard thoughtfully provided in a stoneware pot, and, when the spaniel saw to it he had served himself, she trotted off about her own business.

All that remained to make Beauty's father entirely comfortable was to find, in a curtained recess, not only a telephone but the card of a garage that advertised a twenty-four-hour rescue service; a couple of calls later and he had confirmed, thank God that there was no serious trouble, only the car's age and the cold weather . . . could he pick it up from the village in an hour? And directions to the village, but half a mile away, were supplied, in a new tone of deference, as soon as he described the house from where he was calling.

And he was disconcerted but, in his impecunious[4] circumstances, relieved to hear the bill would go on his hospitable if absent host's account; no question, assured the mechanic. It was the master's custom.

Time for another whisky as he tried, unsuccessfully, to call Beauty and tell her he would be late; but the lines were still down, although, miraculously, the storm had cleared as the moon rose and now a glance between the velvet curtains revealed a landscape as of ivory with an inlay of silver. Then the spaniel appeared again, with his hat in her careful mouth, prettily wagging her tail, as if to tell him it was time to be gone, that this magical hospitality was over.

As the door swung to behind him, he saw the lion's eyes were made of agate.

Great wreaths of snow now precariously curded the rose trees and, when he brushed against a stem on his way to the gate, a chill armful softly thudded to the ground to reveal, as if miraculously preserved beneath it, one last, single, perfect rose that might have been the last rose left living in all the white winter, and of so intense and delicate a fragrance it seemed to ring like a dulcimer on the frozen air.

How could his host, so mysterious, so kind, deny Beauty her present?

Not now distant but close to hand, close as the mahogany front door, rose a mighty, furious roaring; the garden seemed to hold its breath in apprehension. But still, because he loved his daughter, Beauty's father stole the rose.

---

4 **impecunious:** having little or no money.

At that, every window of the house blazed with furious light and a fugal[5] baying, as if a pride of lions, introduced his host.

There is always a dignity about great bulk, an assertiveness, a quality of being more *there* than most of us are. The being who now confronted Beauty's father seemed to him, in his confusion, vaster than the house he owned, ponderous yet swift, and the moonlight glittered on his great, mazy head of hair, on the eyes green as agate, on the golden hairs of the great paws that grasped his shoulders so that their claws pierced the sheepskin as he shook him like an angry child shakes a doll.

This leonine[6] apparition shook Beauty's father until his teeth rattled and then dropped him sprawling on his knees while the spaniel, darting from the open door, danced round them, yapping distractedly, like a lady at whose dinner party blows have been exchanged.

"My good fellow—" stammered Beauty's father; but the only response was a renewed roar.

"Good fellow? I am no good fellow! I am the Beast, and you must call me Beast, while I call you, Thief!"

"Forgive me for robbing your garden, Beast!"

Head of a lion; mane and mighty paws of a lion; he reared on his hind legs like an angry lion yet wore a smoking jacket of dull red brocade and was the owner of that lovely house and the low hills that cupped it.

"It was for my daughter," said Beauty's father. "All she wanted, in the whole world, was one white, perfect rose."

The Beast rudely snatched the photograph her father drew from his wallet and inspected it, first brusquely, then with a strange kind of wonder, almost the dawning of surmise. The camera had captured a certain look she had, sometimes, of absolute sweetness and absolute gravity, as if her eyes might pierce appearances and see your soul. When he handed the picture back, the Beast took good care not to scratch the surface with his claws.

"Take her her rose, then, but bring her to dinner," he growled; and what else was there to be done?

Although her father had told her of the nature of the one who waited for her, she could not control an instinctual shudder of fear when she

---

5 **fugal:** in the style of a fugue, a musical composition based on one or more short themes.

6 **leonine:** like a lion.

saw him, for a lion is a lion and a man is a man and, though lions are more beautiful by far than we are, yet they belong to a different order of beauty and, besides, they have no respect for us: why should they? Yet wild things have a far more rational fear of us than is ours of them, and some kind of sadness in his agate eyes, that looked almost blind, as if sick of sight, moved her heart.

He sat, impassive as a figurehead, at the top of the table; the dining room was Queen Anne,[7] tapestried, a gem. Apart from an aromatic soup kept hot over a spirit lamp, the food, though exquisite, was cold—a cold bird, a cold soufflé, cheese. He asked her father to serve them from a buffet and, himself, ate nothing. He grudgingly admitted what she had already guessed, that he disliked the presence of servants because, she thought, a constant human presence would remind him too bitterly of his otherness, but the spaniel sat at his feet throughout the meal, jumping up from time to time to see that everything was in order.

How strange he was. She found his bewildering difference from herself almost intolerable; its presence choked her. There seemed a heavy, soundless pressure upon her in his house, as if it lay under water, and when she saw the great paws lying on the arm of his chair, she thought: they are the death of any tender herbivore. And such a one she felt herself to be, Miss Lamb, spotless, sacrificial.

Yet she stayed, and smiled, because her father wanted her to do so; and when the Beast told her how he would aid her father's appeal against the judgment, she smiled with both her mouth and her eyes. But when, as they sipped their brandy, the Beast, in the diffuse, rumbling purr with which he conversed, suggested, with a hint of shyness, of fear of refusal, that she should stay here, with him, in comfort, while her father returned to London to take up the legal cudgels again, she forced a smile. For she knew with a pang of dread, as soon as he spoke, that it would be so and her visit to the Beast must be, on some magically reciprocal scale, the price of her father's good fortune.

Do not think she had no will of her own; only, she was possessed by a sense of obligation to an unusual degree and, besides, she would gladly have gone to the ends of the earth for her father, whom she loved dearly.

Her bedroom contained a marvellous glass bed; she had a bathroom, with towels thick as fleece and vials of suave unguents; and a little parlor

---

7 **Queen Anne:** having to do with a style of English architecture and furniture first popular in the reign of Queen Anne in the early 1700s.

of her own, the walls of which were covered with an antique paper of birds of paradise and Chinamen, where there were precious books and pictures and the flowers grown by invisible gardeners in the Beast's hot-houses. Next morning, her father kissed her and drove away with a renewed hope about him that made her glad, but, all the same, she longed for the shabby home of their poverty. The unaccustomed luxury about her she found poignant, because it gave no pleasure to its posses-sor and himself she did not see all day as if, curious reversal, she frightened him, although the spaniel came and sat with her, to keep her company. Today, the spaniel wore a neat choker of turquoises.

Who prepared her meals? Loneliness of the Beast; all the time she stayed there, she saw no evidence of another human presence but the trays of food had arrived on a dumb waiter inside the mahogany cup-board in her parlor. Dinner was eggs Benedict and grilled veal; she ate it as she browsed in a book she had found in the rosewood revolving bookcase, a collection of courtly and elegant French fairy tales about white cats who were transformed princesses and fairies who were birds. Then she pulled a sprig of muscat grapes from a fat bunch for her dessert and found herself yawning; she discovered she was bored. At that, the spaniel took hold of her skirt with its velvet mouth and gave a firm but gentle tug. She allowed the dog to trot before her to the study in which her father had been entertained and there, to her well-disguised dismay, she found her host, seated beside the fire with a tray of coffee at his elbow from which she must pour.

The voice that seemed to issue from a cave full of echoes, his dark, soft rumbling growl; after her day of pastel-colored idleness, how could she converse with the possessor of a voice that seemed an instrument created to inspire the terror that the chords of great organs bring? Fascinated, almost awed, she watched the firelight play on the gold fringes of his mane; he was irradiated, as if with a kind of halo, and she thought of the first great beast of the Apocalypse, the winged lion with his paw upon the Gospel, Saint Mark.[8] Small talk turned to dust in her mouth; small talk had never, at the best of times, been Beauty's forte, and she had little practice at it.

But he, hesitantly, as if he himself were in awe of a young girl who looked as if she had been carved out of a single pearl, asked after her

8 **Apocalypse . . . Saint Mark:** Revelation, the last book of the New Testament in the Bible, is sometimes called the Apocalypse. The symbol of St. Mark is a winged lion.

father's law case; and her dead mother; and how they, who had been so rich, had come to be so poor. He forced himself to master his shyness, which was that of a wild creature, and so, she contrived to master her own—to such effect that soon she was chattering away to him as if she had known him all her life. When the little cupid in the gilt clock on the mantelpiece struck its miniature tambourine, she was astonished to discover it did so twelve times.

"So late! You will want to sleep," he said.

At that, they both fell silent, as if these strange companions were suddenly overcome with embarrassment to find themselves together, alone, in that room in the depths of winter's night. As she was about to rise, he flung himself at her feet and buried his head in her lap. She stayed stock-still, transfixed; she felt his hot breath on her fingers, the stiff bristles of his muzzle grazing her skin, the rough lapping of his tongue and then, with a flood of compassion, understood: all he is doing is kissing my hands.

He drew back his head and gazed at her with his green, inscrutable eyes, in which she saw her face repeated twice, as small as if it were in bud. Then, without another word, he sprang from the room and she saw, with an indescribable shock, he went on all fours.

Next day, all day, the hills on which the snow still settled echoed with the Beast's rumbling roar: has master gone a-hunting? Beauty asked the spaniel. But the spaniel growled, almost bad-temperedly, as if to say, that she would not have answered, even if she could have.

Beauty would pass the day in her suite reading or, perhaps, doing a little embroidery; a box of colored silks and a frame had been provided for her. Or, well wrapped up, she wandered in the walled garden, among the leafless roses, with the spaniel at her heels, and did a little raking and rearranging. An idle, restful time; a holiday. The enchantment of that bright, sad pretty place enveloped her and she found that, against all her expectations, she was happy there. She no longer felt the slightest apprehension at her nightly interviews with the Beast. All the natural laws of the world were held in suspension, here, where an army of invisibles tenderly waited on her, and she would talk with the lion, under the patient chaperonage of the brown-eyed dog, on the nature of the moon and its borrowed light, about the stars and the substances of which they were made, about the variable transformations of the weather. Yet still his strangeness made her shiver; and when he helplessly fell before her to kiss her hand, as he did every night when they parted, she would retreat nervously into her skin, flinching at his touch.

The telephone shrilled; for her. Her father. Such news!

The Beast sunk his great head on to his paws. You will come back to me? It will be lonely here, without you.

She was moved almost to tears that he should care for her so. It was in her heart to drop a kiss upon his shaggy mane but, though she stretched out her hand towards him, she could not bring herself to touch him of her own free will, he was so different from herself. But, yes, she said; I will come back. Soon, before the winter is over. Then the taxi came and took her away.

You are never at the mercy of the elements in London, where the huddled warmth of humanity melts the snow before it has time to settle; and her father was as good as rich again, since his hirsute friend's lawyers had the business so well in hand that his credit brought them nothing but the best. A resplendent hotel; the opera, theaters; a whole new wardrobe for his darling, so she could step out on his arm to parties, to receptions, to restaurants, and life was as she had never known it, for her father had ruined himself before her birth killed her mother.

Although the Beast was the source of this new-found prosperity and they talked of him often, now that they were so far away from the timeless spell of his house it seemed to possess the radiant and finite quality of dream and the Beast himself, so monstrous, so benign, some kind of spirit of good fortune who had smiled on them and let them go. She sent him flowers, white roses in return for the ones he had given her; and when she left the florist, she experienced a sudden sense of perfect freedom, as if she had just escaped from an unknown danger, had been grazed by the possibility of some change but, finally, left intact. Yet, with this exhilaration, a desolating emptiness. But her father was waiting for her at the hotel; they had planned a delicious expedition to buy her furs and she was as eager for the treat as any girl might be.

Since the flowers in the shop were the same all the year round, nothing in the window could tell her that winter had almost gone.

Returning late from supper after the theater, she took off her earrings in front of the mirror; Beauty. She smiled at herself with satisfaction. She was learning, at the end of her adolescence, how to be a spoiled child and that pearly skin of hers was plumping out, a little, with high living and compliments. A certain inwardness was beginning to transform the lines around her mouth, those signatures of the personality, and her sweetness and her gravity could sometimes turn a mite petulant when things went not quite as she wanted them to go. You could not have said that her freshness was fading but she smiled at herself in mirrors a little too often, these days, and the face that smiled back was not quite the one she had seen contained in the Beast's agate eyes. Her face was acquiring, instead of beauty, a lacquer of the invincible prettiness that characterizes certain pampered, exquisite, expensive cats.

The soft wind of spring breathed in from the nearby park through the open window; she did not know why it made her want to cry.

There was a sudden urgent, scrabbling sound, as of claws, at her door.

Her trance before the mirror broke; all at once, she remembered everything perfectly. Spring was here and she had broken her promise. Now the Beast himself had come in pursuit of her! First, she was frightened of his anger; then, mysteriously joyful, she ran to open the door. But it was his liver and white spotted spaniel who hurled herself into the girl's arms in a flurry of little barks and gruff murmurings, of whimpering and relief.

Yet where was the well-brushed, jewelled dog who had sat beside her embroidery frame in the parlor with birds of paradise nodding on the walls? This one's fringed ears were matted with mud, her coat was dusty and snarled, she was thin as a dog that has walked a long way and, if she had not been a dog, she would have been in tears.

After that first, rapturous greeting, she did not wait for Beauty to order her food and water; she seized the chiffon hem of her evening dress, whimpered and tugged. Threw back her head, howled, then tugged and whimpered again.

There was a slow, late train that would take her to the station where she had left for London three months ago. Beauty scribbled a note for her father, threw a coat round her shoulders. Quickly, quickly, urged the spaniel soundlessly; and Beauty knew the Beast was dying.

In the thick dark before dawn, the station master roused a sleepy driver for her. Fast as you can.

It seemed December still possessed his garden. The ground was hard as iron, the skirts of the dark cypress moved on the chill wind with a mournful rustle and there were no green shoots on the roses as if, this year, they would not bloom. And not one light in any of the windows, only, in the topmost attic, the faintest smear of radiance on a pane. The thin ghost of a light on the verge of extinction.

The spaniel had slept a little, in her arms, for the poor thing was exhausted. But now her grieving agitation fed Beauty's urgency and, as the girl pushed open the front door, she saw, with a thrust of conscience, how the golden door knocker was thickly muffled in black crêpe.

The door did not open silently, as before, but with a doleful groaning of the hinges and, this time, on to perfect darkness. Beauty clicked her gold cigarette lighter; the tapers in the chandelier had drowned in their own wax and the prisms were wreathed with dreadful arabesques of cobwebs. The flowers in the glass jars were dead, as if nobody had had the heart to replace them after she was gone. Dust, everywhere; and it was cold. There was an air of exhaustion, of despair in the house and, worse, a kind of physical disillusion, as if its glamor had been sustained by a cheap conjuring trick and now the conjurer, having failed to pull the crowds, had departed to try his luck elsewhere.

Beauty found a candle to light her way and followed the faithful spaniel up the staircase, past the study, past her suite, through a house echoing with desertion up a little back staircase dedicated to mice and spiders, stumbling, ripping the hem of her dress in her haste.

What a modest bedroom! An attic, with a sloping roof, they might have given the chambermaid if the Beast had employed staff. A night light on the mantelpiece, no curtains at the windows, no carpet on the floor and a narrow, iron bedstead on which he lay, sadly diminished, his bulk scarcely disturbing the faded patchwork quilt, his mane a grayish rat's nest and his eyes closed. On the stick-backed chair where his clothes had been thrown, the roses she had sent him were thrust into the jug from the washstand but they were all dead.

The spaniel jumped up on the bed and burrowed her way under the scanty covers, softly keening.

"Oh, Beast," said Beauty. "I have come home."

His eyelids flickered. How was it she had never noticed before that his agate eyes were equipped with lids, like those of a man? Was it because she had only looked at her own face, reflected there?

"I'm dying, Beauty," he said in a cracked whisper of his former purr. "Since you left me, I have been sick. I could not go hunting, I found I had not the stomach to kill the gentle beasts, I could not eat. I am sick and I must die; but I shall die happy because you have come to say goodbye to me."

She flung herself upon him, so that the iron bedstead groaned, and covered his poor paws with her kisses.

"Don't die, Beast! If you'll have me, I'll never leave you."

When her lips touched the meat-hook claws, they drew back into their pads and she saw how he had always kept his fists clenched, but now, painfully, tentatively, at last began to stretch his fingers. Her tears fell on his face like snow and, under their soft transformation, the bones showed through the pelt, the flesh through the wide, tawny brow. And then it was no longer a lion in her arms but a man, a man with an unkempt mane of hair and, how strange, a broken nose, such as the noses of retired boxers, that gave him a distant, heroic resemblance to the handsomest of all the beasts.

"Do you know," said Mr. Lyon, "I think I might be able to manage a little breakfast today, Beauty, if you would eat something with me."

Mr. and Mrs. Lyon walk in the garden; the old spaniel drowses on the grass, in a drift of fallen petals.

QUESTIONS FOR DISCUSSION

1. At what point does this story first begin to take on aspects of fantasy?

2. The King Charles spaniel wears a diamond collar, and meals appear mysteriously in the Beast's wonderful house. What are some other examples of the combination of realism with fantasy?

3. How does the author evoke sympathy for the Beast?

4. What is the climax of the story?

5. What do you think is the theme of the story?

TOPICS FOR WRITING

1. Write a short tale entitled "How Mr. Lyon Became a Beast."

2. Find a version of the original story of Beauty and the Beast and in an essay compare and contrast it with "The Courtship of Mr. Lyon."

THE NINE BILLION NAMES OF GOD

ARTHUR C. CLARKE (born 1917)

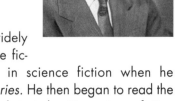

Arthur C. Clarke is one of the most widely read and influential of modern science fiction writers. He first became interested in science fiction when he discovered the pulp magazine *Amazing Stories*. He then began to read the works of Olaf Stapledon and H. G. Wells and started writing science fiction for a school magazine.

He was born in Minehead, Somerset, England, and was an auditor for His Majesty's Exchequer and Audit Department in London from 1936 to 1941, when he enlisted in the Royal Air Force as a radar instructor. After World War II, he received a B.Sc. degree with honors in physics and applied mathematics from Kings College, University of London. After publication of *Childhood's End* (1953), a novel, and *The Exploration of Space* (1951, revised 1979), nonfiction, he began to earn his living as a writer.

He has written over fifty books, fiction and nonfiction, many short stories, and won many awards for his writing. He was named Grand Master by the Science Fiction Writers of America in 1986. He collaborated with film director Stanley Kubrick on *2001: A Space Odyssey* and then wrote the book. He followed *2001* with *2010: Odyssey Two* (1982), *2061: Odyssey Three* (1988), and *3001: The Final Odyssey* (1997).

Other recent books include *Rendezvous with Rama* (1973, 1988) *Rama II* (with Gentry Lee) (1989), *The Garden of Rama* (with Gentry Lee) (1991), *The Ghost from the Grand Banks* (1990), and *The Hammer of God* (1993). *Astounding Days: A Science Fictional Autobiography* was published in 1989.

He has been host of two television series, *Arthur C. Clarke's Mysterious World* (1980) and *Arthur C. Clarke's World of Strange Powers* (1984). "The Nine Billion Names of God" was named to the science fiction hall of fame. Clarke has lived in Sri Lanka since 1956.

■

"This is a slightly unusual request," said Dr. Wagner, with what he hoped was commendable restraint. "As far as I know, it's the first time anyone's been asked to supply a Tibetan monastery with an Automatic Sequence Computer. I don't wish to be inquisitive, but I should hardly have thought that your—ah—establishment had much use for such a machine. Could you explain just what you intend to do with it?"

"Gladly," replied the lama,[1] readjusting his silk robes and carefully putting away the slide rule he had been using for currency conversions. "Your Mark V Computer can carry out any routine mathematical operation involving up to ten digits. However, for our work we are interested in *letters*, not numbers. As we wish you to modify the output circuits, the machine will be printing words, not columns of figures."

"I don't quite understand. . . ."

"This is a project on which we have been working for the last three centuries—since the lamasery[2] was founded, in fact. It is somewhat alien to your way of thought, so I hope you will listen with an open mind while I explain it."

"Naturally."

"It is really quite simple. We have been compiling a list which shall contain all the possible names of God."

"I beg your pardon?"

"We have reason to believe," continued the lama imperturbably, "that all such names can be written with not more than nine letters in an alphabet we have devised."

"And you have been doing this for three centuries?"

"Yes: we expected it would take us about fifteen thousand years to complete the task."

"Oh," Dr. Wagner looked a little dazed. "Now I see why you wanted to hire one of our machines. But exactly what is the *purpose* of this project?"

The lama hesitated for a fraction of a second, and Wagner wondered if he had offended him. If so, there was no trace of annoyance in the reply.

"Call it ritual, if you like, but it's a fundamental part of our belief. All the many names of the Supreme Being—God, Jehovah, Allah, and

---

1 **lama:** a Buddhist monk of Tibet or Mongolia.

2 **lamasery:** a monastery of lamas.

so on—they are only man-made labels. There is a philosophical problem of some difficulty here, which I do not propose to discuss, but somewhere among all the possible combinations of letters that can occur are what one may call the *real* names of God. By systematic permutation of letters, we have been trying to list them all."

"I see. You've been starting at AAAAAAA . . . and working up to ZZZZZZZ. . . ."

"Exactly—though we use a special alphabet of our own. Modifying the electromatic typewriters to deal with this is, of course, trivial. A rather more interesting problem is that of devising suitable circuits to eliminate ridiculous combinations. For example, no letter must occur more than three times in succession."

"Three? Surely you mean two."

"Three is correct: I am afraid it would take too long to explain why, even if you understood our language."

"I'm sure it would," said Wagner hastily. "Go on."

"Luckily, it will be a simple matter to adapt your Automatic Sequence Computer for this work, since once it has been programmed properly it will permute each letter in turn and print the result. What would have taken us fifteen thousand years it will be able to do in a hundred days."

Dr. Wagner was scarcely conscious of the faint sounds from the Manhattan streets far below. He was in a different world, a world of natural, not man-made, mountains. High up in their remote aeries these monks had been patiently at work, generation after generation, compiling their lists of meaningless words. Was there any limit to the follies of mankind? Still, he must give no hint of his inner thoughts. The customer was always right. . . .

"There's no doubt," replied the doctor, "that we can modify the Mark V to print lists of this nature. I'm much more worried about the problem of installation and maintenance. Getting out to Tibet, in these days, is not going to be easy."

"We can arrange that. The components are small enough to travel by air—that is one reason why we chose your machine. If you can get them to India, we will provide transport from there."

"And you want to hire two of our engineers?"

"Yes, for the three months that the project should occupy."

"I've no doubt that Personnel can manage that." Dr. Wagner scribbled a note on his desk pad. "There are just two other points—"

Before he could finish the sentence the lama had produced a small slip of paper.

"This is my certified credit balance at the Asiatic Bank."

"Thank you. It appears to be—ah—adequate. The second matter is so trivial that I hesitate to mention it—but it's surprising how often the obvious gets overlooked. What source of electrical energy have you?"

"A diesel generator providing fifty kilowatts at a hundred and ten volts. It was installed about five years ago and is quite reliable. It's made life at the lamasery much more comfortable, but of course it was really installed to provide power for the motors driving the prayer wheels."[3]

"Of course," echoed Dr. Wagner. "I should have thought of that."

The view from the parapet was vertiginous,[4] but in time one gets used to anything. After three months, George Hanley was not impressed by the two-thousand-foot swoop into the abyss or the remote checkerboard of fields in the valley below. He was leaning against the wind-smoothed stones and staring morosely at the distant mountains whose names he had never bothered to discover.

This, thought George, was the craziest thing that had ever happened to him. "Project Shangri-la,"[5] some wit back at the labs had christened it. For weeks now the Mark V had been churning out acres of sheets covered with gibberish. Patiently, inexorably, the computer had been rearranging letters in all their possible combinations, exhausting each class before going on to the next. As the sheets had emerged from the electromatic typewriters, the monks had carefully cut them up and pasted them into enormous books. In another week, heaven be praised, they would have finished. Just what obscure calculations had convinced the monks that they needn't bother to go on to words of ten, twenty, or a hundred letters, George didn't know. One of his recurring nightmares was that there would be some change of plan, and that the high lama (whom they'd naturally called Sam Jaffe, though he didn't look a bit like him) would suddenly announce that

---

3 **prayer wheel:** a cylinder inscribed with or containing prayers and used in devotions by Tibetan Buddhists.

4 **vertiginous:** tending to produce vertigo or dizziness.

5 **Shangri-la:** in James Hilton's novel *Lost Horizon* (1933), the mythical land of eternal youth, supposedly located somewhere in Tibet. The 1937 movie version starred Ronald Colman and Sam Jaffe.

the project would be extended to approximately A.D. 2060. They were quite capable of it.

George heard the heavy wooden door slam in the wind as Chuck came out onto the parapet beside him. As usual, Chuck was smoking one of the cigars that made him so popular with the monks—who, it seemed, were quite willing to embrace all the minor and most of the major pleasures of life. That was one thing in their favor: they might be crazy, but they weren't bluenoses.[6] Those frequent trips they took down to the village, for instance . . .

"Listen, George," said Chuck urgently. "I've learned something that means trouble."

"What's wrong? Isn't the machine behaving?" That was the worst contingency George could imagine. It might delay his return, and nothing could be more horrible. The way he felt now, even the sight of a TV commercial would seem like manna from heaven. At least it would be some link with home.

"No—it's nothing like that." Chuck settled himself on the parapet, which was unusual because normally he was scared of the drop. "I've just found what all this is about."

"What d'ya mean? I thought we knew."

"Sure—we know what the monks are trying to do. But we didn't know *why*. It's the craziest thing—"

"Tell me something new," growled George.

"—but old Sam's just come clean with me. You know the way he drops in every afternoon to watch the sheets roll out. Well, this time he seemed rather excited, or at least as near as he'll ever get to it. When I told him that we were on the last cycle he asked me, in that cute English accent of his, if I'd ever wondered what they were trying to do. I said, 'Sure'—and he told me."

"Go on: I'll buy it."

"Well, they believe that when they have listed all His names—and they reckon that there are about nine billion of them—God's purpose will be achieved. The human race will have finished what it was created to do, and there won't be any point in carrying on. Indeed, the very idea is something like blasphemy."

"Then what do they expect us to do? Commit suicide?"

"There's no need for that. When the list's completed, God steps in and simply winds things up . . . bingo!"

---

6 **bluenose:** a puritanical person.

"Oh, I get it. When we finish our job, it will be the end of the world."

Chuck gave a nervous little laugh.

"That's just what I said to Sam. And do you know what happened? He looked at me in a very queer way, like I'd been stupid in class, and said, 'It's nothing as trivial as *that*.'"

George thought this over for a moment.

"That's what I call taking the Wide View," he said presently. "But what d'you suppose we should do about it? I don't see that it makes the slightest difference to us. After all, we already knew that they were crazy."

"Yes—but don't you see what may happen? When the list's complete and the Last Trump doesn't blow—or whatever it is they expect—*we* may get the blame. It's our machine they've been using. I don't like the situation one little bit."

"I see," said George slowly. "You've got a point there. But this sort of thing's happened before, you know. When I was a kid down in Louisiana we had a crackpot preacher who once said the world was going to end next Sunday. Hundreds of people believed him—even sold their homes. Yet when nothing happened, they didn't turn nasty, as you'd expect. They just decided that he'd made a mistake in his calculations and went right on believing. I guess some of them still do."

"Well, this isn't Louisiana, in case you hadn't noticed. There are just two of us and hundreds of these monks. I like them, and I'll be sorry for old Sam when his lifework backfires on him. But all the same, I wish I was somewhere else."

"I've been wishing that for weeks. But there's nothing we can do until the contract's finished and the transport arrives to fly us out."

"Of course," said Chuck thoughtfully, "we could always try a bit of sabotage."

"Like hell we could! That would make things worse."

"Not the way I meant. Look at it like this. The machine will finish its run four days from now, on the present twenty-hours-a-day basis. The transport calls in a week. O.K.—then all we need to do is to find something that needs replacing during one of the overhaul periods—something that will hold up the works for a couple of days. We'll fix it, of course, but not too quickly. If we time matters properly, we can be down at the airfield when the last name pops out of the register. They won't be able to catch us then."

"I don't like it," said George. "It will be the first time I ever walked out on a job. Besides, it would make them suspicious. No, I'll sit tight and take what comes."

"I *still* don't like it," he said, seven days later, as the tough little mountain ponies carried them down the winding road. "And don't you think I'm running away because I'm afraid. I'm just sorry for those poor old guys up there, and I don't want to be around when they find what suckers they've been. Wonder how Sam will take it?"

"It's funny," replied Chuck, "but when I said good-by I got the idea he knew we were walking out on him—and that he didn't care because he knew the machine was running smoothly and that the job would soon be finished. After that—well, of course, for him there just isn't any After That. . . ."

George turned in his saddle and stared back up the mountain road. This was the last place from which one could get a clear view of the lamasery. The squat, angular buildings were silhouetted against the afterglow of the sunset: here and there, lights gleamed like port-holes in the side of an ocean liner. Electric lights, of course, sharing the same circuit as the Mark V. How much longer would they share it? wondered George. Would the monks smash up the computer in their rage and disappointment? Or would they just sit down quietly and begin their calculations all over again?

He knew exactly what was happening up on the mountain at this very moment. The high lama and his assistants would be sitting in their silk robes, inspecting the sheets as the junior monks carried them away from the typewriters and pasted them into the great volumes. No one would be saying anything. The only sound would be the incessant patter, the never-ending rainstorm of the keys hitting the paper, for the Mark V itself was utterly silent as it flashed through its thousands of calculations a second. Three months of this, thought George, was enough to start anyone climbing up the wall.

"There she is!" called Chuck, pointing down into the valley. "Ain't she beautiful!"

She certainly was, thought George. The battered old DC3 lay at the end of the runway like a tiny silver cross. In two hours she would be bearing them away to freedom and sanity. It was a thought worth savoring like a fine liqueur. George let it roll round his mind as the pony trudged patiently down the slope.

The swift night of the high Himalayas was now almost upon them. Fortunately, the road was very good, as roads went in that region, and they were both carrying torches. There was not the slightest danger, only a certain discomfort from the bitter cold. The sky overhead was perfectly clear, and ablaze with the familiar, friendly stars. At least there would be no risk, thought George, of the pilot being unable to take off because of weather conditions. That had been his only remaining worry.

He began to sing, but gave it up after a while. This vast arena of mountains, gleaming like whitely hooded ghosts on every side, did not encourage such ebullience. Presently George glanced at his watch.

"Should be there in an hour," he called back over his shoulder to Chuck. Then he added, in an afterthought: "Wonder if the computer's finished its run. It was due about now."

Chuck didn't reply, so George swung round in his saddle. He could just see Chuck's face, a white oval turned toward the sky.

"Look," whispered Chuck, and George lifted his eyes to heaven. (There is always a last time for everything.)

Overhead, without any fuss, the stars were going out.

QUESTIONS FOR DISCUSSION

1. Are the scientific or technological elements in this story plausible?

2. The lamas seem to have acquired knowledge that Dr. Wagner, Chuck, and George don't have. What is that knowledge?

3. What are Chuck and George worried about before they leave the lamasery?

4. How does Clarke build suspense?

5. This is one of two stories in this chapter that has no falling action. Why doesn't it?

TOPICS FOR WRITING

1. In a paragraph or two, explain the advantages of setting this story in Tibet.

2. The end of the world depicted here, with God putting out the lights, is in sharp contrast to the usual stories of apocalypse. What are some other ways that the end of the world is usually predicted in literature and in films? Write an essay, based on research, on the usual treatment in popular fiction and films.

SECTION FOUR

GHOST AND HORROR

Stories that scare people have been popular and profitable for a long time, as current writers Anne Rice and Stephen King would no doubt agree. Ghost and horror stories are types of fantasy and, like other types of fantasy, grew out of the Gothic novels of the 1700s. In Horace Walpole's *The Castle of Otranto: A Gothic Story* (1764), *Gothic* referred to the novel's medieval setting, which in turn meant ruined castles, wild landscapes, supernatural or mysterious events, and young women being preyed upon by evil, or lecherous, men. Walpole's story, considered to be the first Gothic novel, is set in Italy in the 1100s. Nostalgia in the later 1700s for things medieval is often attributed to a rejection of some of the ideas of the Age of Reason, a time when the universe and the things in it were being explored and classified, and the measure of man was his intellect. Still, many people found it hard to give up the popular literature of the day. In her essay "The Supernatural in Fiction," Virginia Woolf observes, "It is worth noticing that the craving for the supernatural in literature coincided in the eighteenth century with a period of rationalism in thought, as if the effect of damming the human instincts at one point causes them to overflow at another."

Subsequent English Gothic novels included *The Mysteries of Udolpho* (1794) by Ann Radcliffe (1764–1823) and *The Monk* (1796) by Matthew Gregory Lewis (1775–1818). Lewis's story is about an abbot, Ambrosio, and a young noblewoman, Matilda, who disguises herself as a monk and enters the monastery to be with him. He is condemned to death, bargains with the devil, and is finally killed. The book was widely condemned as immoral.

The public taste for frightening tales did not abate. Three successful nineteenth-century writers of ghost and horror stories were all Irish: Joseph Sheridan Le Fanu (1814–1873), one of whose stories, "Carmilla" (1872), is about a female vampire; Bram Stoker (1847–1912), whose *Dracula* (1897), the story of a vampire in Transylvania, is known throughout the world—though today, primarily through movies; and Lord Dunsany (1878–1957), many of whose works, such as "Two Bottles of Relish," deal with the macabre.

In the United States, Edgar Allan Poe (1809–1849) excelled at writing horror stories. "The Fall of the House of Usher" (1840),

"The Cask of Amontillado," (1846), and "The Masque of the Red Death" (1842) are all guaranteed to produce chills.

The pulp magazines of the 1920s and 1930s in the United States, notably the short-lived *Ghost Stories*, and *Weird Tales*, which lasted longer, published ghost and horror fiction. American writer H. P. Lovecraft, who in his own words was "very peculiar" as a child and virtually a recluse as an adult, published often in *Weird Tales*, including his stories "The Rats in the Walls" and "The Dunwich Horror."

Many writers not necessarily known for ghost and horror fiction have tried their hand at it. Nathaniel Hawthorne, Edith Wharton, Henry James, Shirley Jackson, Elizabeth Bowen, and Joyce Carol Oates have all written ghost stories. And the popular fiction of Anne Rice, who is still writing vampire stories, and the novels of Stephen King have been frightening readers for years.

The Count Dracula society gives an Ann Radcliffe Award for outstanding achievements in fantasy, horror, terror, and science fiction in television, films, and literature, and the Horror Writers of America gives the Bram Stoker Award.

Most people like being frightened by a story, especially if they are in a safe place with an ordinary, familiar world within reach. In her essay quoted above, Virginia Woolf cautions that "it would be a mistake to suppose that supernatural fiction always seeks to produce fear, or that the best ghost stories are those which most accurately and medically described abnormal states of mind. On the contrary, a vast amount of fiction both in prose and in verse now assures us that the world to which we shut our eyes is far more friendly and inviting, more beautiful by day and more holy by night, than the world which we persist in thinking the real world." Such is not the case with the following stories, however.

ALL BUT EMPTY

GRAHAM GREENE (1904–1991)

Graham Greene's early life was an unhappy one. His father was headmaster of Berkhamsted School in England, which Greene first attended as a boarder at the age of 14, but as son of the headmaster, he was verbally teased by the other boys. He had a nervous breakdown in 1921 and ran away. Despite suffering from some psychological problems for much of his life, he was a prolific writer of nonfiction, novels, short stories, detective stories, dramas, screenplays, and travel books.

He married in 1927 and from 1926 to 1929 was an editor at the London *Times,* a position he left to become a full-time writer. He describes his early years in *A Sort of Life* (1971); *Ways of Escape* (1980) is the second volume of his autobiography. His novels include *The Power and the Glory* (1940); *The Heart of the Matter* (1948); *The End of the Affair* (1951); *A Burnt-Out Case* (1961), set in a leper colony; *The Honorary Consul* (1973), set in Argentina; and *The Human Factor* (1978). He labeled some of his works "entertainments," and these include *Brighton Rock* (1938); *The Confidential Agent* (1939); and *Our Man in Havana* (1958). His dramas include *The Potting Shed* (1937); among his screenplays are *The Third Man* (1949), *Saint Joan* (1957), and *The Comedians* (1967). His short stories are collected in several editions, including *The Portable Graham Greene* (1973, 1977) and *Shades of Greene: The Televised Stories of Graham Greene* (1975, 1977).

■

It is not often that one finds an empty cinema, but this one I used to frequent in the early 1930s because of its almost invariable, almost total emptiness. I speak only of the afternoons, the heavy gray afternoons of late winter; in the evenings, when the lights went up in the Edgware Road and the naphtha flares,[1] and the peep-shows were crowded, this cinema may have known prosperity. But I doubt it.

It had so little to offer. There was no talkie apparatus, and the silent films it showed did not appeal to the crowd by their excitement or to the connoisseur by their unconscious humor. They were merely banal, drawing-room drama of 1925.

I suspect that the cinema kept open only because the owner could not sell or let the building and he could not afford to close it. I went to it because it was silent, because it was all but empty, and because the girl who sold the tickets had a bright, common, venal[2] prettiness.

One passed out of the Edgware Road and found it in a side street. It was built of boards like a saloon in an American western, and there were no posters. Probably no posters existed of the kind of films it showed. One paid one's money to the girl of whom I spoke, taking an unnecessarily expensive seat in the drab emptiness on the other side of the red velvet curtains, and she would smile, charming and venal, and address one by a name of her own; it was not difficult for her to remember her patrons. She may be there still, but I haven't visited the cinema for a long time now.

I remember I went in one afternoon and found myself quite alone. There was not even a pianist; blurred metallic music was relayed from a gramophone in the pay-box. I hoped the girl would soon leave her job and come in. I sat almost at the end of a row with one seat free as an indication that I felt like company, but she never came. An elderly man got entangled in the curtain and billowed his way through it and lost himself in the dark. He tried to get past me, though he had the whole cinema to choose from, and brushed my face with a damp beard. Then he sat down in the seat I had left, and there we were, close together in the wide dusty darkness.

The flat figures passed and repassed, their six-year-old gestures as antique as designs on a Greek coin. They were emotional in great white flickering letters, but their emotions were not comic nor to me

---

1 **Edgware Road . . . naphtha flares:** The Edgware Road is a major thoroughfare in London. Naphtha flares were sometimes used to penetrate the legendary London fogs of an earlier time.

2 **venal:** capable of being obtained for money or of bribery.

moving. I was surprised when I heard the old man next me crying to himself—so much to himself and not to me, not a trace of histrionics in those slow, carefully stifled sobs that I felt sorry for him and did not grudge him the seat. I said:

"Can I do anything?"

He may not have heard me, but he spoke: "I can't hear what they are saying."

The loneliness of the old man was extreme; no one had warned him that he would find only silent pictures here. I tried to explain, but he did not listen, whispering gently, "I can't see them."

I thought that he was blind and asked him where he lived, and when he gave an address in Seymour Terrace, I felt such pity for him that I offered to show him the way to another cinema and then to take him home. It was because we shared a desolation, sitting in the dark and stale air, when all around us people were lighting lamps and making tea and gas fires glowed. But no! He wouldn't move. He said that he always came to this cinema of an evening, and when I said that it was only afternoon, he remarked that afternoon and evening were now to him "much of a muchness." I still didn't realize what he was enduring, what worse thing than blindness and age he might be keeping to himself.

Only a hint of it came to me a moment after, when he turned suddenly towards me, brushing my lips with his damp beard, and whispered.

"No one could expect me to see, not after I've seen what I've seen," and then in a lower voice, talking to himself, "From ear to ear."

That startled me because there were only two things he could mean, and I did not believe that he referred to a smile.

"Leave them to it," he said, "at the bottom of the stairs. The black-beetles always came out of that crack. Oh, the anger," and his voice had a long weary frisson.[3]

It was extraordinary how he seemed to read my thoughts, because I had already begun to comfort myself with the fact of his age and that he must be recalling something very far away, when he spoke again: "Not a minute later than this morning. The clock had just struck two and I came down the stairs, and there he was. Oh, I was angry. He was smiling."

"From ear to ear," I said lightly, with relief.

---

3 **frisson**: shudder.

"That was later," he corrected me, and then he startled me by reading out suddenly from the screen the words, "I love you. I will not let you go." He laughed and said, "I can see a little now. But it fades, it fades."

I was quite sure then that the man was mad, but I did not go. For one thing, I thought that at any moment the girl might come and two people could deal with him more easily than one; for another, stillness seemed safest. So I sat very quietly, staring at the screen and knew that he was weeping again beside me, shivering and weeping and shivering. Among all the obscurities one thing was certain, something had upset him early that morning.

After a while he spoke again so low that his words were lost in the tin blare of the relayed record, but I caught the words "serpent's tooth" and guessed that he must have been quoting scripture.[4] He did not leave me much longer in doubt, however, of what had happened at the bottom of the stairs, for he said quite casually, his tears forgotten in curiosity:

"I never thought the knife was so sharp. I had forgotten I had had it reground."

Then he went on speaking, his voice gaining strength and calmness: "I had just put down the borax for the black-beetles that morning. How could I have guessed? I must have been very angry coming downstairs. The clock struck two, and there he was, smiling at me. I must have sent it to be reground when I had the joint of pork for Sunday dinner. Oh, I was angry when he laughed: the knife trembled. And there the poor body lay with the throat cut from ear to ear," and hunching up his shoulders and dropping his bearded chin towards his hands, the old man began again to cry.

Then I saw my duty quite plainly. He might be mad and to be pitied, but he was dangerous.

It needed courage to stand up and press by him into the gangway, and then turn the back and be lost in the blind velvet folds of the curtains which would not part, knowing that he might have the knife still with him. I got out into the gray afternoon light at last, and startled the girl in the box with my white face. I opened the door of the kiosk and shut it again behind me with immeasurable relief. He couldn't get at me now.

"The police station," I called softly into the telephone, afraid that he might hear me where he sat alone in the cinema, and when a voice

---

4 **serpent's tooth . . . scripture:** Actually the man is quoting from Shakespeare's *King Lear:* "How sharper than a serpent's tooth it is to have a thankless child."

answered, I said hurriedly, "That murder in Seymour Terrace this morning."

The voice at the other end became brisk and interested, telling me to hold the line, and then the seconds drummed away.

All the while I held the receiver I watched the curtain, and presently it began to shake and billow, as if somebody was fumbling for the way out. "Hurry, hurry," I called down the telephone, and then as the voice spoke I saw the old man wavering in the gap of the curtain. "Hurry. The murderer's here," I called, stumbling over the name of the cinema and so intent on the message I had to convey that I could not take in for a moment the puzzled and puzzling reply: "We've got the murderer. It's the body that's disappeared."

QUESTIONS FOR DISCUSSION

1. When does the narrator's reaction to the man who sits next to him change from sympathy to alarm?

2. What kind of person is the narrator and by what method is he characterized?

3. What makes the setting particularly effective?

4. How does the author make the stranger's appearance at the cinema plausible?

TOPICS FOR WRITING

1. Write a script for a radio play based on this story, record the play with a narrator and two or three of your classmates and with appropriate sound effects and music if possible.

2. In a short essay, analyze the sensory images in this story and tell how they contribute to mood.

SUBSOIL

NICHOLSON BAKER (born 1957)

Nicholson Baker was born in New York, attended the Eastman School of Music in 1974–1975, and graduated from Haverford College with a B.A. in 1980. He has been a full-time writer since 1987. His works include *The Mezzanine* (1988), *Room Temperature* (1990), *U and I* (nonfiction, 1991), *Vox* (1992), *The Fermata* (1994), and *The Everlasting Story of Nory* (1998), written from the point of view of a nine-year old girl. Baker writes in his dedication that his "informant" was his daughter Alice.

Baker has been praised for his detailed descriptions of the everyday things that everyone knows about but seldom thinks twice about; reviewer Robert Crum called him "an exquisite literary anatomist." Baker has published in the *Atlantic* and *The New Yorker* magazines, the latter where "Subsoil" first appeared. He lives in upstate New York.

■

For his book-length monograph on the early harrow, Nyle T. Milner, the agricultural historian, decided that he had to pay one more visit to the Museum of the Tractor in Harvey, New York, an inconsequential town not far from Geneva. He had already been to the Museum of the Tractor three times; each time, he left feeling that he had learned everything he needed about the rare implements of harrowage and soil pulverization in its collection, sure that his further photos and sketches would suffice. But always there was some tiny question that lured him back.

The manager of the Harvey Motel took an interest in Nyle's research and wanted him to recall his stay with pleasure; whenever he came she used a headier brand of air freshener in his room. Rather than discuss with her his preference for unflavored air, which might make her regret her earlier acts of kindness, Nyle decided that for this visit he would try to stay someplace else and hope she didn't find out.

Bill Fipton, who owned and curated the Museum of the Tractor, was at first cagey about recommending a bed-and-breakfast close by. "There is one that some people go to," he said, thoughtfully eyeing a 1931 Gilroy & Selvo variable-impact sod-pounder. "I don't want to dump on anyone, but I say stick with the motel." Bill, who had been quite friendly to Nyle on earlier visits, seemed cooler toward him today—he had been evasive, for instance, about which local hobbyist had done the superior restoration work on one of the more fascinating transitional Unterbey harrows. Nyle got the sense that Bill, who had a habit of doing something muscular with his tongue before he said anything, apparently to reseat his dental plate, was perhaps beginning to resent how closely Nyle was scrutinizing the collection.

"Please," Nyle insisted. "I really need to branch out."

"The Taits," said Bill reluctantly. "They'll give you a room." He gave Nyle the address. "It won't be cheap. And keep an eye open there. I've heard some stories. But they're supposed to make an interesting soup."

Mrs. Tait led Nyle up the stairs and down a narrow hall hung with three tiny black-and-white photographs of sliced mushrooms. A cotton runner, striped in purple and black, ran down the middle of the hall. She opened a door.

"This is a surprise," said Nyle, taking it all in. He gestured at a tall tubular brown vase with a single black branch gnarling artily out of it. "It's so . . . spare. I expected cutesy curtains and ruffled bed skirts."

"We are not exactly *of* Harvey," Mrs. Tait said. She was nearly fifty, with an attractive, prematurely ravaged neck and an expensive haircut. A bit of what seemed to be a tattoo, possibly the tail of something, peeped out past the unbuttoned neck of her silvery linen shirt. "But we do love the town."

"Oh, me too," said Nyle. "The tractors drew me here, as usual—where tractors are I must go! But I've grown very fond of Main Street. That sad little Chamber of Commerce."

"And what about dinner?" said Mrs. Tait.

"Do you offer a dinner package?" Nyle asked.

"We could see what we have on hand."

"I've heard high tidings of soup," Nyle said.

"Ah!" said Mrs. Tait, coming alive. "Is that what you would like?"

Nyle said he would, very much, being a soup person—if it wasn't too much trouble. Mrs. Tait left him to settle in. He took off his shoes and scattered his new farm-machinery sketches on the bed. His monograph was taking far too long to finish. Three years was excessive, even for a subject as far-reaching as his. Nyle was disorganized, a trait surprising in a man so short, and he was having exciting insights now about the evolution of rotary-hoe blades and diggers which he later realized were not new to him, ones that he had written down in a state of euphoria and lost in his briefcase and forgotten. So much of what he knew was only in his head, unfortunately, and his head couldn't always be depended on. Driving to Harvey, he had briefly wondered whether, were he to die suddenly, right then, he would have lived his life—not merely as an agricultural historian but even as a human being—entirely in vain. He'd seen it happen recently with the late Raymond Purty, who had known a great deal about early silos—more than anyone else on earth. When Purty was suffocated that muggy April afternoon under three tons of raw soy, everyone in Nyle's circle had expected at least a partial manuscript to come to light. But, sadly, the history of silage had all been in Ray Purty's head.

"This is the last research trip I'll make," said Nyle sternly to himself. "From now on—synthesis, exclusion, and sequential paragraphs." A faint smell of furniture wax and, underneath it, of something earthy and wholesome cheered him. This bed-and-breakfast—in a Greek Revival[1] house with seven thin columns in front—was much better for morale than the well-intentioned instant headache of

---

1 **Greek Revival:** an architectural style imitating elements of Greek temple design.

the Harvey Motel's air freshener. Maybe the town disparaged the Taits just because the Taits had taste.

The room was furnished with extreme, almost oppressive, care. The bureau was an ornamentally incised, Eastlake-style[2] artifact with a large pair of mother-of-pearl wings inlaid in one side. The bed bore puzzling ovoid knobs, about the size of ostrich eggs, on its headboard and footboard. Five tiny safe-deposit-box keys hung next to a tarnished mirror as decoration. Nyle peered closely at the surface of the wall, fascinated by the stippled effect the Taits had achieved. They appeared to have flung or slapped around lengths of thin rope dipped in cinnamon-colored paint. Risky, Nyle felt, but it worked.

Only one pillow was made into the bed, an arrangement that momentarily concerned him, since he always slept with a second between his legs for comfort, having sensitive knees. But in the closet three spares were neatly shelved. Good—no need to bring up matters of ménage[3] with the somewhat intimidating Mrs. Tait. Above the pillows, on the highest closet shelf, Nyle noticed a ziggurat of old children's games. There was a game called Mr. Ree and period Monopoly and Parcheesi boxes. And there was also—the obvious treasure of the collection—an old Mr. Potato Head kit. "Ho!" he cried, gingerly sliding it from its place on the shelf and carrying it to the bed. He had played Mr. Potato Head a few times as a child—back in the days before child safety, when you used a real baking potato and you stabbed the facial features, fitted with sharp points, into it. The joy of the old game came in imposing the stock nose- and ear- and eyepieces on the unique Gothic shape of a real potato. Man and nature in concert; "the encrustation of the mechanical upon the organic," or however it was that Bergson[4] defined laughter. The modern Mr. Potato Head, which included an artificial base potato with holes, was, Nyle felt, a mistake—now you merely joined bought plastic to bought plastic in various fixed permutations. Why continue the affectation of a potato at all?

He pulled the lid slowly off the box, feeling the air slip in to fill the increasing volume. And then he had a nasty shock. Fully prepared for a quick, happy *poof* of nostalgia—needing it, in fact, since he was

---

2 **Eastlake-style:** in the style of Charles Locke Eastlake (1836–1906), British architect, designer, and author.

3 **ménage:** housekeeping.

4 **Bergson:** Henri-Louis Bergson (1859–1941) was a French philosopher.

more than a little discouraged by the progress of his research—he was instead confronted by something unpleasant and even, for a moment at least, outright frightening. A real potato, or a former potato, a now dead potato, still rested within the box. The last person who had played with the set had carelessly left the face he had created inside, with its proptotic[5] yellow eyes and enormous, red-lipped, toothy, Milton Berlesque smile still stabbed in place, and over time—how long Nyle didn't want to guess—the potato's flesh had shrunk to a wizened leer of agonized supplication or self-mockery while it had grown seven long unhealthy sprouts that had curved and wandered around their paper chamber, feeling softly for the earth hold they never found. They resembled sparse hair and gastrointestinal parasites and certain weedy, wormy, albino things that live underwater; Nyle looked on them with disgust. Hurriedly he replaced the top and stuffed the box away in the closet again.

He rested for a moment on the bed, blinking regularly. The expression on the Mr. Potato Head intruded itself several times into his imagination—mummified, it had seemed, but conscious, in a state of sentient misery. The really disturbing thing was that, despite its appliqué grin and hefty comic nose, it had, Nyle felt, looked at him with a fixed intent to do him harm. The apparent animosity, though he could discount it as a trick of decomposition, bothered Nyle; he had never been hated by a potato before.

From downstairs came the cheerful eruption of a blender.

Mrs. Tait held a low green bowl over the table, waiting for Nyle to remove his politely clasped hands from the placemat. "There!" she said, giving the bowl a half turn as she positioned it in front of him. She sat down across from her husband. Mr. Tait had a carefully sculpted silver beard and wore a soft formless jacket over a black sweater with three brown buttons. The two of them were the least likely bed-and-breakfast owners Nyle had run into in a long time.

He turned his attention to his dinner. The soup had a grainy pallor, with parsley shrapnel distributed equitably throughout. "Mm, boy," he said, sniffing deeply. "Leek?"

Mrs. Tait gave him an eighteenth-century smile, "And potato."

Potato! Nyle flinched. On each of his hosts' plates were three dried apricots. "Aren't you having any?" he asked them. Mr. Tait

---

5 **proptotic:** having eyeballs that are pushed forward.

discreetly slipped an apricot in his mouth, as if he were taking a pill, and began dismantling it with toothy care.

"We seldom eat the soup ourselves," Mrs. Tait explained. She put a light finger on her abdomen. "I would like to, but I can't. Potatoes upset me now."

"Juliette makes the soup for our guests only," said Mr. Tait. "It's labor-intensive. Please start."

"Oh, potatoes are not for everyone, that's for sure," said Nyle, his mind racing. "Especially sweet potatoes. I know five, no, more—six—people who hate sweet potatoes."

Mrs. Tait slipped a disk of apricot in her mouth and sucked on it like a cough drop. "Please start," she quietly hissed.

"Pumpkin pie's stock has plunged, don't ask me why," Nyle nattered. "I do enjoy a good boiled potato, though, especially mashed up nicely."

"Oh—you like them mashed?" said Mrs. Tait, with a distant look, as if recalling early felonies. "*Please,* won't you?"

Why was he hesitating? What reason could he possibly have for his sense of vague unease? Suppressing his doubts, the agricultural historian took a big noisy spoonful, feeling immediately juvenile, as he always did when he ate soup as a guest. "Very nice," he said.

Mrs. Tait was pleased. "We're known for it, at least within Harvey."

"I'll tell my colleagues," said Nyle.

By the time he had accepted his second bowl, Nyle's doubts and suspicions were altogether gone. And the Taits, who had been keyed up at first, seemed to relax completely as well. They drank wine and ate their dried fruits and asked Nyle informed questions about his field. When he determined that the term "rear-power takeoff," as applied to the tractor, was not entirely new to them, he grew animated and confessional. As he described his work, he began to think that it was—though obviously influenced (as whose could not be?) by the insights of Chatternan Gough, Paul Uselding, and M. J. French—something well worth finishing. He found himself describing to the Taits his recent fears: he sketched the story of Purty and the terrible soy suffocation, from which the history of "spouted beds" and other fermentational mechanisms might never fully recover.

"I'm feeling unusually mortal at the moment," Nyle was finally drawn to say, wiping his mouth and sitting back. His hosts were arranged in casual poses. Slightly more of Mrs. Tait's tattoo was visible: it now looked like part of a vine, perhaps, rather than like a lizard's tail. "If I were Keats," Nyle went on, "and thankfully I'm not, cough cough, I would be making every attempt to use the word 'glean' in a sonnet."

"I hope your stay here will help," said Mrs. Tait carefully.

"Oh, yes. Although . . ." Hesitating briefly, Nyle decided that he would probably trust the Taits more if he just went ahead and told them. "An oddly upsetting thing happened in my room just before you called me down. I probably shouldn't have, but I took a quick peek inside the Mr. Potato Head box in the closet."

"You opened the box," said Mr. Tait, leaning forward.

"I'm a Curious George sort of person," Nyle explained. "It's the historian in me. Well—there was a highly unattractive dead potato in there. Ugh! Not good."

Mrs. Tait looked thoughtful. "Douglas Grieb was the one who saw that set last, if I remember right," she said. "He was here visiting the Museum of the Tractor, too, from the University of Somewhere—Illinois, was it, Carl?"

"Oh, Grieb," said Nyle, waving dismissively. "A controversial figure, not universally liked. Well, his potato head has not aged well. It scared the starch out of me, quite frankly."

Mrs. Tait rose and removed the plates. "Come with me," she said, and led Nyle into the green-trimmed kitchen. Two Yixing[6] teapots in the shape of cabbages were arranged to the right of a vintage porcelain sink. Mrs. Tait bent and opened all the beautifully mitred doors to the cabinets under the counter. In the shadows were three rotating storage carrousels. Crowded on their round shelves were dozens of silent potatoes. Some were dark-brown; some were deep-red. Some had eyes that looked like bicuspids; some had sprouted and evidently had their sprouts clipped off. A few were extraordinarily large. A smell of earth and rhizomes and of things below consciousness pervaded the room.

Nyle made a whistle of amazement. Then he said, "One or two of those larger gentlemen do not look particularly . . . recent."

"The secret to a good earth-apple soup," explained Mr. Tait, squeezing his wife's arm, "is to age the ingredients."

Nyle sent his sensibility on a little stomach check and then quickly recalled it. All seemed well. "I had no idea," he said.

---

6 **Yixing:** Yixing kilns in Jiangsu Province in China are known for unglazed reddish and brownish stoneware teapots. Traditional Yixing ware is of museum quality. Copies are not.

Mrs. Tait bent and gave one of the carrousels a turn. She leaned forward and lightly caressed a huge russet. "We eat only the fruit of a plant," she said, "and never its tuber, since its tuber is not something it intended to offer the world."

"But—" Nyle began, indicating the gleaming components of the blender which were upended in the black dish drainer. The blender blade sat drying like a blown rose. "You made the soup."

"It was our pleasure," said Mrs. Tait. "It was for you." She closed all but one of the doors to the potato cabinets and turned off the light. The only illumination in the room now came from a small bulb within the oven.

"At this time of evening, we generally watch 'Nick at Nite,' " said Mr. Tait, escorting Nyle into the front hall.

"Oh, thanks—I think I'll head on up," said Nyle. "I've got some more notes that I should expand."

"While the tractor museum is still fresh in your mind?" said Mrs. Tait.

"Exactly," said Nyle. He waved a cheerful good night to his hosts and ascended the stairs, humming. But as he walked down the narrow hallway, paying no notice to the riven mushrooms, he suddenly thought, Why did Mrs. Tait use that particular word; that "fresh"? And were those—could those be—*potato prints* of some kind on the walls of his room?

Nyle had difficulty getting to sleep that night. The Taits had kindly provided some light reading on a shelf by the bed; Nyle got through a short Wilkie Collins story and half of a longer Sheridan Le Fanu.[7] He liked being mildly frightened by fiction when he was uneasy in fact. When he turned out the light, waiting for sleep to come, he was visited by the memory of the now sinister-seeming black rectangle of the half-open kitchen cabinet downstairs. Why hadn't Mrs. Tait closed the last cabinet door? This was like trying to fall asleep after you remembered that you'd left a radio on in the basement, he thought. And the sheer size of some of the potatoes she had shown him! They were phenomenal, unnatural. *Boulders* of carbohydrate. Finally, he was able to worm his way into a fairly satisfactory half sleep by imagining himself tearing up large damp pieces of corrugated cardboard.

---

7 **Wilkie Collins . . . Sheridan Le Fanu:** Collins (1824–1889) was a British writer; Le Fanu (1814–1873) was an Irish writer; both were known for mystery and suspense fiction.

He woke some hours later feeling sorry for a minor engineer named Shelby Hemper Fairchild, whose career had been cut short in the early thirties by the unfortunate inhalation of a cotton ball. (Fairchild—and not Edward Lyrielle, as some wrongly asserted—developed Bleidman & Co.'s famous Guttersnipe, an erratic but groundbreaking turf flail and trencher.) Without moving, Nyle worked his unpillowed eyeball so as to take in as much of his room as he could. Moonlight furbished the brown cylindrical floor vase and its gnarled branch, as well as an aquarium bibelot in the shape of a ruined arch on his bedside table. He felt strange suspicions and recalled the kitchen cabinet. Big hostile pocked things were waiting in there. That cabinet door was open. Wouldn't it be a good idea to nip quickly downstairs and close it himself? Clearly he wasn't going to sleep properly until this state of affairs was resolved.

Pulling the pillow from between his legs, he put on his paper slippers (hospital wear, salvaged from an appendectomy performed several years earlier) and made his way in the half-light toward the door—where he discovered something. A long, glimmering white sprout, with violet accents—a lengthy potato sprout, by all indications—had grown through the keyhole. It curved motionlessly to the floor. Perplexed, on the verge of being horrified, he glanced at his watch, more to steady himself than to check the time. The notion that this sprout had grown its way out of the kitchen cabinet, originating in one of those prodigies of mass storage downstairs, and that it had then worked its way slowly up to him, all while he slept, disturbed Nyle exceedingly. His watch claimed that it was almost three.

"Hello?" he called softly, in case someone or something was on the other side of the door. There was no answer.

Closer up, the feeler appeared harmless. He touched it quickly, testingly. It was cold and didn't move. He grasped it; he wound it around his trembling finger. He pulled.

The soft, unchlorophylled plant flesh gave way against the metal edge of the keyhole, making a tiny rending sound. Carefully Nyle fed the broken mystery frond back out under the doorway. "Out you go," he whispered. He waited for some time, listening. We have scotched the snake, not killed it,[8] he thought to himself, drawing comfort from the scrap of pentameter—and then, reminded that he

---

8 **We have scotched . . . killed it.** Milner is remembering a line from Shakespeare's *Macbeth,* spoken by Macbeth after he has arranged to have Banquo killed (Act III, scene ii). *Scotched* means "slashed."

had some Scotch Tape in his briefcase, he carefully sealed the keyhole. The sensation of the sticky tape on his fingers left him feeling almost brave. It was time to confront the hall.

He turned the knob and peered tentatively out. The long, pale petitioner with the torn end receded kinklessly from his doorway into the shadows along the black-and-purple runner. Nyle tiptoed along it to the head of the stairway and looked down, craning his neck to determine the shoot's route up the stairs. What he then saw, as his gaze penetrated the grainy obscurity of the front hall, made a terror gong go off in his mind.

A dozen or more sinuous emissaries from the kitchen, similar to the first, were just turning the corner from the dining room and beginning the climb toward him.

"Good gravy!" he gasped, hotfooting it back to his room. "They're out to get me!" He slid the bolt and tried to think. The proliferating sprouts, though he suspected that they were up to no good, were none too strong, judging by the one that he had held. They couldn't push their way past the taped-up keyhole. But he had to take reasonable measures to protect himself. If he stuffed something *under* the door, he theorized, these hellish hawsers would never find him.

He took off his pajama bottoms and wedged them into the space between the door and the floor. Immediately he felt much better. No, they were not strong sprouts. They were not robust. They were attenuated and colorless and slow and soft. That was what he didn't like about them, in fact. That and that they seemed, in their blind, tentative way, to want to find him.

Ten minutes went by. Twelve. Nyle craved to know how fast they were growing, if they were growing at all. Maybe they had withdrawn. Were they already at the top of the stairs? Did they grow only while he slept? In that case, he had but to stay awake all night. A watched pot never boils. Or were they already nudging gently against the pajama-bottom buffer—and, if so, would such insistent pushings finally dislodge it entirely? He wheeled around, looking for some backup. A *drawer*. One of the heavy lower drawers from the big ornamental bureau. He seized its two handles and pulled.

Again he heard a soft rending sound, louder this time. The drawer was not empty. Inside was a plastic sack of enormous aging Valley Star potatoes, the biggest Nyle had ever seen. Through the ventilation holes of the plastic had grown a horror whorl of intertwining white shoots and root hairs. Some of the shoots now bore new radish-size dark tubers. The upper surface of the conjoined growth was flat, like a Jackson Pollock,[9] having encountered the plane of the drawer above. Freed and slightly injured, the bureau's brood now began to awaken. Nyle stared for an instant at their sullen stirrings. Then he reverse-salaamed, barking once with shock and revulsion. When he moved, his ankle bone made contact with something more yielding than an electrical cord. He glanced down. A gap in the baseboard molding had allowed entrance to more questing feelers from downstairs. There seemed to be some wispy activity at the window. Something was floating up through a loose floorboard. Nyle stamped on the board, severing the fiendish sucker. Grabbing his briefcase, he backed slowly across the room. "Mr. and Mrs. Tait?" he quavered. But there was no answer.

Sensing his movements and his noise, the sallow stolons[10] began a langourous, low creep toward him. He could see them move now. "No! You're disgusting!" he cried, flicking at them with his fingers. His back bumped against the closet door. I'm doomed, he thought. And yet maybe they feared light. If he could get in the closet and turn on the closet light, maybe they would rethink and withdraw.

He bumbled inside and shut the door. He yanked on the light cord, which sprang away from his hand. A coruscation of bulb yellow filled the space. He waited, squinting, wishing he were wearing his pajama bottoms. A minute or two passed, and he began to think he was safe. And then he heard sounds from the room: his overnight bag seemed to be on the move; softnesses were sweeping the walls. He spotted the tips of three or four lissome elongations peeping under the door. With a terrified, saliva-rich curse, he grabbed a dark-green rubber boot and began pounding their growth tips as they emerged. But the light seemed to stimulate them, and many now vied for entrance. Was there no escape? He looked up. Past the light bulb, which was mounted on the wall, he saw a trapdoor. It must lead to an attic space. He could climb up there, kick out an attic window, climb out onto the porch roof, shimmy down one of the front columns, and run.

He grabbed two clothes hooks and started to hoist himself up toward the closet ceiling. His eyes drew even with the top shelf. From inside the Mr. Potato Head box came a leisurely scrabbling. Its top

---

9   **Jackson Pollock:** (1912–1956) American painter known for his large, abstract paintings.

10   **stolon:** a horizontal branch from a plant that produces new plants from buds at its top.

began to lift. The Parcheesi game slid to one side. The Monopoly game tumbled. The fixed orange eyes of the dead and shrunken Mr. Potato Head appeared from under the rising top, and then one or two—four, *seven*—limply questing spud spawn veered into the air toward Nyle's face, root hairs aquiver.

"Help!" Nyle wailed, and he fell. The floor of the closet was asquirm. Whitish-purple growth enveloped him. He waved his arms and plucked at himself hectically, but the soil-starved delvers were persistent. When they touched his face, he began to feel sad that he would never finish his history of the harrow. A sprout grew smoothly into his right knee, seeking his synovial fluid.[11] Several more penetrated his elbows. These hurt quite a lot, though not nearly as much as the one that found its way into his urethra. One wan ganglion discovered his ear canal, and another a tear duct, and Nyle began to hear only the dim, low pulsation of plant hormones and potato ideology. Let it go, he thought. Let it all go. They found the routes his blood took, and they followed these deeper; by dawn they had grown the fresh, lumpy tuber that burst his heart.

What once was Nyle woke in a very dark place. Many Krebs cycles[12] had passed; many more would pass. He felt himself being slowly turned. His fellows were dozing by the dozen near him. A child's voice was saying, "That one! That big one!" He was lifted and cradled in the child's gentle hand. His vision wasn't working properly—he saw several different views of the world. The child with a cry of happiness, plunged the fake nose into Nyle's crisp body flesh. Nyle screamed, but it was a potato scream, below the hearing of all but tree stumps and extinct volancoes. The child stabbed in the orange pop eyes, and then the big red smiley mouth, and the little black pipe. Each face piece had points. The child wasn't quite sure what it wanted; it rearranged the Potato Head features several times. Nyle leaked a little from his puncture wounds. The child grew bored and put Nyle back in the box, tossing the unused face parts in after. Then there was a long, dark time.

He felt himself shrinking, and the shrinking was agony. He forgot what he had known, he began to know only what potatoes know. He

---

11 **synovial fluid:** In synovial joints, one of three types of joints, a space between the ends of bones is filled with a viscous fluid called the synovial fluid.

12 **Krebs cycles:** a series of chemical reactions in cells for the oxidation of carbohydrates, fat, and protein, first explained by Sir Hans Adolf Krebs (1900–1981), British (German-born) chemist.

sensed the changes of geothermic pressure; he heard the earth's slow resentments. He exhausted himself doing the only thing he could do, which was trying to send out underground shoots to form more potatoes like himself—but the shoots were hindered by a dry, smooth plant product that Nyle dimly remembered as cardboard. Nyle's face collapsed and partially liquefied—an uncomfortable process he did not soon wish to repeat. As moon followed moon he felt long-suffering, and then he forgot how to feel long-suffering and began to feel a crude, incurious misanthropy. When his dark chamber moved, and when suddenly, tumbling, he was swarmed with light prickles that reached down to the few places in his starchy interior that still lived, he made out a looming human face and saw it recoil. There was an exclamation of fear which pleased him. "It's vile!" he heard the face say. *Ah,* soundlessly chuckled the thing that was once Nyle, *it's another historian of agricultural technology.* Emboldened by the fresher air, he readied his pale tentacles for the final gleaning, waiting for nightfall.

QUESTIONS FOR DISCUSSION

1. What seems to be the author's attitude toward Milner?

2. What evidence is there of foreshadowing in this story?

3. When "what once was Nyle woke, . . . he saw several different views of the world." Why does he?

4. Why is the fact that Milner turns into a potato somehow appropriate?

5. Does this story have a theme? If so, what is it?

TOPICS FOR WRITING

1. If potatoes can turn lethal, what about carrots, beans, broccoli, and other vegetables? (What about artichokes?) Choose a vegetable or fruit, and in a paragraph or two describe what method it might use to do away with a human.

2. Fill in the background for the Taits. Who are they? What are their motives? Are they anti-agricultural? anti-tuberians? fruitarians? mad? In an essay, speculate on the reasons for their apparent complicity in the demise of Nyle Milner.

3. In a paper, tell why this story would or would not be a good candidate for a movie.

SYNTHESIS QUESTIONS

1. If there were such a thing as a time machine, and you could take advantage of it, what period of time would you want to visit and why?

2. Make a map of a small country that you invent, naming the country and various geographical features. Then write several paragraphs explaining about the people who live there. For example, tell how they make a living, what kind of dwellings they have, and what they believe in.

3. Write the first paragraph of a story that would fit into any one of the categories of popular fiction in this chapter. Make your first sentence one that will compel a reader to keep reading. You may want to review the opening sentences of the stories in this chapter.

4. Try to recall any superstitions you had as a child or superstitions that you know about. Would any of them be a basis for a story? If so, outline a story based on a superstition.

5. Many people developed interests in various categories of popular fiction as children. If this was true of you, discuss or write about what first led you to read westerns, mysteries, detective stories, fantasy, science fiction, ghost, or horror stories.

GLOSSARY OF
LITERARY TERMS

active character. *See* **character.**

allusion. A reference to a literary, mythological, religious, or historical event, person, or place or to a work of art. In "Paul's Case" by Willa Cather, there is an allusion to the opera *Faust* by Charles Gounod.

analogy. A comparison between two ideas, situations, or objects, usually for the purpose of explaining something unfamiliar by comparing it to something familiar. For example, the expanding universe is often compared to a balloon being filled with air.

antagonist. The character or force in conflict with the **protagonist** or main character in a work of fiction or drama. The antagonist may be a person, a group of people, a force of nature, or an animal. In "The Wedding Gift" by Thomas H. Raddall, the antagonist is the snowy weather. *See also* **protagonist.**

antihero. A main character who does not have the traditional qualities of a hero, such as courage or goodness, but may instead be inept, bumbling, or fearful.

atmosphere. The main tone or mood of a literary work conveyed chiefly through descriptions of setting but also through descriptions of relationships among characters. The atmosphere of "The Rocking Horse Winner" by D. H. Lawrence is tense.

character. A person created for a work of fiction. An **active character,** also known as a **dynamic character,** is one who changes during the course of a story. An active character is the opposite of a **static character,** who remains unchanged throughout the course of a story. A **flat character** is a two-dimensional character only briefly described. The father in "The Water-Faucet Vision" by Gish Jen is a flat character. A **major character** is the main or central character in fiction or drama. A **minor character** is any character other than a major character. A **piece of furniture character** is a minor character without much personality but essential to the story. In "The Man Who Shot Liberty Valance" by Dorothy M. Johnson, the reporter is such a character. A **round character** is a fully developed or three-dimensional character, such as Paul in "Paul's Case" by Willa Cather. A **stereotyped character,** also known as a **stock character,** represents a category of people, such as hen-pecked husbands, gum-chewing waitresses, or absent-minded professors. A **foil** is a minor character who is in contrast to a main character and points up the strengths or weaknesses of that character. In "Why I Live at the P.O." by Eudora Welty, Stella Rondo serves as a foil to the narrator.

447

characterization. The method by which an author depicts a character. Characters may be depicted by what they say or how they say it, how they act, or through their appearance. In **direct characterization,** the narrator tells what the character looks like, what kind of person he or she is, and, usually, the narrator's own reaction. In "Tamar" by Mark Helprin, the first-person narrator describes Tamar and then says, "I was breathless." A character may also describe himself or herself. In **indirect characterization,** a narrator or a character may describe a character's appearance or actions without comment, as E. Annie Proulx frequently does in "Electric Arrows."

cliché. An overused expression, such as "last but not least," or a hackneyed plot or theme in fiction or drama. A story about a young person who saves the life of an elderly rich person and is rewarded with substantial sums of money has a clichéd plot.

climax. The moment of highest interest and the turning point in a story. In "The Wedding Gift" by Thomas Raddall, the turning point is when Kezia and Mr. Mears decide to marry.

conflict. The struggle between the main character and opposing forces. **External conflict** occurs between the central character and another character or society or natural forces, including fate. In "Borders" by Thomas King, the conflict is between the narrator's mother and the customs officials at the U.S. and Canadian border. **Internal conflict** occurs when the main character is in conflict with himself or herself.

connotation. The feelings associated with a word such as *homesick* or *campfire*. Connotations may be shared by many people or they may be highly personal.

denotation. The literal or dictionary definition of a word, as opposed to the **connotation.**

denouement. Literally, "unravelling," meaning the final resolution of the conflict in a story. The term is often synonymous with the term **resolution.**

deus ex machina. An artificial device used to solve some problem with the resolution of a story—for example, someone may be rescued from certain execution by an earthquake or a bolt of lightning. The term originally referred to the mechanical device in Greek drama that lowered gods onto the stage to provide the solution to a problem.

dialogue. The conversation between people in a story or play.

diction. An author's choice of words and a basic component of an author's style.

didactic literature. Literature whose primary purpose is to teach.

direct characterization. *See* **characterization.**

dynamic character. *See* **character.**

epiphany. A moment of enlightenment or revelation. In "Paul's Case" by Willa Cather, the protagonist has an epiphany as he begins to spend the money he has stolen.

exposition. The explanatory information a reader needs to understand the situation in a story. Exposition establishes setting, the major characters, and any necessary background that happened before the story began.

external conflict. *See* **conflict.**

falling action. The events following the climax of a story.

figurative language. Language that contains **figures of speech.**

figures of speech. Expressions that make nonliteral comparisons between two slightly similar but unlike things. "The road was a ribbon of moonlight" is a figure of speech. "The road was brightly lighted" is not a figure of speech. *See also* **simile** and **metaphor.**

first-person point of view. *See* **point of view.**

flashback. The interruption in a narrative to show what happened before the time setting of the story. "The Lemon Tree Billiards House" by Cedric Yamanaka contains a flashback to the day when the narrator believes he was cursed.

flat character. *See* **character.**

foreshadowing. A hint or clue to the reader of what is to come.

formula story. A kind of story that adheres to standard characters and plot devices. Western and detective stories are often formula stories.

genre. A type of literary work, such as short story, novel, drama, and so on.

hero/heroine. The main character of a literary work.

imagery. The sensory details that appeal to the five senses as well as to internal feelings.

indirect characterization. *See* **characterization.**

inference. A conclusion about the actions of a character or the meaning of an event based on limited information provided by the author.

initiating incident. The event that changes the situation established in the exposition and sets the conflict in motion. In "The Lemon Tree Billiards House" by Cedric Yamanaka, the initiating incident occurs when a girl asks the narrator whether he wants to play billiards with her dad.

internal conflict. *See* **conflict.**

irony. The contrast between what is or appears to be and what really is. In **verbal irony,** the intended meaning of a statement is different from the actual meaning. If someone says, for example, "George would make a wonderful senator" and means just the opposite, the statement is ironic. **Situational irony** refers to an occurrence that is contrary to what is expected. **Dramatic irony** occurs when the audience at a play knows more about a situation than a character or characters on stage.

limited omniscience. *See* **point of view.**

local color. The depiction of setting, attitudes, or customs of a particular region such as the Old South.

magic realism. A type of literature that describes magical or fantastic events within ordinary, real-world settings.

metaphor. A figure of speech that makes a comparison without the words *like* or *as.* "The lake is a cloudy mirror" is a metaphor.

mood. The overall atmosphere of a work. The mood of "The Wedding Gift" by Thomas Raddall is generally hopeful.

motif. An image, incident, idea, or object that appears over and over in a work.

motivation. The cause of a character's actions, feelings, or thinking. In "Sweat" by Zora Neale Hurston, for example, the motivation for the actions the main character takes against her husband are quite clear.

naive narrator. A narrator who does not fully understand the meaning of the events he or she is telling about.

narrative. A story or account of an event or several events.

narrator. The teller of a story. The narrator may be a character in the story, as in "Tamar" by Mark Helprin, or a voice outside the story, as in "The Rocking-Horse Winner" by D. H. Lawrence.

objective point of view. *See* **point of view.**

omniscient point of view. *See* **point of view.**

persona. The voice or mask through which a story is told. For example, the "I" in "Why I Live at the P.O." by Eudora Welty is not Welty, but a voice through which she speaks.

piece of furniture character. *See* **character.**

plot. The arrangement of incidents in a narrative. The incidents are related by cause and effect and form a sequence of events with a beginning, middle, and end. In most short-story plot structures, the action begins with **exposition,** continues with **rising action,** which contains a complication, and moves to a **climax,** followed by **falling action** and a **resolution.**

point of view. The vantage point from which a story is told. The first-person narrator (*I, we*) may be a main character, a minor character, or merely an observer of the action and not a participant in the story. When a story is told from the third-person point of view (*he, she, they*), the narrator may be **omniscient,** revealing the thoughts and characters of all the characters; or the point of view may be **limited omniscient,** in which the narrator focuses on the thoughts of a single character. The narrator who assumes the **objective point of view** merely reports on the incidents, much like a newspaper reporter, and does not comment on events or characters.

protagonist. The main character in a work of fiction.

regional literature. Writing that focuses on a specific locality or geographic region.

resolution. The final resolving or the conclusion of the plot.

rising action. The various episodes that develop, complicate, or intensify the plot.

round character. *See* **character.**

setting. The time and place in which a story takes place.

simile. A figure of speech that makes a comparison using the words *like* or *as*. "He looks like a scarecrow" is a simile.

static character. *See* **character.**

stereotyped character. *See* **character.**

stock character. *See* **character.**

stream of consciousness. The continuous, usually fast-paced re-creation of a character's thoughts, memories, and feelings.

structure. The arrangement of events in a literary work.

style. The way a writer handles language. Style includes word choice, **syntax, imagery, figurative language,** and **tone.**

suspense. Uncertainty or anticipation about the outcome of events. Suspense is often created by an author's use of **foreshadowing.**

symbol. Anything concrete that stands for something else. Some symbols are universal, such as darkness signifying evil. Some symbols, perhaps a necklace or a ring, are specific to a particular work.

symbolism. The use of one object, action, or character to suggest another; the use of symbols.

syntax. The arrangement of words, phrases, and clauses in sentences. Syntax is a distinctive aspect of an author's style.

theme. The main idea in a literary work. Theme is not the same as the subject or topic of a work and is not usually stated by an author. Instead, theme must usually be inferred by the reader. The subject of a work might be the relationship between a father and son, but the theme of such a work might be that a son's understanding of a father's past is necessary to the relationship. Some works, such as detective stories, do not usually have a theme.

thesis. An attitude or position taken by a writer in support of a topic. It is usually expressed in the first sentence of a speech or composition.

third-person point of view. *See* **point of view.**

tone. The author's attitude toward his or her subject. Tone may be mocking, ironic, playful, or serious. The tone of "Bright Winter" by Anna Keesey, for example, is quite serious.

turning point. The point in a plot when the action or protagonist's situation changes. It is usually, but not always, the same as the climax.

villain. An antagonist. The term is usually used for a character in a melodrama who is in conflict with the hero or heroine.

ACKNOWLEDGMENTS

Alexie, Sherman. "This Is What It Means to Say Phoenix, Arizona" from *The Lone Ranger and Tonto Fistfight in Heaven* by Sherman Alexie. Copyright ©1993 by Sherman Alexie. Used by permission of Grove/Atlantic, Inc.

Ardizzone, Tony. "Holy Cards" by Tony Ardizzone from *Taking It Home: Stories from the Neighborhood*. Copyright ©1996 by Tony Ardizzone. Reprinted by permission.

Baker, Nicholson. "Subsoil" by Nicholson Baker. Copyright ©1994 by Nicholson Baker. Originally appeared in *The New Yorker* June 27/July 4, 1994. Reprinted by permission of Melanie Jackson Agency.

Callahan, Barbara. "The Mists of Ballyclough" by Barbara Callahan. Reprinted by permission of the author.

Carter, Angela. "The Courtship of Mr. Lyon" by Angela Carter, first published in *UK Vogue*. Copyright ©1995 by The Estate of Angela Carter. Reproduced by permission of the Estate of Angela Carter c/o Rogers, Coleridge & White Ltd., 20 Powis Mews, London W11 1JN.

Clarke, Arthur C. "The Nine Billion Names of God" from *The Nine Billion Names of God*, copyright ©1967 and renewed 1995 by Arthur C. Clarke, reprinted by permission of Harcourt Brace & Company.

Dubus, Andre. "The Intruder" from *Dancing After Hours* by Andre Dubus. Copyright ©1996 by Andre Dubus. Reprinted by permission of Alfred A. Knopf, Inc.

Greene, Graham. "All But Empty" originally titled, "A Little Place Off the Edgeware Road" from *Collected Stories* by Graham Greene (Penguin). Reprinted by permission of David Higham Associates, Ltd.

Helprin, Mark. "Tamar" from *Ellis Island & Other Stories* by Mark Helprin. Copyright ©1976, 1977, 1979, 1980, 1981 by Mark Helprin. Used by permission of Delacorte Press/Seymour Lawrence, a division of Bantam Doubleday Dell Publishing Group, Inc.

Hunter, Evan. "Snowblind" by Evan Hunter. Copyright ©1953, 1981 by Hui Corporation. Reprinted by permission of the Author.

Hurston, Zora Neale. "Sweat" is taken from *The Complete Stories* by Zora Neale Hurston. Introduction copyright ©1995 by Henry Louis Gates, Jr. and Sieglinde Lemke. Compilation copyright ©1995 by Vivian Bowden, Lois J. Hurston Gaston, Clifford Hurston, Lucy Ann Hurston, Winifred Hurston Clark, Zora Mack Goins, Edgar Hurston, Sr., and Barbara Hurston Lewis. Afterword and Bibliography copyright ©1995 by Henry Louis Gates. Reprinted by permission of HarperCollins Publishers, Inc. "Sweat" was originally published in *Fire*, November 1926.

Jen, Gish. "The Water Faucet Vision" by Gish Jen. Copyright ©1987 by Gish Jen. First published in *Nimrod*, Fall/Winter 1987. Reprinted by permission of the author.

Johnson, Dorothy M. "The Man Who Shot Liberty Valance" from *Indian Country* by Dorothy M. Johnson. Copyright ©1949 by Dorothy M. Johnson. Reprinted by permission of McIntosh and Otis, Inc.

Keesey, Anna. "Bright Winter" by Anna Keesey. First published in *Grand Street*. Copyright ©1995 by Anna Keesey. Reprinted by permission of the author.

King, Thomas. "Borders" by Thomas King from *One Good Story, That One*. Copyright ©1993 by Thomas King. Reprinted by permission of HarperCollins Publishing Ltd. and the author. Published by HarperCollins Publishing Ltd.

Lawrence, D.H. "The Rocking-Horse Winner" by D.H. Lawrence, copyright 1933 by the Estate of D.H. Lawrence, renewed ©1961 by Angelo Ravagli and C.M. Weekley, Executors of the Estate of Frieda Lawrence, from *Complete Short Stories of D.H. Lawrence* by D.H. Lawrence. Used by permission of Viking Penguin, a division of Penguin Books USA Inc.

Lively, Penelope. "The French Exchange" from *Pack of Cards and Other Stories* by Penelope Lively. Copyright ©1984 by Penelope Lively. Used by permission of Grove/Atlantic, Inc. and David Higham Associates Limited.

Narayan, R.K. "Like the Sun" from *Under the Banyan Tree* by R.K. Narayan. Copyright ©1985 by R.K. Narayan. Used by permission of Viking Penguin, a division of Penguin Books USA Inc.

O'Connor, Frank. "First Confession" from *Collected Stories* by Frank O'Connor. Copyright 1951 by Frank O'Connor. Reprinted by permission of Alfred A. Knopf, Inc. Also reprinted by arrangement with Harriet O'Donovan Sheehy, c/o Joan Daves Agency as agent for the proprietor. Copyright 1931 by Frank O'Connor; Copyright last renewed 1981 by Harriet O'Donovan Sheehy, Executrix of the Estate of Frank O'Connor.

Porter, Katherine Anne. "The Jilting of Granny Weatherall" from *Flowering Judas and Other Stories,* copyright 1930 and renewed 1938 by Katherine Anne Porter, reprinted by permission of Harcourt Brace & Company.

Proulx, E. Annie. "Electric Arrows" reprinted with the permission of Scribner, a Division of Simon & Schuster from *Heart Songs And Other Stories* by E. Annie Proulx. Copyright ©1988 E. Annie Proulx.

Raddall, Thomas H. "The Wedding Gift" by Thomas H. Raddall is reprinted with permission of Dalhousie University.

Rendell, Ruth. "Inspector Wexford and the Winchurch Affair" by Ruth Rendell as appeared in *Murder Intercontinental* edited by Cynthia Manson & Kathleen Halligan. Reprinted by permission of the Peters Fraser & Dunlop Group Ltd.

Walker, Alice. "Roselily" from *In Love & Trouble: Stories of Black Women*, copyright ©1972 by Alice Walker, reprinted by permission of Harcourt Brace & Company.

Welty, Eudora. "Why I Live at the P.O." from *A Curtain of Green and Other Stories*, copyright 1941 and renewed 1969 by Eudora Welty, reprinted by permission of Harcourt Brace & Company.

Yamanaka, Cedric. "The Lemon Tree Billiards House" by Cedric Yamanaka origi nally appeared in *Into The Fire*, an anthology published by The Greenfield Review Press. Reprinted by permission.

ILLUSTRATION CREDITS

Dubus, Andre	7: Marion Ettlinger/Outline
O'Connor, Frank	20: Elliott Erwitt/Magnum Photos
Hurston, Zora Neale	30: Library of Congress/Corbis
Raddall, Thomas H.	50: Dalhousie University Archives/Thomas Raddall Collection
King, Thomas	66: Paul McDonald
Proulx, E. Annie	78: Wilson/Gamma Liaison
Jen, Gish	101: Marion Ettlinger/Outline
Lively, Penelope	112: Jerry Bauer
Cather, Willa	127: Corbis
Helprin, Mark	155: Deborah Feingold/Outline
Narayan, R. K.	166: Jerry Bauer
Yamanaka, Cedric	172: Courtesy of the author
Welty, Eudora	184: Janice Rubin/Black Star
Alexie, Sherman	205: Marion Ettlinger/Outline
Walker, Alice	218: Lawrence Barns/Black Star
Lawrence, D. H.	224: Hulton-Deutsch Collection/Corbis
Ardizzone, Tony	248: (no credit required)
Anderson, Sherwood	270: Archive Photos
Keesey, Anna	282: Courtesy of the author
Porter, Katherine Anne	303: Jerry Bauer
Johnson, Dorothy M.	320: Lacy's Studio/Whitefish, Montana
Hunter, Evan	336: Frank Capri/SAGA/Archive Photos
Callahan, Barbara	350: Courtesy of the author
Rendell, Ruth	372: Miriam Berkley
Carter, Angela	401: Miriam Berkley
Clarke, Arthur C.	414: Corbis
Greene, Graham	425: Corbis
Baker, Nicholson	431: C. Cumming/Gamma Liaison

INDEX OF AUTHORS
AND TITLES